Beyond Doctrine

FROM THE SAME AUTHOR

Cybersecurity & Emerging Technologies:
A Pocket Dictionary for Students and Professionals.

Cybersecurity Governance, Risk, and Compliance:
Foundations for Secure and Resilient Organizations.

Effective Communication in the Modern World:
Academic, Workplace, and Digital Skills.

Forced Unity: A Critical Appraisal of the Ambazonia Struggle
for Emancipation and Self-Determination.

Hidden Selves:
Triple Masking and the Mental Health Crisis in the Church.

Holistic Resilience:
Counseling at the Intersection of Faith, Family, and Identity.

Strategic Corporate Social Responsibility in Practice:
Institutions, Strategy, Innovation, Marketing, and Global
Legitimacy. 2nd ed.

The Graduate Research Companion:
A Step-by-Step Handbook for Thesis Writers.

The Human Firewall:
How Organizational Culture Shapes Cybersecurity Behavior.

The Modern MBA:
Core Concepts and Strategies for Global Business Leaders.

(These are all published by Saint Monica University Press and available through Amazon.)

BEYOND DOCTRINE

A Critical-Liberative Theology
of Faith and Emancipation

Januarius Asongu

WIPF & STOCK · Eugene, Oregon

BEYOND DOCTRINE
A Critical-Liberative Theology of Faith and Emancipation

Copyright © 2026 Januarius Asongu. All rights reserved. Except for brief quotations in critical publications or reviews, no part of this book may be reproduced in any manner without prior written permission from the publisher. Write: Permissions, Wipf and Stock Publishers, 199 W. 8th Ave., Suite 3, Eugene, OR 97401.

Wipf & Stock
An Imprint of Wipf and Stock Publishers
199 W. 8th Ave., Suite 3
Eugene, OR 97401

www.wipfandstock.com

PAPERBACK ISBN: 979-8-3852-7204-4
HARDCOVER ISBN: 979-8-3852-7205-1
EBOOK ISBN: 979-8-3852-7206-8

For my son, Jude Jingwa Ngangsic-Asongu—whose quiet strength, moral courage, and unwavering integrity continue to inspire my own journey.

Contents

Preface ix

Acknowledgements xiii

Introduction: Faith Seeking Emancipation —
  The Vision of Critical-Liberative Theology (CLT) xv

PART I — *Foundations of Critical-Liberative Theology*

  1 Roots of Critical-Liberative Theology: Boff, Newman, Popper, and CSR 3

  2 Methodological Framework: Faith, Reason, and Emancipatory Praxis 28

  3 Liberation Theology: A Global History from Latin America to Africa and Asia 64

  4 Biblical Paradigms for Liberation: Exodus, Prophets, Jesus, Cross & Resurrection 141

PART II: *Church, Power, and Prophecy: The Crisis of Institutional Sin*

  5 The Silence of the Shepherds: The Collapse of Prophetic Witness in Africa 199

  6 The Collapse of Prophetic Witness: African Church Elites and Political Complicity 239

  7 The Crucified Body: Clerical Sexual Abuse as a Systemic Theological Crisis 248

  8 Christian Nationalism and the Failure of Orthopraxy in the American Church 276

9   Theology of Institutions: Why Churches Drift Into Self-Preservation   312

PART III: *Liberation, Justice, and the Oppressed*

10   Liberation Theology and the Ambazonia Struggle: Justice, Peace, and Moral Legitimacy   325

11   Witchcraft, Fear, and the Demonization of the Poor in Africa   346

12   Economic Oppression and the Theology of Structural Sin   379

13   Migration, Exile, and the Theology of Forced Displacement   389

PART IV — *Faith, Gender, and the Body: Toward a Liberative Anthropology*

14   The Human Person in Critical-Liberative Theology: Body, Embodiment, Freedom, and Moral Agency   401

15   Women, Power, and the Structural Sin of Ecclesial Exclusion   411

16   Contraception, Women's Health, and Moral Freedom   433

17   Celibacy as Structural Injustice: Vocation, Freedom, and Reform   444

18   Neither Do I Condemn You: LGBTQ+ Inclusion as a Christological Imperative   455

PART V — *Cosmic Liberation: Ecology, Technology, and the Future of Humanity*

19   Cosmic Liberation: Ecology, African Cosmology, and Intergenerational Justice   473

20   AI, Technology, and Digital Oppression: A New Frontier of Liberation Theology   497

Conclusion — Beyond Doctrine: A Manifesto for a Church of the Poor and the Planet   507

Bibliography   519

Index   531

Preface

SINCE CHILDHOOD, I HAVE carried within me a quiet but unwavering desire: to become a saint. Not a figure of pious fantasy, but a life shaped by truth, courage, and radical fidelity to God. That aspiration has remained with me, though I eventually learned that sanctity is not achieved through passive obedience or unthinking conformity. True holiness requires the disciplined listening of conscience, the willingness to wrestle with difficult truths, and the courage to speak honestly even when one stands in tension with established doctrine. My work in this book emerges from that vocation.

My spiritual formation began in earnest during the five years I spent as a Catholic seminarian in the Diocese of Buea, Cameroon. I studied for the priesthood, served in parish communities, and encountered Christian faith in its raw, lived, and sacrificial form. Many of the parishioners I met—women carrying impossible burdens, families persevering through economic hardship, young people navigating uncertainty with resilient hope—were, in many ways, holier than many of their priests. Their witness forced me to confront profound theological questions about justice, suffering, and dignity. The tensions I wrestled with then have become the foundation of this book.

Over time, my intellectual and spiritual journey aligned me with the tradition of John Henry Newman, the great theologian whom Pope Leo XIII named a Doctor of the Church. Newman taught that doctrine develops—that the Church deepens its understanding through conscience, history, and the movement of the Holy Spirit. His insistence that conscience is the "aboriginal Vicar of Christ" remains central to my own method. Equally formative is Anselm's vision of *fides quaerens intellectum*—faith seeking understanding—which inspires me to see inquiry not as a departure from faith but as its natural expression.

Though many of my ideas may be considered unorthodox, my love for the Church has never wavered. As an Extraordinary Minister of the Eucharist and a catechist, I have faithfully taught the Church's doctrine to catechumens and candidates preparing for the sacraments. Teaching the tradition with integrity does not prevent me from interrogating it; rather, it grounds my theological exploration in humility, responsibility, and service.

As an American citizen, however, I have become increasingly troubled by the rise of white nationalism and its infiltration into segments of American Catholic life. These forces distort the Gospel and undermine the Church's universal mission. At the same time, demographic reality tells another story: the future of Catholicism in the United States depends profoundly on immigrant communities, even as many of these very communities feel unwelcome or invisible. Countless African and Latin American Catholics have quietly drifted away from the Church, seeking recognition and spiritual vitality in evangelical congregations.

Because I experienced firsthand the vibrancy of African Catholicism—its music, communal warmth, expressive liturgy, and theological depth—I recognized the pastoral crisis unfolding around me. In response, I helped found African Catholic communities in Texas and the Washington, DC area. Over the years, many have testified that without these communities, they would have left the Church entirely. The contrast is stark: African liturgy is lively and incarnational, while many American parishes offer a worship style that feels sterile, subdued, and emotionally distant. Add to this the reality that many immigrants do not feel fully welcomed in predominantly white parishes, and the spiritual cost becomes clear.

My home has become its own theological workshop—a place where I test ideas with my wife, a conservative Catholic Christian whose faith challenges and refines my own thinking, and where my children listen with thoughtful reserve. Their presence reminds me that theology is intergenerational, and that the Church we build today must be a home for them tomorrow.

I do not expect everyone to agree with every argument in this book. If agreement were my goal, there would be no need to write. Theology advances when faithful people articulate new insights, confront inherited limitations, and name truths that have not yet been integrated into doctrine. My aim is not rebellion but renewal; not rupture but deeper fidelity; not destruction but growth for a Church that I love.

Beyond Doctrine: A Critical-Liberative Theology of Faith and Emancipation is offered in that spirit—born from conscience, sharpened by encounter, nurtured in pastoral experience, and sustained by hope. If this work helps even one reader envision a more just, compassionate, and liberated Church, then it will have honored the desire that first awakened in me as a child: the longing, however imperfectly realized, to become a saint.

—Januarius Jingwa (JJ) Asongu, PhD
Townsend, DE, USA

Acknowledgements

THIS BOOK IS WOVEN from the threads of many lives, communities, and graces that have shaped my journey. I begin by thanking my children—Jude, Maria, and Bernard—whose moral courage, quiet strength, and joyful presence continually renew my sense of purpose. To my wife, Christine Ngangsic, I owe more gratitude than words can contain. Your steadfast support, intellectual honesty, spiritual depth, and unyielding love have carried me through every stage of this work. You have been my closest partner in discernment and my companion in hope.

I am deeply grateful to my parents, Dr. Nicholas Asongu Jingwa and Lady Monique Nkengbeza, whose unwavering faith and devotion to the Church formed the earliest contours of my spiritual imagination. Their simplicity, fidelity, and love for God and neighbor remain grounding forces in my life. I also thank all my siblings, each of whom has remained faithful to the Church in ways that honor the dreams of our parents. Their quiet perseverance in faith is a blessing.

My years preparing for the Catholic priesthood were profoundly formative. I thank all the Christians I was privileged to minister to during my five years of seminary formation. Their resilience, faith, and generosity left an indelible mark on me. I remain forever grateful for the rigorous intellectual training, spiritual discipline, and pastoral experience that shaped my vocation—even though my path ultimately took a different direction.

I offer special thanks to the mentors who shaped my early theological and philosophical formation. Bishop Immanuel B. Bushu, my former rector and philosophy professor, remains the humblest person I have encountered and the priest par excellence. His simplicity and authenticity continue to inspire me. Fr. Henri Peeters, who has taught at STAMS for over fifty years, embodied fidelity to formation and intellectual rigor.

Fr. Henry Dinayen, with his passion for research and inculturation, expanded my understanding of the Church's mission. And I remain grateful to Bishop Francis Teke Lysinge, my former spiritual director and later Bishop of Mamfe, whose humble witness of faith still guides me. Finally, I thank Fr. William Tardze, and Prof. Bongasu Tala-Kishani (RIP) who supervised my thesis in Bambui with patience and scholarly generosity.

My gratitude also extends to my classmates and schoolmates at St. Thomas Aquinas Major Seminary (STAMS), Bambui. The camaraderie, debates, shared struggles, and spiritual brotherhood we cultivated shaped my character and sharpened my theological instincts. I am equally thankful for all my fellow seminarians across the years who contributed to an environment of prayer, discipline, humor, and intellectual growth.

Long before seminary, my leadership in the Young Christian Students (YCS) movement in the Diocese of Kumbo profoundly influenced my faith and social consciousness. I thank my fellow YCS members—many of whom remain lifelong friends—for the formative conversations, youthful zeal, and shared commitment to justice and service. I also thank my schoolmates and teachers at GHS Kumbo, who contributed to the intellectual and social foundation upon which much of my early thinking was built.

Among those who shaped my youth, Fr. Robert Tanto stands out as an extraordinary inspiration. As the energetic, charismatic, and intellectually gifted youth chaplain, he modeled a faith that was rigorous, fearless, intellectual, and deeply engaged with the world. His clarity of thought and pastoral dynamism awakened in me a lifelong desire to think critically, love deeply, and serve faithfully.

To all these communities and individuals—family, mentors, classmates, parishioners, friends, and spiritual guides—I express my heartfelt gratitude. This book is, in many ways, a testament to your influence. Whatever good it contains belongs as much to you as to me.

INTRODUCTION

Faith Seeking Emancipation — The Vision of Critical-Liberative Theology (CLT)

CHRISTIAN THEOLOGY BEGINS IN liberation. The God of Scripture is not a distant abstraction but the One who hears the cry of the oppressed (Exod. 3:7), who brings captives out of bondage, who proclaims justice to the nations, and who in Jesus Christ announces good news to the poor (Luke 4:18). Yet across centuries, the emancipatory heart of Christian faith has often been obscured by doctrinal rigidity, institutional self-protection, and alliances with systems of domination. Theology became more invested in defending propositions than in transforming lives, more concerned with guarding boundaries than with healing the wounds of history.

Beyond Doctrine is a call to retrieve the liberating center of Christian faith and to reimagine theology as a practice of emancipation—intellectually rigorous, historically conscious, and prophetically engaged. The vision advanced here is what I call Critical-Liberative Theology (CLT), a theological method shaped by the integration of critical rationality, liberative praxis, and faithful discernment. It is a theology that seeks not merely to *understand* faith, but to *enact* it. If classical theology defined itself as *fides quaerens intellectum*—"faith seeking understanding"—CLT insists that faith today must also be understood as faith seeking emancipation.

This introduction outlines the intellectual journey, methodological commitments, and historical contexts that gave birth to CLT. It describes why theology must confront structural injustice, how CSR (Critical Synthetic Realism) informs theological method, and what liberation means in a globalized and technologized world. It also offers a preview of the themes explored in the pages that follow: ecclesial complicity, human dignity, ecological devastation, gendered and sexualized oppression, political violence, and the emancipatory struggles of marginalized communities in Africa and beyond.

1. THE GENESIS OF A THEOLOGICAL VISION

My theological formation began at St. Thomas Aquinas Major Seminary in Bambui, Cameroon—an environment steeped in scholastic clarity, metaphysical precision, and doctrinal loyalty. Yet the world outside the classroom spoke a different language: the grinding poverty of my people, the suffocating effects of colonial legacies, the silencing of dissent, and the spiritual resilience woven into African communal life.

I learned early that theology divorced from the lived suffering of the people becomes an intellectual ornament—beautiful, but powerless.

The liberative writings of Gustavo Gutiérrez, Jon Sobrino, and Leonardo Boff introduced an alternative horizon in which God's preferential option for the poor becomes the standard by which all theology is judged. Their insistence that orthopraxy is the criterion of orthodoxy resonated deeply with the African context, where faith must continually confront the injustices of corrupt governance, patriarchal tradition, neo-colonial economics, and the demonization of vulnerable populations.

Two other thinkers profoundly shaped the emergence of Critical-Liberative Theology. John Henry Newman taught me that doctrine develops historically—that fidelity requires the courage to reinterpret tradition as the Church encounters new questions. Karl Popper's critical rationalism challenged me to embrace the humility of self-correction: truth unfolds through dialogue, critique, and engagement with experience.

These three streams—liberationist praxis, historical development, and critical rationalism—flowed together into what I now call Critical-Liberative Theology, a method that is:

- faithful to revelation yet open to critique,
- rooted in tradition yet alive to history,
- committed to the Church yet prophetic in conscience,
- intellectually rigorous yet oriented toward liberation.

This book is the fruit of that journey.

2. THE CRISIS OF DOCTRINE WITHOUT EMANCIPATION

Doctrines matter—they anchor belief, safeguard memory, and offer continuity across generations. But doctrine can also become an idol, especially when it is insulated from experience or weaponized to protect institutional privilege. Too often, the Church has defended ideas at the expense of people and preserved structures at the expense of justice.

The crisis of contemporary Christianity is not merely doctrinal confusion; it is the collapse of credibility that occurs when the Church proclaims the Gospel of freedom yet tolerates, perpetuates, or collaborates with systems of oppression.

When theology fails to confront:

- political tyranny,
- clerical abuse and systemic cover-up,
- misogyny and patriarchal exclusion,
- homophobic violence,
- economic exploitation,
- environmental destruction,

...then it betrays its own foundations. Doctrine becomes a shield for injustice rather than a catalyst for liberation.

Critical-Liberative Theology invites the Church to move beyond doctrine not by abandoning belief, but by refusing to reduce faith to intellectual assent. It insists that doctrine finds its truth only in how it shapes the world—whether it liberates or enslaves, includes or excludes, reconciles or divides.

3. THE METHOD OF CRITICAL-LIBERATIVE THEOLOGY (CLT)

CLT rests on three mutually reinforcing pillars: critical reason, liberative praxis, and faithful discernment.

a) Critical Reason: The Courage to Question

Guided by Popper's epistemology and the spirit of Vatican II, CLT affirms that no theological claim is exempt from scrutiny. Revelation is fixed, but its interpretation is historical—and fallible. Critical reason protects the Church from totalizing ideologies, internal corruption, and the illusion of infallible human systems.

This is not relativism; it is fidelity to a God who leads the Church "into all truth" (John 16:13) through ongoing engagement with science, culture, and human experience.

b) Liberative Praxis: The Criterion of Truth

Gutiérrez's insight remains foundational: theology is not written *about* liberation but arises *from* the practice of liberation.

Every theological claim must be tested by one question: Does this promote human and cosmic flourishing? If not, it must be rethought.

Liberation, for CLT, includes political, economic, cultural, bodily, ecological, and spiritual dimensions. It envisions not only the freeing of oppressed peoples but the healing of creation itself.

c) Faithful Discernment: Prophetic Loyalty

CLT remains rooted in the life of the Church even as it challenges the Church's failures. Authentic fidelity requires both respect for tradition and the courage of prophetic dissent. The saints, martyrs, mystics, and reformers embody this paradox: loyalty expressed through critique, and critique grounded in love.

4. LIBERATION IN A GLOBALIZED AND TECHNOLOGIZED WORLD

The world of the 21st century introduces new forms of oppression—digital surveillance, algorithmic bias, economic precarity, ecological collapse, migration crises, and authoritarian populisms. Liberation theology must extend its analysis beyond traditional political structures into the social, technological, and economic forces reshaping human life.

CLT confronts:

- digital colonialism and the exploitation of African data;
- AI-driven inequality, social scoring, and algorithmic injustice;
- planetary crisis as both ecological and theological catastrophe;
- forced displacement, war, and the commodification of human beings;
- the fragility of truth in an era of misinformation and ideologized religion.

Liberation today must be both local and planetary, both historical and eschatological, both personal and political.

5. CONTEXTS OF EMANCIPATION: THEMES OF THE BOOK

Each part of this book applies CLT to concrete crises in the Church and the world:

Church and Power

A critical examination of African ecclesial complicity, clerical sexual abuse, and the rise of Christian nationalism in the United States.

Justice and the Oppressed

The demonization of the poor through witchcraft accusations, economic exploitation, migration as modern crucifixion, and the Ambazonia struggle.

Gender, Sexuality, and the Body

The structural exclusion of women, debates on contraception, the harms of mandatory clerical celibacy, and the call for full LGBTQ+ inclusion.

Creation and Cosmic Liberation

Eco-theology, African cosmology, and the moral challenge of the climate crisis and emerging technologies.

These are not isolated issues; they form a single tapestry of intersecting oppressions, each demanding theological engagement grounded in liberation.

6. TOWARD A CHURCH OF THE POOR AND THE PLANET

What emerges from these reflections is a vision of the Church not as a fortress of doctrine but as a community of justice, a sanctuary for the marginalized, and a steward of creation.

A Church of the Poor and the Planet listens before it speaks, accompanies before it judges, and embodies mercy before asserting power. It recognizes that salvation is not the escape from history but its transformation.

Liberation is not peripheral to the Gospel; it is the Gospel.

7. FAITH SEEKING EMANCIPATION

Faith that seeks understanding must today also seek emancipation. Faith longs for freedom—from fear, domination, falsehood, and the many crucifixions of our age.

Critical-Liberative Theology is a theology of hope: the hope that another Church and another world are possible, one in which every person and all of creation can flourish in dignity.

These pages are offered in fidelity to the Church that formed me and in solidarity with all who labor for justice. Beyond doctrine lies not rebellion but renewal; not abandonment of faith but its deepest realization. There, in the risky terrain of love and liberation, theology becomes not merely an intellectual pursuit but a spiritual and moral vocation.

PART I — FOUNDATIONS OF CRITICAL-LIBERATIVE THEOLOGY

Part I lays the intellectual and spiritual groundwork for Critical-Liberative Theology (CLT) by tracing its historical roots, methodological commitments, and biblical foundations. It begins in Chapter 1 with an autobiographical reflection on how liberationist thinkers such as Gustavo Gutiérrez, Leonardo Boff, and Jon Sobrino intersected with the developmental theology of John Henry Newman and the critical rationalism of Karl Popper. These influences converge with Critical Synthetic Realism (CSR) to form a theological method that is faithful to tradition yet fearless in critique. The chapter argues that faith requires critical realism—a willingness to acknowledge historical development, question unjust structures, and engage conscience as a site of prophetic dissent. A brief case study of Vatican II illustrates how the Church itself embodies liberation when it opens its windows to the world.

Chapter 2 develops the formal methodology of CLT. It presents a hermeneutic in which Scripture becomes a call to action, not a static text. Epistemologically, truth is seen as tested, provisional, and ordered toward liberation. Social analysis becomes essential to theological reflection, requiring engagement with economics, culture, and political power. Human beings are moral agents responsible for resisting oppression. The chapter then outlines the methodological tools of CLT—critical inquiry, prophetic praxis, and communal discernment—and illustrates them through the theology of accompaniment practiced in Latin America and emerging African ecclesial movements.

Chapter 3 situates CLT within the global history of liberation theology, moving from its Latin American origins under dictatorship to the contributions of African theologians such as Jean-Marc Ela, Engelbert Mveng, Laurenti Magesa, and Charles Nyamiti, and Asian movements including Dalit, Minjung, and feminist liberation theologies. Liberation is shown to be ecumenical, diverse, and globally resonant.

Chapter 4 turns to biblical paradigms, grounding emancipation in the Exodus, prophetic denunciation, the liberating ministry of Jesus, the Cross as God's solidarity with the crucified, and the Resurrection as the triumph of justice and hope. Together, these chapters establish CLT as a theology rooted in Scripture, history, reason, and the lived struggles of oppressed peoples.

CHAPTER 1

Roots of Critical-Liberative Theology: Boff, Newman, Popper, and CSR

1. INTRODUCTION: THEOLOGY AS A JOURNEY TOWARD EMANCIPATION

EVERY THEOLOGIAN'S WORK BEGINS as a response—sometimes to wonder, sometimes to suffering, and often to contradiction. My own theological journey emerged from all three. Raised in an upper-middle-class family in Cameroon, I knew comfort, security, and opportunity. Yet stepping beyond the boundaries of my home and social circle, I encountered poverty so pervasive and normalized that it seemed invisible to many who were not touched by it. I could not understand how a society so devoutly Christian—where churches filled each Sunday with hymns of praise—coexisted so comfortably with such deep material deprivation. I began to wonder: *What good is theology if it cannot speak to the wounds of the world? What is faith if it does not heal?*

This question followed me into the seminary at St. Thomas Aquinas Major Seminary in Bambui. Like so many young seminarians, I entered with a zeal to serve God and the Church. I expected to find clarity, holiness, and moral conviction. Instead, I encountered profound contradictions—holiness and hypocrisy, beauty and brokenness, fidelity and failure. Already in my first year of seminary formation, I was confronted with the unsettling reality that the institutional Church, revered in doctrine and liturgy, carried deep patterns of sin within its own structures. Stories of clerical corruption, sexual misconduct, and moral inconsistency were whispered in corridors or spoken with resignation by ordinary Catholics. And even more painful was the fact that many faithful Christians—those whom I had expected to draw inspiration from ecclesial leadership—were instead being scandalized, confused, and spiritually wounded.

I watched as ordinary Catholics, many of them striving sincerely for holiness amid difficult lives, felt betrayed by the very leaders entrusted with their care. Increasingly, they began seeking spiritual nourishment elsewhere. Evangelical and Pentecostal churches, with their emphasis on personal conversion, accessible preaching, healing, and community support, attracted those who felt unseen or marginalized within Catholic structures. I realized that the Church was losing its credibility not because of its doctrines, but because of its inability to embody them.

This awakening led me to a conviction that has shaped my entire theological vocation: the Church must be reformed internally before it can evangelize externally. Evangelization without conversion—moral, institutional, and structural—is merely performance. I began to believe that salvation must be understood not only in celestial terms but also in terrestrial ones. Faith must speak to hunger, injustice, social inequality, and political violence. The Church must offer liberation in this world if it hopes to speak credibly of liberation in the next.

This realization did not turn me against theology; it deepened my hunger for it. But I could no longer be satisfied with a theology concerned only with abstract metaphysics. I needed a theology that could illumine both heaven and earth—one that could explain the world as it is and inspire the world as it ought to be.

My longing for such a theology found resonance in thinkers like Karl Rahner, Hans Küng, Leonardo Boff, Jean-Marc Ela, Karl Popper, and John Henry Newman. Each offered a different piece of the puzzle: Rahner's transcendental anthropology, Küng's insistence on truthfulness and reform, Boff's prophetic critique of ecclesial power, Ela's African cry for justice, Popper's humility of critical rationalism, and Newman's theology of doctrinal development.

As I gradually integrated their insights, something new began to emerge: a theological method that would become Critical-Liberative Theology (CLT). CLT seeks truth with the humility of critical realism, evaluates tradition through conscience and historical experience, and views faith as a call to emancipatory praxis. It is a theology that insists that God is found not only in the sanctuary but also in the streets—in the cries of the poor, the disillusionment of the betrayed, and the struggles of communities seeking dignity.

This chapter narrates the origins of that theological synthesis. It begins with my early scholastic formation and the first cracks that appeared in its intellectual edifice. It then traces the influence of key thinkers—Popper, Boff, Newman, Rahner, Küng—whose ideas opened new horizons. Finally, it situates Vatican II as a pivotal example of critical liberation within the Church's own history.

2. EARLY FORMATION: BETWEEN SCHOLASTIC CERTAINTY AND ECCLESIAL CONTRADICTION

My years in the seminary were intellectually enriching but spiritually disorienting. On the one hand, the scholastic tradition offered a theological framework that was elegant, rational, and coherent. We studied Augustine's penetrating introspection and Aquinas's majestic synthesis of faith and reason. I was taught, as Aquinas famously wrote, that grace does not destroy nature but perfects.[1] Augustine's *Confessions* moved me deeply, especially his recognition that the human heart is restless until it rests in God.[2]

Yet even as I absorbed these profound insights, something troubled me. Scholastic theology had answers for metaphysical questions—the nature of the Trinity, the attributes of God, the categories of sin, the logic of sacraments—but it had little to say about the concrete injustices shaping the African world outside our seminary walls. The intellectual grandeur of scholasticism began to feel discordant with the lived reality of poverty, inequality, and corruption.

Meanwhile, the Church that had nurtured my vocation revealed its own brokenness. As a young seminarian, I was unprepared for the moral inconsistencies I witnessed among clergy—instances of financial mismanagement, arrogance, exploitation, and, in some cases, the early hints of what I would later recognize as sexual misconduct. These were not isolated events but symptoms of deeper structural problems: clericalism, lack of accountability, and a culture of silence.

I realized—to my shock and sorrow—that the Church was losing moral authority not because people rejected its doctrines, but because

---

1. Aquinas, *ST* I-I, q. 1
2. Augustine, *On Christian Doctrine*.

they felt abandoned, exploited, or dismissed by its representatives. If evangelization was failing, it was because Christians were not being fed, healed, or uplifted. Many were instead being wounded.

This realization marked a crucial turning point in my thinking: authentic theology must begin with reality, not abstraction. It must listen to the experiences of God's people—especially the wounded, the poor, and the disillusioned—before speaking to them.

The "radical priests" of Latin America and Africa appealed to me precisely because they embodied this conviction. Figures like Oscar Romero, Helder Câmara, Jean-Marc Ela, and Engelbert Mveng spoke not from academic ivory towers but from the crucible of suffering. Their theology began with the cry of the people, not the logic of textbooks.

For the first time, I began to imagine a theology that was not merely descriptive but transformative—a theology that could speak to injustice, inspire reform, and awaken the Church to its prophetic mission.

3. ENCOUNTERING KARL POPPER: A PROVIDENTIAL DISRUPTION OF CERTAINTY

My introduction to Karl Popper was not the result of a formal philosophy curriculum, nor did it arise from any structured academic requirement. It came instead through an unexpected and, in retrospect, providential encounter—one that would ultimately reshape the entire trajectory of my intellectual and theological life. During my freshman year (1990/91) at St. Thomas Aquinas Major Seminary in Bambui, our rector and philosophy lecturer, Father Immanuel Balanjo Bushu (who would later become the Bishop of Yagoua and then that of Buea), called me into his office and handed me a book written by Professor Godfrey B. Tangwa, one of Cameroon's most distinguished philosophy professors and an ex-seminarian himself.

Tangwa's book, entitled *Karl Popper: A Thematic Critical Introduction*, was a brief philosophical study of Karl Popper's critical rationalism. Bushu, a traditional Thomist and scholastic to the core, had received the monograph directly from Tangwa for his perusal. Knowing my voracious appetite for reading and philosophical inquiry, he entrusted the document to me with the instruction: *"Read this carefully and come back so we can discuss it."*

At the time, I did not realize the significance of that moment. Bushu, who adhered firmly to scholastic metaphysics and Aristotelian logic, was not the kind of thinker one expected to promote Popper's epistemology—an epistemology that questioned the very foundations of absolute certainty and emphasized the provisional nature of human knowledge. I suspect, looking back, that he offered me the monograph less because he endorsed its contents and more because he trusted my intellectual curiosity. Yet this simple gesture became one of the most transformative events of my formation.

Popper through the eyes of Tangwa

Reading Tangwa's monograph was like entering a different philosophical universe. Tangwa presented Popper not as a destructive skeptic but as a philosopher committed to truth through openness, critique, and the continual testing of ideas. He explained Popper's famous principle of falsifiability—the notion that a statement or theory is scientific only if it can, in principle, be proven false.[3] This introduced me to a radically different understanding of knowledge, one in which certainty was not the goal but the enemy of intellectual progress.

Tangwa's exposition was lucid, rigorous, and generous. He presented Popper as a defender of rational inquiry against dogmatism—whether political, scientific, or religious. The more I read, the more I felt the ground shift beneath the neat scholastic categories I had been taught. Popper insisted that knowledge grows through the identification of errors, not through the accumulation of dogmatic truths. As he famously put it, "We may become the makers of our fate when we have ceased to pose as its prophets."[4]

This was not just an epistemological claim; it was a moral one. Popper viewed openness to critique as an ethical imperative, a safeguard against tyranny and intellectual totalitarianism.

A dialogue with my rector

After finishing the monograph, I returned to Bushu's office for the promised discussion. True to his scholastic formation, he questioned many

---

3. Popper, *The Logic of Scientific Discovery*.
4. Popper, *The Open Society and Its Enemies*, 13.

of Popper's premises. He challenged Popper's rejection of induction, defended the value of metaphysical certainty, and expressed concern that Popper's epistemology risked undermining the stability of theological truth. Yet despite these reservations, he listened attentively as I explained how Popper's ideas had expanded my horizons. Our conversation was respectful but animated, and although we never reached agreement, that exchange with my rector marked the beginning of my intellectual maturation.

What remains most striking to me now is the irony—and perhaps divine irony—of that moment. Bushu, who would have disagreed with Popper on nearly every philosophical point, nonetheless became the person through whom Popper entered my life. His decision to give me that monograph opened a door that had previously been invisible to me.

Had I not encountered Popper through Tangwa, and had Bushu not placed the monograph in my hands, my intellectual path might have unfolded differently. Instead, this encounter planted a seed that would eventually grow into Critical Synthetic Realism (CSR)—my own epistemological framework—and later into the methodological foundations of Critical-Liberative Theology (CLT).

Why Popper mattered so deeply

Popper's work answered a question that had quietly troubled me since my first months in the seminary: *How can we speak of theological truth in a world where interpretations multiply and contradictions abound?*

I had been taught to view Catholic doctrine as immutable, grounded in revelation, and safeguarded by ecclesial authority. Yet I could see that doctrines had developed over time—sometimes dramatically. Popper provided a conceptual vocabulary that made sense of this evolution. If all human knowledge remains open to correction, then doctrinal development is not a failure of stability but a sign of vitality. Newman had articulated this theologically decades earlier, but Popper gave me the philosophical lens to understand it more deeply.

For Popper, truth is objective but never fully grasped. Human formulations of truth are always partial, revisable, and historically conditioned. The key to intellectual integrity is not certainty but critical openness. Knowledge grows through error elimination, not through dogmatic closure. This insight resonated with my growing awareness that the Church, as a historical institution composed of fallible human beings, must also remain open to critique, reform, and renewal.

A new way of seeing the Church

Popper also helped me reinterpret my painful encounters with ecclesial weakness—corruption, sexual scandals, and abuse of power. Before Popper, these failures had shaken my faith in the institution itself. After Popper, I began to see them not as anomalies but as signs of what happens when an institution treats its formulations as immune to question.

Popper wrote that closed systems—whether political or religious—inevitably foster oppression, because they suppress critique in the name of protecting truth.[5] This insight clarified something I had observed: when the Church operates in a closed, defensive posture, prioritizing institutional preservation over moral accountability, it inevitably produces harm.

At the same time, Popper helped me resist the temptation toward cynicism. If all human institutions err, and if all knowledge is provisional, then the Church is not uniquely corrupt—it is simply human. What distinguishes a healthy institution from a pathological one is not perfection but its willingness to reform.

Popper as a bridge to liberation theology

Curiously, Popper's secular rationalism became a stepping stone toward the very theological tradition that would later define my spiritual and intellectual identity: liberation theology. Popper taught me that:

- Truth must remain open to correction
- Institutions must remain accountable
- Critique is a moral obligation
- Knowledge grows from confronting suffering and error

These insights harmonized almost seamlessly with the central claims of liberation theologians like Gustavo Gutiérrez and Leonardo Boff. Liberation theology insists that theology must begin with lived experience—especially the experience of the poor—and must critique unjust

5. Popper, *The Open Society and Its Enemies*.

structures in light of the Gospel. Popper provided the epistemological scaffolding for this theological intuition.

I came to realize that critical rationalism and liberative praxis are not opposites; they are complementary. Critical rationalism guards theology against authoritarianism and intolerance. Liberation praxis guards theology against irrelevance and abstraction. Together, they formed the intellectual soil from which both CSR and CLT would later grow.

4. DISCOVERING LIBERATION THEOLOGY: WHEN THEOLOGY MEETS THE WOUNDS OF THE WORLD

If Popper shattered the illusion of epistemological certainty, liberation theology shattered the illusion of ecclesial innocence. It offered a theological language for what I had long felt but had lacked the confidence to articulate: the institutional Church was itself implicated in the suffering of ordinary people, and theology must address this reality rather than obscure it.

My first real encounter with liberation theology came through reading Leonardo Boff's *Church, Charism, and Power* (1981). I can still remember the experience vividly. As a seminarian steeped in scholastic categories, I approached the book expecting to disagree with everything; instead, I felt as though someone had turned on a light in a room I had been fumbling through in darkness. Boff articulated with clarity, courage, and compassion what I had only sensed intuitively: the Church's structures of power often betray the Gospel they claim to serve. As Boff bluntly put it, "The Church must pass through a process of conversion if it wishes to remain faithful to Christ."[6]

That sentence shook me. It named what I had seen but had feared to acknowledge.

I had witnessed priests living in comfort while parishioners struggled to feed their children; bishops cultivating political alliances while ignoring the cries of the poor; seminarians discussing vocation while exploiting vulnerable parishioners; and communities being spiritually starved by leaders more concerned with image, wealth, or hierarchy than with mercy.

Boff gave me language for this moral dissonance. He described how ecclesial power can become "sinful structures" that distort the Church's

---

6. Boff, *Church: Charism and Power*, 28.

witness.[7] His critique was not an attack on the Church; it was a call to conversion—precisely the conversion I felt the Church desperately needed.

A Church Losing Its People

During this same period, I witnessed many Catholics—devout, sincere, morally upright—leaving the Church for evangelical communities. I never believed they left because Catholic doctrine was too difficult; they left because Catholic *practice* was too distant. Evangelical churches offered what they felt the Catholic Church did not: community, belonging, support, and spiritual enthusiasm. Meanwhile, some Catholic clergy behaved like distant lords, not shepherds.

This exodus was heartbreaking yet understandable. Ordinary Christians were being scandalized by the moral failures of their leaders; their trust in the Church was eroding. Evangelicals flourished not because of theological superiority but because they embodied pastoral care and lived holiness in ways many Catholics found lacking.

This reality helped me understand a truth that has become central to my theology:

Before the Church can evangelize others, it must first evangelize itself.

No amount of theological precision can compensate for the lack of credibility that comes from scandal, corruption, or indifference to suffering.

5. MEETING RAHNER: THE MYSTERY OF GOD IN THE DEPTHS OF HUMAN EXPERIENCE

If Boff awakened my sense of ecclesial injustice, Karl Rahner awakened my sense of theological depth. His masterpiece, *Foundations of Christian Faith*,[8] introduced me to a transcendental approach to theology—one that understood human beings as inherently oriented toward God, and God as present in the very structure of human existence.

Rahner's famous claim that "the Christian of the future will be a mystic or will not exist at all"[9] struck me with particular force. He was not

---

7. Boff, *Church: Charism and Power*.
8. Rahner, *Foundations of Christian Faith*.
9. Rahner, *Theological Investigations*, 12.

rejecting doctrine; he was insisting that authentic faith must be rooted in lived experience of God, not merely intellectual assent. Rahner helped me recognize that the crisis of the Church was not merely moral or institutional—it was existential. Catholics were leaving not only because of clerical scandals but because theology had become too distant from human experience.

Rahner's transcendental method was critical for my developing thought in several ways:

1. He affirmed the dignity and agency of the human person, grounding theology in the freedom and responsibility of conscience.
2. He emphasized God's presence in history, reminding me that salvation is not merely otherworldly but begins in the concrete realities of life.
3. He linked theology to anthropology, insisting that every theological claim must illuminate human existence.

Rahner opened within me a deeper appreciation that liberation is not only social but spiritual. The Church must address both the earthly and heavenly dimensions of salvation—or it fails in its mission.

6. ENCOUNTERING HANS KÜNG: TRUTH, REFORM, AND THE COURAGE OF CONSCIENCE

While Rahner deepened my understanding of mystery, it was Hans Küng who emboldened my commitment to truth-telling within the Church. Küng's writings—especially *On Being a Christian*[10] and *Infallible? An Inquiry*[11]—were electrifying. Küng believed passionately in the Church but refused to remain silent about its failures. For him, authentic theology required both fidelity and honesty.

In *On Being a Christian*, Küng wrote that Jesus' message demands a "radical change of heart"[12]—a change that must begin within the Church itself. His willingness to critique ecclesial structures, even at great personal cost, helped me understand that prophetic dissent is not a betrayal of the Church but an act of love. His courage reassured me that the

---

10. Küng, *On Being a Christian*.
11. Küng, *Infallible? An Inquiry*.
12. Küng, *On Being a Christian*, 93.

questions stirring in my heart were not signs of disloyalty but signs of genuine faith seeking integrity.

Küng taught me that theological critique is not rebellion; it is a service to the truth. His example strengthened the moral dimension of my developing theology: without structural reform, the Church cannot fulfill its mission.

7. THE AFRICAN PROPHETS: JEAN-MARC ELA AND ENGELBERT MVENG

My theological awakening would not have been complete without the voices of African liberation thinkers—especially Jean-Marc Ela and Engelbert Mveng. Ela's *African Cry*[13] was a revelation. He argued that theology in Africa must begin with the lived suffering of the people, not with imported doctrinal formulations. His critique of ecclesial elitism in Africa—where clergy often live far more comfortably than their congregations—mirrored exactly what I had witnessed.

Mveng's analysis of "anthropological poverty" exposed how colonialism and economic exploitation dehumanize African peoples at the deepest level.[14] His writings helped me see that liberation theology in Africa must address not only social injustice but also cultural and psychological structures that perpetuate oppression.

Both Ela and Mveng convinced me that the Gospel cannot be authentically proclaimed in Africa unless it confronts:

- poverty
- political oppression
- cultural alienation
- economic exploitation
- ecclesial elitism

Their theological witness validated my early intuition that the Church must offer terrestrial salvation—justice, dignity, freedom—as much as celestial hope.

---

13. Ela, *African Cry*.
14. Mveng, *L'Afrique dans L'Église*.

8. WHY "RADICAL PRIESTS" APPEALED TO ME

The more I read Boff, Rahner, Küng, Ela, Mveng, Romero, and others, the more I felt drawn to those whom the institutional Church sometimes labeled "radical." They spoke honestly about injustice. They refused to separate the spiritual from the political. They lived among the people. They prioritized the cry of the poor over the privileges of hierarchy.

I realized that my affinity for these theologians was not accidental. Their concerns aligned perfectly with the contradictions I had seen in the Church:

- A clergy living in comfort while preaching poverty
- Bishops allied with political elites rather than the oppressed
- Seminars filled with scholastic speculation while villages endured hunger
- Masses celebrated with grandeur while communities lacked clean water
- Pious language masking institutional failures

These contradictions awakened within me a deep conviction: the Church must change—from the inside out—if it is to be credible.

Liberation theology offered me a way to imagine such change. It asked the most important question of all:

How can we proclaim the Gospel of love while participating in structures of injustice?

9. MEETING JOHN HENRY NEWMAN: HISTORY, CONSCIENCE, AND THE LIVING CHURCH

If Popper provided the philosophical humility I needed, and liberation theology awakened my moral consciousness, John Henry Newman offered the missing bridge between them. Newman showed me that faith could embrace historical development without losing fidelity; that conscience could be honored without undermining ecclesial unity; and that reform could emerge from within tradition rather than in opposition to it.

Reading Newman, especially *An Essay on the Development of Christian Doctrine*[15] and *Letter to the Duke of Norfolk*,[16] was like discovering a theological map for a terrain I had been wandering intuitively. He articulated with clarity what I had long felt but could not yet express: the Church lives in history, and therefore its understanding of truth must grow, mature, and sometimes radically shift as new questions emerge.

This insight was liberating because it affirmed something my seminary experience had already revealed: the Gospel is eternal, but its articulation is not.

Doctrinal Development as Fidelity, Not Betrayal

Newman argues that doctrine develops in the same way that a living idea unfolds across time—organically, coherently, and in response to new challenges. He writes:

> "In a higher world it is otherwise, but here below to live is to change, and to be perfect is to have changed often."[17]

For a mind shaped by scholasticism, this sentence struck with almost volcanic force. I had been formed in an atmosphere that treated doctrinal formulations as pristine, timeless, and unalterable. Yet the historical record—church councils, patristic debates, moral shifts—told a different story. Newman provided the interpretive key: change does not mean contradiction; it means maturation.

His theory of development opened the door for me to recognize that:

- The Church's moral teachings can evolve
- New contexts require new theological insights
- The Holy Spirit does not cease speaking in history
- The Church is faithful not because it never changes, but because it listens

This perspective became indispensable as I wrestled with contemporary issues—women's roles, sexual ethics, political injustice, economic

---

15. Newman, *An Essay on the Development of Christian Doctrine*.
16. Newman, *Letter to the Duke of Norfolk*.
17. Newman, *An Essay on the Development of Christian Doctrine*, 40.

inequality, and ecological crisis. Newman gave me theological permission to believe that the Church must grow beyond its current understanding in order to remain faithful to Christ.

10. CONSCIENCE: THE VOICE OF GOD IN THE HUMAN HEART

If Newman revolutionized my understanding of doctrinal development, his insights on conscience transformed my understanding of moral agency. In *Letter to the Duke of Norfolk*, Newman famously calls conscience the "aboriginal Vicar of Christ."[18] This meant that conscience is not merely a private feeling or a rational deduction; it is the privileged place where the human person encounters God's call.

This insight resonated deeply with my seminary experience. I had witnessed priests and even bishops act against what many ordinary Christians clearly recognized as morally wrong. I had seen faithful Catholics question the actions of their leaders but silence themselves out of fear or misplaced obedience. Newman gave me a theological language for this disquiet: obedience that violates conscience is not virtue—it is distortion.

For Newman, conscience and authority are not enemies but partners. Authority guides, but conscience discerns. Authority teaches, but conscience judges. Authority proposes, but conscience responds.

This approach helped me understand why I felt compelled to question the Church even as I loved it. Newman affirmed a paradox I had been living: faithfulness sometimes requires dissent—not dissent for its own sake, but dissent born of fidelity to the deeper truth of the Gospel.

11. PROPHETIC DISSENT: LOVING THE CHURCH ENOUGH TO CRITIQUE IT

My growing awareness of clerical corruption, sexual scandal, economic elitism, and political complicity within the Church created a profound internal struggle. On the one hand, I revered the Church as the sacrament of Christ's presence in the world. On the other hand, I could not ignore how its leaders sometimes betrayed that very mystery. Newman helped me resolve this tension by showing that dissent—when grounded in conscience and charity—is not rebellion but reform.

---

18. Newman, *Letter to the Duke of Norfolk*, 258.

He writes:

> "I shall drink to the Pope, if you please, still, to Conscience first."[19]

This declaration did not undermine the papacy; it clarified its purpose. The authority of the Church exists to serve truth, not to replace it. The Church's credibility does not rest on its ability to silence critique, but on its willingness to be purified by it.

This insight became crucial as I witnessed the Church losing members to evangelical communities. Many Catholics were not leaving because they rejected doctrine; they were leaving because they felt abandoned, dismissed, or scandalized. Their departure was an indictment not of faith but of failed leadership.

Prophetic dissent, therefore, became for me not merely a theoretical possibility but a pastoral necessity. If the Church is to be credible—especially among the poor, the young, and the wounded—it must first confront its own sin.

12. NEWMAN, LIBERATION THEOLOGY, AND THE SEEDS OF CSR

Although Newman lived in a very different context, his theological instincts aligned remarkably well with the core principles of liberation theology:

- Theology must respond to historical reality
- The poor have a privileged place in God's revelation
- The Church must undergo continual conversion
- Spiritual truths must have ethical consequences

Where Popper provided an epistemological humility and Boff provided a prophetic moral voice, Newman offered a theological coherence that connected them. His approach to development foreshadowed my later formulation of Critical Synthetic Realism (CSR), which likewise affirms:

1. Reality is objective and knowable, but only partially grasped by finite human minds.

---

19. Newman, *Letter to the Duke of Norfolk*, 261.

2. Knowledge grows through dialogue, correction, and synthesis.
3. Tradition is dynamic, not static.
4. Truth reveals itself through history, human freedom, and communal discernment.

CSR would become the philosophical scaffolding for Critical-Liberative Theology, offering a theoretical justification for why theology must remain responsive to new social, cultural, and scientific developments.

Newman's influence on my ecclesiology

Perhaps Newman's greatest gift to my theology was his understanding that the Church is a living organism. As he writes:

> "A great idea takes a different view of things as time goes on."[20]

This means that theological growth is not a deviation from truth but its unfolding. It also means that the Church can—and must—change in response to new insights about human dignity, justice, and the demands of the Gospel.

In this sense, Newman provided the courage to believe that confronting corruption and injustice within the Church is not disloyal—it is essential to the Church's mission. Reform is not optional; it is intrinsic to ecclesial life.

13. CONSCIENCE AND COURAGE AMID ECCLESIAL SCANDAL

As reports of clerical sexual abuse and systemic cover-up began to surface—first in whispers within African seminaries, later in global headlines—I found Newman's theology indispensable. The more I learned, the more emotionally shaken I became. The institution I loved and hoped to serve was implicated in profound moral failures. The Church's instinct to protect itself at the expense of victims revealed not only a failure of leadership but also a crisis of conscience.

Newman helped me understand that such crises demand not silence but courage. Authentic fidelity requires the willingness to confront darkness. In this sense, Newman strengthened my emerging conviction

---

20. Newman, *An Essay on the Development of Christian Doctrine*, 39.

that theology must not shy away from institutional critique. The Church cannot credibly proclaim the Gospel of liberation while ignoring the injustices it commits or tolerates.

Faithful dissent, grounded in conscience and love for the Church, became a central pillar of my theological vocation.

14. VATICAN II AS A MOMENT OF CRITICAL LIBERATION

As I moved deeper into theology, I became increasingly fascinated by the Second Vatican Council (1962–1965). Though it occurred decades before my seminary formation, its effects were still being debated in classrooms, parish halls, and clerical circles. Vatican II represented, for me, the clearest historical example of what I now call critical liberation within the Church itself—a moment when the Church looked into the mirror of the modern world, acknowledged its failings, and sought renewal.

Vatican II did not change doctrine so much as change the Church's posture:

from defensive to dialogical,

from insular to engaged,

from authoritarian to pastoral.

I was particularly struck by the Council's insistence that the Church must read "the signs of the times."[21] This phrase reverberated in my consciousness. It implied that theology is not merely deductive but responsive. It must listen to reality, not simply impose abstract principles upon it.

A Church willing to critique itself

For the first time in centuries, the Church publicly acknowledged that its structures, practices, and attitudes needed reform. The Council fathers recognized that the Church had in many ways aligned itself with power rather than the Gospel, privileged clerical authority over the people of God, and failed to address the deep yearning for justice present in the modern world.

---

21. *Gaudium et Spes,* §4.

The council documents are filled with luminous lines that called the Church to conversion:

- The Church is "in constant need of purification."[22]
- Christians must "scrutinize the signs of the times and interpret them in the light of the Gospel."[23]
- Human dignity is the foundation of all social.[24]

These were not merely pastoral statements. They were a theological revolution—an admission that truth unfolds historically and that the Church must reform itself to remain faithful to Christ.

Why Vatican II resonated so deeply with me

In the face of clerical scandals, elitism, and the suffering of the poor, Vatican II gave me language and authority to believe that critique is not betrayal but participation in the Church's own self-renewal.

For a young seminarian struggling with the contradictions between Gospel ideals and ecclesial realities, Vatican II functioned as a theological anchor. It showed that the Church could change—and change profoundly—when the Spirit demanded it.

Vatican II confirmed what I had learned from Newman and Küng:

the Church's credibility depends not on its power but on its willingness to convert.

15. THE INTERNAL TENSION: BETWEEN FIDELITY AND REFORM

Even as Vatican II inspired me, I felt an internal tension. On one hand, I loved the Church deeply. It nurtured my childhood faith, inspired my vocation, and gave me an intellectual home. On the other hand, I could not ignore the structural injustices and moral failures that wounded both the Church and its people.

---

22. *Lumen Gentium*, §8.
23. *Gaudium et Spes*, §4.
24. *Gaudium et Spes*, §26.

This tension—between faithful belonging and prophetic critique—would become a defining feature of my theology. On many days, it felt like a spiritual burden. On other days, it felt like a calling.

I came to understand that reform is itself an act of fidelity. Reformers like Francis of Assisi, Teresa of Ávila, John XXIII, Romero, and countless unnamed priests and laypeople did not love the Church less; they loved it so much that they dared to challenge it. They believed that the Church must resemble Christ, not only in doctrine but in practice—especially in its treatment of the poor and the vulnerable.

My own anger at ecclesial injustice was, in this sense, a form of love: love for the Church as it is, and hope for the Church as it could be.

16. THE BIRTH OF CRITICAL SYNTHETIC REALISM (CSR): AN EPISTEMOLOGY FOR A LIVING CHURCH

As my theological and philosophical reflections deepened, I realized that I needed a conceptual framework that could hold together the diverse influences shaping me:

- Popper's critical rationalism
- Newman's doctrinal development
- Rahner's transcendental theology
- Küng's commitment to truth and reform
- Boff's and Ela's prophetic liberationist voices

What emerged from this synthesis was Critical Synthetic Realism (CSR)—my attempt to articulate a comprehensive epistemological model that honors both the objectivity of truth and the limitations of human knowing.

CSR is built on several convictions:

1. Reality exists independently of perception, yet we only grasp it partially.
2. Human knowledge grows through critical engagement, not unquestioned acceptance.
3. Tradition is a living process, not a static archive.
4. Dialogue between disciplines and between cultures enriches understanding.

5. Errors, contradictions, and crises are not obstacles but catalysts for growth.

CSR allowed me to anchor theology in both critical realism and synthetic openness. It provided a philosophical foundation for understanding why doctrines develop, why ecclesial structures can fail, and why reform is not a deviation from tradition but a continuation of it.

CSR and the poor

As I began applying CSR to the real conditions of African life—the crushing poverty, political marginalization, corruption, and ecclesial elitism—I realized that knowledge divorced from suffering is incomplete. Suffering is a mode of revelation; it exposes dimensions of reality that abstract reasoning cannot reach.

CSR therefore requires not only philosophical critique but existential empathy and historical awareness. Any adequate theology must account for:

- The lived experiences of the poor
- The cry of the oppressed
- The wounds inflicted by corrupt institutions
- The silent suffering of those betrayed by their pastors
- The degradation of the earth

CSR, as it matured, became increasingly ethical. It pointed me beyond theoretical concerns toward the urgent question:

How must theology respond to injustice?

The answer began to take the shape of Critical-Liberative Theology (CLT).

17. CRITICAL-LIBERATIVE THEOLOGY: THE CHILD BORN OF EXPERIENCE AND REFLECTION

CLT emerged not from academic speculation alone but from the convergence of my spiritual journey, intellectual influences, and social experiences. It is the theological flowering of CSR in a world marked by inequality and suffering.

CLT rests on three foundational pillars:

1. Critical Reason (from Popper and Küng):

All theological claims must remain open to critique. Authority is not diminished by accountability; it is strengthened by it.

2. Historical Development (from Newman and Vatican II):

Doctrine grows through encounter with new questions. The Spirit speaks through history, culture, science, and conscience.

3. Liberation (from Boff, Gutiérrez, Ela, and Mveng)

Faith that does not confront injustice is not Christian faith. Theology must prioritize the poor, the marginalized, and the wounded.
CLT integrates these insights into a single conviction:
Faith seeks emancipation—not only through spiritual salvation but through justice, dignity, and the flourishing of all creation.

CLT and internal Church reform

The earliest intuitions of CLT formed the moment I realized that the Church must undergo its own liberation. It is not only society that needs transformation; the Church itself must be healed of elitism, corruption, clericalism, and silence in the face of injustice.
CLT therefore insists that:

- The Church must reform its structures
- Theology must confront painful truths
- The voices of the poor must shape doctrine
- Conscience must be respected
- Transparency and accountability must replace clerical privilege

This is not a theology *against* the Church but a theology *for* the Church—a Church more faithful to Christ, more credible to the world, and more attuned to the Spirit.

18. THE MORAL IMPERATIVE OF EMANCIPATORY THEOLOGY

As I synthesized these insights, one truth became central: theology that does not liberate is inadequate for our time. The Church must offer salvation not only in the eschatological sense but also in the historical sense. People today hunger for liberation from:

- poverty
- corruption
- systemic injustice
- spiritual emptiness
- political oppression
- clerical abuse
- ecological destruction

A credible theology must speak to these wounds.

Critical-Liberative Theology is my response—a theology that honors tradition but refuses to be imprisoned by it; that respects authority but questions abuses of power; that accepts doctrine but demands development; that loves the Church but insists on its conversion; and that seeks both earthly and heavenly liberation.

19. CONCLUSION: TOWARD A THEOLOGY THAT LIBERATES BOTH CHURCH AND WORLD

The journey traced in this chapter—intellectual, spiritual, and existential—reveals how my theology emerged not from abstract speculation but from the lived experience of contradiction, suffering, discovery, and hope. Critical-Liberative Theology did not spring forth fully formed. It grew through the friction between faith and reality, between tradition and conscience, between the ideals of the Gospel and the wounds inflicted by the very institution meant to embody it.

From my earliest days in the seminary, I sensed a tension that I could not yet articulate. I loved the Church profoundly, but I could not ignore the dissonance between its teachings and its actions. Clerical arrogance, sexual scandals whispered in corridors, financial impropriety, and pastoral indifference—all of these realities pierced my youthful idealism. And beyond the seminary walls, the crushing poverty of Cameroon stood in stark contrast to the comfortable lives of many clergy. The Church, called to be the sacrament of Christ's presence among the poor, often resembled the elites who exploited them.

My encounter with poverty was not abstract. Coming from an upper-middle-class family, I lived a sheltered life in my early years. But once exposed to the harshness of poverty, especially in rural communities, something in me shifted permanently. It became clear that religion that does not address earthly suffering fails in its heavenly mission. Salvation must be both terrestrial and celestial. A theology that cannot feed the hungry, heal the wounded, or confront oppression is a theology that has betrayed its vocation.

These painful realizations set the stage for the transformative intellectual encounters that followed.

Popper taught me that certainty is an illusion and that truth emerges through critique, humility, and the willingness to be corrected. His critical rationalism shattered the rigid scholastic frameworks that could not account for real-world complexity. Yet Popper also empowered me to believe that questioning does not weaken faith—it purifies it.

Newman then entered my life as a bridge-builder between my yearning for doctrinal fidelity and my awakening to historical development. His insight that "to live is to change"[25] provided the theological grounding that Popper's epistemology needed. Newman taught me that tradition is alive, that doctrine unfolds like an idea gaining clarity, and that conscience is the Church's truest compass.

Rahner deepened my understanding of God as Mystery—ever-present, ever-near, and encountered not in formulas but in the depths of human experience. His transcendental theology reminded me that every person is oriented toward the divine and that grace saturates history. He helped me appreciate the spiritual dimension of liberation and the sacredness of human dignity.

Küng, with his fearless critique of ecclesial pretensions and his unwavering commitment to truth, gave me the moral courage to believe that reform is not an act of rebellion but an act of fidelity. His work affirmed what I felt in my bones: love for the Church sometimes demands that we challenge it.

---

25. Newman, *An Essay on the Development of Christian Doctrine*, 40.

Boff, Ela, and Mveng completed the picture by revealing the inseparable link between faith and justice. They spoke openly about clerical elitism, ecclesial complicity, and the crushing weight of poverty. They taught me that God's preferential option for the poor is not a slogan but the heart of the Gospel. They reignited my theological imagination, turning me toward the cry of the oppressed as a source of revelation.

Then there was Vatican II—the great council that called the Church to convert herself, to become a servant church, a poor church, a listening church. Vatican II legitimized my emerging convictions: that the Church must read the signs of the times, that it must reform its structures, and that its credibility depends on its willingness to undergo purification. The council fathers reminded us that the Church does not exist for herself but for the world.

Out of the convergence of these influences came Critical Synthetic Realism (CSR)—my attempt to articulate an epistemology capable of holding together truth and history, objectivity and humility, tradition and reform. CSR became the philosophical scaffolding upon which I would construct Critical-Liberative Theology (CLT).

CLT emerged from the recognition that theology must not merely interpret reality; it must transform it. It insists that:

- Truth unfolds through critical engagement with reality.
- Doctrine must develop in response to conscience and experience.
- The Church must undergo continual reform.
- Liberation—spiritual, social, economic, ecological—is intrinsic to the Gospel.
- The cries of the poor and wounded are theological texts.
- Faith without justice is dead; justice without love is incomplete.

CLT is both a continuation of the Church's tradition and a challenge to it. It seeks not to destroy but to fulfill. It calls the Church to become what it proclaims: a community of mercy, justice, humility, and solidarity.

Personal Integration: A Theology Shaped by Life

What becomes clear in retrospect is that my theology was not produced in a library alone. It was forged in the seminary pews where disillusionment met hope, in the dusty streets where poverty revealed the limits of abstract doctrine, in late-night conversations with mentors who challenged me to think deeply, and in the pages of thinkers who dared to imagine a more just Church and world.

CLT is not a rejection of the Church. It is an act of fidelity to the Church's deepest calling. It echoes the courage of saints and prophets who loved the Church enough to confront its sins. It affirms that the Gospel's power is not diminished by critique; it is unleashed by it.

Toward the Rest of the Book

This first chapter sets the stage for the theological project developed in the rest of the book. The next chapters will examine:

- how doctrine develops,
- how power operates within the Church,
- how the poor reveal the face of Christ,
- how gender, sexuality, and embodiment must be rethought in light of human dignity,
- how ecological destruction demands theological response,
- and how the Church can reclaim its prophetic voice in a world hungry for justice.

Critical-Liberative Theology begins with a simple conviction:

Faith must seek emancipation—of persons, societies, the Church, and the entire creation.

It is my hope that the journey traced in this chapter becomes an invitation: to think courageously, to listen deeply, to question lovingly, and to believe that transformation is possible.

Not in some distant future.

Not only in heaven.

But here, now, in the fragile, beautiful, wounded world that God so loves.

CHAPTER 2

Methodological Framework: Faith, Reason, and Emancipatory Praxis

A) INTRODUCTION

1. Theology as a Way of Knowing and Acting

Every theology, whether acknowledged or not, operates with a method—a particular way of approaching truth, discerning meaning, and evaluating the relationship between God and the world. For centuries, Catholic theology relied primarily on scholastic method, emphasizing logical clarity, metaphysical categories, and deductive reasoning. While these tools remain valuable, they prove insufficient in a world marked by profound social injustice, political turmoil, sexual abuse scandals, ecological crisis, and existential homelessness.

As the Church confronts this wounded world, theology must likewise undergo a methodological conversion. The questions facing Christian communities today cannot be answered solely by appealing to metaphysical definitions or canonical formulations. They require a method that listens to experience, respects human dignity, integrates historical consciousness, and confronts structures of power. They require a methodology that embraces both critical humility and liberative courage.

This chapter outlines the methodological foundations of Critical-Liberative Theology (CLT). These foundations draw from my intellectual encounters with figures like Popper, Newman, Rahner, Küng, Boff, Ela, and Mveng; from my experiences of ecclesial contradiction; and from the social realities that press urgently upon African and global Christianity.

CLT rests on three core commitments:

1. Hermeneutical openness: Scripture must be read not only as text but as *call to action* in concrete history.
2. Epistemological humility: Truth is real yet always mediated, partial, and calling for further discernment.
3. Emancipatory praxis: Theology is accountable to lived experience and must promote justice, dignity, and the flourishing of creation.

These commitments converge into a coherent method grounded in critical inquiry, prophetic praxis, and communal discernment. The result is a way of doing theology that is not merely descriptive but transformative—not only contemplative but active, not only faithful but free.

2. Hermeneutics: Scripture as a Call to Action

At the heart of Christian theology lies Scripture. But how we read Scripture determines whether theology becomes an agent of liberation or an instrument of oppression. Too often, the Church has treated Scripture as a repository of timeless propositions rather than a living encounter with the God who acts within history. In contrast, liberation theologians insist that the Bible is best understood when read through the lens of the oppressed.

The Gospel of Luke records Jesus' proclamation:

> "He has sent me to bring the good news to the poor,
> to proclaim liberty to captives
> and recovery of sight to the blind."
> (Luke 4:18, Jerusalem Bible)

This is not merely a theological statement; it is a programmatic declaration. The hermeneutical method of CLT begins with this recognition: the Word of God summons us to concrete action for justice.

The inadequacy of purely literal or purely spiritual readings

Many scriptural interpretations have historically fallen into two extremes:

Literalism, which reduces Scripture to its surface meaning, ignoring cultural, linguistic, and historical context.

Spiritualism, which evacuates Scripture of concrete ethical demands by allegorizing it into vague moral principles.

CLT rejects both extremes. Scripture must be taken seriously both in its historical context and in its ethical urgency. It must be read "from below"—from the viewpoint of those who suffer—because that is the place from which God chooses to speak most forcefully in the biblical narrative.

Hermeneutics of liberation

Liberation hermeneutics has several core features:

- Preference for narratives of oppression and deliverance (Exodus, Prophets, Gospels).
- Attention to socio-political contexts of biblical communities.
- Interpretation grounded in contemporary struggles for justice.
- Recognition that Scripture critiques religious hypocrisy, including that of the Church.

This method acknowledges that God does not speak uniformly through the entire Bible; God speaks most clearly where human beings are most vulnerable.

The role of African experience

African theology brings its own hermeneutical riches: communal identity, reverence for ancestors, sensitivity to suffering, and a deep connection to land and ecology. These experiences expand liberation hermeneutics by insisting that Scripture must address not only economic poverty but also:

- cultural dislocation
- postcolonial trauma
- ethnic and religious conflict
- ecological devastation
- anthropological marginalization

A hermeneutical method that ignores African realities is not merely incomplete; it is unfaithful.

3. Epistemology: Truth as Tested, Provisional, and Oriented Toward Liberation

Critical-Liberative Theology adopts an epistemology rooted in Critical Synthetic Realism (CSR)—a synthesis of critical rationalism, historical consciousness, and a realist commitment to objective truth.

a. Truth exists, but we grasp it gradually

Against postmodern relativism, CSR asserts that truth is real and objective. Against fundamentalism, it asserts that our understanding of truth is always mediated, limited, and subject to correction.

This echoes St. Paul's recognition that:

> "Now we see only reflections in a mirror, mere riddles."
> *(1 Corinthians 13:12, Jerusalem Bible)*

We grasp truth, but not fully. Our theological statements point toward divine mystery; they do not capture it exhaustively.

b. The role of critique in theological growth

Following Popper, CSR holds that knowledge grows when it is tested—especially by the harsh realities of life. Theological claims that do not survive encounter with:

- the suffering of the poor
- the voices of women and marginalized groups
- the cry of the earth
- the historical evidence of injustice
- the moral judgments of conscience

must be revised or abandoned.
This does not relativize faith; it refines it.

c. Tradition as dynamic

Newman's insight is crucial: doctrine develops. Tradition is not a museum but a living organism. The Holy Spirit speaks through history, science, culture, and experience. Epistemology therefore must be dynamic, allowing room for:

- doctrinal growth
- moral maturation
- ecclesial reform
- new categories of human dignity

  If doctrine cannot respond to new insights, it becomes an idol.

d. Liberation as epistemic criterion

Liberation theologians argue that truth is recognized not only through rational coherence but through its capacity to set people free. A theology that perpetuates oppression—even unintentionally—is epistemologically flawed. Jesus' teachings are credible not because they are logically impeccable, but because they heal, reconcile, liberate, and restore.

Thus, epistemology and ethics are inseparable.

4. Social Analysis: Seeing the World Truthfully

Theological method must include robust social analysis. Too often, theologians have treated social realities—poverty, politics, economics, patriarchy, ecological crisis—as secular subjects outside theology's domain. Liberation theology rejects this false divide.

To speak of God in a suffering world is to analyze:

- economic structures that impoverish
- political systems that oppress
- cultural norms that discriminate
- ecclesial structures that exclude
- global forces that dehumanize

Catholic Social Teaching has long emphasized the need for structural analysis. *Gaudium et Spes* (§1) states that "the joys and hopes, the griefs and anxieties" of the poor are the Church's own. Theology that ignores social reality becomes, at best, irrelevant; at worst, complicit.

The African context

African social analysis must confront:

- postcolonial exploitation
- corruption
- ethnic tensions
- gender inequality
- predatory capitalism
- religious fundamentalism
- ecological destruction (forests, rivers, land-grabs)

African theology is inherently socio-political because African life is shaped by socio-political wounds.

The ecclesial context

The Church must also analyze itself. Structures of clericalism, patriarchal exclusion, financial opacity, sexual abuse, and elitism are not merely moral problems; they are theological problems that distort the Church's witness.

5. Moral Agency and Responsibility: The Human Person as Co-Worker in Liberation

Any credible theological method must take seriously the moral agency of the human person. In classical Catholic theology, moral agency was often discussed abstractly: the will, the intellect, natural law, and virtue. Liberation theologians do not reject these categories, but they insist on grounding them in historical responsibility. The human person is not simply a moral agent in private life but a co-worker with God in transforming the world.

This insight resonates with Rahner's claim that every person is a "hearer of the Word" and oriented toward God through free, responsible decisions (Rahner, 1978). It also resonates with Newman's insistence that conscience is the primary authority guiding human responsibility.

Beyond the individualistic view of morality

Traditional catechesis often reduced morality to personal sins—lying, stealing, sexual misconduct—while ignoring the structural injustices that shape entire societies. Liberation theology expands moral reflection by teaching that:

- participating in unjust systems
- remaining silent in the face of injustice
- benefiting from oppression
- ignoring the suffering of others

are moral failures just as real as personal sin.

Jesus' parable of the Last Judgment (Matthew 25), in the Jerusalem Bible translation, makes this clear:

> "In so far as you neglected to do this to one of the least of these, you neglected to do it to me."

Neglect, silence, indifference—these are theological failures, not merely ethical ones.

Global examples of moral agency and ecclesial crisis

To illustrate this, consider three global examples where moral agency is at the center of theological discernment:

1. The clerical abuse crisis in Europe and North America
2. The crisis revealed not only individual crimes but systemic failures: bishops covering up abuse, dioceses protecting institutional reputation over victims, and cultures of clericalism that silenced questioning. Here moral agency demanded whistleblowing, transparency, truth-telling, and structural reform—not simply personal repentance.

3. Migration and xenophobia in Europe

4. As millions flee war, persecution, and poverty, European churches face the moral question of hospitality versus nationalism. Pope Francis' famous plea—"Who is my neighbor if not the migrant?"—demands a global moral imagination.

5. Racial injustice in the United States

6. After George Floyd's murder in 2020, many U.S. churches recognized their complicity in racial structures. The call for repentance was not simply personal but institutional. Theologians such as Bryan Massingale have shown how racism is a "soul-sickness," requiring radical conversion at all levels of society and church.

These examples show why CLT emphasizes moral agency as social responsibility.

6. Methodological Tools of CLT

CLT is not a loose collection of ideas; it is a structured methodology rooted in three interrelated tools:

1. Critical inquiry
2. Prophetic praxis
3. Communal discernment

Each of these tools emerges from the Christian tradition yet responds to contemporary needs.

6.1 Critical Inquiry: Thinking Faithfully and Honestly

Critical inquiry insists that theology must:

- ask difficult questions
- interrogate power
- examine tradition with humility
- evaluate moral and doctrinal claims in light of experience
- differentiate between divine revelation and human error

This method reflects Popper's insight that knowledge grows through critique, as well as Küng's belief that the Church must always be engaged in self-examination.

Examples from the Global Church

Hans Küng's challenge to papal infallibility demonstrated the role of critical inquiry in doctrinal development.

- The Synodal Path in Germany is engaging critical questions on power, clericalism, gender, sexuality, and authority.
- Theological debates on LGBTQ inclusion in North America and Europe show the need for honest inquiry into both Scripture and human experience.
- Asian feminist theologians—such as Chung Hyun Kyung—critically interrogate patriarchy in church and culture.

Theology that forbids critique becomes ideology. Theology that embraces critique becomes a path to truth.

6.2 Prophetic Praxis: Theology as Action

If critical inquiry is the head of CLT, prophetic praxis is its heart.

Praxis is not simply "action"; it is reflective action grounded in faith and directed toward liberation. It is the recognition that theology becomes credible only when it generates transformation in the real world.

This approach echoes the biblical prophets, who constantly linked worship with justice:

> "Let justice flow like water, and integrity like an unfailing stream."
> *(Amos 5:24, Jerusalem Bible)*

Praxis insists that the credibility of theology does not lie in its internal coherence alone, but in its ability to:

- defend the oppressed
- challenge unjust systems
- comfort victims
- promote ecological stewardship

- foster reconciliation

Global examples of prophetic praxis

Óscar Romero in El Salvador, who denounced state violence from the pulpit and was martyred for it.

- Dorothy Day and the Catholic Worker Movement in the United States, combining radical hospitality with political resistance.
- Catholic social activists in the Philippines, especially during resistance to dictatorship.
- German and Polish priests who resisted Nazism—such as Alfred Delp or Maximilian Kolbe.
- Indigenous theologians in Latin America and Oceania, whose ministry includes protecting ancestral lands against extractive industries.

These examples show that prophetic praxis is not confined to one geographical region; it is the lifeblood of the global Church.

6.3 Communal Discernment: Hearing the Spirit in the People of God

Vatican II restored an ancient truth: the entire People of God shares in Christ's prophetic office.[1]

Communal discernment recognizes that the Holy Spirit speaks:

- through the poor
- through marginalized voices
- through the sensus fidelium
- through local communities
- through interfaith partners
- through victims of injustice
- through scientific insight and secular wisdom

This means theology must be dialogical. It cannot be imposed from above.

---

1. *Lumen Gentium*, §12.

Global movements in communal discernment

Latin American ecclesial base communities, which read Scripture together through the eyes of the poor.

- Synodal assemblies in Europe and Australia, seeking structural reform.
- The Amazon Synod (2019), which elevated indigenous voices in theological reflection.
- Catholic social movements in India, emphasizing interreligious dialogue, especially with Dalit and tribal communities.
- The U.S. Black Catholic Congress, articulating a theology of justice, healing, and racial equality.

Communal discernment anchors CLT in the lived experience of the global Church.

7. Case Study: The Theology of Accompaniment in Latin America and Beyond

One of the richest contemporary examples of CLT's methodological principles is the theology of accompaniment—an approach rooted in Latin America but now global.

Accompaniment means:

- walking with people in their struggles
- listening before teaching
- allowing the poor to shape moral and pastoral priorities
- recognizing that grace is encountered through presence

This method influenced:

- pastoral ministry in U.S. immigrant communities
- ministry with Indigenous peoples in Canada
- European refugee ministries
- LGBTQ outreach in Germany, Belgium, and parts of the U.S.
- Asian "minjung theology," which accompanies the suffering masses of Korea

Accompaniment integrates hermeneutics, ethics, and pastoral practice. It embodies Pope Francis' vision of a Church that is a "field hospital after battle."

8. Liberation Theology: A Global History of Faith in Struggle

Liberation theology is often associated with Latin America, but its roots, resonances, and impact extend far beyond a single region. It is a global Christian phenomenon, emerging wherever suffering people read Scripture with expectant hope and prophetic anger. It is a theological methodology born from the cry of the oppressed—a cry that echoes across continents, cultures, and historical moments.

The purpose of reviewing this history is methodological: liberation theology teaches us *how* to do theology in contexts of injustice. Its global manifestations demonstrate that theology must be rooted in lived experience, communal discernment, and a commitment to emancipation.

9. Latin America: The Birthplace of Liberation Theology

a. Gustavo Gutiérrez and the foundational vision

Liberation theology's most well-known articulation emerged with Peruvian priest Gustavo Gutiérrez, whose groundbreaking book *A Theology of Liberation* (1973) argued that Christian faith demands:

- analysis of structural sin
- solidarity with the poor
- transformation of unjust social systems
- historical praxis inspired by the Gospel

Gutiérrez introduced the famous definition:

> "Theology is critical reflection on Christian praxis in the light of the Word of God."
> (Gutiérrez, A Theology of Liberation, p. 11)

This definition revolutionized theological method. Theology was no longer simply contemplation; it became active, participatory, historical.

b. Liberation theologians under authoritarian regimes

Liberation theology matured under oppressive political conditions. In Brazil, Argentina, Chile, El Salvador, and Guatemala, theologians and pastoral agents confronted:

- military dictatorships
- disappearances and kidnappings
- torture
- economic inequality
- death squads

Figures such as Jon Sobrino, Leonardo Boff, Freire in education, and Archbishop Óscar Romero became champions of justice. Romero's martyrdom in 1980 symbolized the theological courage of the region.

c. Ecclesial base communities

Small Christian communities (CEBs) emerged where Scripture was read collectively through the lens of local suffering. These groups became the pastoral backbone of liberation theology—schools of discipleship that merged faith with social consciousness.

The Latin American experience offers a methodological lesson: the poor are not merely recipients of theology; they are its producers.

10. Africa: Liberation as Decolonization, Cultural Revival, and Social Justice

While liberation theology in Africa shares an option for the poor, it evolved within the context of colonialism, apartheid, economic exploitation, and cultural alienation.

a. Jean-Marc Ela

Ela's *African Cry* (1986) insists that theology must address the concrete suffering of African communities—poverty, hunger, political repression. He famously wrote that African Christians "pray in the language of Europe while dying in the language of Africa." His critique exposed the mismatch between imported theological categories and African lived realities.

b. Engelbert Mveng

Mveng coined the phrase "anthropological poverty" to describe the dehumanization inflicted by colonial powers. He asserted that liberation must be cultural, economic, and ecclesial.

C. South Africa and apartheid

The Kairos Document (1985), written during apartheid, argued that Christian theology cannot remain neutral in the face of systemic injustice. The document distinguished three theologies:

- State theology (justifying oppression)
- Church theology (neutral but complicit)
- Prophetic theology (rejecting injustice in God's name)

This remains one of the clearest methodological statements in liberation theology.

Africa teaches the global Church that liberation includes identity, culture, land, and memory—elements often neglected in Western discourse.

11. Asia: Liberation as Interfaith Dialogue, Cultural Resistance, and Struggle Against Caste

Asian liberation theologies reflect the continent's religious pluralism, communal suffering, and cultural complexity.

a. Minjung theology (Korea)

Minjung theology emerged during Korea's authoritarian era. "Minjung" means "the people," especially the oppressed masses. Theologians like Ahn Byung-mu interpreted Jesus as standing with the suffering people against corrupt elites. The minjung became the locus of divine revelation.

b. Dalit theology (India)

India's caste system prompted Dalit Christians to articulate a theology of dignity, liberation, and cultural affirmation. Arvind P. Nirmal argued that Jesus identifies with the Dalits because he too experienced social rejection. Dalit theology critiques not only Hindu caste structures but also casteism within Christian churches.

c. Feminist theologies across Asia

Asian feminist theologians—such as Chung Hyun Kyung—expand liberation's scope by incorporating gender, ecology, and indigenous wisdom.

Asia teaches that liberation theology must adapt to cultural and religious plurality, and that oppression takes many forms—not only economic but also caste-based, patriarchal, and militaristic.

12. Europe: Liberation in a Post-Christian, Postcolonial, and Migrant Age

Liberation theology in Europe may seem paradoxical, given Europe's wealth and its role as the seat of colonial power. Yet significant liberation movements have emerged there, especially around:

- migration
- racism
- secular alienation
- the rise of far-right nationalism
- economic austerity
- clerical abuse crisis

a. Migrant theology

As Europe receives millions of refugees from Africa, the Middle East, and Eastern Europe, Christian communities face the moral question of hospitality.

The Sant'Egidio Community in Rome models a "theology of welcome," grounded in prayer and solidarity. Their method illustrates a liberation theology suited to a pluralistic environment.

b. Political theology in Germany

The postwar German theological landscape (Metz, Moltmann) responded to the Holocaust and totalitarianism. Johann Baptist Metz emphasized "dangerous memory"—the duty of the Church to remember the suffering of victims. Jürgen Moltmann insisted on the "crucified God" who stands with the oppressed.

c. Liberation and ecclesial reform

Europe's clergy abuse crisis sparked new forms of liberation theology focused on ecclesial transparency, accountability, and the dismantling of clericalism.

Europe teaches that liberation must confront historical sins, institutional failures, and the marginalization created by modernity.

13. North America: Liberation as Anti-Racism, Feminism, and LGBTQ Inclusion

In North America, liberation theology took shape in diverse forms.

a. Black liberation theology

James Cone's seminal *A Black Theology of Liberation* (1970) asserts that "God is Black"—meaning God identifies with those persecuted by racism. Black liberation theology interprets Scripture through the experience of slavery, segregation, violence, and systemic injustice.

b. Latinx and migrant liberation theology

Theologies arising from Mexican-American and Central American communities emphasize accompaniment, sanctuary movements, and the Gospel as solidarity with migrants.

c. Feminist and womanist theologies

Feminist theologians (Ruether, Schüssler Fiorenza) and womanist theologians (Katie Cannon, Delores Williams) critique patriarchy and racialized sexism. They push the Church to confront its complicity in misogyny and racialized exclusion.

d. LGBTQ-inclusive theologies

These movements explore liberation for those marginalized because of sexual orientation or gender identity. They argue for theological frameworks based on dignity, conscience, and the primacy of love.

North America teaches the global Church that liberation includes dismantling racism, sexism, homophobia, and xenophobia—and that theology must listen to those wounded by religious institutions.

14. Methodological Lessons from the Global Church

Across continents, certain methodological themes emerge:

1. Oppression has many faces—economic, political, cultural, racial, sexual, ecological, ecclesial.
2. The poor and marginalized are theological subjects, not objects.
3. Theology must confront structural sin, not only personal sin.
4. Liberation requires interdisciplinary analysis, including economics, sociology, politics, and psychology.
5. Local contexts matter, but global solidarity enriches understanding.
6. The Church itself must undergo liberation, becoming transparent, humble, and just.

Liberation theology, therefore, is not a regional movement but a global methodological orientation—a way of doing theology that responds to suffering wherever it is found.

15. Introduction: Scripture as the Library of Liberation

Liberation theology is not an invention of the 20th century. It arises from the deepest currents of biblical revelation. The Bible is the sustained narrative of God's engagement with human suffering and God's redemptive commitment to justice. Liberation is not a theological afterthought—it is the beating heart of Scripture.

Critical-Liberative Theology reads the Bible through the lens of God's preferential care for the oppressed, not as an ideological projection but as a hermeneutical recognition of Scripture's central themes. The Exodus, the prophetic tradition, the ministry of Jesus, the crucifixion, and the resurrection each provide paradigms that shape theology's method.

Here we explore these paradigms using the Jerusalem Bible translation for scriptural references.

B) THE EXODUS: THE FOUNDATIONAL STORY OF EMANCIPATION

16. Exodus as the Archetype of Liberation

No narrative has shaped liberation theology more deeply than the Exodus. It is the primal story of God siding with the oppressed against the structures of empire. God hears the cry of enslaved laborers and intervenes in history.

> "I have seen the miserable state of my people... I have heard their appeal... Yes, I am well aware of their sufferings."
> *(Exodus 3:7, JB)*

Three elements of this passage form the foundation of a liberationist hermeneutic:

1. God sees oppression
2. God hears the cry of the oppressed
3. God takes action in history

   Liberation is not merely spiritual; it is socio-political.
   The methodological implications

- God's revelation is tied to historical suffering.
- The oppressed are the privileged recipients of God's concern.

- Theology must ask: *Where is contemporary Egypt? Who is Pharaoh today? Who are the enslaved?*

Exodus as global template

Latin America applied Exodus to peasants under oligarchic regimes.

- Black liberation theologians applied it to slavery and segregation.
- Asian theologians applied it to caste oppression.
- European theologians used it to interpret resistance against Nazism and fascism.
- North American immigrant communities see it in the struggle for safety and dignity.

Wherever oppression exists, Exodus becomes a theological grammar.

C) THE PROPHETS: GOD'S CRITIQUE OF RELIGIOUS AND POLITICAL POWER

17. Prophetic Denunciation: God on the Side of Justice

The prophets are the biblical tradition's most explicit critique of injustice, exploitation, and religious hypocrisy. Their method is uncompromising honesty before God and society.

Amos, addressing a wealthy elite indifferent to the poor, declared:

> "Let justice flow like water, and integrity like an unfailing stream."
> *(Amos 5:24, JB)*

Isaiah, confronting corrupt rulers, proclaimed:

> "Cease to do evil. Learn to do good; search for justice, help the oppressed."
> *(Isaiah 1:16–17, JB)*

Prophets as methodological models

1. They read social reality through God's eyes.
2. They link worship to ethics.
3. They confront both kings and priests.
4. They refuse neutrality in the face of injustice.

Liberation theology adopts this prophetic stance, insisting that theology must hold both Church and society accountable to God's justice.

Prophetic critique of religious institutions

This is crucial:
The prophets criticize *religion itself* when it becomes complicit in oppression.

> "I hate your festivals… Away with the noise of your chants!"
> *(Amos 5:21, 23, JB)*

The implication for theological method is clear:
Authentic faith cannot coexist with injustice.

D) JESUS: THE LIBERATOR WHO INAUGURATES THE KINGDOM

18. Jesus' Mission Statement in Luke 4

In the synagogue at Nazareth, Jesus reads from Isaiah and declares the fulfillment of the prophecy:

> "The spirit of the Lord has been given to me…
> He has sent me to bring the good news to the poor,
> to proclaim liberty to captives
> and new sight to the blind,
> to set the downtrodden free."
> *(Luke 4:18–19, JB)*

This is not a metaphor. It is a public proclamation of Jesus' mission. Liberation is woven into the Christological identity of Jesus.

Jesus' method: accompaniment and confrontation

Jesus' ministry includes:

- Healing the sick
- Eating with sinners
- Touching the untouchable
- Challenging religious leaders
- Defending the marginalized
- Naming hypocrisy

Jesus does theology on the move, in the streets, among the wounded—not primarily in academic or priestly elites.

This challenges theologians to reject any method that abstracts faith from the suffering of real people.

19. The Kingdom of God as Social, Spiritual, and Political Reality

Jesus announces the Kingdom of God, not as an otherworldly dream but as a concrete reordering of relationships, priorities, and structures.

The Kingdom upends social hierarchies

The poor are blessed.

- The last become first.
- The meek inherit the earth.
- The hungry are filled.
- The weeping rejoice.

This is a theological revolution that challenges wealth, privilege, and exclusion.

The Kingdom confronts empire

Jesus' message was politically dangerous. His proclamation of God's reign directly threatened Roman imperial ideology and the local religious elite. Therefore, liberation theology emphasizes that:

Announcing the Kingdom entails resisting oppressive powers.

E) THE CROSS: THE VICTIM OF SYSTEMIC VIOLENCE

20. The Cross as Public Execution, Not Only Spiritual Symbol

Christian tradition often spiritualizes the cross, focusing on personal sin. Liberation theology insists on its historical and political dimensions.

Jesus was executed because he threatened unjust systems:

- Roman political power
- Temple economic interests
- Priestly authority
- Social boundaries

The cross is the place where all oppressive forces converge.

The crucified peoples of history

Jon Sobrino speaks of "the crucified peoples"—those whose suffering mirrors the unjust death of Jesus. The cross reveals:

- God's solidarity with victims
- God's judgment on oppressive structures
- The cost of prophetic witness

A theology that ignores these realities does not take the cross seriously.

F) THE RESURRECTION: GOD'S YES TO JUSTICE AND HOPE

21. Resurrection as Cosmic Liberation

The resurrection is not merely the vindication of Jesus; it is the victory of life over death, justice over injustice, and hope over despair.

The resurrection proclaims:

- The world can change.
- Oppression is not the last word.
- Death-dealing systems crumble.
- God's power is life-giving, not dominating.

Methodological implications

Theology must be hopeful without being naïve.

5. Liberation is possible because God transforms history.
6. Ecclesial reform is not optional but grounded in resurrection hope.
7. Justice movements reflect God's ongoing work.

The resurrection gives CLT its horizon:
Emancipation is both a present struggle and a promised future.

22. Summary: Scripture as Methodological Grounding

The biblical paradigms show that:

- Exodus teaches that God liberates the oppressed.
- Prophets model critique of power.
- Jesus embodies liberation.
- The Kingdom reorders society.
- The Cross exposes systemic violence.
- The Resurrection affirms hope and transformation.

Thus, Scripture is not merely a text to interpret—it is a method to imitate, a theological compass pointing toward liberation.

23. Introduction: Why Case Studies Matter in Methodology

Theology does not exist in a vacuum. It is always embedded in a concrete social context. If a theological method cannot address the lived experience of suffering, injustice, and human longing, it fails to fulfill its purpose. Case studies are essential for CLT because they show how method becomes praxis—how critical inquiry, biblical paradigms, and ethical discernment converge in real-world struggles.

The following global examples illustrate CLT's methodological usefulness and adaptability.

G) CASE STUDY 1: THE CLERICAL ABUSE CRISIS (UNITED STATES, IRELAND, GERMANY)

24. Liberation Through Truth-Telling

Few crises have shaken the global Church as profoundly as the clerical sexual abuse scandal. It is not only a moral catastrophe but a theological one, because it calls into question:

- ecclesial authority
- structures of secrecy
- clerical privilege
- misuse of spiritual power
- the Church's credibility

How CLT interprets this crisis

A. Critical Inquiry:

CLT demands a fearless examination of institutional structures that enabled systemic abuse. The methodological question is not merely *who sinned*, but *what structures allowed this sin to flourish?* Silence and denial are incompatible with the Gospel.

52   BEYOND DOCTRINE

B. Prophetic Praxis:

The Church's response must prioritize victims over institutional preservation. Justice requires transparency, reparation, and structural reform.

C. Communal Discernment:

Listening to survivors becomes a theological act. Their voices reveal the wounds of Christ in the body of the Church.

Methodological lesson

The clerical abuse crisis demonstrates why theology must question power. Any method that protects institutions over persons betrays the Gospel. CLT provides a framework for confronting this systemic failure and promoting conversion.

H) CASE STUDY 2: REFUGEES AND MIGRATION (EUROPE, MIDDLE EAST, GLOBAL SOUTH)

25. Liberation as Hospitality

Europe's ongoing migration crisis—shaped by conflicts in Syria, Afghanistan, Iraq, Eritrea, Sudan, and elsewhere—has created a theological crossroads. Millions of refugees seek safety while populist rhetoric fuels fear and hostility.

How CLT interprets this crisis

A. Hermeneutics:

Biblical narratives of migration—Abraham, Moses, Ruth, the Holy Family fleeing to Egypt—challenge xenophobic attitudes. Scripture sees the migrant as a sacred guest.

B. Social Analysis:

Migration is often the result of economic injustice, war, climate change, or political instability—issues that require structural solutions, not charity alone.

C. PRAXIS:

Movements like the Sant'Egidio Community and Jesuit Refugee Service embody CLT by offering housing, legal aid, and advocacy.

Methodological lesson

Liberation theology teaches that the stranger is a locus of revelation. The Church's stance toward migrants reveals the integrity of its faith.

I) CASE STUDY 3: THE FIGHT AGAINST RACISM (UNITED STATES, BRAZIL, SOUTH AFRICA, UNITED KINGDOM)

26. Liberation as Anti-Racism

The murder of George Floyd in 2020 catalyzed global calls for racial justice. Churches confronted their complicity in racial structures and their failure to address inequality.

How CLT interprets this crisis

A. CRITICAL INQUIRY:

Racism is a structural sin embedded in institutions, not merely a personal prejudice. It demands systemic analysis.

B. TRADITION:

Biblical teachings on human dignity and equality directly oppose racial hierarchy.

C. PRAXIS:

Black churches in the U.S., Afro-Brazilian Christian movements, and South African reconciliation initiatives draw on liberation themes to promote justice and healing.

D. Communal Discernment:

The theology of *lament*—truth-telling, mourning, naming injustice—becomes a path toward repentance and hope.

Methodological lesson

Anti-racism is not an optional social issue but a theological imperative grounded in creation, incarnation, and redemption.

J) CASE STUDY 4: GENDER JUSTICE AND WOMEN'S EMPOWERMENT (GLOBAL)

27. Liberation Feminism

Across continents, women challenge patriarchal interpretations of Scripture and ecclesial structures that exclude them from leadership.

How CLT interprets this crisis

A. Hermeneutics:

Biblical texts are reread in light of women's experience, revealing themes of equality, inclusion, and prophetic leadership (from Miriam to Mary Magdalene).

B. Social Analysis:

Feminist theologians show how patriarchal cultures shape theology and church practices, often distorting the Gospel.

C. Praxis:

Women religious in the U.S., Europe, India, and Latin America lead anti-trafficking initiatives, ecological missions, and ministries to the poor—often outperforming male-dominated structures.

Methodological lesson

Liberation theology insists that full human dignity requires full participation. Any theology or ecclesial structure that excludes women is methodologically flawed.

K) CASE STUDY 5: ECOLOGICAL CRISIS AND CLIMATE JUSTICE (AMAZON, PACIFIC ISLANDS, ASIA, EUROPE)

28. Liberation for Creation

Ecological destruction is now one of the greatest moral crises of our time. Rising seas threaten Pacific islands; the Amazon is devastated by deforestation; pollution suffocates cities in Asia; climate refugees multiply.

How CLT interprets this crisis

A. HERMENEUTICS:

Genesis portrays humans as caretakers, not conquerors. The Psalms describe creation as God's beloved work. Romans 8 speaks of creation "groaning" for liberation.

B. SOCIAL ANALYSIS:

Environmental harm is often tied to economic exploitation, extractive industries, and neoliberal structures.

C. PRAXIS:

The Amazon Synod (2019) exemplifies CLT by integrating indigenous voices, ecological wisdom, and critiques of colonialism.

D. GLOBAL MOVEMENTS:

European ecological movements, Filipino climate justice initiatives, and U.S.-based Catholic ecological networks embody this method.

Methodological lesson

Ecology is not a new topic but a new lens. Liberation includes the earth itself.

M) CASE STUDY 6: INDIGENOUS RIGHTS AND CULTURAL LIBERATION (CANADA, AUSTRALIA, PHILIPPINES, LATIN AMERICA)

29. Liberation as Cultural Survival

Indigenous peoples around the world have faced systemic dispossession, forced assimilation, destroyed traditions, and violated lands.

How CLT interprets this crisis

A. HERMENEUTICS:

Biblical themes of land, covenant, and identity take on new meaning when read through colonized communities.

B. CRITICAL INQUIRY:

Missionary history must be evaluated honestly, including the Church's complicity in cultural oppression (e.g., residential schools in Canada).

C. PRAXIS:

Indigenous theologians articulate liberation as cultural revival, ecological protection, and historical truth-telling.

Methodological lesson

Liberation must restore not only justice but cultural identity, memory, and sovereignty.

N) CASE STUDY 7: THE LGBTQ+ QUESTION (NORTH AMERICA, EUROPE, GLOBAL SOUTH VARIANTS)

30. Liberation as Inclusion and Conscience

The struggle for LGBTQ+ dignity within the global Church has become a pressing theological frontier. The debate is often polarized, but at its core lies a methodological question:

How do we interpret doctrine in light of human experience, conscience, and scientific knowledge?

How CLT interprets this crisis

A. CONSCIENCE:

Newman's teachings emphasize that conscience is the primary moral authority in the believer's life.

B. SOCIAL ANALYSIS:

LGBTQ persons face violence, discrimination, homelessness, and rejection—clear markers of social sin.

C. PRAXIS:

Pastoral accompaniment, as encouraged by Pope Francis, becomes the methodological norm.

D. GLOBAL VARIATION:

- In Germany and the U.S., inclusive ministries flourish.
- In parts of Africa and Asia, social stigma intensifies, requiring theological courage to defend human dignity.

Methodological lesson

Any theology that produces unjust suffering demands reevaluation.

31. Summary of Global Lessons

Across continents, liberation theology provides tools to analyze:

- power
- oppression
- conscience
- structural sin
- ecclesial failure
- social transformation

These global case studies demonstrate that CLT is not tied to one context; it is a method adaptable to every context where God's people seek justice.

32. The Francis Pontificate: Renewal of Method Without Structural Transformation

No contemporary figure has shaped the methodological imagination of the global Church more than Pope Francis. From the moment of his election in 2013, Francis signaled a pastoral and theological shift toward mercy, inclusion, ecological justice, transparency, and synodality. His papacy is deeply resonant with the methodological foundations of Critical-Liberative Theology (CLT), especially in its:

- emphasis on listening
- prophetic critique of clerical privilege
- preferential option for the poor
- global ecological consciousness
- insistence that doctrine develops through discernment

a. Evangelii Gaudium (2013): A Program for a Missionary, Liberative Church

In *Evangelii Gaudium*, Francis issued a sweeping call for ecclesial reform, famously declaring:

METHODOLOGICAL FRAMEWORK 59

"I prefer a Church which is bruised, hurting and dirty because it has been out on the streets." *(EG, §49)*

This vision challenges a defensive, self-enclosed Church. Methodologically, Francis insists that:

- evangelization must be grounded in the lived realities of the poor,
- the Church must be decentralized and synodal,
- pastoral practices must adapt to human experience,
- theology must serve mission, not ideology.

This resonates profoundly with CLT's insistence that theology must begin with praxis and respond to injustice.

b. Laudato Si' (2015): Ecological Conversion as Theological Method

Laudato Si' is arguably the most significant magisterial text in the environmental era. Francis links ecological devastation to economic injustice, colonial exploitation, and spiritual blindness. He teaches that:

- "the cry of the earth and the cry of the poor" are one.[2]
- ecological conversion must transform hearts and structures.
- science, indigenous wisdom, and theology must work together.

This multi-disciplinary, justice-oriented approach is precisely the methodological synthesis at the heart of CLT.

c. Amoris Laetitia (2016): Conscience and Discernment

Francis recovered Newman's theology of conscience. In *Amoris Laetitia*, he writes:

"We have been called to form consciences, not replace them." *(AL, §37)*

This represents a methodological revolution. Conscience again becomes the primary agent of moral decision, echoing Rahner and Newman.

---

2. *Laudato Si'*, §49.

d. *The Synodal Process: Communal Discernment as Method*

Francis has emphasized synodality—not as an event but as a method of being Church.

Key methodological principles:

- listening to the laity, especially those on the margins
- elevating women's voices (though without structural equality yet)
- involving local cultures in theological reflection
- acknowledging clergy abuse survivors
- dialoguing with scientific and indigenous knowledge

Synodality embodies CLT's insistence that theology arises from the whole People of God.

33. Yet the Limits Remain: Minimal Structural Change in Africa and Elsewhere

Despite the pope's bold rhetoric, real change has been uneven and sometimes nonexistent, especially in parts of Africa, Asia, and Eastern Europe.

a. Resistance from bishops' conferences

Many episcopal leaders—particularly in Africa—are wary or openly critical of Francis's reforms:

- They resist discussions on LGBTQ inclusion.
- They oppose revisiting celibacy or women's roles.
- They are cautious about ecological critiques that threaten extractive economic partnerships.
- They reject synodal openness on divorced and remarried Catholics.

Francis has spoken prophetically, but episcopal practice often remains unchanged.

b. Clericalism remains entrenched

Few regions have embraced Francis's call to dismantle clerical privilege. In many African dioceses:

- priests control parish resources with minimal transparency
- bishops maintain hierarchical distance
- lay leadership, especially among women, is limited
- accountability structures are weak

CLT sees this as a methodological failure: the structures of power remain unchallenged.

c. Ecclesial patriarchy persists

The papacy has opened new pathways for women's theological leadership, but:

- women are still excluded from ordained ministry
- many local churches resist even basic pastoral participation
- theological contributions from women are minimized or dismissed

Francis has changed the conversation, but not the structure.

d. LGBTQ pastoral practice remains stagnant

While Francis's rhetoric is compassionate—"Who am I to judge?"—local practice in many regions has remained punitive or hostile. In some African and Asian countries, bishops have supported or tolerated anti-LGBTQ legislation.

This underscores why CLT insists on hermeneutics of experience and social analysis. Rhetoric alone is insufficient; pastoral and structural transformation are required.

34. The Methodological Legacy of Francis

Despite the limits, Francis has permanently shifted the Church's methodological horizon.

His papacy established that:

1. The Church must prioritize the poor.
2. Reform is intrinsic to fidelity.
3. Doctrine develops through discernment and history.
4. Conscience is primary in moral decision-making.
5. Theology must listen before speaking.
6. Ecology is a core theological category.
7. Synodality—not clericalism—is the Church's future.

These principles align deeply with the methodological structure of CLT.

Francis did not create liberation theology. But he rehabilitated it, normalized it, and placed many of its concerns at the center of global Catholic discourse.

Whether Church leaders will translate this into structural action remains unresolved.

35. Synthesis: The Method of Critical-Liberative Theology

We can now articulate the full methodological structure of CLT:

1. Hermeneutics of Liberation
   Scripture is read as a call to justice, beginning from the perspective of the oppressed.
2. Critical Epistemology (CSR)
   Truth is objective but always mediated, tested in praxis, and open to development.
3. Social and Cultural Analysis
   Theology must analyze structures of power, economics, gender, race, ecology, and ecclesial systems.
4. Moral Agency and Conscience
   Human dignity and responsibility require active participation in liberation.
5. Prophetic Praxis
   Theology becomes credible only when it leads to transformative action.

6. Communal Discernment
   The People of God—especially the marginalized—are co-authors of theology.
7. Methodological Hope
   The Resurrection grounds a realistic but unwavering hope for justice and reform.

36. Conclusion: Method as Mission

Critical-Liberative Theology emerges as a method shaped by:

- history
- Scripture
- conscience
- global struggles for justice
- the Church's own woundedness
- the Spirit's call to renewal

CLT insists that theology must be accountable to the suffering of the world. This accountability demands intellectual courage, pastoral compassion, and prophetic risk-taking.

Pope Francis has revived this vision rhetorically, placing liberation themes at the center of global Catholic discourse. Yet real transformation depends not only on papal words but on the collective conversion of the whole Church.

The method of CLT prepares the Church for that conversion.

CHAPTER 3

Liberation Theology: A Global History from Latin America to Africa and Asia

1. INTRODUCTION: LIBERATION THEOLOGY AS A GLOBAL AWAKENING

Liberation theology did not erupt suddenly in the 1960s and 1970s; it emerged from centuries of Christian struggle for justice, from the prophetic witness of martyrs, and from the cry of oppressed peoples across continents. Though the term *"liberation theology"* was popularized by Gustavo Gutiérrez's 1971 lecture (published as *A Theology of Liberation* in 1973), the substance of the movement—Scripture interpreted through suffering, faith wedded to justice, theology undertaken from below—has deep biblical and historical roots.

This chapter explores liberation theology as a global phenomenon, expanding across Latin America, Africa, Asia, and the wider world. Unlike earlier movements of Catholic reform, liberation theology emerged not from ecclesiastical elites or theological faculties but from the poor themselves. It was forged in:

- the slums of Lima and São Paulo
- the villages of El Salvador and Guatemala
- the mines of Bolivia
- the apartheid townships of South Africa
- the colonized communities of Cameroon and Kenya

- the Dalit neighborhoods of India
- the military dictatorships of Korea and the Philippines

As a theological method, liberation theology is revolutionary because it relocates the center of reflection. Instead of theology emerging from abstract metaphysics or scholastic categories, it emerges from:

- hunger
- poverty
- political repression
- racial violence
- gender oppression
- caste discrimination
- cultural destruction
- state-sponsored terror

This chapter traces how liberation theology developed, diversified, and globalized, becoming one of the most influential Christian movements of the 20th and 21st centuries.

2. SEEDS OF LIBERATION BEFORE GUTIÉRREZ: THE PREHISTORY OF A MOVEMENT

While Gutiérrez systematized the movement, liberationist impulses existed long before him.

a. The biblical foundations

The Exodus, prophets, Jesus' ministry, and the early Christian communities were inherently liberationist. Patristic figures such as John Chrysostom and Ambrose criticized economic injustice. The medieval tradition produced voices like Bartolomé de las Casas who defended Indigenous peoples against colonial brutality.

b. The Catholic social tradition

Beginning with *Rerum Novarum* (1891), the Church articulated a consistent teaching on workers' rights, economic justice, and the dignity of labor. These encyclicals provided conceptual support for later liberation theologians.

c. Anti-colonial movements in Africa and Asia

Christian thinkers fighting colonial rule—such as Simon Kimbangu in the Congo, Julius Nyerere in Tanzania, and the leaders of the African Independent Churches—recognized that faith had social and political consequences.

d. The Second Vatican Council

Vatican II (1962–1965) laid the groundwork for liberation theology with its insistence on:

- reading the signs of the times
- the Church's responsibility to the poor
- historical consciousness
- human dignity
- social engagement

Especially important were:

- *Gaudium et Spes*
- *Lumen Gentium*
- *Ad Gentes*

These documents encouraged theologians to link doctrine with history, faith with justice, and spirituality with social transformation.

3. GUSTAVO GUTIÉRREZ AND THE BIRTH OF LIBERATION THEOLOGY

a. The Peruvian context

Gustavo Gutiérrez, a Dominican priest born in Lima, lived amid staggering inequality. Urban slums, rural poverty, and political instability provided the backdrop for his theological work. Gutiérrez's early pastoral experience among the poor convinced him that traditional theology—focused on abstract metaphysics or moral casuistry—was inadequate.

b. The foundational insight

In his landmark book *A Theology of Liberation*, Gutiérrez proposed a radical idea:

> "Theology is critical reflection on Christian praxis in the light of the Word of God." *(Gutiérrez, A Theology of Liberation, p. 11)*

This redefinition reversed centuries of theological methodology. Instead of beginning with doctrine and applying it to life, theology begins with life—especially the life of the oppressed—and rereads Scripture from that perspective.

c. The "preferential option for the poor"

Borrowing from biblical tradition, Gutiérrez articulated what became the core principle of liberation theology:

- God is committed to the oppressed
- The poor reveal God's presence
- Faith must include socio-political transformation

This was not a sentimental love for the poor but a theological conviction: the poor occupy a privileged position in God's plan because their suffering reveals the world's injustice.

d. Praxis before theory

Gutiérrez emphasized praxis—reflective action—as the essence of theology. Faith is not simply believed; it is lived through actions:

- organizing communities
- resisting injustice
- defending human rights
- transforming structures

e. Gutiérrez's global impact

Within a decade, liberation theology spread to:

- Brazil (Boff)
- El Salvador (Sobrino, Romero)
- Nicaragua (Fernando Cardenal)
- Chile (Pablo Richard)
- Argentina (poor communities under military dictatorship)

Liberation theology became the theological language of resistance for millions.

4. LATIN AMERICAN DICTATORSHIPS AND CHRISTIAN RESISTANCE

Liberation theology matured in a context of political violence. Military dictatorships in Argentina, Chile, Brazil, Uruguay, Guatemala, and El Salvador suppressed dissent, tortured activists, and executed clergy who sided with the poor.

a. The Church divided

In many countries:

- conservative bishops aligned with military regimes
- progressive priests defended human rights

- religious women ran literacy programs and shelters
- base communities formed networks of solidarity

The Church became a battleground between complicity and prophecy.

b. The martyrs

The blood of martyrs authenticated liberation theology:

- Óscar Romero, Archbishop of San Salvador, murdered at the altar (1980)
- The Jesuit martyrs of UCA (1989), killed for defending human rights
- Sister Dorothy Stang, murdered in Brazil for defending Amazonian communities
- Countless catechists, peasants, women, and activists

These martyrs embodied the method of liberation: Scripture interpreted through the willingness to die for justice.

c. Base communities (CEBs)

Christian base communities read the Bible collectively, identifying parallels between:

- Exodus and their struggle against landowners
- the prophets and their denunciation of corruption
- Jesus' ministry and their own resistance

This was theology from below—communal, participatory, and transformative.

d. Vatican tensions

In the 1980s and 1990s, the Vatican (under John Paul II and Benedict XVI) expressed concern about Marxist influences in liberation theology.

Yet even during this period, liberation theology continued to grow and diversify.

Under Pope Francis—a Latin American himself—liberation theology has been rehabilitated and affirmed as a legitimate theological method (without all its earlier political associations).

5. BEYOND GUTIÉRREZ: A PLURAL LATIN AMERICAN MOVEMENT

Latin American liberation theology soon expanded into diverse expressions:

- Indigenous liberation theology (Victor Montejo, Eleazar López Hernández)
- Afro-Latin theology (Clodovis Boff, black coastal communities in Brazil)
- Feminist and womanist liberation theology
- Liberationist biblical scholarship (Carlos Mesters)

Liberation theology is not a school but a movement with multiple voices, all united by the conviction that:
God's revelation occurs in the struggle for justice.

6. TRANSITION TO AFRICA AND ASIA

The global expansion of liberation theology demonstrates that its method resonates wherever human beings suffer. While Latin America provided the initial articulation, Africa and Asia adapted the movement to their own histories, cultures, and wounds.

The next sections will examine:

- African liberation theologians (Ela, Mveng, Magesa, Nyamiti)
- Asian liberation movements (Dalit, Minjung, feminist theologies)
- Ecumenical and interfaith contributions
- Liberation theology in Europe and North America
- Liberation theology's influence on Pope Francis

This chapter will thus show that liberation theology is not a historical footnote:
it is a global reshaping of Christian theology.

7. INTRODUCTION: THE AFRICAN CONTEXT OF LIBERATION

Liberation theology in Africa did not simply imitate Latin America. It emerged from unique historical wounds:

- centuries of colonial domination
- racism and cultural dehumanization
- economic exploitation
- postcolonial dictatorship and corruption
- ecclesial paternalism
- racialized missionary theology
- the marginalization of African cultures, languages, and spirituality

While Latin America struggled against capitalist oligarchies and military dictatorships, Africa contended simultaneously with:

- external domination (colonial and neo-colonial)
- internal oppression (autocratic regimes, elite capture)
- ecclesial coloniality (a Church structured like a foreign extension of Rome)

Liberation theology in Africa thus had a triple task:

1. theological decolonization
2. socio-political liberation
3. cultural and anthropological restoration

Four figures—Jean-Marc Ela, Engelbert Mveng, Laurenti Magesa, and Charles Nyamiti—stand out as pioneers, representing different streams within African liberation thought.

8. JEAN-MARC ELA: THE CRY OF THE AFRICAN VILLAGE

Jean-Marc Ela, the Cameroonian priest and sociologist, is perhaps the most radical African liberation theologian. His seminal works—*African Cry* (1980) and *My Faith as an African* (1989)—articulate a theology arising from the daily struggles of rural communities.

a. Theology from Below—Literally

Ela lived among the Kirdi people in northern Cameroon. His theology began not in seminaries or universities but in:

- famine
- forced labor
- illiteracy
- corrupt local officials
- indifferent ecclesial leadership
- the crushing weight of poverty

He wrote:

> "We must read the Gospel with the eyes of the poor, with dusty feet planted in the African soil."[1]

b. Critique of Ecclesial Colonialism

Ela denounced a Church that behaved like a colonial administrator:

- imported liturgies
- foreign languages
- European spirituality
- hierarchical distance
- clerical privilege

---

1. Ela, *African Cry*.

He saw a Church more concerned with internal order than with liberating God's people. His critique resonates powerfully with your own seminary experiences.

c. Scripture interpreted in African suffering

Ela emphasized:

- the Exodus as an African story
- Jesus' ministry as empowerment of the oppressed
- the prophets as warriors against injustice

For Ela, *all theology must begin in the village,* among the poor, not in the cathedral or chancery.

d. Social analysis and political critique

Ela was unafraid to challenge authoritarian regimes—something many African bishops avoided.

His insistence on praxis and prophetic witness placed him in conflict with both Church and state, leading eventually to exile in Canada.

9. ENGELBERT MVENG: THE THEOLOGY OF ANTHROPOLOGICAL POVERTY

Engelbert Mveng, another Cameroonian Jesuit theologian, produced one of the most profound concepts in African theological thought: anthropological poverty.

a. Anthropological poverty vs. material poverty

Mveng argued that Africa suffers not only economically but spiritually and culturally:

Africa is "a continent torn from its identity," deprived of its history, dignity, and self-worth.

b. Colonialism as theological violence

Mveng contended that colonialism inflicted not only political domination but theological destruction:

- African religions were demonized
- cultures dismissed as primitive
- languages suppressed
- European Christianity imposed as "universal"
- African subjectivity erased

Thus, liberation must address *the dignity of the African person*, not merely economic systems.

c. Christ as liberator of African identity

Mveng proposed a Christology rooted in African experience:

- Christ restores damaged identities
- Christ heals cultural wounds
- Christ empowers Africans to reclaim their history

d. Martyrdom and resistance

Mveng's later life was marked by tension with government and Church structures. He was mysteriously killed in 1995—seen by many as a martyr for the African poor.

10. LAURENTI MAGESA: THE MORAL TRADITION OF AFRICAN PEOPLES

The Tanzanian theologian Laurenti Magesa reframed African liberation theology through ethics, culture, and spirituality.

a. African religion as foundation

In works like *African Religion: The Moral Traditions of Abundant Life* (1997), Magesa argued that African traditional religions are not primitive systems to be replaced but rich moral worlds that seek:

- harmony
- community
- life
- justice
- balance

Thus, liberation includes reclaiming indigenous morality.

b. Critique of ecclesial authoritarianism

Magesa observed that African Catholicism often suppresses indigenous expression:

- liturgy is European
- moral norms are Roman legalisms
- clergy hold absolute authority
- inculturation is minimal or symbolic

He saw the need for an African Catholic imagination—a Church that respects African wisdom and not merely tolerates it.

c. Liberation as restoring abundant life

For Magesa, liberation is not only political but spiritual, moral, and ecological. The African worldview, which emphasizes interconnectedness, anticipates the ecological theology of Pope Francis's *Laudato Si'*.

11. CHARLES NYAMITI: INCULTURATION AND THE SEARCH FOR AFRICAN CHRISTOLOGY

Charles Nyamiti of Tanzania produced a sophisticated system of African theology by rooting Christian doctrine in African kinship structures.

a. Christ as "Ancestor"—a liberative model

In his well-known "Ancestor Christology," Nyamiti proposed that:

- in African thought, ancestors mediate life, unity, and blessing
- Christ fulfills and transforms the role of the ancestor
- thus, Christianity enters African culture from within, not from above

This approach was liberative because it affirmed African categories as theologically valid.

b. Inculturation as liberation from Eurocentric theology

Nyamiti demonstrated that theology can:

- speak African languages
- use African symbols
- engage African anthropology
- critique colonial impositions

c. Complement to socio-political critique

Nyamiti's work complements Ela and Mveng:

- Ela: liberation from political and economic oppression
- Mveng: liberation from cultural and anthropological oppression
- Nyamiti: liberation within religious imagination, Christology, and worship

Together, these thinkers formed a multifaceted African liberation theology.

12. BROADER AFRICAN MOVEMENTS IN LIBERATION THEOLOGY

Though Cameroon and East Africa produced influential voices, the movement is continent-wide.

a. South Africa: Apartheid and Black Theology

Black Theology in South Africa, influenced by James Cone, interpreted Christian faith through the struggle against apartheid.

Key figures:

- Steve Biko (Black Consciousness Movement)
- Allan Boesak
- Desmond Tutu
- The Kairos Document authors

The 1985 *Kairos Document* denounced:

- state theology (legitimizing apartheid)
- church theology (abstract spirituality)
- called for prophetic theology (justice and resistance)

This is one of the clearest examples of theology directly confronting structural sin.

b. East Africa: Liberation and nation-building

Figures like John Mbiti explored African religiosity in ways that affirmed African dignity, though not overtly political. Others, like Jesse Mugambi, argued that "reconstruction" should replace liberation after apartheid and colonialism.

c. Nigeria and Ghana: Liberation in a pluralistic context

In West Africa's multi-religious environment, Christian theologians engage:

- political corruption
- economic inequalities
- inter-religious tensions
- gender injustice

Liberation theology here often intersects with peacebuilding and anti-corruption work.

d. North Africa and the Arab world

Though predominantly Muslim, liberation movements rooted in Christian thought influenced human rights activism in Egypt, Tunisia, and Algeria—especially through Jesuit centers of social reflection.

13. THE AFRICAN CHURCH AND ITS INTERNAL CONTRADICTIONS

African liberation theology emerged not only from external oppression but also from the failures of the Church itself.

a. Ecclesial complicity and silence

Many African bishops supported:

- authoritarian governments
- military rulers
- corrupt elites

This mirrored your own early recognition of ecclesial moral failure and the need for internal reform.

b. Clerical elitism

Priests often enjoy:

- economic privilege
- social status
- political protection

Meanwhile, the laity—especially women—provide the Church's labor and resources while lacking structural power.

c. The unfulfilled promise of Vatican II

Although Vatican II called for inculturation and social justice, African implementation remained superficial:

- European vestments and rituals persisted
- theological education remained Western
- prophetic critique of oppression was often muted

Liberation theologians challenged this stagnation.

14. SYNTHESIS: THE AFRICAN CONTRIBUTION TO GLOBAL LIBERATION THEOLOGY

African liberation theology contributed three distinctive emphases to the global movement:

1. Liberation as cultural and anthropological restoration
   Freedom from oppression includes reclaiming identity, history, and dignity.
2. Liberation as community-centered spirituality
   African theologies emphasize communal life, relationality, and ecological harmony.
3. Liberation as critique of Church and state
   Ela, Mveng, and others insisted that the Church must examine its own complicity in oppression.

15. ASIA'S VAST LANDSCAPE OF OPPRESSION AND FAITH

Asian liberation theologies arose in some of the world's most complex environments—vast populations shaped by caste hierarchies, religious pluralism, military dictatorships, economic disparities, Indigenous marginalization, gendered violence, and cultural suppression.

Asia is not a monolith. Liberation theology here took many forms:

- Dalit theology in India confronted caste apartheid.
- Minjung theology in Korea interpreted the struggles of ordinary people under dictatorship.
- Filipino liberation theology emerged through resistance to the Marcos regime and People Power movements.

- Asian feminist theology confronted patriarchal cultures and ecclesial exclusion.
- Indigenous and minority theologies in Japan, Taiwan, Myanmar, and the Philippines fought for cultural survival.
- Catholic, Protestant, and ecumenical voices collaborated across denominational lines.

While Latin America rooted liberation in class struggle and Africa in decolonization and cultural affirmation, Asia expanded liberation theology to include caste, peoplehood, gender, and communal identity.

16. DALIT THEOLOGY: LIBERATION FROM CASTE APARTHEID

Dalit theology, emerging in the 1980s and 1990s, is one of the most powerful liberation movements in global Christianity. It confronts the caste system—a 3,000-year-old structure of hierarchy that has oppressed millions of people deemed "untouchable."

a. Dalit experience as locus theologicus

The foundational insight of Dalit theology is that God is revealed in the story of the Dalit people—the poorest of the poor, systematically excluded from:

- education
- religious spaces
- land ownership
- political representation
- human dignity

Arvind P. Nirmal, a key Dalit theologian, wrote that true theology must begin with "the Dalit situation," not with elite philosophical categories.

Dalit theology reads the Exodus, prophets, and Jesus through the lens of caste oppression. The cry of the Dalits becomes a contemporary expression of the Hebrew slaves in Egypt.

b. Jesus as the Dalit Christ

Dalit theologians argue that in Jesus' rejection, suffering, and solidarity with the marginalized, he identifies with Dalit experience.

Jesus is not simply a liberator; He is a Dalit—a rejected one who transforms rejection into liberation.

c. Critique of Indian Christianity

Dalit theology exposes how:

- the Indian Church internalized caste prejudice
- clergy from higher castes dominate leadership
- Dalit Christians are segregated even in burial grounds
- theological institutions ignore caste issues

Liberation requires restructuring the Church, not merely society.

d. Methodological insights

Dalit theology contributed several methodological breakthroughs:

- *social location* as theological starting point
- *caste as structural sin*
- *cultural and religious critique* of Indian Christianity
- *use of Dalit literature, songs, and symbols* in theology
- *interfaith engagement with Buddhism, Sikhism, and reformist Hindu traditions*

Dalit theology is one of the clearest examples of liberation theology transcending class and focusing on identity-based oppression.

17. MINJUNG THEOLOGY (KOREA): THE PEOPLE AS SUBJECTS OF HISTORY

Korean Minjung theology arose in the 1970s–1980s during an era of military dictatorship, rapid industrialization, labor exploitation, and violent repression of democratic movements.

Minjung means "the people"—specifically, the oppressed masses.

a. Historical context

Key events shaped this theology:

- Gwangju Uprising (1980)
- student movements for democracy
- labor strikes in textile and manufacturing industries
- imprisonment and torture of activists
- repression of intellectuals and artists

Christian pastoral workers, many Protestant, stood with the Minjung in their struggle.

b. Theologically, who is the Minjung?

The Minjung are not simply the poor. They are:

- socially oppressed
- politically silenced
- economically exploited
- culturally devalued

They are the biblical "people of God" reimagined in modern Korean context.

c. Reinterpretation of Jesus

Minjung theologians (Suh Nam-dong, Ahn Byung-mu) interpret Jesus as:

- *the suffering servant* who identifies with oppressed Koreans
- *the one who gathers the excluded* (e.g., tax collectors, prostitutes)
- *the one executed by an imperial collaborationist regime*

Jesus becomes a symbol of political resistance and hope.

d. Reinterpretation of the Bible

Minjung theology reads Scripture as a story of the oppressed masses reclaiming their agency. For example:

- Exodus = liberation from imperialism
- Prophets = critique of corrupt rulers
- Gospel healings = restoration of dignity

The "people" are the subjects, not the objects, of salvation history.

e. Methodological contributions

Minjung theology expands liberation methodology by:

- centering historical trauma
- combining political protest with spiritual identity
- using cultural arts (poetry, theater, traditional music) as theology
- engaging Marxism critically but not uncritically
- integrating Confucian and Shamanistic insights

This is a theology of the people's movement, not merely of the academy.

18. FILIPINO LIBERATION THEOLOGY: PEOPLE POWER AND POSTCOLONIAL FAITH

The Philippines offers a unique site for liberation theology because it is one of the few places where a peaceful, mass uprising—People Power (1986)—became explicitly theological.

a. Dictatorship under Ferdinand Marcos

Marcos's regime (1965–1986) was marked by:

- martial law (1972–1981)
- imprisonment of opponents
- torture centers

- corruption and plunder
- rural displacement
- collusion with foreign military powers

The Church was initially divided but increasingly became the voice of resistance.

b. Cardinal Jaime Sin and the prophetic Church

Cardinal Sin used Catholic radio stations to mobilize millions of Filipinos in nonviolent resistance. Priests and religious women stood between tanks and civilians. The Church became:

- mediator
- moral compass
- political actor
- sanctuary for activists

c. People Power as a theological event

Liberation theologians in the Philippines interpreted the uprising as a *kairos* moment—a dramatic eruption of God's justice through ordinary citizens.

d. Theological themes

Filipino liberation theology highlights:

- nonviolent resistance
- community solidarity (bayanihan)
- postcolonial identity
- critique of Western imperialism
- preferential option for the poor
- martyrdom (e.g., Fr. Pops Tentorio, Ninoy Aquino)

e. Post-dictatorship challenges

After Marcos, theologians recognized:

- structural injustices persisted
- globalization produced new forms of exploitation
- human trafficking and labor migration intensified

Thus liberation theology shifted from anti-dictatorship struggle to global economic critique.

19. ASIAN FEMINIST THEOLOGIES: GENDER, PATRIARCHY, AND THE DIVINE

Asian feminist theology arose because liberation theology, as first articulated by men, did not fully address the oppression of women in patriarchal cultures.

a. The social reality of Asian women

Women across Asia face:

- forced marriages
- dowry-related violence
- exclusion from religious leadership
- human trafficking
- domestic abuse
- economic exploitation
- cultural silencing

b. Feminist theological insights

Asian feminist theologians such as Chung Hyun Kyung, Kwok Pui-lan, Virginia Fabella, and Agnes Brazal articulate several principles:

- God's presence is found in women's survival and resistance.

- Patriarchy is a structural sin embedded in Church and culture.
- The divine includes feminine metaphors suppressed by male theologians.
- Women's bodies and work are loci of theological reflection.
- Liberation must include gender justice.

c. Dialogue with Asian religious traditions

Asian feminist theologians engage:

- Buddhism (notions of compassion and suffering)
- Confucianism (critiques of hierarchical order)
- Hindu Shakti traditions (divine feminine)

This interreligious dialogue deepens liberation methodology, showing that justice must engage cultural and spiritual diversity.

20. INDIGENOUS AND MINORITY THEOLOGIES ACROSS ASIA

a. Japanese Burakumin Liberation Theology

The Burakumin—historically marginalized caste-like communities in Japan—developed a Christian and Buddhist-inspired liberation movement addressing discrimination and cultural erasure.

b. Taiwanese Indigenous Theology

The Amis, Bunun, and other Indigenous peoples developed contextual theologies emphasizing land, ancestors, colonial trauma, and ecological stewardship.

c. Myanmar and Thailand

Christian minorities facing religious and ethnic persecution articulate liberation as:

- cultural survival
- political autonomy
- reconciliation
- resistance to militarization

d. Chinese Context

Though the Chinese Church operates under severe state controls, underground Catholic and Protestant communities incorporate liberation themes in:

- resilience
- secret worship
- advocacy for human dignity

21. METHODOLOGICAL CONTRIBUTIONS OF ASIAN LIBERATION THEOLOGIES

Asian liberation theology enriched global liberation thought in several ways:

1. Liberation as identity-based (not only class-based)
   Caste, ethnicity, gender, and peoplehood shape oppression.
2. Theology rooted in suffering communities
   The Minjung and Dalits embody theology-in-history.
3. Interreligious dialogue as liberation method
   Justice requires learning from Buddhist compassion, Hindu nonviolence, Confucian ethics, Indigenous cosmologies.
4. Cultural and symbolic liberation
   Myth, story, ritual, dance, and community are sources of theology.
5. Political and spiritual nonviolence
   People Power and Korean democratic movements shaped theology as peaceful resistance.

22. TRANSITION

Let's now examine liberation movements in:

- Europe (peace theology, resistance to fascism, anti-austerity movements)
- North America (Black theology, feminist/womanist theology, Indigenous liberation)
- Oceania (Maori, Aboriginal, and islander theologies)
- and the emerging role of Pope Francis in uniting these threads

23. LIBERATION THEOLOGY COMES TO THE WEST

While liberation theology is often perceived as a Global South movement, Europe and North America became essential sites of reflection, activism, and theological innovation. In these regions, liberation theology confronted:

- racism and white supremacy
- colonial histories and Indigenous dispossession
- gender and sexual oppression
- economic injustice under capitalism
- immigration and refugee crises
- state violence and mass incarceration
- religious nationalism

Oceania added its own distinctive contribution, centered on Indigenous struggle and ecological spirituality.

As liberation theology matured globally, the West became both a critic of the movement and, ironically, one of its expanding frontiers.

24. EUROPE: FROM RESISTANCE THEOLOGY TO ECONOMIC AND MIGRANT JUSTICE

a. Anti-fascist and resistance roots (1930s–1940s)

Before liberation theology had a name, Europe experienced its own liberationist theologies during the fight against fascism:

- Dietrich Bonhoeffer resisted Nazi totalitarianism.
- The French worker-priest movement confronted industrial exploitation.
- Catholic and Protestant resistance networks sheltered Jews.

These were early expressions of theological praxis confronting systemic evil.

b. Post-war Europe and the critique of capitalist injustice

In the late 20th and early 21st centuries, European theologians began applying liberation insights to:

- unemployment
- austerity policies
- housing and migration crises
- rising nationalism and xenophobia

Jürgen Moltmann emphasized hope as a political force, interpreting the resurrection as the horizon of emancipation. Johann Baptist Metz articulated a "political theology" that confronted suffering and memory—especially the Holocaust.

c. The migration crisis and theological transformation

The arrival of millions of refugees from Syria, Iraq, Africa, and Afghanistan forced European churches to reexamine:

- hospitality
- identity
- borders

- human dignity
- racism

The Sant'Egidio Community, Caritas Europe, and numerous Jesuit networks became key actors in migrant support.

Pope Francis made this crisis central to his papacy:

> "Every migrant has a name, a face, and a story." *(Francis, 2018)*

Despite resistance from many European governments and bishops, Francis has insisted that migration is not merely political but theological—a test of Christian integrity.

d. Liberation themes in secular Europe

Even in highly secular environments such as Scandinavia, the Netherlands, and parts of France, Christian liberationist thought shaped:

- anti-racist activism
- ecological movements
- anti-poverty campaigns
- sanctuary city initiatives

European liberation thought thus emerged at the intersection of Church and civil society.

25. NORTH AMERICA: BLACK, WOMANIST, INDIGENOUS, MIGRANT, QUEER, AND ECOLOGICAL LIBERATION THEOLOGIES

North America became a major center for liberation theology, particularly through the Black struggle for freedom and civil rights.

A. Black Liberation Theology: James Cone and the Struggle for Freedom

James Cone is to North America what Gutiérrez is to Latin America. In *A Black Theology of Liberation* (1970), Cone argued:

"God is Black because God stands with the oppressed Black community."

This was not a racial essentialism but a theological claim: God identifies with those crushed by white supremacy.

Key themes:

- America's original sin is racism.
- Jesus is Black in His solidarity with the oppressed.
- Liberation is inseparable from political struggle.
- Theology must confront lynching, segregation, and modern policing.

Later Black theologians—Kelly Brown Douglas, Dwight Hopkins, M. Shawn Copeland—expanded this tradition.

Pope Francis and racial justice

During his visit to the United States (2015), Francis acknowledged America's racial wounds, but his interventions have been restrained. Still, his emphasis on structural sin resonates with Black liberation theology.

B. Womanist Theology: Liberation from Racism, Sexism, and Classism

Womanist theologians exposed a limitation in both Black theology (too male) and feminist theology (too white).

Key voices:

- Delores Williams
- Jacquelyn Grant
- Katie Cannon

Womanist theology insists:

- Liberation must include Black women's bodies, labor, and historical trauma.
- The Church must confront patriarchy within African American communities and ecclesial structures.

- Biblical interpretation must center the experience of Black women.

Womanism significantly influenced Catholic feminist theologians and global liberation thought.

C. Indigenous Theologies: Land, Memory, and Survival

Indigenous theologians in the United States and Canada developed liberation frameworks rooted in:

- land dispossession
- genocide
- forced assimilation
- residential schools
- desecration of sacred sites
- ecological devastation

Key themes:

1. Land is sacred and cannot be commodified.
2. Liberation involves cultural resurgence and sovereignty.
3. Christianity must repent for colonial violence.
4. Indigenous cosmologies enrich Christian spirituality.

Pope Francis's 2022 apology in Canada for residential schools was a historic moment, though many Indigenous leaders criticized its limitations.

D. Migrant and Latinx Theologies

Latinx theologians in the United States (Virgilio Elizondo, Ada María Isasi-Díaz) developed liberation thought rooted in:

- border violence
- labor exploitation
- cultural hybridity
- undocumented immigration

- racism against Hispanic communities/

Isasi-Díaz coined mujerista theology, focusing on the liberation of Latina women.

Pope Francis's advocacy for migrants strongly aligns with Latinx liberation theology—though U.S. Church structures remain divided.

E. Queer and LGBTQ+ Liberation Theologies

Queer theologians developed liberation frameworks grounded in:

- exclusion from Church sacraments
- queerphobic violence
- homelessness among LGBTQ+ youth
- ecclesial silence on mental health
- the need for a theology of embodiment and love

Pope Francis's statements—"Who am I to judge?"—opened pastoral doors, though structural change remains stalled. Even more significant is *Fiducia Supplicans* ("Supplicating Trust"), a groundbreaking 2023 Vatican declaration from the Dicastery for the Doctrine of the Faith (DDF) that permits Catholic priests to offer spontaneous, non-liturgical blessings to couples in "irregular situations," including same-sex couples, without changing church doctrine on marriage or validating their unions as marriage. Approved by Pope Francis, it distinguishes between formal rites (like marriage) and informal blessings, allowing pastoral closeness to those seeking God's help, but it has caused varied reactions, with some seeing it as a major shift and others as a pastoral nuance.

F. Ecological Liberation Theology

Inspired by Thomas Berry, Sallie McFague, and Indigenous theologians, North American ecological theology emphasizes:

- interconnectedness
- planetary justice
- critique of extractive capitalism
- climate grief and hope

Francis's *Laudato Si'* strongly resonated with these movements.

26. CANADA: INDIGENOUS LIBERATION AND DECOLONIZING CHRISTIANITY

Because Canada's Christian history is deeply entangled with colonial violence, liberation theology here takes the form of truth-telling and decolonization.

Key themes:

- healing from residential schools
- restoring Indigenous languages and ceremonies
- land acknowledgments as spiritual acts
- reinterpreting Christianity through Indigenous cosmologies
- confronting systemic racism in Church and society

Francis's apology (2022) acknowledged "grave abuses," but survivors continue to demand:

- full disclosure of records
- repatriation of land
- reparations
- structural reform in religious orders

This struggle exemplifies liberation theology's challenge to institutional power.

27. OCEANIA: INDIGENOUS AND ECOLOGICAL LIBERATION

Liberation theology in Oceania centers on:

- land sovereignty
- climate change
- cultural survival
- anti-colonial resistance
- Indigenous spirituality

a. Māori Theology (Aotearoa/New Zealand)

Māori liberation thought emphasizes:

- land as sacred (whenua)
- genealogy and identity (whakapapa)
- communal spirituality
- resistance to colonial legal systems
- ecological guardianship (kaitiakitanga)

Christianity is reinterpreted through Indigenous cosmology.

b. Aboriginal Australian Theology

Key themes include:

- trauma of colonization
- stolen generations
- racism and economic exclusion
- Dreamtime spirituality as theological lens
- land rights and sacred sites

The Uluru Statement from the Heart (2017) reflects a theological call for voice, treaty, and truth.

c. Pacific Islander Theologies

Pacific Islander theologians (Fiji, Samoa, Tonga, Marshall Islands) emphasize:

- climate justice
- rising sea levels
- displacement
- ecological stewardship

For these communities, liberation is literally a struggle for survival.

Pope Francis and Oceania

Francis has consistently elevated island nations' voices, stating:

> "The climate crisis is claiming lives, homes, and cultures." Francis, address to Pacific bishops (2019)

This alignment illustrates how liberation theology has shaped papal priorities.

28. THE ROLE OF POPE FRANCIS IN WESTERN LIBERATION MOVEMENTS

Pope Francis has not merely engaged liberation movements; he has often amplified them:

a. On racial justice

Condemned George Floyd's killing.

- Called racism a "sin that denies human dignity."
- Encouraged U.S. bishops to address structural racism.

b. On Indigenous rights

Apologized for residential school abuses.

- Supported Amazonian Indigenous communities.
- Affirmed Indigenous ecological knowledge.

c. On migrants and refugees

Francis's first papal trip was to Lampedusa, where he declared: "The globalization of indifference must end."

d. On women

While structural change is slow, Francis has:

- appointed women to high Vatican roles
- opened liturgical ministries to women
- encouraged synodal dialogue on women's participation

e. On LGBTQ+ persons

Francis emphasizes accompaniment and inclusion, reshaping pastoral theology—though doctrine remains unchanged.

f. On ecology

Laudato Si' is the single most influential ecological theological document in Christian history.

g. On capitalism and economic oppression

Francis critiques neoliberal capitalism as a system that "kills," echoing Latin American liberation theologians.

Limitations remain

Despite powerful rhetoric:

- African and Asian episcopacies often reject Francis's reforms.
- U.S. bishops are divided.
- Curial resistance slows structural change.

Francis represents a liberationist papacy, but liberation is not yet institutionalized.

29. SYNTHESIS: THE WESTERN CONTRIBUTION TO GLOBAL LIBERATION THEOLOGY

Western liberation movements contributed:

1. A theology of race and structural injustice

Cone, womanist theologians, and Indigenous scholars expanded liberation beyond class.

2. Gender and sexuality as central liberation themes

Feminist, mujerista, and queer theologies reshaped global Catholic discourse.

3. Ecological liberation as planetary mission

North American and Oceanian theologians influenced Francis's ecological vision.

4. Theology as resistance to empire and nationalism

Bonhoeffer, peace movements, and migrant justice networks brought liberation into political contexts.

5. Decolonizing Christianity

Truth and reconciliation movements challenge the Church to confront its own sins.

6. Papal engagement

Francis unites global liberation themes, though practice lags behind rhetoric.

30. LIBERATION THEOLOGY BECOMES A GLOBAL CONVERSATION

One of the most extraordinary outcomes of liberation theology is that it inspired parallel movements beyond Christianity. The "liberation paradigm"—reading sacred texts through the lens of injustice, grounding theology in lived suffering, and viewing religious practice as political transformation—found resonance in Judaism, Islam, Buddhism, Indigenous spiritualities, and secular social movements.

Liberation theology became a method shared across religions, not a Christian monopoly.

This section surveys these interfaith developments.

31. JEWISH LIBERATION THOUGHT: COVENANT, EXODUS, AND SOCIAL JUSTICE

Jewish liberation theology has deep biblical roots. The Exodus story, central to Jewish identity, became a major interpretive lens for social and political justice.

a. Post-Holocaust theology and liberation

In the aftermath of the Shoah (Holocaust), Jewish theologians such as Emil Fackenheim, Abraham Joshua Heschel, and Elie Wiesel emphasized:

- the dangerous consequences of theological passivity
- the ethical imperative to resist dehumanization
- the necessity of moral vigilance against injustice

Heschel famously marched with Martin Luther King Jr., arguing:

"When I marched in Selma, I felt my legs were praying."

This embodied a liberationist spirituality grounded in covenantal responsibility.

b. Exodus as paradigm of resistance

Jewish thinkers applied the Exodus to contemporary struggles:

- Soviet Jewry
- civil rights
- economic inequality
- Palestinian justice movements
- global Jewish ethics

c. Jewish-Palestinian liberation theologies

Some Jewish theologians—Marc Ellis, Yehuda Amital, Jeremy Milgrom—integrated liberation theology with Israeli–Palestinian peace activism.

This movement emphasizes:

- justice for both peoples
- critique of state power
- fidelity to prophetic ethics

Marc Ellis coined the phrase "a Jewish theology of liberation," calling for resistance to injustice committed by or against Jews.

d. Methodological contributions

Jewish liberation thought contributes:

1. Covenantal ethics — justice as obligation, not option.
2. Historical memory — liberation rooted in remembrance of suffering.
3. Prophetic resistance — challenging one's own community.

32. MUSLIM LIBERATION THOUGHT: ANTI-COLONIALISM, JUSTICE, AND THE UMMAH

Islamic liberation movements emerged from anti-colonial struggle and Qur'anic ethics of justice (*adl*) and community (*ummah*).

a. Anti-colonial Islamic thought

Islamic theologians and activists resisted Western imperial domination in:

- North Africa
- the Middle East
- South Asia
- Indonesia
- West Africa

Figures like Jamal al-Din al-Afghani, Hassan al-Banna, and Ali Shariati framed liberation as:

- cultural revival
- resistance to exploitation
- renewal of Islamic ethics

Ali Shariati's "Islamic liberation theology" in Iran emphasized:

- social justice
- equality
- critique of oppressive rulers
- prophetic resistance (using Imam Husayn as model)

b. Qur'anic ethics and social justice

Key Qur'anic themes align with liberation theology:

- God sides with the oppressed (*mustada'fin*)
- justice is a divine command[2]
- wealth redistribution is a moral obligation (*zakat, sadaqa*)
- tyranny must be confronted

c. Muslim-Christian liberation dialogue

In the Philippines, South Africa, and parts of the Middle East, Muslim and Christian leaders collaborated in social justice movements—often inspired by liberation theology's method.

d. Limitations and challenges

Islamic liberation movements face:

- authoritarian regimes
- sectarian politics

2. Qur'an 4:135.

- patriarchal religious structures

But the fundamental conviction remains: faith requires social transformation.

33. BUDDHIST ENGAGED LIBERATION: COMPASSION MEETS SOCIAL ETHICS

Buddhism historically emphasized personal enlightenment, but modern Buddhist leaders rediscovered the social dimension of liberation.

a. Thich Nhat Hanh and Engaged Buddhism

Thich Nhat Hanh, the Vietnamese monk, developed Engaged Buddhism during the Vietnam War, combining:

- mindfulness
- nonviolence
- social justice
- interbeing (relational ontology)

He insisted that meditation and activism belong together:

> "When bombs fall, do not think meditation halls are safe."

This parallels liberation theology's insistence on praxis.

b. Buddhist liberation movements

Liberation–oriented Buddhist activism emerged in:

- Vietnam (peace and reconstruction)
- Tibet (cultural survival, nonviolent resistance)
- Sri Lanka (social justice, anti-war movements)
- Myanmar (women's rights, anti-military activism)
- Thailand (ecology monks protecting forests)

c. Buddhist economics and liberation

Buddhist thinkers critique consumerism and inequality, proposing "right livelihood" and sustainable development.

d. Methodological contributions

Buddhist insights enrich liberation theology:

1. Interdependence strengthens ecological liberation.
2. Nonviolence offers alternatives to political militancy.
3. Mindfulness grounds activism in interior transformation.
4. Compassion becomes a political ethic.

34. INDIGENOUS LIBERATION SPIRITUALITIES: LAND, ANCESTORS, AND RESISTANCE

Across the world, Indigenous communities created liberation theologies rooted in land, memory, and sacred cosmology.

a. Core features

Indigenous liberation spirituality emphasizes:

- land as sacred (not property)
- ancestors as living presence
- ecological harmony
- communal identity
- resistance to colonial structures

Unlike Western theology, Indigenous liberation blends religion, ecology, culture, and politics seamlessly.

b. Examples

Maori theology (Aotearoa) grounded in *whakapapa* and *kaitiakitanga*.

- Aboriginal Australian theology centered on Dreamtime, land, and trauma.
- First Nations in Canada invoking treaty rights and spiritual sovereignty.
- Ainu of Japan reviving land-based cosmologies.
- Igorot and Lumad peoples in the Philippines resisting mining and militarization.
- Indigenous Taiwanese theologians integrating ancestral rituals with Christian faith.

c. Theological themes

1. Liberation as cultural survival.
1. Mission as decolonization—not conversion.
2. Truth-telling as healing.
3. Ancestors as theological interlocutors.
4. Ecological liberation as spiritual duty.

d. Pope Francis and Indigenous struggles

Francis has been receptive to Indigenous concerns:

- *Laudato Si'* affirms Indigenous ecological wisdom.
- The Amazon Synod elevated Indigenous voices.
- He apologized in Canada for residential school abuses.

Yet many Indigenous leaders see these efforts as symbolic without structural restitution.

35. SECULAR LIBERATION MOVEMENTS AND THEIR DIALOGUE WITH THEOLOGY

Liberation theology has influenced—and been influenced by—secular movements.

a. Human rights frameworks

Human rights discourse often parallels liberation theology in affirming:

- dignity
- equality
- participation
- justice

Liberation theologians (e.g., Sobrino, Boff) frequently use human rights language.

b. Marxism and socialist thought

Early liberation theologians drew on Marxist analysis:

- class struggle
- ideology critique
- structural oppression

Though controversial, this dialogue sharpened the theological critique of capitalism.

c. Feminism, queer theory, and intersectionality

These frameworks enriched liberation theology by emphasizing:

- bodily autonomy
- systemic sexism
- heteronormativity
- layered oppression

d. Ecological movements

Secular environmentalists influenced theological ecology, especially in:

- systems thinking

- climate activism
- sustainability frameworks

e. Anti-colonial struggles

Secular anti-colonial movements (Fanon, Nkrumah, Cabral) deepened theological insights about:

- oppression
- cultural dehumanization
- liberation as psychological and spiritual healing

36. LIBERATION THEOLOGY AND INTERFAITH COALITIONS

Liberation theology helped birth interfaith coalitions for justice:

- Christian–Jewish refugee initiatives in Europe
- Muslim–Christian solidarity in Nigeria and Indonesia
- Buddhist–Christian partnerships for peace in Sri Lanka
- Jewish–Muslim–Christian feminist networks
- Indigenous–Christian ecological alliances
- Catholic–secular collaborations in Latin America during dictatorships

These movements highlight that liberation transcends doctrinal boundaries.

37. METHODOLOGICAL CONTRIBUTIONS OF INTERFAITH LIBERATION MOVEMENTS

Interfaith liberation perspectives expanded liberation methodology by adding:

1. Multiple sacred narratives of liberation

Exodus, Hijra, Buddhist compassion, Indigenous creation stories—all become sources.

2. Shared ethics of justice

Interfaith cooperation emphasizes universal moral principles.

3. Decolonization of theology

Indigenous and Muslim scholars challenge Christian theological imperialism.

4. Nonviolent resistance and spiritual activism

Drawing from Gandhi, Buddhist practice, and Christian pacifism.

5. Ecological cosmologies

Indigenous and Buddhist traditions strengthen theological ecology.

6. Universalizing the preferential option for the oppressed

Oppression is global; liberation must be global.

38. CATHOLIC CHURCH'S RELATIONSHIP WITH LIBERATION THEOLOGY

Having explored liberation theology across religions and continents, we now examine the Catholic Church's complex relationship with liberation theology:

- initial suspicion and condemnation (1970s–1990s)
- partial rehabilitation
- the Francis revolution

- ongoing resistance
- contested futures

39. A MOVEMENT THE CHURCH COULD NOT IGNORE

Liberation theology, from its birth in the 1960s, forced the Catholic Church to confront questions it had long deferred:

- What is the Church's responsibility toward the poor?
- Is faith inherently political?
- How should Christians resist unjust structures?
- Can theology be done from below rather than from ecclesial centers of power?
- What is the relationship between evangelization and social transformation?

These questions inevitably brought liberation theologians into tension with Rome.

The global Church's reaction to liberation theology is best understood as a three-act drama:

1. Suspicion and Condemnation (1970s–1990s)
2. Cautious Reconciliation and Reformulation (1990s–2013)
3. The Francis Revolution: Rehabilitation and Renewal (2013–present)

This section narrates each act in detail.

40. ACT I — SUSPICION AND CONDEMNATION (1970S–1990S)

Liberation theology emerged during a period of geopolitical tension, economic upheaval, and massive Church transformation following Vatican II.

Rome's reaction was shaped by:

- the Cold War
- concerns about Marxist influence

- desire to maintain ecclesial unity
- fear of politicizing the Gospel
- resistance from conservative episcopal conferences

a. The Marxism controversy

Many liberation theologians utilized Marxist social analysis to interpret:

- class conflict
- structural oppression
- ideology
- capital accumulation

Rome feared this signaled theological relativism and political radicalization.

b. The Congregation for the Doctrine of the Faith (CDF) Steps In

Under Cardinal Joseph Ratzinger, the CDF issued two instructions:

1. The 1984 Instruction on Certain Aspects of the "Theology of Liberation"

This document:

- warned against Marxist analysis
- cautioned that liberation should not be reduced to political revolution
- emphasized spiritual liberation
- criticized interpretations of Jesus as a political activist

2. The 1986 Instruction on Christian Freedom and Liberation

More balanced, this text:

- affirmed the preferential option for the poor

- recognized structural sin
- accepted the need for social critique
- situated liberation within the broader Gospel

The two documents represent Rome's struggle to balance orthodoxy and justice.

c. Silencing and disciplinary actions

Several theologians faced silencing or sanctions:

- Leonardo Boff (Brazil)
- Jon Sobrino (El Salvador, censured in 2007)
- Gustavo Gutiérrez faced scrutiny
- Ernesto Cardenal (Nicaragua) was suspended
- Brazilian base communities were restricted

The Vatican viewed liberation theology as destabilizing to ecclesial authority.

41. ACT II — CAUTIOUS RECONCILIATION AND REINTERPRETATION (1990S–2013)

As political landscapes shifted—dictatorships fell, the Cold War ended—Rome began to soften its stance.

a. Liberation theology survived because the poor survived

Despite Vatican criticism, liberation theology did not die because:

- poverty increased
- dictatorships continued or mutated
- globalization created new inequalities
- community struggles persisted
- martyrs gave the movement moral legitimacy

People kept doing liberation theology long after the controversy faded.

b. Theological refinement

Liberation theologians responded by:

- clarifying their relationship to Marxism
- deepening spirituality and biblical focus
- expanding into feminist, ecological, Indigenous, and Afro-Latin forms
- strengthening ties with Catholic social teaching

The movement matured, diversified, and became more explicitly theological.

c. Selective acceptance by the Vatican

Popes John Paul II and Benedict XVI gradually recognized the validity of:

- the preferential option for the poor
- structural sin
- social justice
- critique of unjust systems

But they insisted that liberation must remain evangelically grounded and free of secular ideologies.

d. Bishops and religious orders quietly embraced liberation themes

Across Latin America, Africa, and Asia:

- Jesuits
- Franciscans
- Maryknoll missionaries
- Vincentians

- Dominican sisters
- Local pastors and catechists

continued liberative work even when official theology remained cautious.

e. The voices of the martyrs

Canonizations such as:

- Óscar Romero (2018)
- Rutilio Grande (2022)

signaled that liberation martyrs were slowly being recognized as saints.

This paves the way for the next act.

42. ACT III — THE FRANCIS REVOLUTION (2013-PRESENT)

Pope Francis, a Jesuit formed in the context of Latin American poverty, became the first pope to speak the language of liberation theology with ease—albeit in his own distinctly pastoral style.

a. A Pope Formed by the Poor

As Archbishop of Buenos Aires, Francis:

- lived simply
- rode public transportation
- worked closely with slum communities (villas miseria)
- resisted clerical privilege
- prioritized pastoral encounter

He was not a liberation theologian in the academic sense, but he absorbed liberation theology's ethos.

b. His first papal act: Lampedusa

Francis's pontificate began with a symbolic gesture: he traveled to Lampedusa, the site of migrant drownings in the Mediterranean, and condemned:

> "The globalization of indifference."

This framed his entire papacy as a critique of systems that abandon the poor.

c. Evangelii Gaudium (2013): Liberation in papal voice

His apostolic exhortation *Evangelii Gaudium* includes unmistakable liberation themes:

- denunciation of "an economy of exclusion"
- critique of consumerism
- call for structural reform
- affirmation of missionary discipleship among the poor

Francis writes:

> "The poor are the privileged recipients of the Gospel."

This is pure liberation theology in spirit.

d. Laudato Si' (2015): Liberation Ecology

Laudato Si' reframed environmental destruction as a moral issue and placed it within the Church's teaching authority:

- ecological devastation and poverty are linked
- Indigenous wisdom is essential
- global capitalism must be critiqued
- creation awaits liberation

This document brought theological ecology into mainstream Catholicism.

e. Amoris Laetitia (2016): Liberation of Conscience

Francis emphasized:

> "We have been called to form consciences, not replace them."

Here he channels John Henry Newman and liberation theology's emphasis on personal agency.

f. The rehabilitation of liberation theologians

Under Francis:

- Gustavo Gutiérrez was received warmly by the Vatican
- Leonardo Boff's ecological insights influenced *Laudato Si'*
- Jon Sobrino's work regained credibility
- Cardinal Müller (CDF prefect) visited Gutiérrez in Lima
- CELAM began a liberationist renewal

Francis re-legitimized liberation theology without reviving earlier ideological tensions.

g. Synodality: Liberation as Church practice

The Synod on the Amazon (2019) embodied liberation principles:

- dialogue
- listening
- Indigenous leadership
- critique of extractive industries
- proposals for pastoral creativity (*viri probati*, ministries for women)

This synod reflects Francis's belief that liberation is not only a theological idea but a method of Church governance.

43. ONGOING RESISTANCE WITHIN THE GLOBAL CHURCH

Despite Francis's advocacy, liberation theology remains contested—especially in Africa, Asia, and parts of Eastern Europe.

a. African episcopal resistance

Many African bishops oppose:

- LGBTQ inclusion
- women's leadership
- criticism of authoritarian regimes
- economic critiques of multinational corporations

The African Church often:

- upholds conservative morality
- maintains clerical privilege
- aligns with political elites
- remains wary of social movements

This limits liberation theology's impact.

b. U.S. episcopal division

In the United States:

- some bishops embrace Francis
- others resist him fiercely
- political polarization distorts reception of liberation themes

Issues such as racism, migration, and poverty become politicized rather than theological.

c. Curial inertia

Even under Francis:

- structural reform is slow
- clerical culture remains deeply embedded
- women remain excluded from ordained ministry
- decisions about LGBTQ persons divide bishops' conferences

Liberation theology has a papal advocate but not yet institutional backing.

44. LIBERATION THEOLOGY'S CONTRIBUTION TO CATHOLIC DOCTRINE

Despite tensions, liberation theology has quietly reshaped key doctrines:

1. The Preferential Option for the Poor

Now an official part of Catholic social teaching.

2. Structural Sin

The Church recognizes that injustices exist within systems, not only individuals.

3. Evangelization as social transformation

Proclaimed in *Evangelii Nuntiandi* (1975), reinforced by Francis.

4. Theological significance of experience

Communities of the poor are loci of revelation.

5. Ecology as moral and theological category

Advocated by Francis.

6. Synodality as liberation praxis

Consultation and participation echo base community methodology.

45. LIBERATION THEOLOGY AND THE FUTURE OF THE CHURCH

The future of liberation theology is tied to the future of the Church itself.

a. Francis's legacy: a turning point but not a conclusion

Francis introduced liberation themes into the mainstream papacy, but:

- he has not changed doctrine on women or LGBTQ persons
- structural reform remains incomplete
- successor popes may reverse or deepen his trajectory

His pontificate is an inflection point, not the final word.

b. The next battles

The Church must confront:

- the global clerical abuse crisis
- climate collapse
- mass migration
- digital inequality
- authoritarian politics
- patriarchal church structures

Liberation theology offers tools for navigating these crises.

c. A more global Catholicism

The demographic center of Catholicism is moving:

- to Africa

- to Asia
- to Latin America

These continents face profound injustices. Liberation theology provides the grammar for their theological future.

d. Synodal Catholicism

If adopted sincerely, synodality could institutionalize liberation methodologies:

- listening
- participation
- decentralization
- accountability
- prophetic witness

This could be the most enduring fruit of the Francis era.

46. THE CHURCH IN TENSION BETWEEN EMPIRE AND EXODUS

The history of the Church's engagement with liberation theology reveals a profound internal contradiction:

- The Church preaches Exodus but often practices empire.
- The Church proclaims resurrection but fears transformation.
- The Church canonizes martyrs of justice yet silences prophets.

And yet, liberation theology persists because the cry of the poor persists.

In every age, God raises prophets—whether in Latin American villas, African villages, Asian slums, Native territories, migrant camps, or refugee tents—who insist that faith without justice is idolatry.

Liberation theology is not a chapter in theological history. It is the ongoing conversion of the Church to the Gospel of Jesus Christ.

47. A NEW ERA OF OPPRESSION AND LIBERATION

The world of the 21st century is profoundly different from the one that birthed liberation theology. Traditional forms of oppression—poverty, dictatorship, racism, patriarchy—remain, but new systems of domination have emerged:

- digital surveillance
- algorithmic discrimination
- artificial intelligence and automation
- climate collapse
- mass displacement and forced migration
- global pandemics
- new racisms and nationalisms
- economic precarity in the gig economy
- epistemic injustice and misinformation

Liberation theology has adapted to these new realities, expanding its method and deepening its ethical horizon.

This section explores these new frontiers.

48. LIBERATION THEOLOGY AND THE DIGITAL WORLD

Technology has become one of the primary sites of oppression and liberation.

a. Surveillance capitalism

Companies like Google, Meta, Amazon, and global data brokers collect vast amounts of personal data. Shoshana Zuboff calls this *surveillance capitalism*—a political-economic system where human experience is turned into data for monetization.

Liberation theologians argue:

- surveillance violates human dignity
- privacy is essential to freedom

- the poor and minorities are disproportionately surveilled
- powerful corporations wield quasi-sovereign authority

b. Algorithmic oppression

AI systems can:

- reinforce racial bias (predictive policing)
- deny benefits to the poor
- exacerbate inequality in hiring
- suppress dissent through content moderation
- shape political opinion through algorithmic curation

Liberation theology must ask: Who designs the algorithm? Who benefits? Who is harmed?

c. Digital divide and epistemic inequality

Access to technology determines access to:

- education
- political participation
- employment
- information

The digital divide—between rich and poor, urban and rural, global north and south—creates new forms of structural injustice.

d. Technology and human dignity (CSR relevance)

Your own framework—Critical Synthetic Realism—offers valuable insight:

- knowledge is tested, provisional, and socially conditioned
- digital ecosystems shape epistemic authority
- truth is manipulated through technology

- liberation requires critical rationality and emancipation from digital illusion

Liberation theology must therefore incorporate digital ethics.

49. LIBERATION THEOLOGY, GLOBAL CAPITALISM, AND THE GIG ECONOMY

The globalization of capitalism has transformed labor, producing:

- precarious work
- unstable income
- the gig economy (Uber, DoorDash, Amazon Flex)
- wage stagnation
- exploitation of migrant workers

a. The working poor

Millions cannot survive even with full-time work. Liberation theology sees this as a violation of economic justice.

b. The theology of labor revisited

Building on John Paul II's *Laborem Exercens*, Francis critiques:

- "the deification of the market"
- profit without ethics
- economic systems that discard people

    Liberation theologians reinterpret:

- the Exodus as God's refusal of exploitative economies
- Sabbath as resistance to capitalist productivity
- the Eucharist as community-solidarity against commodification

c. Modern slavery

Human trafficking, forced labor, and debt bondage persist across continents. Liberation theology confronts these new forms of enslavement.

50. CLIMATE COLLAPSE AND ECOLOGICAL LIBERATION

No issue defines the 21st century more than ecological destruction.

a. Climate change and the poor

The poor bear:

- extreme heat
- drought
- flooding
- loss of farmland
- health consequences

    Climate injustice is class injustice.

b. *Laudato Si'* as ecological liberation theology

Francis reframed ecology as:

- spiritual
- ethical
- economic
- political

    The encyclical emphasizes:

- "integral ecology"
- "ecological conversion"
- "ecological sin"
- "the cry of the earth and the cry of the poor" as one

This directly aligns with liberation theology.

c. Indigenous ecological wisdom

Indigenous communities protect 80% of the world's remaining biodiversity. Liberation theology increasingly engages Indigenous cosmologies as partners in ecological justice.

d. Climate migration

Millions are displaced by:

- rising seas
- desertification
- drought
- storms

Migration is becoming the defining humanitarian crisis of the century.

51. LIBERATION THEOLOGY AND MASS MIGRATION

Migration is now global and structural, not episodic.

a. Drivers of migration

conflict

- climate change
- economic inequality
- political instability
- religious persecution

Liberation theology interprets migration through Scripture:

- the Holy Family's flight to Egypt
- Israel's sojourning identity
- hospitality as divine command

b. Pope Francis: a global advocate for migrants

Francis consistently elevates migrants' rights:

> "Every migrant is an opportunity to encounter Jesus Christ." (Francis, 2019)

He has spoken against:

- anti-immigrant nationalism
- border cruelty
- refugee detention
- trafficking networks
- exploitation of migrant labor

c. Migrant churches as new theological spaces

Migrant communities in Europe, North America, and Asia produce:

- new ecclesial cultures
- intercultural liturgies
- grassroots pastoral networks
- ministries of resilience

Liberation theology must place migrants at the center of theological method.

52. POPULISM, NATIONALISM, AND THE RETURN OF STRONGMEN

Around the world, authoritarian leaders and nationalist movements have gained power:

- the United States
- Brazil
- India
- Turkey

- Hungary
- Russia
- the Philippines
- parts of Africa and Latin America

a. Liberation theology's critique of authoritarianism

Drawing from Latin American dictatorships, liberation theology indicts:

- racism
- xenophobia
- misogyny
- state violence
- rule by fear
- religious nationalism

b. Christian nationalism as heresy

Christian nationalism in the U.S., Brazil, and parts of Europe:

- merges faith with political identity
- idolizes national myths
- sanctions violence
- erases the Gospel's universal love

Francis has condemned this ideology implicitly, calling it a distortion of Christianity.

c. Silence of bishops

In many countries, bishops:

- support nationalist regimes
- remain silent about police violence

- bless political strongmen
- suppress prophetic priests

This remains a major obstacle to liberation.

53. GENDER AND SEXUALITY: EXPANDING LIBERATION'S HORIZON

21st-century liberation theology has expanded to include:

- women
- LGBTQ+ persons
- survivors of abuse
- gender-nonconforming people

a. Feminist liberation theology

Women theologians emphasize:

- bodily autonomy
- patriarchy as structural sin
- sexual violence
- domestic labor
- reproductive justice
- inclusive language for God

b. LGBTQ+ liberation theologies

LGBTQ theologians focus on:

- belonging
- sacramental access
- human dignity
- critique of heteronormativity

- spiritual trauma
- healing

Francis has shifted pastoral tone but not doctrine:

- endorses civil protections for LGBTQ people
- denounces criminalization
- calls for pastoral accompaniment
- rejects violence and discrimination

But full inclusion remains unrealized.

c. Gender as a theological prism

Liberation now sees gender as a site of:

- power
- identity
- vulnerability
- injustice

This is a major shift from earlier liberation theology, which was largely male.

54. LIBERATION THEOLOGY AND GLOBAL YOUTH MOVEMENTS

Young people across the world challenge:

- climate inaction
- racial injustice
- gender inequality
- economic precarity
- authoritarianism

Movements such as *Black Lives Matter, Fridays for Future, End SARS,* Hong Kong activism, and Latin American student protests have deeply theological dimensions—even when secular.

Liberation theologians increasingly engage these movements, seeing them as:

- expressions of moral conscience
- signs of the times
- loci of revelation
- catalysts for ecclesial reform

55. PANDEMIC, HEALTH INEQUALITY, AND BIO-LIBERATION THEOLOGY

The COVID-19 pandemic exposed:

- inequitable access to healthcare
- racial disparities in mortality
- vaccine apartheid
- the vulnerability of essential workers

a. Theology of vulnerability

Liberation theologians argue:

- vulnerability is a theological category
- suffering exposes structural sin
- solidarity is the Christian response

b. Theology of public health

Health is:

- communal
- political
- social
- spiritual

Liberation theology increasingly incorporates public health ethics.

56. LIBERATION THEOLOGY AND THE INFORMATION CRISIS: POST-TRUTH, CONSPIRACY, AND EPISTEMIC JUSTICE

Modern oppression is also epistemic.

a. Misinformation as structural sin

Propaganda, conspiracy theories, and political manipulation undermine:

- free will
- informed conscience
- democracy
- social cohesion

b. Truth as a theological imperative (CSR influence)

Your CSR framework's emphasis on:

- critical testing
- provisional knowledge
- rational accountability
- synthesis of evidence

aligns well with liberation theology's need to navigate post-truth environments.

Truth-oriented theology becomes a form of liberation from ignorance.

57. LIBERATION THEOLOGY IN GLOBAL CATHOLIC PRACTICE: NEW FORMS

Liberation theology has taken new shapes:

- popular Bible reading movements

- youth ecological networks
- digital communities of resistance
- feminist liturgy groups
- social justice podcasts and media
- refugee-led ecclesial communities
- Amazonian and African synodal networks
- LGBTQ-inclusive Catholic spaces

Liberation is no longer confined to seminaries—it is lived in digital, ecological, and intercultural communities.

58. SYNTHESIS: THE 21ST CENTURY AS A LIBERATION CENTURY

Today liberation theology confronts:

- artificial intelligence
- global capitalism
- ecological crisis
- migration
- racism
- patriarchy
- authoritarianism

It does so with tools shaped by:

- Scripture
- tradition
- critical reason
- communal praxis
- interfaith wisdom
- scientific insight
- Indigenous knowledge

Liberation theology's core insight remains unchanged:

God is found where people struggle for dignity, justice, and life. But its methods have expanded exponentially.

59. INTRODUCTION: A THEOLOGY THAT REFUSES TO DIE

Liberation theology is one of the most influential—and contested—theological movements of the 20th and 21st centuries. From its birth in the barrios and favelas of Latin America, the movement has expanded to encompass the cries of oppressed peoples around the world:

- Indigenous communities
- women
- the African poor
- Dalits
- Afro-descendants
- LGBTQ+ persons
- migrant workers
- ecological refugees
- victims of digital surveillance and exploitation

What began as a regional theological project is now a global, multifaceted framework for understanding salvation as both historical and transcendent, both terrestrial and celestial.

Liberation theology refuses to die because the structures of sin it confronts refuse to disappear. As long as the poor are crushed, as long as women are excluded, as long as political elites manipulate religion, as long as the earth groans under extractive capitalism, liberation theology will continue to speak.

But beyond resistance, liberation theology also offers a positive vision: a world reconciled to justice, a Church aligned with the oppressed, and a faith that seeks not only understanding but emancipation.

60. A GLOBAL VISION ROOTED IN THE LOCAL

One of the central insights of liberation theology is that universal theology begins with concrete experience.

a. Particularity as a path to universality

Latin American theologians insisted:

- theology is done *from* the place where one stands
- all theology begins with the cry of a particular people
- the Church must listen to the poor before speaking to them

This principle has been embraced globally. African, Asian, and Indigenous theologians do not imitate Latin America; instead, they practice liberation theology in their own cultural and historical contexts.

b. Global resonance, local expression

While the theological grammar varies, certain themes recur worldwide:

- God's preferential love for the poor
- structural sin
- communal discernment
- prophetic resistance
- hope as a historical force

In this sense, liberation theology is not a school of thought limited to Spanish-speaking Catholicism; it is a method grounded in:

1. critical analysis of oppression
2. conscientization
3. praxis of justice
4. biblical re-reading from below

These steps have been adopted in diverse communities across continents.

61. LIBERATION THEOLOGY'S CONTRIBUTION TO CHRISTIAN THOUGHT

Liberation theology has reshaped global Christianity—Catholic and Protestant, Pentecostal and ecumenical—in ways that would have been unimaginable in the early 1970s.

a. The preferential option for the poor

This concept, once controversial, is now foundational in Catholic social teaching. It asserts:

- God stands with the oppressed
- the Church must make the poor central to its mission
- justice is not optional for Christian discipleship

Pope John Paul II affirmed it in *Sollicitudo Rei Socialis* (1987), and Francis has made it the heart of his papacy.

b. Structural sin and social analysis

Before liberation theology, Catholic moral teaching emphasized:

- personal sin
- individual morality
- private charity

After liberation theology, the Church acknowledges:

- systems and structures can be sinful
- institutions produce injustice
- conversion must be both personal and societal

c. Scripture read from the margins

Biblical interpretation is transformed when:

- the poor

- women
- migrants
- enslaved peoples
- Indigenous communities

read themselves into the biblical narrative. Liberation hermeneutics has become a powerful tool for pastoral ministry and theological reflection.

d. Interdisciplinarity as theological method

Liberation theology brought:

- sociology
- economics
- political theory
- psychology
- anthropology

into theological discourse. This method is now standard across academic theology.

e. Martyrdom as theological witness

The blood of liberation martyrs—Romero, the UCA Jesuits, Ita Ford, Jean Donovan, and thousands of unnamed catechists and activists—gave moral authority to the movement and changed the Church's self-understanding.

Their witness embodies Jesus' words from the Jerusalem Bible translation:

> "No one can have greater love than to lay down his life for his friends." *(John 15:13, JB)*

Their lives made liberation theology a theology of martyrdom, not ideology.

62. POPE FRANCIS AND THE REDISCOVERY OF LIBERATION THEOLOGY

Pope Francis constitutes the most significant ecclesial opening for liberation theology since Vatican II. His pontificate has:

- rehabilitated liberation theologians
- embraced ecological, Indigenous, and pastoral liberation themes
- condemned economic injustice
- prioritized migrants and refugees
- promoted synodality as a liberation method
- challenged clericalism, colonialism, and spiritual worldliness

a. A pastoral liberation theology

Francis does not teach liberation theology in academic terms. Instead, he embodies its ethos:

- simplicity
- closeness to the poor
- preference for pastoral encounter
- distrust of elitism
- denunciation of "an economy that kills"
- call for synods that listen to people

  This makes liberation theology accessible to ordinary Catholics.

b. Rhetoric vs. reality

Despite Francis' support, little has changed in many regions:

- African bishops remain resistant to feminist and LGBTQ-theological perspectives
- political elites still dominate episcopal appointments
- clericalism persists
- local churches often silence prophetic voices

- sexual abuse cover-ups continue globally
- economic elites still enjoy de facto ecclesial privilege

Francis has opened a door, but most bishops have not walked through it.

c. A shift in global Catholic consciousness

Francis' papacy has:

- normalized liberation language
- revived Vatican II's spirit
- strengthened synodal practices
- foregrounded the cry of the poor and earth
- reconnected doctrine with pastoral life

Even if institutional reform is slow, the theological and spiritual climate of the Church has changed significantly.

63. CRITIQUES OF LIBERATION THEOLOGY: THEN AND NOW

Liberation theology has its critics—then and now.

a. Early critiques

The Vatican's concerns in the 1970s–1980s included:

- Marxist influence
- reduction of salvation to politics
- potential for ideological violence
- risk of replacing spirituality with activism

Some of these critiques reflected Cold War tensions more than theology.

b. Postmodern and contemporary critiques

More recent critics argue:

- liberation theology is outdated
- it overemphasizes class conflict
- it ignores identity struggles
- it underplays spirituality
- it lacks a global framework

But most of these critiques misunderstand the movement's adaptability.

c. Pentecostal and evangelical challenges

In Latin America and Africa, Pentecostalism grew rapidly because:

- it offered healing ministries
- it addressed emotional and economic suffering
- it mobilized lay leadership
- it empowered women
- it created vibrant worship

Catholic liberation theology often failed to provide comparable spiritual depth or charismatic experience.

d. Internal critique: the movement must evolve

Liberation theology itself recognizes:

- the need for deeper spirituality
- attention to gender and sexuality
- attention to youth and digital culture
- ecological urgency
- interreligious collaboration

The movement has always thrived on critical self-reflection.

64. LIBERATION THEOLOGY'S FUTURE: FOUR EMERGING TRAJECTORIES

The next decades will determine whether liberation theology remains a major theological movement. Four trajectories appear most promising:

Trajectory 1: Integral Liberation

Liberation theology is moving toward a holistic approach that integrates:

- economic justice
- gender justice
- racial justice
- ecological sustainability
- Indigenous sovereignty
- digital ethics
- psychological and spiritual healing

    This is liberation theology for a complex world.

Trajectory 2: Decolonial and Indigenous Theologies

Across the globe, theologians are embracing:

- Indigenous cosmologies
- decolonial hermeneutics
- postcolonial critique
- land-based spirituality
- anti-extractive activism

    Indigenous theology connects liberation with:

- land
- body
- memory
- communal identity

This is a major shift beyond classical Marxist analysis.

Trajectory 3: Digital Liberation Theology

Given the rise of:

- misinformation
- algorithmic bias
- surveillance states
- AI-driven economies

liberation theology must address the ethics of:

- technology
- data exploitation
- digital inequality
- cyber-authoritarianism

The Critical Synthetic Realism (CSR) framework provides a powerful epistemological tool for this new field.

Trajectory 4: Synodal Ecclesiology as Liberation Praxis

Synodality offers a new ecclesial form of liberation:

- participation
- listening
- accountability
- decentralization of power
- communal discernment

If fully implemented, synodality could institutionalize liberation theology within the Church's governance structures.

65. FINAL SYNTHESIS: LIBERATION AS THE HEART OF THE GOSPEL

Liberation theology is not a theological trend; it is a reading of Christianity that insists:

- God hears the cry of the poor
- Jesus identifies with the oppressed
- the Spirit animates communities seeking justice
- salvation includes historical transformation
- the Eucharist demands solidarity
- the Church must be a sacrament of liberation

  As the Jerusalem Bible translation so beautifully puts it:

  "I have indeed seen the misery of my people... I mean to deliver them." *(Exodus 3:7–8, JB)*

This is the hermeneutical key. Liberation theology is not an innovation; it is a return to the biblical God.

66. CONCLUSION: THE GOSPEL IS ALWAYS ON THE SIDE OF LIFE

Liberation theology survives because it articulates a truth Christianity too often forgets:

The Gospel demands justice.

Christ did not call the Church to maintain empire, but to proclaim good news to the poor, release to captives, sight to the blind, and freedom to the oppressed (Luke 4:18–19, JB).

The future of Christianity depends on whether it takes this call seriously.

Liberation theology reminds the Church of who it is—and who it must become.

CHAPTER 4

Biblical Paradigms for Liberation: Exodus, Prophets, Jesus, Cross & Resurrection

A) SCRIPTURE AS THE FIRST LIBERATION TEXT

1. Introduction: Scripture as an Emancipatory Narrative

The Bible is, fundamentally, a story of liberation. Its central testimonies arise not from philosophers in ivory towers, but from enslaved laborers in Egypt, exiles in Babylon, oppressed peasants in Galilee, and a persecuted minority within the Roman Empire. As Walter Brueggemann observes, Scripture is "a sustained contest between the claims of empire and the promises of God."[1] Its pages pulse with the energy of protest, lament, resistance, and hope. The God revealed in Scripture is not a distant deity of abstract metaphysics but the One who sees, hears, and responds to human suffering.

The foundational self-revelation of God in Exodus reads:

> "I have indeed seen the misery of my people in Egypt. I have heard them crying for help on account of their taskmasters. Yes, I am well aware of their sufferings. And I mean to deliver them."
> *(Exod 3:7-8, Jerusalem Bible)*

This divine declaration establishes the biblical grammar of liberation. God's identity is inseparable from the act of emancipation.

---

1. Brueggemann, *The Prophetic Imagination*, 3.

Liberation theology does not impose a political agenda upon Scripture; rather, it retrieves Scripture's own original thrust.

For Critical-Liberative Theology (CLT), Scripture is not a collection of doctrinal propositions but a testimony to:

- God's preferential love for the oppressed
- the demand for justice
- the exposure of structural sin
- the call to prophetic resistance
- the promise of reconciliation
- the hope of new creation

This chapter explores the major biblical paradigms that ground CLT: the Exodus, the Prophets, the ministry of Jesus, the Cross, and the Resurrection. Each paradigm reveals a God acting in history to confront injustice and restore human dignity.

2. Scripture as Liberation: The Hermeneutics of the Poor

2.1. *The Word of God from the Underside of History*

The Bible was written largely by and for communities who lived under conditions of oppression:

- enslaved Israelites in Egypt
- refugees exiled to Babylon
- peasants under foreign occupation
- marginalized sinners and outcasts
- early Christians persecuted by Rome

Thus, Scripture frequently adopts the perspective of the powerless. As Jean-Marc Ela argues, "The Word of God becomes Good News only when it is heard in the cries of the oppressed."[2] Liberation theology follows this hermeneutical trajectory by interpreting Scripture from below — from the vantage point of those who today live under systems of violence, exclusion, or exploitation.

---

2. Ela, *African Cry*, 12.

This approach does not distort Scripture; it aligns with its original sociopolitical context.

2.2. The Poor as Hermeneutical Subjects

The poor are not merely objects of charity in Scripture; they are subjects of revelation. The Psalms consistently affirm that God listens most attentively to the cries of the poor:

> "This poor man called, and Yahweh heard him and rescued him from all his troubles." *(Ps 34:7, JB)*

Liberation theology therefore asserts that genuine theological insight emerges when the experiences of the marginalized shape biblical interpretation. This approach aligns with *Lumen Gentium* (§12), which teaches that the Holy Spirit guides the whole People of God in discerning truth.

2.3. Scripture as Resistance Literature

Many biblical texts were written under imperial domination — Assyrian, Babylonian, Persian, Greek, or Roman. They can be read as resistance literature, offering alternative visions of justice, community, and divine sovereignty that challenge prevailing political orders.[3] The Exodus, prophetic oracles, apocalyptic visions, and Jesus' parables all undermine the ideology of empire.

Scripture does not ask the poor to accept suffering as fate. It equips them to resist.

2.4. The Unity of Spiritual and Social Liberation

Western theology often separates "spiritual" salvation from "material" liberation. Scripture does not. The God of the Bible saves by:

- breaking chains
- healing bodies
- restoring communities

---

3. Brueggemann, *The Prophetic Imagination*.

- forgiving sins
- dismantling unjust systems

As Boff asserts, "To fragment salvation is to betray the holistic vision of Scripture."[4] The Bible unites transcendence and historical transformation in a single movement of divine love.

2.5. Critical Reason and Biblical Interpretation

CLT integrates Scripture with critical rationality. Building on Popper's insight that all human knowledge is provisional,[5] CLT affirms that biblical interpretation must remain open to:

- historical-critical insight
- scientific understanding
- ethical critique
- the sensus fidelium
- the demands of justice

This complements Newman's (1845) idea of doctrinal development: the Spirit leads the Church into deeper understanding over time. Scripture is therefore dynamic — not in itself, but in our ever-maturing grasp of its liberating implications.

3. The Foundations of Liberation in the Hebrew Scriptures

3.1. Creation as the Affirmation of Dignity

The Bible begins not with sin or judgment, but with dignity. Human beings are created "in the image and likeness of God" *(Gen 1:26, JB)*. This imago Dei establishes the theological foundation for human rights. Any system that degrades human beings — slavery, racism, colonialism, patriarchy, homophobia, economic exploitation — also violates God.

Karl Rahner emphasizes that human dignity is essential to theology because God's self-communication is directed toward persons capable

---

4. Boff, *Church: Charism and Power*, 62.
5. Popper, *The Logic of Scientific Discovery*.

of receiving divine love.[6] Liberation theology expands this insight: systemic injustice is a theological affront because it distorts the possibility of human flourishing before God.

3.2. Creation as Liberation

Creation is an act of liberation: order out of chaos, life out of formlessness. The God who creates is the God who frees. The biblical cosmos itself reflects divine intention for justice, harmony, and abundant life.

Creation theology thus becomes ethical: humans must steward creation, not exploit it. This insight anticipates ecological liberation theologies developed by Boff, Francis, and others.

3.3. Covenant as Social Justice

The Sinai covenant binds Israel not merely to religious obligations but to social transformation. Laws protecting widows, orphans, debtors, and the poor (Exod 22–23; Deut 24) demonstrate that covenant fidelity is inseparable from justice.

The Jubilee (Lev 25) is perhaps the most radical structural reform in antiquity:

- cancellation of debts
- restoration of land
- release of slaves
- economic equality

The Torah refuses to sanctify permanent inequality. This vision remains vital in today's world where global capitalism produces extreme wealth for a few and unrelenting poverty for many.

3.4. Memory as Moral Imperative

Israel's ethics emerge from memory:

> "Remember that you were slaves in Egypt." *(Deut 5:15, JB)*

---

6. Rahner, *Foundations of Christian Faith*.

Memory prevents the oppressed from becoming oppressors. As Segundo argues, liberation requires "hermeneutical suspicion" — awareness of how easily religion can justify domination.[7] The People of God must remain vigilant against repeating the sins of Egypt.

This is especially relevant for postcolonial contexts, where elites sometimes replicate colonial patterns of rule after independence.

4. Scripture and Critical-Liberative Theology (CLT)

4.1. Faith Seeking Emancipation

Anselm defined theology as *fides quaerens intellectum* ("faith seeking understanding"). CLT reframes this: faith seeking emancipation. Scripture becomes the catalyst for social transformation.

4.2. Praxis as Interpretation

For liberation theology, praxis — reflective action — is a mode of interpretation. Meaning emerges as communities struggle to embody biblical justice. Gutiérrez puts it succinctly: "Theology is critical reflection on praxis in the light of the Word of God."[8]

4.3. Community Discernment

Interpretation is not the monopoly of scholars. Vatican II affirms that truth unfolds through the whole People of God. The poor, the excluded, and the suffering play a central role in discerning the Gospel's meaning today.

4.4. Scripture as Mirror and Critique of the Church

Biblical liberation not only critiques oppressive states but also exposes ecclesial injustice. When Church leaders mimic the Pharisees by prioritizing power over compassion, Scripture calls the Church back to fidelity.

As Jesus declares:

---

7. Segundo, *Theology for the Art of Living*.
8. Gutiérrez, *A Theology of Liberation*, 11.

"This people honors me only with lip-service, while their hearts are far from me." *(Mark 7:6, JB)*

CLT applies this critique to clericalism, abuse cover-ups, gender exclusion, homophobia, and alliances with political elites.

B) EXODUS AS THE TEMPLATE OF EMANCIPATION

1. Introduction: The Exodus as Theology's Original Liberation

Among all biblical narratives, none has exercised more influence on liberation theology than the Exodus. For Gutiérrez, the Exodus is "the foundational salvific event,"[9] the first great drama in which God reveals God's character through decisive action in history. The story of Israel's deliverance from Egyptian bondage is not peripheral to biblical faith; it is the theological and ethical center from which all later revelation unfolds.

The Exodus narrative is not merely a chronicle of the past. It is a paradigmatic event — a theological archetype — that shapes how believers understand God, human dignity, justice, oppression, community, and mission. As Brueggemann argues, the Exodus is "the primal narrative of God's emancipatory resolve and Israel's identity as a liberated people."[10] It sets the standard for how God acts and how the people of God must live.

For CLT, Exodus is not optional biblical content; it is the template for understanding salvation, politics, and spirituality.

2. The Socio-Political World of the Exodus: God Confronts Empire

2.1. Egypt as Symbol of Structural Oppression

The book of Exodus situates the people of Israel under a system of imperial domination:

- forced labor
- economic exploitation
- population control
- structural discrimination

---

9. Gutiérrez, *A Theology of Liberation*, 84.
10. Brueggemann, *The Prophetic Imagination*, 25.

- ideological manipulation
- state-sanctioned violence

Pharaoh's policies represent a sophisticated machinery of oppression. Egypt is the prototype of all exploitative systems — colonial, neocolonial, racist, patriarchal, and authoritarian. Its significance is less historical reconstruction than theological symbolism. Egypt is empire; Pharaoh is the archetype of every ruler who treats human beings as tools in service of power.

The biblical text describes Israel's dehumanization starkly:

> "The Egyptians made the sons of Israel work to the point of exhaustion… ruthlessly." *(Exod 1:13–14, JB)*

2.2. The Cry of the People: The Beginning of Liberation

Liberation begins not with God's action but with human lament. The enslaved Israelites cry out:

> "The sons of Israel groaned because of their bondage and cried for help." *(Exod 2:23, JB)*

Liberation theology emphasizes the theological importance of this cry. It is the cry of the poor — the oppressed refusing to accept suffering as fate. Human agency initiates divine engagement; God responds to the cry.

As Ela notes in the African context, "Whenever the poor cry out, God listens; their protest becomes the locus of revelation."[11] The cry of the oppressed is thus an act of resistance and a summons to God.

2.3. God's Self-Revelation: Seeing, Hearing, Knowing, Delivering

God responds with one of the most powerful declarations in Scripture:

> "I have seen the misery of my people… I have heard them crying… I know their sufferings. I mean to deliver them." *(Exod 3:7-8, JB)*

This fourfold affirmation — *seeing, hearing, knowing, delivering* — defines the biblical God's relationship to history.

---

11. Ela, *African Cry*, 14.

God's knowledge is not abstract; it is relational, embodied, compassionate. Rahner writes that divine knowledge is always "self-involving," meaning God does not observe suffering from a distance but participates in the suffering of the oppressed.[12]

2.4. Exodus as Divine Judgment on Injustice

The Exodus is not merely liberation for Israel; it is judgment on Egypt. God confronts oppressive systems directly. Liberation is inherently political. It requires dismantling the structures that inflict suffering.

This divine confrontation is symbolized in the plagues. While modern readers debate historicity, liberation theologians interpret the plagues symbolically as God's judgment against:

- unjust power
- exploitative economics
- religious idolatry
- imperial arrogance

God is not neutral. God takes sides — with the oppressed against the oppressor.

3. Moses: The Calling of a Reluctant Liberator

3.1. Moses as Refugee and Resister

Moses' biography is itself a liberation story. Raised in Pharaoh's household yet identifying with enslaved Hebrews, Moses becomes a refugee fleeing state violence. God chooses not a perfect hero but a flawed, fearful man lacking eloquence:

> "Please, Lord, send someone else." *(Exod 4:13, JB)*

Moses' reluctance underscores that liberation is not driven by charisma but by vocation. God calls reluctant prophets, not bystanders.

---

12. Rahner, *Foundations of Christian Faith*, 112.

3.2. The Burning Bush: Revelation in the Margins

The burning bush appears in the wilderness, not in Pharaoh's palace. Revelation comes on the periphery. Liberation theology thus locates divine presence in the margins of society — slums, refugee camps, impoverished villages — where suffering is acute and faith is tested.

3.3. God's Name: "I Am Who I Am" as Promise of Faithfulness

God reveals the divine name as:

> "I Am who I Am." *(Exod 3:14, JB)*

Scholars debate its meaning, but liberation theology reads it as a declaration of reliability:

- "I will be with you."
- "I will be who I need to be for your liberation."

God identifies not through abstract ontology but through faithful presence.

3.4. Moses' Confrontation with Power

Moses' mission demands confrontation:

> "Let my people go." *(Exod 5:1, JB)*

Liberation theology insists that true faith requires speaking truth to power. The Church must echo Moses, not Pharaoh. Where bishops or priests align with oppressive governments, they betray the Exodus God.

4. Exodus as Paradigm for Structural Liberation

4.1. Liberation as More Than Escape

The Exodus is not simply a jailbreak from Egypt. Liberation includes:

- emancipation from forced labor
- dismantling oppressive structures
- formation of a new community

- covenantal commitment to justice
- restoration of dignity

It is a comprehensive transformation — political, social, economic, and spiritual.

4.2. The Sea Crossing: God's Power Against Imperial Violence

The crossing of the Red Sea is the climax of liberation. As the narrative says:

> "Yahweh fought for Israel." *(Exod 14:25, JB)*

This divine combat imagery symbolizes God's commitment to defeating systems of violence. Empire falls not by human strength alone but by divine solidarity with the oppressed.

For contemporary contexts — apartheid, slavery, colonialism, neocolonial economic exploitation — the sea crossing represents divine disruption of seemingly invincible systems.

4.3. Liberation and the Journey Through the Wilderness

Freedom is not instantaneous perfection. It is a journey fraught with:

- uncertainty
- complaint
- temptation to return to slavery
- need for communal formation

The wilderness teaches Israel:

- dependence on God (manna)
- radical equality (no hoarding allowed)
- rejection of nostalgia for oppression

Liberation theology interprets the wilderness as a metaphor for transitional societies seeking justice. After revolutions, civil rights advances, or social movements, the wilderness represents the difficult work of building just structures.

5. Exodus and the Formation of a Just Community

5.1. Revelation at Sinai: Justice as Covenant

At Sinai, liberation becomes law. The Ten Commandments reflect the moral architecture of a just society. They are not restrictive prohibitions but the ethical scaffolding for freedom.

As Brueggemann writes, "The law is the shape of liberated life."[13]

5.2. Laws Protecting the Vulnerable

Biblical law repeatedly protects:

- widows
- orphans
- strangers (migrants)
- debtors
- the poor

> "You must not molest or oppress the stranger, for you were once strangers in the land of Egypt." *(Exod 22:21, JB)*

The memory of oppression becomes moral imperative. Liberation is not complete until society is structured to prevent future oppression.

5.3. The Jubilee: God's Economics of Restoration

Leviticus 25 introduces the Jubilee:

- cancellation of debts
- restoration of lost land
- liberation of slaves
- rest for the land

The Jubilee reveals divine concern for structural justice — not merely charity. As Boff notes, "Jubilee is God's project for economic equality."[14]

---

13. Brueggemann, *The Prophetic Imagination*, 42.
14. Boff, *Church: Charism and Power*, 90.

Modern liberation theologians see the Jubilee as a model for addressing crushing debt in the global South.

5.4. *The Golden Calf: Freedom's Fragility*

Even after liberation, Israel succumbs to idolatry. The Golden Calf is the temptation to worship security, wealth, or political power. Liberation theology warns that communities can revert to oppressive patterns if vigilance lapses.

The Church likewise faces the temptation to abandon prophetic mission for institutional comfort.

6. Exodus as Counter-Narrative to Every Empire

6.1. *Egypt as Timeless Symbol*

Egypt is not merely ancient history. It symbolizes:

- colonial exploitation
- corporate greed
- racist systems
- patriarchal order
- political despotism

As long as such systems persist, the Exodus remains a living text.

6.2. *Exodus and Liberation Movements*

The Exodus has inspired:

- African American spirituals ("Go Down, Moses")
- abolitionists
- the Civil Rights Movement
- anti-apartheid activism
- Latin American campesino struggles
- Ambazonian demands for justice

- feminist liberation movements
- Indigenous land rights campaigns

The cry "Let my people go!" resounds across continents.

6.3. *Exodus and the Church Today*

When Church leaders:

- ally with corrupt regimes
- silence survivors of abuse
- exploit the poor
- deny women full dignity
- marginalize LGBTQ+ persons
- prioritize wealth over justice

they stand with Pharaoh, not Moses.
Exodus calls the Church to repentance, courage, and solidarity.

7. Exodus, Critical Rationality, and CLT

7.1. *Popper and the Open-Ended Nature of Liberation*

Karl Popper emphasizes that human knowledge progresses through critique. Liberation is likewise open-ended.[15] Exodus does not describe one final emancipation but inaugurates a continuous struggle for freedom.

This aligns with CSR's epistemological humility: truth unfolds in history as communities test, refine, and expand their understanding of God's liberating will.

7.2. *Newman and Doctrinal Development*

Newman affirms that doctrine develops organically.[16] Liberation theology applies this insight to salvation history: God's liberating intention

---

15. Popper, *The Open Society and Its Enemies*.
16. Newman, *An Essay on the Development of Christian Doctrine*.

becomes clearer across time — from Exodus to prophets to Jesus to the Cross and Resurrection.

7.3. Rahner and the Universal Offer of Freedom

Rahner's anthropology underscores that every person is called into God's self-communication. Oppression violates this vocation. Exodus reveals God's will that all humanity experience freedom in its fullness.

8. Exodus: A Theological Map

Exodus is not a story about the past; it is a theological map for the present. It shows:

- who God is
- where God stands
- what God desires
- how oppression must be confronted
- how community must be shaped
- how memory sustains justice

For CLT, Exodus is the foundational paradigm for understanding salvation as liberation — historical, spiritual, social, and cosmic.

C) PROPHETIC DENUNCIATION AS DIVINE COMMAND

1. Introduction: The Prophets as God's Voice for Justice

If the Exodus is the foundational act of liberation in Scripture, the prophets are the guardians and interpreters of that liberating memory. Their task is not primarily to foretell the future but to judge the present. As Abraham Heschel famously wrote, "The prophet's word is a scream in the night."[17] It is the cry of God echoing through human conscience, indicting systems of injustice and calling for repentance.

The prophets are the continuation of the Exodus. They confront kings who forget the poor, priests who hoard privilege, merchants who

---

17. Heschel, *The Prophets*, 16.

exploit laborers, and elites who normalize corruption. As Brueggemann notes, their mission is to "nurture, nourish, and evoke an alternative consciousness"[18] — a consciousness rooted in God's covenant and God's unwavering concern for the oppressed.

For CLT, the prophets reveal that denunciation is not optional. It is a divine command. The Church cannot preach the Gospel while ignoring injustice; silence is complicity.

2. The Social World of the Prophets: When Religion and Power Collude

2.1. Israel's Descent into Injustice

After settling in the land, Israel gradually adopted patterns of inequality reminiscent of Egypt:

- concentration of land and wealth
- exploitation of labor
- judicial corruption
- unchecked royal power
- oppression of foreigners
- patriarchy and gender violence
- economic injustice and debt slavery

The prophets arise in this context, not as polite moralists but as fierce defenders of the poor. They speak God's anger at a society that betrays the very liberation that formed its identity.

2.2. The Prophets as Critics of Both State and Temple

Prophetic denunciation targets two intersecting structures:

1. The State (kings, nobles, elites)
2. The Temple (priests, religious authorities)

---

18. Brueggemann, *The Prophetic Imagination*, 3.

This dual critique makes prophecy a threat to power. As Gustavo Gutiérrez argues, prophets represent "the conscience of a people that has forgotten the demands of justice."[19]

When religion blesses injustice, the prophets declare divine judgment upon religion itself.

2.3. Prophecy as a Dangerous Vocation

Prophets are not institutional leaders. They are outsiders, marginal figures, often persecuted for their message:

- Jeremiah is beaten and imprisoned *(Jer 20:2)*
- Amos is expelled from the sanctuary *(Amos 7:12–13)*
- Elijah flees from political assassination *(1 Kings 19)*
- Zechariah is murdered in the Temple court *(2 Chron 24:20–21)*

The prophetic voice is hated precisely because it calls for transformation.

Today, those who prophetically challenge Church and society — whistleblowers, survivors of abuse, feminist theologians, LGBTQ+ Catholics, anti-corruption activists — often suffer similar resistance.

3. Prophetic Denunciation: The Content of God's Fury

3.1. Amos: The Economist of God's Justice

Amos is perhaps the most explicit biblical voice against structural injustice. A humble shepherd and dresser of sycamores, he confronts a wealthy and religiously complacent society.

He condemns:

- the exploitation of the poor
- the corruption of courts
- economic inequality
- oppression funded by luxury
- religious rituals detached from justice

---

19. Gutiérrez, *On Job*, 57.

His most famous declaration rings with divine indignation:

> "I hate and despise your festivals…
> Let justice flow like water, and integrity like an unfailing stream."
> *(Amos 5:21, 24, JB)*

Amos insists that worship without justice is idolatry. Liberation theology draws directly from this critique when confronting Church practices that prioritize ritual over compassion.

3.2. Isaiah: Condemning Legal and Social Corruption

Isaiah exposes how law itself becomes an instrument of oppression:

> "Woe to those who enact unjust laws…
> who rob the poor of their rights and prey on widows and orphans!" *(Isaiah 10:1–2, JB)*

Isaiah shows that injustice is not only personal but systemic. Structures can be sinful when they perpetuate inequality. This distinction between personal sin and structural sin becomes central to liberation theology.

3.3. Micah: The Essence of God's Will

Micah distills prophetic ethics into one of the most concise and powerful statements in Scripture:

> "This is what Yahweh asks of you:
> only this, to act justly, love tenderly,
> and walk humbly with your God." *(Micah 6:8, JB)*

Justice, tenderness, humility — three dimensions of liberation theology.

3.4. Jeremiah: The Prophet of Truth-Telling

Jeremiah denounces religious leaders who manipulate the faithful:

> "They dress my people's wounds without concern, saying 'Peace, peace,' when there is no peace." *(Jer 6:14, JB)*

The false promise of "peace" becomes a theological deception. Today the Church commits similar error when it seeks institutional quiet over transparency regarding clerical abuse or corruption.

3.5. Ezekiel: Shepherds Who Feed Themselves

Ezekiel 34 condemns leaders who serve themselves instead of the flock:

> "You have fed yourselves, not my sheep." *(Ezek 34:8, JB)*

This indictment applies wherever:

- bishops protect abusers
- clergy accumulate wealth
- religious leaders silence dissent
- Church structures shield privilege

Liberation theology insists that ecclesial authority is legitimate only when it protects the vulnerable.

4. Prophetic Critique of Religion: When God Rejects Worship

4.1. The Prophets Against Religious Hypocrisy

The prophets reserve their harshest judgment not for foreign nations but for religious communities that betray justice. Isaiah declares:

> "I am sick of holocausts…
> Cease doing evil, learn to do good.
> Seek justice, relieve the oppressed." *(Isaiah 1:11, 16–17, JB)*

Temple worship becomes offensive to God when it coexists with exploitation. This reveals a fundamental biblical theology: ethics precede liturgy. Ritual is meaningful only when grounded in justice.

4.2. Religious Idolatry as Political Complicity

When the Temple becomes aligned with the monarchic state, religion becomes an agent of oppression. Amos warns priests who conflate God with nationalistic power. Liberation theology identifies similar patterns today:

- clergy aligned with authoritarian regimes
- prosperity gospel that sanctifies wealth
- Churches benefitting from unjust political structures
- religious nationalism (e.g., Christian nationalism in the U.S., Hindu nationalism in India)

Prophetic denunciation unmasks these idolatries.

4.3. Prophecy and Ecclesial Corruption

Contemporary scandals in the Church — sexual abuse, financial misconduct, clergy living in luxury — find their biblical critique in the prophets. Ezekiel's condemnation of shepherds who exploit their flock, Isaiah's denunciation of unjust leaders, and Jeremiah's exposure of deceptive priests echo painfully in our time.

Liberation theology insists that the Church must undergo internal purification before it can credibly evangelize.

This aligns with your own experience of seminary formation, where witnessing corruption, clerical arrogance, and cover-ups raised profound questions about the Church's fidelity to its liberating mission.

4.4. Prophecy as Self-Critique and Ecclesial Renewal

The prophets remind Israel of its vocation. Their denunciation is not destructive but restorative. As Heschel observed, prophetic anger is "born of compassion," the compassionate demand that God's people be faithful to justice.[20]

For the Church, prophetic critique is essential for renewal. As Pope Francis (2013) states:

> "I prefer a Church that is bruised, hurting and dirty because it has been out on the streets."[21]

---

20. Heschel, *The Prophets*.
21. Francis, *Evangelii Gaudium*, §49.

5. Prophetic Symbols: Imagination as Resistance

5.1. Symbolic Action as Public Theology

Prophets often perform symbolic actions:

- Jeremiah breaks a pot (Jer 19)
- Ezekiel lays on his side for 390 days (Ezek 4)
- Isaiah walks naked to symbolize exile (Isa 20)
- Hosea marries a prostitute as symbol of Israel's infidelity (Hos 1–3)

These acts are public theology — prophetic dramatizations of social truth.

Liberation movements likewise employ symbolic resistance:

- marches
- sit-ins
- hunger strikes
- civil disobedience
- protest art and music

Symbolic action awakens society to injustice.

5.2. Poetic Imagination: A Different World Is Possible

Prophets do not merely condemn; they imagine. They articulate alternative visions of society:

"They shall beat their swords into ploughshares." *(Isaiah 2:4, JB)*

This imagination is crucial for liberation. As Brueggemann writes, "The task is not only to expose injustice but to nurture the possibility of a new social reality."[22]

Today this includes imagining:

---

22. Brueggemann, *The Prophetic Imagination*, 44.

- economies centered on human dignity
- politics rooted in common good
- Churches that welcome all
- communities free from racism, patriarchy, homophobia
- ecological cultures of sustainability

Prophecy opens a horizon of hope.

6. Prophetic Themes that Shape Liberation Theology

6.1. *The Preferential Option for the Poor*

Although the phrase originates in contemporary theology, its biblical roots lie in prophetic concern for:

- widows
- orphans
- foreigners
- the poor
- victims of injustice

Prophets consistently affirm God's special care for the vulnerable.

6.2. *Social Sin and Structural Injustice*

Prophets attack:

- unjust laws
- corrupt courts
- exploitative economies
- violence against the marginalized

Structural sin is not a modern Marxist concept; it is biblical.

6.3. Community Ethics Over Individual Piety

Prophets stress collective responsibility. Israel's sin is communal; its repentance must be social.

Today, liberation theology applies this insight to systemic racism, global capitalism, environmental destruction, and political oppression.

6.4. Prophecy as Revelation of God's Character

God is not indifferent:

> "For I, Yahweh, love justice." *(Isaiah 61:8, JB)*

Justice is not merely divine command; it is divine identity.

7. Prophecy and the Church Today: A Call to Courage

7.1. The Church's Prophetic Vocation

The Church is called to be prophetic — not domesticated, not aligned with empire, not obsessed with self-preservation. Vatican II redefined the Church as the People of God (Lumen Gentium) and affirmed the prophetic mission of all baptized persons.

CLT extends this:

Every Christian must discern how to speak God's truth in a world of inequality.

7.2. Obstacles to Prophetic Witness

Contemporary obstacles include:

- clericalism
- fear of controversy
- institutional self-protection
- theological rigidity
- political alliances with the powerful
- internal corruption

These hinder the Church from confronting injustice.

7.3. Prophetic Voices Today

Modern prophetic figures include:

- Óscar Romero (El Salvador)
- Ita Ford, Maura Clarke, Dorothy Kazel (martyred religious sisters)
- Jean-Bertrand Aristide (Haiti, before political capture)
- Berta Cáceres (Honduras, Indigenous activist)
- Desmond Tutu (South Africa)
- Sister Stan Mumuni (Ghana, missionary serving vulnerable children)

They echo the biblical prophets in courage and compassion.

7.4. Pope Francis as Prophetic Pastor

Francis's papacy reflects prophetic commitment:

- denunciation of "an economy that kills"[23]
- critique of clerical power
- strong stance against abuse cover-ups
- solidarity with migrants
- ecological justice[24]
- promotion of synodality
- pastoral openness to LGBTQ+ persons
- rehabilitation of liberation theologians

While structural reform is slow, Francis has reawakened the prophetic imagination of the Church.

---

23. Francis, *Evangelii Gaudium*.
24. *Laudato Si'*.

8. Conclusion: Prophesy Is Essential

Prophetic denunciation is not merely biblical history; it is a divine imperative that shapes the identity and mission of God's people. The prophets teach that:

- justice is the heart of worship
- religion must confront, not bless, oppression
- silence is complicity
- imagination is powerful
- God sides with the oppressed

For CLT, prophecy is essential to ecclesial integrity. Without prophetic courage, the Church becomes an institution of Egypt rather than a community of Exodus.

D) JESUS AS LIBERATOR AND RECONCILER

1. Introduction: The Liberating Horizon of the Incarnation

Liberation theology does not begin with ideology but with Christology. Jesus is not only teacher, healer, and savior; he is liberator, one who enters a world of oppression to inaugurate God's reign of justice, reconciliation, and peace. As Jon Sobrino observes, "The Jesus of history is the crucified God of the poor."[25] His mission is not spiritual abstraction but concrete solidarity with those marginalized by social, religious, and political structures.

Every Gospel scene is embedded in the socio-political tensions of first-century Palestine—Roman occupation, economic exploitation, religious legalism, and social stratification. Jesus' ministry responds directly to these realities. The proclamation of the Kingdom is a confrontation with empire.

In CLT, the Incarnation means God takes sides—not in a partisan sense but in solidarity with the oppressed so that all may be restored to dignity. As the Jerusalem Bible puts it, Jesus proclaims:

> "The Spirit of the Lord has been given to me...
> He has sent me to bring the good news to the poor,

---

25. Sobrino, *Jesus the Liberator*, 19.

> to proclaim liberty to captives,
> and to the blind new sight,
> to set the downtrodden free. *(Luke 4:18-19, JB)*

This manifesto is the programmatic core of Jesus' mission.

2. The Social World of Jesus: Empire, Hierarchy, and Exclusion

2.1. Roman Occupation and Exploitation

Jesus lived in a land dominated by the Roman Empire. The imperial system:

- imposed heavy taxation
- used crucifixion as terror
- occupied land through military force
- collaborated with local elites
- extracted wealth from rural peasants

Rome ruled through violence masked as order. Liberation theology understands Jesus' proclamation of the Kingdom as a direct alternative to imperial domination.

2.2. Religious Elites and Exclusionary Purity Codes

In addition to Roman oppression, Jesus confronted religious exclusion. Purity laws and temple practices created social hierarchies:

- categorizing people as clean/unclean
- excluding the sick, the disabled, the poor
- marginalizing women and foreigners
- treating Gentiles as inferior
- equating physical suffering with moral failure

Jesus' ministry repeatedly dismantles these structures.

2.3. Economic Inequality and Debt Slavery

First-century Palestine was plagued by:

- land dispossession
- debt bondage
- food insecurity
- exploitative landlords
- unemployment

The parables of Jesus assume a world where peasants struggle to survive. His message is therefore inseparable from economic justice.

3. Jesus' Mission in Luke 4: Liberation as the Heart of the Gospel

Luke presents Jesus' inaugural sermon at Nazareth as the theological foundation of his mission. Quoting Isaiah, Jesus proclaims:

> "He has sent me to bring the good news to the poor...
> to set the downtrodden free." *(Luke 4:18, JB)*

This is not metaphorical. Jesus announces:

- good news to the poor → economic justice
- liberty to captives → political freedom
- sight to the blind → healing and social restoration
- freedom to the oppressed → dismantling structures of exclusion
- the Lord's year of favor → Jubilee economics

The "year of favor" alludes to the Jubilee cycle (Leviticus 25), including debt cancellation and restitution of land. Jesus therefore aligns his ministry with the economic justice envisioned in the Torah.

As Leonardo Boff insists, "Jesus' first word is liberation; his first gesture is solidarity."[26]

---

26. Boff, *Introducing Liberation Theology*, 14.

4. Jesus' Table Fellowship: Reconstituting Community

4.1. Eating With the Marginalized as Prophetic Symbol

One of Jesus' most subversive acts is table fellowship. He eats with:

- tax collectors
- prostitutes
- sinners
- the sick
- Gentiles
- women
- the poor

This practice violates purity laws and challenges social hierarchy. As the Jerusalem Bible records, the Pharisees complain:

> "Why do you eat and drink with tax collectors and sinners?" *(Luke 5:30, JB)*

Jesus responds:

> "It is not the healthy who need the doctor, but the sick." *(Luke 5:31, JB)*

Table fellowship becomes a sacrament of liberation—redefining community not by exclusion but by compassion.

4.2. Dignity as the Basis of Belonging

In Jesus' community, dignity precedes purity. Belonging is not earned; it is bestowed. This is a radical reversal of social norms. Women, children, foreigners, and sinners find welcome in Jesus.

Liberation theology interprets table fellowship as critique of contemporary ecclesial exclusion—such as the marginalization of LGBTQ+ persons, divorced Catholics, or the poor who feel unwelcome in wealthier parishes.

5. Jesus' Healing Ministry: Restoring Bodies, Souls, and Social Participation

5.1. Healing as Liberation

Healing is central to Jesus' mission. Yet healings are not mere miracles; they are acts of social restoration. In first-century Judaism, illness often meant:

- exclusion from community
- loss of livelihood
- spiritual stigma
- ritual impurity

Healing therefore returns people to full participation in life.

5.2. Confronting Stigma and Structural Exclusion

When Jesus touches lepers, he violates purity laws:

> "He stretched out his hand and touched him." *(Mark 1:41, JB)*

Touching the untouchable exposes the injustice of systems that blame victims.

5.3. Healing the Woman with a Hemorrhage

This woman has suffered twelve years, excluded due to ritual impurity. Jesus reverses her stigma:

> "My daughter, your faith has restored you to health." *(Mark 5:34, JB)*

Healing includes:

- physical restoration
- personal affirmation
- social reintegration

Jesus names her "daughter," giving her dignity and belonging.

6. Jesus and Economic Justice

6.1. The Rich Young Man: Confronting Economic Attachment

Jesus demands that the rich young man redistribute wealth:

> "Go and sell what you own and give the money to the poor." (Mark 10:21, JB)

Economic justice is integral to discipleship.

6.2. Zacchaeus: Repentance as Restitution

Zacchaeus offers a model for economic conversion:

> "I am going to give half my property to the poor… and if I have cheated anyone, I will pay him back fourfold." (Luke 19:8, JB)

Restitution, not sentiment, defines repentance.

6.3. The Workers in the Vineyard: Equality and Social Grace

Jesus' parable defends equal dignity:

> "Are you envious because I am generous?" (Matt 20:15, JB)

God's justice surpasses human notions of merit and hierarchy.

7. Jesus and Women: Liberation from Patriarchy

7.1. Women as Disciples

Women accompany Jesus (Luke 8:1–3), support his ministry financially, and remain faithful through the Passion. Liberation theology emphasizes:

- women are first witnesses to the Resurrection
- Jesus accepts women as theological dialogue partners (John 4)
- Mary of Bethany is affirmed for choosing contemplation (Luke 10:42)

Jesus overturns patriarchal norms.

7.2. The Samaritan Woman: Breaking Social, Ethnic, and Gender Barriers

Jesus speaks with a Samaritan woman, violating religious norms:

> "How is it that you, a Jew, ask me, a Samaritan woman, for a drink?" *(John 4:9, JB)*

He reveals himself to her as the Messiah—giving theological revelation to a marginalized woman. This challenges modern ecclesial exclusion of women from leadership.

8. Jesus and Social Outsiders

8.1. The Gerasene Demoniac: Liberation from Social Death

This man is isolated, naked, imprisoned by chains, and living among tombs—symbolizing total dehumanization. Jesus restores him to community:

> "He was sitting, clothed and in his right mind." *(Mark 5:15, JB)*

8.2. The Blind Beggar: The Cry for Justice

The blind man cries out:

> "Son of David, have pity on me!" *(Luke 18:38, JB)*

Despite attempts to silence him, he insists on being heard. Jesus hears the cry of the oppressed, echoing Exodus.

9. Jesus' Parables: A New Imagination for Justice

9.1. The Good Samaritan

The Samaritan breaks ethnic hatred, religious prejudice, and social hierarchy by embodying compassion. Jesus identifies this outsider as the true model of discipleship.

9.2. The Prodigal Son: Radical Forgiveness

The father restores the prodigal's dignity:

> "This son of mine was dead and has come back to life." *(Luke 15:24, JB)*

Liberation includes reconciliation and healing of relationships.

9.3. The Unforgiving Servant: Condemning Power Without Mercy

Jesus condemns authoritarianism that demands obedience but offers no compassion (Matt 18:23–35).

10. Jesus' Confrontation With Empire and Religious Authority

10.1. *Confrontation in the Temple: Economic and Spiritual Liberation*

Jesus drives out exploiters from the Temple:

> "You have turned it into a robbers' den." *(Mark 11:17, JB)*

Temple commerce oppressed the poor. Jesus' act is political and prophetic.

10.2. Challenging Hypocrisy and Clericalism

Jesus condemns leaders who burden others:

> "They tie up heavy burdens and lay them on people's shoulders." *(Matt 23:4, JB)*

This critique applies today where ecclesial power becomes oppressive rather than pastoral.

10.3. The "Woes" Against Religious Elites

Jesus pronounces woes on leaders who:

- prioritize rules over compassion
- exploit spiritual authority

- love honor more than justice
- "shut the kingdom of heaven in people's faces" *(Matt 23:13, JB)*

This parallels modern ecclesial failures—clerical abuse, secrecy, exclusion, corruption.

11. Jesus' Kingdom: A New Social Order

11.1. Not Spiritual Escapism

The Kingdom of God is not an otherworldly abstraction but a social reality breaking into history. It includes:

- justice
- compassion
- healing
- reconciliation
- inclusion
- liberation

11.2. Reversals: The Logic of God's Justice

Jesus proclaims radical reversals:

> "The last shall be first, and the first last." *(Matt 20:16, JB)*

The Beatitudes bless the poor, mourners, the persecuted (Matt 5:1–12). These reversals oppose the logic of empire.

11.3. Community Ethics

Jesus' teaching shapes a new society grounded in:

- forgiveness
- economic sharing
- care for the poor
- nonviolence

- truth
- hospitality

This is the new community of liberation.

12. Jesus as Reconciler: Liberation Through Healing of Relationships

12.1. Reconciliation With God

Jesus offers forgiveness freely (Mark 2:5). Liberation is spiritual as well as political.

12.2. Reconciliation of Communities

He breaks barriers:

- Jew/Samaritan
- male/female
- clean/unclean

    citizen/foreigner

12.3. Reconciliation and Nonviolence

Jesus rejects violent revolution (Matt 26:52) yet confronts injustice boldly. Liberation includes transformation without retaliation.

13. Conclusion: Christology is liberation

Jesus embodies liberation in every aspect of his ministry:

- preaching
- healing
- table fellowship
- parables
- exorcisms

- solidarity
- confrontation
- reconciliation

For CLT, Christology is liberation. Jesus reveals a God whose reign overturns empire, heals the broken, restores dignity, and forms a community of justice and compassion.

E) THE CROSS AS CONFRONTATION OF SYSTEMIC SIN

1. Introduction: Why the Cross Must Be Re-Read Through Liberation

Classical theology has often emphasized the Cross as personal atonement: Christ dies to reconcile individuals to God. While this is deeply true, liberation theology expands the meaning of the Cross to include structural sin, state violence, religious complicity, and the suffering of oppressed peoples throughout history.

As Sobrino argues, the Cross reveals not only God's love but also "the sinful mechanisms that crucify peoples."[27] Jesus dies not as an abstract sacrifice but as a victim of empire, religious hypocrisy, and political expediency.

The Cross is therefore:

- God's judgment against unjust systems
- solidarity with victims of oppression
- exposure of structural evil
- the cost of prophetic ministry
- a call for the Church to stand with the crucified peoples of history

The Cross is where liberation theology confronts the darkest realities of human sin — not merely individual wrongdoing, but systemic injustice that destroys lives and communities.

---

27. Sobrino, *Jesus the Liberator*, 45.

2. The Political and Religious Dynamics Leading to the Cross

2.1. Jesus Was Executed by the State as a Political Threat

Crucifixion was a Roman punishment reserved for rebels and slaves. Jesus is executed under the charge:

> "This is the King of the Jews." *(Luke 23:38, JB)*

This is not a religious accusation. It is a political one: Jesus is perceived as a rival to Caesar, a threat to imperial order. His proclamation of the Kingdom — an alternative society grounded in justice, equality, and compassion — is inherently subversive.

Rome crucifies him because he imagines a world beyond empire.

2.2. Religious Authorities Participate in the Condemnation

The Gospels make clear that certain religious leaders collaborate with Rome:

> "The chief priests and the whole Sanhedrin were looking for evidence against Jesus." *(Mark 14:55, JB)*

Their motivations include:

- protection of institutional power
- fear of Roman reprisal
- concern for doctrinal control
- jealousy and resentment
- preservation of economic privilege

Here the Cross exposes religious institutions that betray their prophetic mission.

2.3. The "Crowd" as Symbol of Manipulated Conscience

The Gospel scene of the crowd shouting for Barabbas ("Crucify him!") illustrates how collective conscience can be manipulated by powerful actors.

Mark describes:

"The chief priests incited the crowd." *(Mark 15:11, JB)*

Liberation theologians see this dynamic in modern populist movements, state propaganda, religious nationalism, and politicized fear. The Cross reveals how societies can be persuaded to destroy the innocent.

3. The Cross and Structural Sin

3.1. Structural Sin Defined

Structural sin refers to social, political, economic, and religious systems that perpetuate injustice. These are:

- unjust legal systems
- exploitative economic policies
- patriarchal structures
- racism and ethnic oppression
- colonial and neocolonial domination
- institutional corruption
- clerical abuse and cover-up

Jesus is killed by a convergence of such structures.

3.2. The Cross Exposes the Mechanisms of Oppression

In the Passion narratives, we see structural sin at work:

- arbitrary arrest (Matt 26:47–56)
- false witnesses (Mark 14:56)
- manipulated justice (John 18:28–32)
- political calculation (John 11:50)
- public humiliation (Matt 27:27–31)
- torture (John 19:1)
- execution designed to terrorize others

Crucifixion is the empire's tool to crush hope.

In CLT, the Cross is the ultimate revelation of how power destroys prophetic truth.

3.3. From "Jesus Died for Our Sins" to "Human Sin Killed Jesus"

Liberation theology does not deny atonement, but reframes it. Instead of seeing God demanding a sacrifice, it sees humanity demanding violence.

As theologian James Cone argues, "The death of Jesus was the cross of a condemned criminal, a lynched victim of empire."[28]

Salvation is not God requiring a sacrifice but God entering into the suffering caused by injustice — and overcoming it.

4. Jesus as the Innocent Victim: Solidarity With the Crucified Peoples

4.1. Jesus Among Today's Crucified Peoples

In liberation theology, the Cross represents the suffering of:

- victims of war
- political prisoners
- impoverished communities
- exploited workers
- trafficked children
- survivors of sexual abuse
- LGBTQ+ persons rejected by families or Church
- Indigenous peoples stripped of their lands
- women harmed by patriarchal structures
- African youth oppressed by corrupt regimes
- Ambazonian civilians caught in conflict

Jesus is present wherever human beings are crucified by injustice.

---

28. Cone, *A Black Theology of Liberation*, 113.

4.2. God Suffers With the Oppressed

The Jerusalem Bible expresses Jesus' cry of abandonment:

> "My God, my God, why have you forsaken me?" *(Mark 15:34, JB)*

This is not despair but profound solidarity. God enters the deepest human suffering, experiencing what victims experience — isolation, humiliation, abandonment.

Rahner emphasizes that in the Cross, God's self-communication reaches its depth: God is present even where God seems absent.[29]

4.3. The Cross and Survivors of Abuse

For many Catholics — particularly those who have endured clerical sexual abuse — the Cross reveals both the depth of human sin and God's solidarity with victims. Jesus was also betrayed by a trusted insider (Judas), abandoned by leaders (disciples), and condemned by corrupt religious power.

Liberation theology insists that the Church cannot preach the Cross without bearing responsibility for its own crucifixions.

5. The Cross as Prophetic Consequence

5.1. Jesus Did Not Seek Death — He Sought Justice

Jesus' death is not the result of passive fate. It is a consequence of his prophetic mission:

- defending the poor
- challenging purity laws
- confronting religious power
- exposing hypocrisy
- resisting empire
- proclaiming a new social order

---

29. Rahner, *Foundations of Christian Faith*.

As Gutiérrez explains, Jesus died "for the cause of the Kingdom," which is inseparable from justice.[30]

5.2. Prophetic Ministry Always Leads to Conflict

In Luke's Gospel, Jesus warns:

> "A prophet is never accepted in his own country." *(Luke 4:24, JB)*

Prophets disturb the status quo. They name what society suppresses. They identify the idolatries of wealth, power, and privilege. They defend the marginalized.

Such truth-telling provokes violent response. The Cross is the predictable outcome of prophetic fidelity in a world structured by injustice.

6. The Cross and the Failure of Discipleship

6.1. The Disciples Flee

At the moment of truth, even Jesus' closest followers abandon him. Mark recounts:

> "All deserted him and ran away." *(Mark 14:50, JB)*

This is a sobering reality for the Church. Christians often fail to stand with the oppressed. They protect themselves, not justice.

6.2. Peter's Denial: Fear and Institutional Failure

Peter denies Jesus three times out of fear. This mirrors how Church leaders today often remain silent in the face of injustice. Silence is a form of participation in structural sin.

6.3. The Women Remain

The women disciples stay at the Cross:

> "There were also women watching from a distance." *(Mark 15:40, JB)*

---

30. Gutiérrez, *A Theology of Liberation*, 103.

Women embody the fidelity and courage that male disciples lack. Liberation theology emphasizes that women have historically preserved the Church's moral conscience.

7. The Cross, Empire, and the Church: A Mirror for Today

7.1. When the Church Aligns with Empire

The Cross condemns every alliance between the Church and oppressive political power. History offers painful examples:

- Catholic complicity with colonialism
- Church silence during slavery
- support for dictatorships in Latin America
- racism within Christian communities
- clerical protectionism over justice for abuse survivors
- political alliances that marginalize the poor

The Cross unmasks these betrayals.

7.2. Pope Francis and the Reopening of the Prophetic Imagination

Pope Francis has re-emphasized the Cross as God's solidarity with the marginalized:

- denouncing "an economy that kills"[31]
- naming clericalism as the root of abuse
- calling for reform of power structures
- centering mercy over rigidity
- upholding migrants and refugees
- challenging ecological destruction

While institutional change proceeds slowly, Francis restores the prophetic meaning of the Cross as confrontation with systemic evil.

---

31. Francis, *Evangelii Gaudium*.

7.3. The Cross and African Contexts

In Africa, the Cross confronts:

- political corruption
- exploitative elites
- foreign economic domination
- conflict zones like the Ambazonian crisis
- gender violence
- exploitation by some religious leaders
- structural poverty

In many African Churches, the crucified Christ stands with those betrayed by both government and ecclesial authority.

8. The Cross as Divine Protest Against Injustice

8.1. God Does Not Will Oppression

The Cross is not a divine endorsement of suffering. It is God's protest against the systems that kill the innocent.

8.2. The Cry of Jesus as Reflection of Every Oppressed Voice

Jesus' cry from the Cross mirrors the laments of:

- abused children
- persecuted minorities
- the homeless
- victims of war
- exploited workers
- abandoned women
- LGBTQ+ persons driven from their families
- oppressed peoples seeking justice

The Cross is God listening to — and participating in — humanity's deepest cries.

8.3. The Cross and the Hope of Transformation

The Cross does not end the story. It opens the possibility of transformation. The Resurrection redefines the Cross as victory, not defeat — hope, not despair.

9. Conclusion: The Cross and Liberation

The Cross, viewed through liberation theology, reveals:

- Jesus' solidarity with the oppressed
- the exposure of systemic evil
- the consequences of prophetic courage
- the cost of justice in a violent world
- the failure of religious institutions
- God's unwavering presence in suffering

It challenges the Church to become the community of those who stand at the Cross — not with empire, not with religious hypocrisy, not with silent complicity, but with the crucified peoples of the world.

The next movement in the chapter will reflect on the Resurrection as God's definitive answer to injustice and violence — the triumph of hope over despair, life over death, justice over oppression.

F) THE RESURRECTION AS THE TRIUMPH OF JUSTICE AND HOPE

1. Introduction: Resurrection as God's Defiance of Death and Injustice

If the Cross confronts the full brutality of human injustice, the Resurrection reveals God's definitive response. It is not merely the reversal of death; it is the vindication of the oppressed, the exposure of falsehood, and the inauguration of a new creation grounded in justice, compassion, and restored dignity.

As the Jerusalem Bible recounts:

> "Why look among the dead for someone who is alive? He is not here; he has risen." *(Luke 24:5–6, JB)*

These words signify the most radical claim in Christian faith: history is not closed by violence, injustice does not have the last word, and God's life is stronger than the forces that crucify. Liberation theology reads the Resurrection not as spiritual escapism but as God's decisive intervention in history — raising up the innocent victim and overturning the verdicts of empire.

The Resurrection is not consolation. It is revolution: the opening of a new horizon of hope for all crucified peoples.

2. The Resurrection as God's Vindication of the Innocent

2.1. God Overturns the Judgment of Empire

Rome condemned Jesus as a criminal. The religious authorities labeled him a blasphemer. The crowd rejected him. The disciples abandoned him. By every earthly metric, Jesus' movement should have died with him.

But the Resurrection reverses every human judgment. It is God's declaration that:

- innocence cannot be permanently silenced
- prophetic truth cannot be buried
- justice ultimately triumphs over violence
- victims will be vindicated
- history is redeemable

As Sobrino argues, "The Resurrection is God's proclamation that the victim is right."[32] Rome executed Jesus; God raised him. The Resurrection is the ultimate divine NO to oppression and divine YES to life, justice, and liberation.

2.2. The Resurrection as Restoration of Human Dignity

When Jesus appears to Mary Magdalene, he calls her by name:

"Mary." *(John 20:16, JB)*

The first word of the risen Christ is recognition — restoring dignity to one who had been marginalized by society and dismissed by the male

---

32. Sobrino, *Christology at the Crossroads*, 72.

disciples. The Resurrection begins with a woman, placing her at the center of the new creation.

This has profound implications for liberation theology:

The Resurrection elevates those whom society marginalizes — women, foreigners, the poor, the excluded — and makes them bearers of divine revelation.

2.3. The Wounds of the Risen Christ: Memory and Justice

When the risen Jesus appears to Thomas, he shows his wounds:

> *"Put your finger here... Doubt no longer but believe." (John 20:27, JB)*

Resurrection does not erase suffering. The wounds remain visible. They become signs of:

- God's solidarity with the oppressed
- the memory of injustice
- the continuing call to resist systems that wound
- the transformation of violence into hope

Theologian Johann Baptist Metz calls this the "dangerous memory" of the Passion[33] — a memory that compels the Church toward justice.

3. Resurrection as Transformation of Fear Into Mission

3.1. From Fearful Disciples to Courageous Witnesses

Before the Resurrection, the disciples hide behind locked doors (John 20:19). They are paralyzed by fear — fear of Rome, fear of death, fear of failure. The Resurrection transforms their fear into courage.

Peter becomes the bold proclaimer of Christ in Acts; the disciples move from hiding to public ministry. This transformation is a model for the Church: fear must never impede liberation. Resurrection empowers the oppressed to become agents of change.

---

33. Metz, *Faith in History and Society*.

3.2. The Commissioning: Resurrection Activates Liberation

Jesus says:

> "As the Father sent me, so am I sending you." *(John 20:21, JB)*

Just as Jesus was sent to proclaim liberty, heal the afflicted, challenge injustice, and reveal God's reign, the Church is sent to continue this liberating mission. Resurrection is the basis of Christian action in the world.

4. Resurrection as the Birth of a New Community of Equals

4.1. The Community of the Resurrection as Counter-Empire

The early Church does not organize itself around hierarchy or power but around fellowship, equality, and shared resources. Acts describes:

> "The whole group of believers was united, heart and soul...
> They shared all their possessions." *(Acts 4:32, JB)*

This is not primitive socialism; it is resurrection politics — a transformed community where economic justice is fundamental.

4.2. The Breaking of Social Barriers

The Resurrection inaugurates a community where:

- Jews and Gentiles eat together
- men and women share leadership
- slaves and free persons worship as equals
- the poor are honored members
- wealth is redistributed

Paul proclaims:

> "There is neither Jew nor Greek, slave nor free, male nor female."
> *(Gal 3:28, JB)*

Resurrection destroys social hierarchies grounded in exclusion.

4.3. Eucharist as the Meal of Resurrection Justice

Paul criticizes the Corinthians for celebrating the Eucharist while neglecting the poor:

> "One goes hungry while another is drunk." *(1 Cor 11:21, JB)*

The Eucharist becomes a judgment on the community unless it embodies justice. The Resurrection transforms liturgy into a demand for equality.

5. The Resurrection and Hope for the Oppressed

5.1. Hope as Resistance

In liberation theology, hope is not blind optimism. It is active resistance against despair. Resurrection hope empowers communities to struggle for justice, knowing that oppression cannot defeat God's purposes.

As Moltmann asserts, "The resurrection of Christ is the foundation of all Christian hope."[34] It is hope based on divine action in history.

5.2. Hope for Communities Living Under Oppression

For communities suffering:

- dictatorship
- war and displacement
- structural poverty
- racism
- political marginalization (e.g., Ambazonia, Palestine, Amazonia)
- economic exploitation
- patriarchal domination
- clerical abuse

The Resurrection proclaims that injustice is temporary, not eternal. God is already at work undoing systems of death.

---

34. Moltmann, *Theology of Hope*, 36.

5.3. The Cry of Survivors and the Promise of Resurrection

Survivors of abuse, violence, and exclusion often experience the Cross more than the Resurrection. Liberation theology insists that the Resurrection promises:

- healing
- restoration of dignity
- justice
- truth-telling
- community solidarity

God's vindication belongs first to the wounded.

6. Resurrection as Rejection of Violence

6.1. Jesus Does Not Seek Revenge

After rising, Jesus does not punish the disciples who abandoned him or the authorities who condemned him. Instead he says:

> "Peace be with you." *(John 20:21, JB)*

This is not passive acceptance of injustice. It is the refusal to reproduce the cycle of violence.

6.2. Resurrection as Nonviolent Victory

Jesus overcomes violence not by greater violence but by transforming death into life. This transforms the ethics of resistance. Liberation does not require war or domination; it requires courage, truth, solidarity, and nonviolent power.

6.3. The State's Weapon of Terror Is Defeated

Rome used crucifixion to terrorize dissenters. By raising Jesus, God empties empire's ultimate weapon of its power. This is deeply political: the Resurrection is the collapse of the empire's ideological monopoly.

7. Resurrection and the Cosmic Dimension of Liberation

7.1. New Creation: Liberation Extends Beyond Humanity

Paul and the New Testament writers envision the Resurrection as cosmic transformation:

> "The whole creation is eagerly waiting for God to reveal his sons." *(Rom 8:19, JB)*

Ecological liberation — a theme central to CLT — is grounded in the Resurrection. Creation itself participates in God's salvific liberation.

7.2. The Final Defeat of Death

Paul declares:

> "Death is swallowed up in victory." *(1 Cor 15:54, JB)*

This eschatological promise affirms that God will abolish all forms of death — physical, spiritual, social, ecological.

7.3. The "Already and Not Yet" of Resurrection Hope

The Resurrection inaugurates a transformed world, yet its fullness is still to come. This tension animates liberation theology:

- struggle continues
- injustice persists
- hope sustains action

The Resurrection guarantees that history bends toward justice.

8. The Resurrection and the Church's Mission Today

8.1. Resurrection Calls the Church to Prophetic Witness

A resurrection Church must:

- stand with victims of abuse
- challenge unjust governments

- defend the poor and marginalized
- embrace LGBTQ+ persons with dignity
- advocate for ecological justice
- dismantle patriarchal structures
- reform clerical systems of power
- promote peace and human rights

The Church can no longer hide behind doctrine divorced from compassion.

8.2. Pope Francis and Resurrection Hope

Pope Francis' pastoral approach reflects resurrection values:

- mercy over judgment
- accompaniment over exclusion
- synodality over clericalism
- ecological conversion (*Laudato Si'*)
- solidarity with migrants and refugees
- compassion toward LGBTQ+ persons

Francis' message revives the early Christian conviction that the Resurrection demands radical hospitality, justice, and conversion.

8.3. Resurrection and African Christian Contexts

In African theology, the Resurrection holds special resonance:

- communities devastated by war long for peace
- victims of political oppression seek justice
- women challenge patriarchal traditions
- the poor resist structures of exploitation
- ecological devastation calls for spiritual renewal

The Resurrection is God's promise that Africa's suffering will not define its future.

9. Resurrection as Liberation From Fear, Fatalism, and Oppression

9.1. Liberation From Fear

The risen Jesus tells his disciples:

> "Do not be afraid." *(Matt 28:10, JB)*

Fear is a major tool of oppression:
fear of rulers, poverty, exclusion, punishment, failure, rejection.
Resurrection breaks fear's power.

9.2. Liberation From Fatalism

Oppressive systems teach resignation:
"Nothing can change."
"Power is eternal."
"The poor must accept their fate."
Resurrection is God's refutation of fatalism. History is open.

9.3. Liberation From Internalized Oppression

The Resurrection restores the self-worth of the oppressed. It announces:

- you are loved
- you are dignified
- your suffering matters
- God stands with you
- you will rise

This psychological liberation is as important as political liberation.

10. Conclusion: Resurrection and Biblical Liberation

The Resurrection is the climax of the biblical liberation narrative. It proclaims:

- God vindicates the innocent

- injustice will not have the final word
- death is defeated
- a new world is possible
- hope is stronger than despair
- love is stronger than violence
- truth is stronger than empire

For CLT, the Resurrection is the ultimate affirmation that liberation is not merely human aspiration but God's own work in history.

It is the anchor of Christian hope — the assurance that every crucified people will one day rise.

G) CHAPTER CONCLUSION

1. The Arc of Liberation: From Exodus to Resurrection

Chapter 4 has traced the liberative arc of Scripture—from the cries of enslaved Israelites to the risen Christ who inaugurates a new creation. This arc is not accidental or peripheral. It is the spine of biblical revelation, the theological grammar through which God is known and experienced in history.

We have seen that the Exodus stands as the foundational template for understanding God's relation to injustice. The God who sees, hears, knows, and delivers (Exod 3:7–8) is the same God who calls prophets, stands with the poor, confronts oppressive structures, and raises the crucified Jesus from the dead. The Scriptures do not merely contain liberation themes; they are liberation texts.

The prophets carried the memory of Exodus forward, revealing God's ongoing concern for justice, righteousness, and the dignity of the marginalized. Their fiery denunciations of unjust rulers, corrupt priests, dishonest merchants, and complacent religious communities remind every generation that liberation is fragile and must be continually reclaimed. Prophetic denunciation is not a historical curiosity but a constitutive dimension of the faith community's vocation.

Jesus of Nazareth embodies the fullness of this liberative trajectory. His preaching, table fellowship, healing ministry, parables, confrontation with oppressive power, and solidarity with the rejected reveal a God whose reign breaks open the boundaries of exclusion and reverses the hierarchies of empire. His mission is not a departure from the prophetic tradition but its most radical fulfillment.

The Cross exposes the mechanisms of systemic sin—political violence, religious complicity, economic exploitation, and the fear-driven distortions of human conscience. Jesus' execution is not an isolated event; it is the crucifixion of God by the world's unjust systems. Liberation theology recognizes that Christ dies *because* of his fidelity to the liberating will of God. The Crucified One is the God of the oppressed.

The Resurrection, finally, is the triumph of justice and hope. It is God's ultimate "No" to oppression and God's "Yes" to life, dignity, and liberation. The Resurrection vindicates Jesus, condemns unjust structures, restores dignity to the marginalized, and opens a new horizon where communities are transformed into agents of justice and reconciliation.

Taken together, these biblical paradigms form the heart of Critical-Liberative Theology (CLT) and demonstrate that liberation is not an optional theological theme but the very essence of Christian revelation.

2. Theological Synthesis: Liberation as Divine Identity and Human Vocation

The God revealed in Scripture is not a distant sovereign but a liberating presence immersed in human history. Liberation is not something God does occasionally; it is who God is. As Isaiah declares:

"For I, Yahweh, love justice." *(Isa 61:8, JB)*[/EXT[

Justice is not merely a divine command; it is divine identity. God's nature is relational, compassionate, and committed to human flourishing. CLT builds on this foundation to articulate a vision of faith grounded in:

- liberation as the lens of interpretation
- critical rationality (CSR) as method
- prophetic praxis as response
- communal discernment as ethical foundation
- hope as spiritual resilience

Scripture shows that God calls ordinary people—Moses, Amos, Mary Magdalene, Peter, the Samaritan woman—to participate in this liberating mission. This means liberation is not only divine initiative but human vocation.

For modern contexts, this vocation demands attention to:

- the cries of the poor
- systemic injustice
- gender exclusion
- ecological destruction
- racial and ethnic oppression
- economic inequality
- the wounds inflicted by corrupt or abusive religious structures
- the aspirations of oppressed peoples seeking self-determination

Liberation is both interior and exterior, personal and structural, spiritual and socio-political.

3. Implications for the Church: Becoming a Resurrection Community

For the Church, these biblical paradigms pose challenging questions:

- Can a Church aligned with unjust powers proclaim the Gospel of liberation?
- Can clergy who live like elites credibly preach Exodus solidarity?
- Can a Church that silences the oppressed embody the prophetic mission?
- Can a Church that hides its wounds be healed by the Crucified and Risen One?

The answer, increasingly clear, is no.

The Church is called to become a Resurrection community, characterized by:

- justice as its organizing principle
- solidarity with the poor as sacramental identity
- radical hospitality toward the excluded
- courageous self-critique and reform

- transparent accountability
- ecological stewardship
- genuine empowerment of women
- defense of human dignity in all forms

Pope Francis has attempted to reorient Catholic consciousness toward these values, especially in *Evangelii Gaudium*, *Laudato Si'*, and *Fratelli Tutti*. He emphasizes mercy, synodality, compassion, care for creation, economic justice, and the Church's responsibility to listen rather than condemn.

Yet he also acknowledges that structural change within the Church is slow, uneven, and resisted—particularly in regions where clericalism remains deeply entrenched. Africa, for example, continues to face challenges in addressing corruption, political complicity, gender exclusion, and inadequate responses to clerical abuse. The Resurrection calls the global Church to move beyond mere rhetoric and embody the liberating power of Christ.

4. Liberation as the Heartbeat of Scripture and the Soul of CLT

The biblical paradigms explored in this chapter reveal a consistent theological rhythm:

- Exodus: God hears the cry of the oppressed.
- Prophets: God demands justice and denounces corruption.
- Jesus: God walks with the marginalized and challenges oppressive power.
- Cross: God confronts structural sin and suffers with humanity.
- Resurrection: God vindicates victims and inaugurates a new world.

CLT arises from this rhythm. It insists that theology must not remain trapped in abstraction but must enter the wounds of the world with compassion and courage.

Scripture, read through this liberative lens, becomes:

- an invitation to solidarity
- a summons to resistance

- a call to conversion
- a promise of hope
- a guide for building just communities
- a source of prophetic imagination

To follow the God of Exodus, the prophets, Jesus, the Cross, and the Resurrection is to join the ongoing struggle for liberation in every corner of the world.

5. Final Reflection: The Triumph of Justice and Hope

In an age marked by inequality, violence, ecological crisis, corruption, and deep spiritual hunger, the liberative message of Scripture is more urgent than ever. Exodus tells us that oppression is not destiny. The prophets tell us that injustice is intolerable. Jesus tells us that God walks with the marginalized. The Cross tells us that oppressive systems can be exposed and defeated. The Resurrection tells us that hope is stronger than despair.

For CLT, these paradigms shape a vision in which faith seeks not only understanding but emancipation—the liberation of all creation into the fullness of God's justice and peace.

As the risen Christ proclaims:

"I am with you always, yes, to the end of time." *(Matt 28:20, JB)*

This promise sustains the struggle for liberation. It assures us that justice will triumph, dignity will be restored, and hope will rise again and again.

PART II: CHURCH, POWER, AND PROPHECY: THE CRISIS OF INSTITUTIONAL SIN

Part II exposes one of the most painful contradictions within global Christianity: the Church that proclaims liberation often becomes an agent of oppression through silence, complicity, and institutional self-preservation. Across four chapters, this section offers a critical-liberative analysis of how ecclesial power can betray the Gospel and what a renewed prophetic Church might require.

Chapters 5 and 6 examine the collapse of prophetic witness in Africa, where bishops and clergy frequently align with authoritarian regimes in Cameroon, DR Congo, Nigeria, and Zimbabwe. Through this alignment, the Church's moral authority erodes, replaced by a "theology of silence" that prioritizes political access and comfort over solidarity with the oppressed. These chapters call for a theology of ecclesial courage rooted in the prophetic tradition.

Chapter 7 turns to the global clerical sexual abuse crisis, describing abuse as an "anti-sacrament" that desecrates bodies and destroys trust. The U.S. Church's systemic failures reveal patterns now emerging in Africa: secrecy, clericalism, and institutional protection over victims' dignity. The chapter argues for a restorative ecclesiology grounded in truth, accountability, and structural reform.

Chapter 8 analyzes Christian nationalism in the United States, especially the MAGA movement, where race, politics, and distorted messianic identity undermine Gospel ethics. Evangelical and Catholic complicity expose a profound failure of orthopraxy—right action—revealing how faith is weaponized against the poor and marginalized. The chapter proposes a liberative Christian citizenship rooted in justice and the common good.

Chapter 9 addresses the deeper theology of institutions themselves. Churches drift into self-preservation through sociological patterns of bureaucracy and theological habits that sanctify hierarchy. Case studies from the Vatican, African dioceses, and megachurches show how sinful structures produce moral blindness. The chapter concludes with pathways toward transparency, democratization, and Spirit-led institutional conversion.

CHAPTER 5

The Silence of the Shepherds: The Collapse of Prophetic Witness in Africa

1. INTRODUCTION: WHEN THE CHURCH FORGETS ITS PROPHETIC SOUL

Modern African Christianity stands at a moment of profound contradiction. Numerically vibrant and spiritually expressive, the Church occupies a central role in civil society across the continent. Yet this very institution, whose mission proclaims liberation to the poor (Luke 4:18), often fails to confront the political systems that manufacture poverty, violence, and exclusion. In many contexts—from Cameroon and the DR Congo to Nigeria and Zimbabwe—the institutional Church has drifted into structural accommodation, carefully calibrating its public witness to avoid conflict with authoritarian regimes. The result is a widespread moral crisis: the collapse of prophetic witness.

The prophetic vocation is not an optional feature of ecclesial identity. It is constitutive of the Church itself. As theologians such as Jean-Marc Ela insist, Christian faith loses its credibility when it becomes blind to the cries of the oppressed and complicit in the structures that crush human dignity.[1] Yet despite Africa's long tradition of resistance to colonial violence, apartheid, and dictatorship, much of the contemporary episcopate practices what this chapter calls a "theology of silence"—a strategic preference for neutrality, coded statements, and pastoral ambiguity rather than direct confrontation with injustice.

1. Ela, *African Cry*.

This chapter critically examines the theological, sociopolitical, and institutional mechanisms that have led to this collapse. Drawing on liberation theology, African political history, and ecclesiological analysis, it explores how Church leaders frequently negotiate moral influence in exchange for political access, social stability, and institutional preservation. Through detailed case studies in Cameroon, DR Congo, Nigeria, and Zimbabwe, it shows how the Church's silence reproduces suffering, undermines public trust, and betrays the Gospel's demand for truth.

The chapter then outlines a constructive vision for a theology of ecclesial courage—a renewed model of prophetic leadership rooted in the biblical tradition, the example of courageous African Christian reformers, and the ethical demands of contemporary democratic struggles.

The goal is not to condemn the Church but to recall it to its deepest identity. As Gustavo Gutiérrez notes, "the Church must be where the poor are, or it will not be the Church of Jesus Christ."[2] Africa stands in need of a prophetic Church—one that listens to the cries of its people, speaks truth to power, and risks institutional comfort for the sake of justice.

2. PROPHETIC TRADITION AND THE AFRICAN MEMORY OF RESISTANCE

2.1. Prophecy as a Biblical Mandate

The prophetic tradition of the Hebrew and Christian Scriptures is marked by uncompromising truth-telling directed toward political and religious authorities. Prophets such as Amos, Isaiah, Jeremiah, and John the Baptist embraced a vocation defined not by institutional loyalty but by fidelity to divine justice. They confronted kings (1 Kings 21), denounced corrupt priests (Jer. 23), and exposed the mechanisms of exploitation (Amos 5:10–15). Their authority lay not in their office but in their courage.

Jesus stands within this tradition. His ministry challenged imperial power, religious hypocrisy, and economic oppression. The Gospels portray him as deeply political—not partisan, but committed to liberation. His proclamation of the Kingdom of God was a direct challenge to systems that dehumanize (Luke 4:18–19). Any Church that claims continuity with this mission must embrace the same prophetic courage.

---

2. Gutiérrez, *A Theology of Liberation*.

2.2. The African Legacy of Prophetic Resistance

Africa possesses a rich historical memory of Christian resistance to tyranny:

- St. Augustine, though often misappropriated to justify state authority, insisted that unjust regimes are no true commonwealths.[3]
- St. Cyprian denounced systemic greed and the corruption of elites in vivid terms.
- In the modern period, Desmond Tutu embodied prophetic leadership during apartheid, declaring that neutrality in the face of oppression is itself a moral failure.[4]
- Jean-Marc Ela argued that African Christianity must refuse cooptation by elites, insisting that the Gospel demands critical engagement with political realities.[5]

Ela's critique remains particularly relevant. He argued that African churches risk becoming chaplaincies to the state—offering ritual comfort without structural challenge. For Ela, a Church that refuses to confront injustice has abandoned its mission: "Faith does not flee conflict; it interrogates history in the name of the poor."[6]

The tragedy of contemporary ecclesial Africa is not a lack of theological resources for prophecy, but a profound hesitation to use them.

3. THE THEOLOGY OF SILENCE: WHEN INSTITUTIONAL PRUDENCE DISGUISES COMPLICITY

3.1. Silence as a Political Strategy

In many African contexts, bishops and clergy have adopted a strategy of *measured silence* in the face of authoritarianism. This silence is rationalized through a variety of theological and pastoral arguments:

1. Preservation of unity – Fear that open criticism might divide the Church.

---

3. Augustine, *City of God*, XIX.
4. Tutu, *Hope and Suffering*.
5. Ela, *African Cry*.
6. Ela, *My Faith as an African*.

2. Protection of institutions – Schools, hospitals, and seminaries often depend on state goodwill.

3. Avoidance of retaliation – Regimes in Central Africa and parts of West Africa have historically targeted outspoken clergy through intimidation, surveillance, or legal harassment.

Yet these rationalizations mask a deeper crisis: a shift from moral leadership to institutional diplomacy. As Ela observes, the Church's role becomes distorted when "pastoral caution serves as an alibi for the refusal to confront injustice."[7]

3.2. The Rewards of Silence

In exchange for silence, Church leaders often gain:

- Invitations to state ceremonies
- Protection from government interference
- Preferential access to political elites
- Social prestige as mediators rather than agitators
- Financial benefits for Church-run institutions

This dynamic creates a *moral transaction* in which ecclesial actors sacrifice prophetic clarity for political stability.

3.3. When Silence Becomes Theological

A particularly dangerous development is the theologization of silence. Some Church leaders invoke "prudence," "dialogue," or "peace" as spiritual values that prohibit strong confrontation. Others misuse Romans 13 to claim that criticizing a government undermines divine order.

This misinterpretation ignores both the biblical tradition and the long-standing Christian teaching that unjust authority has no moral legitimacy.[8]

A Church that teaches obedience without justice becomes a theological instrument of oppression.

---

7. Ela, *African Cry*.
8. Aquinas, *ST* I-II, Q. 96.

4. FOUR AFRICAN WOUNDS: CASE STUDIES IN PROPHETIC FAILURE

If the crisis of African Catholicism were merely theoretical, it would wound only theologians. But it is not theoretical; it is historical, political, bloody, and brutally concrete. The collapse of prophetic witness is written in the lives of the poor, the bodies of the oppressed, the tears of mothers burying sons, and the despair of youth fleeing collapsing nations.

The prophetic wound can be traced across the continent, but four case studies illustrate it with heartbreaking clarity: Cameroon, DR Congo, Nigeria, and Zimbabwe. In each, the Church's silence—or selective courage—has shaped national destinies.

4.1 Cameroon: Silence in the Time of Dying

Cameroon is a nation where the earth groans under the weight of fear. Since 2016, the Anglophone regions have been engulfed in a deadly conflict marked by burned villages, massacred civilians, arbitrary arrests, and the displacement of nearly a million people. International organizations have documented atrocities committed by both state forces and armed separatists. And yet, at the height of national agony, a deafening silence hovered over the episcopal leadership.

Only the outspoken Cardinal Tumi, before his passing, showed sustained prophetic clarity. Most issued vague communiqués, urging "peace" and "dialogue," without naming perpetrators, systemic injustice, structural marginalization, or the political roots of the conflict.

The faithful asked:

"If our shepherds cannot weep with us, who will?"

Jean-Marc Ela warned that the African Church often behaves like "an institution more committed to maintaining order than announcing liberation."[9] Cameroon embodies this critique. As villages were razed and children shot in their sleep, many Catholics felt the hierarchy cared more about maintaining diplomatic neutrality with the regime than defending human lives.

The consequences have been spiritual and demographic. In the Anglophone regions, Catholics flock to Pentecostal churches where pastors pray boldly against oppression and speak openly about injustice,

---

9. Ela, *African Cry*, 54.

corruption, and suffering. These pastors address trauma with spiritual immediacy. Meanwhile, diaspora Cameroonians form independent Catholic-inspired churches—from Brussels to Texas—because they perceive the official Church as absent in their hour of need.

Silence became a wound from which many will never return.

4.2 DR Congo: The Church of Two Souls

If Cameroon reveals a silent Church, DR Congo reveals a divided one. The Catholic Church in Congo is massive, influential, educated—and torn between the prophetic fire of CENCO (The National Episcopal Conference of Congo) and the complacency of segments of the hierarchy compromised by ties to political and economic elites.

CENCO has been a rare light in African Catholicism. In 1997, in 2006, and again in the tumultuous elections of 2018, CENCO courageously monitored elections, mediated political transitions, and refused to legitimize fraud. In 2018 it famously declared that the results announced by the regime "did not correspond with the observations of its 40,000 observers."[10] This act was nothing short of prophetic.

Yet Congo's ecclesial landscape is more complex. Many local bishops and clergy have close ties to provincial leaders, mining interests, or political factions. The Catechism may condemn corruption, but in Congo, clergy sometimes bless it with their silence.

The contradictions are stark:

- Some priests preach bold sermons against injustice.
- Others collaborate with militia-backed politicians.
- Some bishops accompany protestors.
- Others dine with oligarchs who pillage the nation's minerals.

As Kä Mana lamented, Congolese Christianity often suffers from "a profound moral schizophrenia."[11]

Meanwhile, Pentecostalism explodes in Kinshasa, Lubumbashi, Goma, and diaspora communities in Paris, London, and Montreal. Catholics leave because Pentecostal pastors name what they suffer: exploitation, demonic cycles, political violence, and despair. These pastors

---

10. CENCO. *Déclaration des Evêques...*
11. Kä Mana. *Christians and the Social Question in Africa*, 17.

address Congo's spiritual wounds with a power the people feel, not just hear.

Congo proves an important truth:

Prophetic witness cannot be occasional; it must be consistent.

Wherever the Church fails in consistency, Pentecostalism fills the void.

4.3 Nigeria: When Corruption Infects the Sanctuary

Nigeria is Africa's spiritual giant—Catholic, Pentecostal, Muslim, and traditionalist in equal measure. Its Catholic Church is vibrant, intellectually rich, and globally influential. Yet it is also deeply wounded by corruption, ethnic divisions, political infiltration, and clerical ambition.

Nigeria's Catholic bishops have, at times, spoken courageously—against Boko Haram, against state brutality, and against electoral fraud. Yet their voice is fragmented and inconsistent. Some dioceses thunder with liberation; others whisper with caution. Some priests live among the poor; others flaunt wealth indistinguishable from that of corrupt politicians.

Young Nigerians see the contradictions. They see priests arriving at church in convoys. They see clergy who preach moral purity yet practice tribal favoritism. They see bishops who condemn youth protests but not the political elite responsible for their suffering.

This fosters disillusionment.

The 2020 #EndSARS protests—driven primarily by young Nigerians resisting police brutality—exposed the Church's hesitation. While Pentecostal and Anglican voices rose quickly, Catholic leadership responded slowly and cautiously. Many Catholics felt unseen.

As a result, Nigeria has experienced one of the largest Catholic-to-Pentecostal migrations in Africa. Churches like Winners Chapel, RCCG, MFM, and SCOAN attract former Catholics seeking:

- spiritual warfare
- socio-economic empowerment
- emotionally expressive worship
- courageous preaching
- dynamic community

These churches speak to Nigeria's existential crisis: corruption, unemployment, insecurity, and spiritual fear. The Catholic Church often appears too formal, bureaucratic, or detached to address these wounds with equal force.

Ela's prophetic insight again proves accurate: "The Church that refuses to let the cry of the poor enter its theology will become irrelevant to their faith."[12] Nigeria's Church risks precisely this irrelevance.

4.4 Zimbabwe: Prophecy in Chains

Zimbabwe stands as a tragic example of a Church that once spoke boldly but grew fearful under decades of authoritarian rule. Robert Mugabe, though educated by Catholic institutions, learned how to intimidate and divide the Church.

A few brave voices—such as Archbishop Pius Ncube—spoke boldly against tyranny, land seizures, and state violence. But the regime's retaliation was swift, public, and humiliating. Many bishops recoiled in fear, retreating into diplomatic communiqués and ambiguous appeals for "dialogue."

Zimbabwean Catholics watched as:

- elections were rigged
- the economy collapsed
- inflation devoured salaries
- activists disappeared
- soldiers shot protestors

Yet homilies remained cautious. Pastoral letters avoided naming the regime. The people were not fooled. They left.

Pentecostalism in Zimbabwe offers not only spiritual vitality but psychological survival. It becomes a refuge of hope in a collapsing nation, a space where God still feels powerful and present. Catholicism, by contrast, often feels institutional, distant, and passive.

Tutu's iconic warning hangs over Zimbabwe like a judgment:
"Our silence is complicity."

---

12. Ela, *African Cry*, 102.

4.5 What These Four Nations Reveal

Across Cameroon, Congo, Nigeria, and Zimbabwe, a clear pattern emerges:

(1) Where the Church clings to political privilege, prophecy dies.

(2) Where bishops fear rulers more than God, the people lose trust.

(3) Where the Church spiritualizes suffering, the poor seek churches that confront it.

(4) Where the Church is silent, Pentecostalism speaks.

These nations reveal not isolated failures but a continental crisis:
The African Catholic Church is losing its children because it has lost its voice.

5. WHY PENTECOSTALISM THRIVES WHERE CATHOLICISM COLLAPSES

The rise of Pentecostal and charismatic Christianity across Africa is not an accident. It is not a temporary emotional wave, nor a mere stylistic preference. It is, instead, a profound theological revolt—a spiritual protest against a Church that has become too silent, too cautious, too comfortable, too clerical, and too institutional to meet the urgency of African suffering.

> Jean-Marc Ela predicted this exodus long ago when he wrote:
> "The Christian faith will be reborn in Africa when it learns to speak the language of the people's struggles."[13]

Pentecostalism learned that language. The Catholic Church, in many places, did not.

To understand why Catholics leave, we must explore the sociological, theological, spiritual, and psychological forces that make Pentecostalism a compelling refuge for millions.

---

13. Ela, *My Faith as an African*, 5.

5.1 Pentecostalism Gives People Their Voice Back

Catholic liturgy—beautiful, ancient, universal—can also feel rigid and impersonal when lived in contexts of trauma. African Catholics often experience:

- homilies that avoid real issues
- worship that feels emotionally restrained
- pastors who remain distant from daily suffering
- hierarchical structures that silence lay initiative

Pentecostalism reverses this dynamic entirely.

In Pentecostal spaces, the people speak. They pray aloud, testify, cry, lament, rejoice, shout, confess, prophesy, and claim God's promises. Worship becomes a collective uprising of hope, not a ritual of quiet endurance. The poor rediscover their voice—spiritual, emotional, and communal.

As Birgit Meyer observes, Pentecostalism allows Africans to "reclaim agency in a world where they feel increasingly powerless."[14] Agency is empowerment—and Catholics crave it.

5.2 Pentecostalism Preaches a God Who Acts Today

In many African Catholic parishes, sermons are theological reflections, catechetical exhortations, or moral reminders. But Pentecostal preaching is existentially urgent. It proclaims a God who:

- heals
- delivers
- breaks chains
- intervenes in history
- lifts the poor
- destroys the works of evil
- promotes human flourishing

A God who acts now, not only after death.

---

14. Meyer, *Christianity in Africa*.

Allan Anderson notes that Pentecostalism grew because it "resonated with the African worldview of a dynamic spiritual universe."[15] Africans live with the reality of spirits, curses, ancestors, misfortune, and invisible forces. Pentecostalism treats this worldview seriously and theologically.

Catholicism, in many places, has not. It often treats these realities as superstition or pastoral complications, offering doctrinal abstraction instead of spiritual tools. The sacramental system is powerful, but when it is not communicated in ways that address existential fear, it can feel distant.

The people leave because they want a Church that takes the invisible world as seriously as they do.

5.3 Pentecostalism Names Injustice Without Fear

Pentecostal pastors in Africa do something Catholic bishops often do not: They name the sins of the nation aloud.

They preach against:

- corrupt politicians
- unjust police
- ethnic violence
- exploitation
- abuse of women
- economic inequality

They call out injustice with prophetic clarity.

In Uganda, Kenya, Nigeria, Ghana, and South Africa, Pentecostal leaders have become some of the most vocal critics of state violence and corruption.[16] They speak as if the prophets of Israel were alive again.

Meanwhile, Catholic bishops often speak in guarded, bureaucratic language, with carefully negotiated statements designed not to provoke the state.

Africans, especially youth, can tell the difference between courage and caution.

One young Nigerian convert put it plainly:

"Pentecostals speak the truth. Catholics speak in code."

---

15. Anderson, *An Introduction to Pentecostalism*, 29.
16. Englund, *Christianity and Public Culture in Africa*.

5.4 Pentecostalism Meets Everyday Material Needs

Liberation theology has long insisted that the Gospel must address not only spiritual salvation but also material conditions. Yet many African Catholics feel that their Church preaches morality while Pentecostal churches help them survive.

Pentecostal churches often provide:

- job networks
- business training
- mutual aid groups
- emotional counseling
- healing ministries
- prayer against fear, anxiety, depression
- daily encouragement

Rather than telling believers to "offer their suffering to God," Pentecostalism teaches them to fight suffering with faith, community, and practical strategies.

In contexts of unemployment, illness, debt, and fear, this is not prosperity theology—it is pastoral realism.

5.5 Pentecostalism Expands the Imagination of the Poor

For generations, African Catholics were taught a theology of endurance:
Suffer now, rejoice later.
Be patient.
God will reward you in heaven.
Offer your trials to the Lord.
Obey your pastors.
Trust the Church.

But Pentecostalism teaches a theology of expectation:
Breakthrough is possible.
Healing is possible.
Deliverance is possible.
Restoration is possible.
Change is possible.
God hears your cry today.

This shift from endurance to expectation expands the imagination of the poor. It makes them actors in God's transformative plan, not passive observers of their own suffering.

As Gifford argues, Pentecostalism "gives people a sense of mastery over their circumstances."[17] Catholics crave this mastery, especially in nations where government corruption and social collapse rob them of control.

5.6 Pentecostal Leadership Is Close to the People

The Catholic hierarchy is often:

- distant
- formal
- clerical
- hard to access
- culturally rigid

In contrast, Pentecostal pastors:

- answer their phones
- visit members' homes
- pray with families in crisis
- mentor youth
- speak in local idioms
- dress like ordinary people
- share personal struggles

They embody a pastoral intimacy many Catholics have never experienced.

One Cameroonian woman put it this way:

"In the Catholic Church, I know the sacraments. In the Pentecostal church, I know my pastor."

The Church of Christ was meant to feel like a family. Too often, Catholic parishes feel like administrations.

---

17. Gifford, *Christianity and Politics in Doe's Liberia*, 178.

5.7 Pentecostalism Offers Emotional Healing

Trauma is widespread in Africa:

- war
- displacement
- domestic violence
- poverty
- hopelessness
- communal fear
- political instability

The Catholic Church, with its formal rituals and clerical reserve, frequently struggles to address these wounds directly. Pentecostal worship, on the other hand, provides emotional catharsis:

- crying
- shouting
- laying on of hands
- deliverance rituals
- singing with abandon
- communal prayer

These practices help people process trauma in ways cognitive theology cannot. They give voice to pain, allowing the Spirit to touch the wound.

In this sense, Pentecostalism functions as both church and therapy.

5.8 Catholicism Often Appears More Institutional Than Spiritual

Africans do not reject Catholic sacramental theology—they reject Catholic institutionalism when it becomes:

- bureaucratic
- slow
- impersonal
- elitist

- disconnected from their reality

When priests live like elites, the Church becomes suspect. When bishops dine with dictators, the Church becomes compromised. When parishes seem like offices rather than communities, the Church becomes irrelevant.

Meanwhile, Pentecostalism offers:

- spiritual spontaneity
- pastoral accessibility
- charismatic energy
- strong leadership
- community solidarity

It feels alive.

> As one Ghanaian youth told researchers:
> "In Pentecostalism, God feels near. In Catholicism, God feels far."[18]

This perception, true or not, drives conversions.

5.9 Pentecostalism Embodies What Catholicism Has Forgotten

At its origin, Christianity was:

- charismatic
- prophetic
- emotionally expressive
- communal
- anti-imperial
- healing-centered
- poor-centered

Pentecostalism has rediscovered this early Christian fire. Catholicism once had it too, but centuries of institutional layering have obscured it.

African Catholics are not abandoning Catholic theology.

18. Meyer, *Sensational Movies*, 62.

They are abandoning Catholic timidity.

6. THE ECCLESIOLOGY OF COMPLICITY: CLERICALISM, FEAR, AND INSTITUTIONAL SELF-PRESERVATION

If the Church in Africa were only silent because it did not understand the suffering of its people, that would be a tragedy. But the truth is more painful: the Church is silent because it fears losing the privileges it has acquired through its proximity to power. This fear is the root of what liberation theologians call *institutional sin*, a deep spiritual disorder that distorts the Church's mission from within.

Jean-Marc Ela warned that "the African Church risks becoming an auxiliary of the state instead of the sacrament of liberation."[19] His warning has proven prophetic. This section examines the theological and sociopolitical structures that keep the Church trapped in complicity—clericalism, fear, bureaucracy, dependency, and a distorted theology of authority.

6.1 Clericalism: When the Shepherd Becomes a Lord

Clericalism is not simply a bad habit; it is a theological mutation. It transforms pastors into princes, bishops into barons, and parishes into fiefdoms. Pope Francis has called clericalism "the greatest perversion in the Church,"[20] and Africa suffers deeply from this disease.

Clericalism manifests in:

- exaggerated reverence for bishops and priests
- authoritarian leadership styles
- insulation from criticism
- financial opacity
- disdain for lay participation
- suppression of dissenting voices
- distance from the poor

---

19. Ela, *African Cry*, 67.
20. Francis, *Address of His Holiness Pope Francis to the Roman Curia.*

Clericalism makes prophets impossible. Prophets must be *vulnerable*, but clericalism teaches priests to be *untouchable*. It teaches bishops to expect privilege rather than accountability.

The People Suffer in Silence, Because Their Shepherds Love Comfort

In many African countries, priests live better than the average citizen. Bishops travel in government vehicles, attend elite gatherings, and consult political leaders more than they consult the poor. This creates a psychological distance that makes prophetic solidarity difficult.

Laurenti Magesa notes that "the Church in Africa has too often absorbed the colonial mentality of domination rather than the Gospel spirit of service."[21] Colonial bishops once lived like administrators of empire; their successors sometimes unconsciously reproduce these patterns.

A Church that behaves like an elite class cannot defend the oppressed.

6.2 Fear: The Silent Dictator of the Church

Fear rules the Church more effectively than any canon law.

Bishops fear:

- government retaliation
- losing state subsidies
- expulsion of missionaries
- division within their dioceses
- being labeled "political"
- Vatican disciplinary intervention

Priests fear:

- being transferred to remote parishes
- losing stipends
- being ostracized by their bishops
- accusations of disobedience

---

21. Magesa, *African Religion*, 142.

- reprisals from local politicians

Lay Catholics fear:

- being denied the sacraments
- losing Church positions
- community backlash

Fear explains much of the Church's paralysis.

Fear Destroys Prophecy Before It Is Born

Jeremiah said, "Do not be afraid of them, for I am with you to protect you" (Jer 1:8, JB). But many African Church leaders fear earthly rulers more than divine judgment. They fear presidents more than prophets. They fear conflict more than complicity.

In Cameroon, bishops privately admit they fear government surveillance and reprisal. In Zimbabwe, clergy fear losing their parishes, pensions, and safety. In Nigeria, priests fear ethnic backlash or attacks by extremists. In DR Congo, some fear militia retaliation.

Fear has become a spiritual master—and the Gospel leaves no room for such a master.

6.3 Bureaucracy: The Church That Drowns the Spirit in Paper

The Catholic Church is a global institution with immense administrative machinery. But in Africa, bureaucracy has become a spiritual chokehold. Many bishops manage dioceses like civil service departments, not missionary communities.

Bureaucratic features include:

- endless committees and meetings
- slow decision-making
- rigid protocols for public statements
- fear of "embarrassing the Church"
- formalism in pastoral responses
- reluctance to act without consensus

This bureaucracy kills prophetic urgency. The prophets did not form committees before speaking truth. Jesus did not consult advisory boards before confronting injustice.

Liberation theology teaches that the people's suffering demands immediate moral clarity, not procedural delay.

Under bureaucracy, prophetic statements must be drafted, edited, approved, softened, reviewed, and re-approved until they lose all force. By the time a pastoral letter appears, the people's crisis has worsened.

This institutional slowness contrasts sharply with Pentecostal dynamism. A Pentecostal pastor can preach a bold sermon about injustice on Sunday; a bishop may need six months to issue a neutral statement about "restoring harmony."

6.4 Dependency: When the Church Lives by Caesar's Bread

African Catholicism is deeply dependent on:

- state funding
- foreign donors
- missionary resources
- Catholic NGOs
- development partnerships
- elite benefactors

This creates vulnerabilities that silence prophecy.

State Dependency Silences the Prophetic Imagination

If a government pays for:

- school construction
- hospital renovations
- priestly salaries
- land titles
- visas for missionaries

…it expects loyalty—or at least silence—in return.

Bishops know that a prophetic statement could cost millions in subsidies. The ethics of justice become entangled with the economics of survival.

This is the Church's version of what political scientists call neopatrimonialism: the blending of public responsibility with personal or institutional patronage. As Chabal and Daloz argue, African institutions often depend on informal networks of power and favor; the Church is not immune.[22]

Foreign Dependency Creates Diplomatic Paralysis

European and American missionary societies fund seminaries, build schools, and support dioceses. Many bishops rely on these partnerships to maintain their institutions. They fear that prophetic stances could upset donors, especially when Western political interests are involved.

As long as the Church depends on external actors, it struggles to speak with an independent, prophetic voice.

6.5 A Distorted Theology of Authority: Obedience Without Conscience

Many African Catholics—especially seminarians—are formed in an atmosphere of authoritarian obedience. Questioning a bishop is treated as rebellion; expressing dissent is labeled disloyal; critical thinking is discouraged.

This contradicts the teaching of Vatican II:

> "Conscience is the most secret core and sanctuary of the human person...there he is alone with God."[23]

But African clerical culture often elevates hierarchical authority above conscience.

> John Henry Newman warned of this danger:
> "Conscience is the aboriginal Vicar of Christ."[24]

---

22. Chabal and Daloz. *Africa Works*.
23. *Gaudium et Spes*, §16.
24. Newman, *Letter to the Duke of Norfolk*.

Yet African seminarians are often taught the opposite—that obedience to superiors defines holiness more than fidelity to conscience.

This theological deformation fosters:

- passive clergy
- fearful curates
- unreflective obedience
- intellectual stagnation
- moral blindness

A Church that trains its leaders to fear authority cannot expect them to confront political power.

6.6 The Church's Self-Preservation Instinct: Choosing Survival Over Truth

Institutions fear collapse more than sin. The African Catholic Church, like all large institutions, often prioritizes:

- protecting its image
- preserving its assets
- maintaining internal unity
- avoiding scandal
- sustaining diplomatic relations

This instinct is understandable but spiritually fatal. When the Church chooses survival over truth, it becomes incapable of prophecy.

The People See the Hypocrisy

Africans see bishops who condemn sexual immorality but remain silent about political immorality. They hear priests preach about honesty but avoid condemning corrupt leaders sitting in the front pew. They watch Church leaders attend national events while ignoring political prisoners.

The result is a spiritual crisis:

"If the Church does not defend us, who will?"

The Church's moral authority evaporates when its actions contradict its preaching.

6.7 The Theological Cost: A Church Without a Cross

A silent Church is not merely ineffective; it is un-Christian. Jesus was crucified precisely because He confronted injustice. The prophets were persecuted because they dared to speak. A Church that avoids conflict cannot claim to follow Jesus.

The African Church's complicity through silence reveals a deeper theological wound:
It prefers the safety of the palace to the danger of Calvary.
But there is no resurrection without the cross.

> Oscar Romero's martyrdom stands as a judgment against episcopal fear. He said:
> "A Church that does not provoke crises, a Gospel that does not unsettle, a Word of God that does not stir the conscience…such a Gospel is not the Gospel of Christ."[25]

African Catholicism must decide whether it wants to be safe or faithful.
It cannot be both.

7. TOWARD A PROPHETIC AFRICAN CATHOLICISM: COURAGE, CONVERSION, AND THE FIRE OF LIBERATION

If the Church in Africa is to regain its soul, it must pass through a profound ecclesial conversion—a return not to institutional security, but to the dangerous memory of the Gospel. A prophetic African Catholicism will not emerge from new pastoral letters, synodal statements, or diplomatic gestures. It will emerge from fire. From courage. From the rediscovery that God sides with the oppressed and that the Church must stand where God stands or cease to be the Church at all.

As Gustavo Gutiérrez insisted, "The Church must make an option for the poor—a real, existential option, not a rhetorical one."[26] Africa re-

---

25. Romero, *The Violence of Love*.
26. Gutiérrez, *A Theology of Liberation*, xxv.

quires this option with urgency, not because poverty is romanticized, but because injustice is dehumanizing. A prophetic Church is not one that speaks occasionally about justice; it is one that places justice at the center of its identity.

This part outlines the contours of a renewed ecclesial imagination—one that embraces prophetic courage, institutional humility, structural reform, pastoral intimacy, and the moral audacity to confront injustice with the boldness of Christ Himself.

7.1 Prophetic Courage: Relearning the Theology of Risk

The African Church will rediscover its prophetic voice only when it accepts that the Gospel is inherently risky. The prophets were not diplomats. They were disturbers of comfort, breakers of silence, voices crying in the wilderness. The prophetic vocation is incompatible with episcopal caution or clerical privilege.

Prophecy Requires Naming Names

African bishops often speak about "peace," "security," and "dialogue," yet avoid identifying the perpetrators of corruption, oppression, and violence. But biblical prophecy is never vague.

- Nathan named David.
- Elijah named Ahab.
- Isaiah named unjust rulers.
- John the Baptist named Herod.
- Jesus named the Pharisees and temple elites.

A Church that merely "invites all parties to restraint" cannot claim the legacy of these prophets. As Ela warns, "Christianity becomes irrelevant when it speaks in abstractions while people suffer in specificity."[27]

Prophecy Requires Losing Something

The Church cannot be prophetic if it fears losing:

27. Ela, *African Cry*, 75.

- political access
- government funding
- elite relationships
- institutional safety
- public reputation

A prophetic Church must be ready to lose all of these.

For what does it profit the Church to gain state favor but lose its soul?

Prophecy Demands Solidarity, Not Sympathy

Solidarity is not simply caring about the poor; it is sharing their fate.

Romero did not simply preach about injustice; he walked with the poor until he died with them. Tutu did not merely condemn apartheid; he stood publicly with its victims until he became a target himself.

African bishops must ask whether they are willing to stand so closely with the oppressed that they risk suffering alongside them.

Without this solidarity, there can be no prophecy.

7.2 Ecclesial Conversion: From Palace to Periphery

The Church cannot be prophetic while living near the palace. It must relocate—physically, spiritually, institutionally—from privileged centers to marginalized peripheries.

Pope Francis called this the Church of the "field hospital": a Church that rushes to the wounded, not one that waits behind fortress walls.[28]

The Church Must Relearn to Listen

Too often African bishops speak in polished statements written far from the lived realities of the people. A prophetic Church begins by listening—not in auditoriums, but in:

- slums
- refugee camps

---

28. Francis, *Evangelii Gaudium*.

- conflict zones
- rural communities
- prisons
- marketplaces
- youth gatherings

The poor must shape the Church's theological imagination.

The Church Must Reclaim Poverty as Evangelical Witness

This does not mean romanticizing suffering. It means rejecting clerical luxury:

- lavish bishop residences
- expensive vehicles
- elite social circles
- elaborate church constructions while communities starve

Laurenti Magesa warns that the people lose faith when "the Church lives far above their conditions."[29] Poverty, simplicity, and humility are not mere virtues—they are prophetic necessities.

7.3 Structural Reform: Dismantling Sinful Ecclesial Structures

Prophetic witness requires structural change, not simply personal conversion. Sin in the Church is not only moral; it is institutional. Structural sin must be dismantled through concrete reforms.

Transparency and Accountability

The Church must adopt practices that reduce corruption and clerical privilege, including:

- public financial audits
- independent lay-led financial councils
- transparency in diocesan spending

---

29. Magesa, *African Religion*, 142.

- clear processes for addressing misconduct
- accountability for political entanglements

Where transparency exists, trust grows. Where secrecy dominates, credibility dies.

Democratization of Ecclesial Life

The African Church often marginalizes lay voices, especially women and youth. A prophetic Church must:

- include laypeople in decision-making
- empower theologians and pastoral leaders
- encourage open dialogue and dissent
- welcome youth leadership
- elevate women to real positions of authority

Vatican II envisioned a People of God, not a clerical caste. The African Church must recover this vision.

Independence from State Patronage

The Church must refuse financial dependency that compromises its moral integrity. If a bishop cannot speak prophetically because the government funds his projects, he is not free.

Freedom is the soil in which prophecy grows.

7.4 Pastoral Renewal: A Church Close to the People

A prophetic Church must rediscover pastoral intimacy. The clergy must become once again shepherds who "smell like their sheep,"[30] not administrators of sacramental transactions.

Shepherds Must Walk With Their People

Priests and bishops must be present in:

---

30. Francis, *Evangelii Gaudium*.

- funerals of victims
- protests against injustice
- communities struck by hunger
- conflict-ravaged villages
- youth unemployment gatherings
- migrant communities

Not as observers, but as companions.

Homilies Must Speak to the Wounds of the People

The people hunger for:

- sermons on corruption
- sermons on justice
- sermons on violence
- sermons on hope
- sermons on racism, tribalism, inequality
- sermons on faith in the midst of suffering

The prophetic homily is not a theological essay; it is a word that ignites courage.

Sacraments as Instruments of Liberation

The sacraments must be presented not as rituals disconnected from life, but as means of liberation:

- Baptism as a call to resist all forms of bondage
- Eucharist as a protest against systems that exclude
- Reconciliation as a critique of structural sin
- Anointing of the Sick as a sign of God's solidarity with the suffering
- Holy Orders as a commission to serve, not to rule

The sacraments must regain their prophetic meaning.

7.5 The Role of Theologians, Laity, and Prophetic Communities

Renewal will not come from bishops alone. The Spirit speaks through the entire Body of Christ.

Theologians Must Dare to Think Dangerously

African theologians must continue the legacy of:

- Jean-Marc Ela
- Kä Mana
- Engelbert Mveng
- Bénézet Bujo
- Kwame Bediako
- Mercy Amba Oduyoye

They must analyze, critique, expose, imagine, and dream—without fear. Theology is not safe; it is a dangerous vocation when done honestly.

Lay Movements Must Become Engines of Prophecy

Lay Catholics—especially youth—are often more prophetic than the hierarchy. They must:

- form justice movements
- demand accountability
- challenge clerical culture
- create spaces for liberative spirituality
- support victims of injustice

In Africa, the future of prophecy belongs not only to bishops, but to courageous laypeople.

Religious Orders Must Be Frontlines of Liberation

Historically, religious orders led the Church's prophetic missions. Africa needs:

- Dominican preachers speaking truth
- Jesuit intellectuals confronting injustice
- Franciscans living among the poor
- Sisters leading community empowerment
- Monastics offering spaces of resistance and prayer

The consecrated life must regain its prophetic daring.

7.6 A Prophetic Church Is a Persecuted Church

Let African Catholicism accept a truth the saints always knew:

If the Church is not being persecuted, it is probably not being prophetic.

A prophetic Church will face:

- hostile governments
- angry elites
- suppressed publications
- revoked privileges
- smear campaigns
- internal division

But persecution is not a sign of failure—it is a sign of fidelity.

Romero, Tutu, and Ela all faced hostility because they told the truth. The African Church must abandon the illusion that it can please both God and authoritarian rulers.

One must choose.

8. A THEOLOGICAL VISION FOR REFORM: CRITICAL-LIBERATIVE ECCLESIOLOGY

If the African Catholic Church is to rise again with prophetic fire, it must undergo not only moral renewal and institutional reform but also deep theological transformation. The crisis of prophetic witness is fundamentally a crisis of ecclesiology—of what the Church believes itself to be, of how it understands its mission, of how it exercises authority, and of how it imagines God's presence in the struggles of the poor.

Critical-Liberative Theology (CLT) insists that the Church must become a community of liberation oriented toward justice, not a guardian of the status quo. It demands that theology speak to history—not abstractly, but concretely, in the cries of those who suffer under political oppression, poverty, corruption, and silence. It insists that every ecclesial structure, sacrament, doctrine, and pastoral act be measured by its liberative capacity.

As Leonardo Boff argued, "The Church must be the continuation of Jesus' liberating presence in history."[31] If the Church ceases to liberate, it ceases to represent Christ.

The task before African Catholicism, therefore, is not simply to *restore* prophecy but to reimagine the Church from the ground up, using a liberative lens grounded in Scripture, tradition, and lived African reality.

8.1 The Church as Sacrament of Liberation

a. The Church Is Not an Institution First, but a Movement

Classical Catholic theology emphasizes the Church as sacrament, institution, mystical body, and communion. These images are valuable, but in contexts of political repression and social suffering, they risk becoming abstractions. CLT insists that the Church must first be understood as:

- a movement of liberation,
- a community of resistance,
- a people walking with the poor,
- a prophetic sign against injustice,
- a visible contradiction to oppressive systems.

The Church must exist not for itself, but for the transformation of the world.

Ela insists that for Africans, "the Church must be useful to life, or it will have no reason to exist."[32] If the Church cannot liberate bodies and communities, its claims to liberate souls ring hollow.

---

31. Boff, *Church: Charism and Power*, 27.
32. Ela, *My Faith as an African*, 14.

b. Biblical Foundations for a Liberative Ecclesiology

The early Church grew not because it was institutionally powerful but because it embodied:

- radical equality ("There is neither Jew nor Greek, slave nor free"—Gal 3:28)
- resistance to imperial brutality (Revelation as anti-imperial text)
- communal sharing of goods (Acts 4:32–35)
- healing the sick (Mark 1:34)
- liberation of captives (Luke 4:18)
- confrontation with oppressive authorities (Acts 5:29)

This ecclesiological DNA must be rediscovered.

A prophetic African Church must reinterpret these biblical paradigms in light of contemporary challenges such as:

- authoritarian regimes,
- economic exploitation,
- ethnic divisions,
- youth unemployment,
- trauma and violence,
- women's exclusion,
- and systemic corruption.

The Bible does not permit neutrality in such contexts.

8.2 Authority Reimagined: From Domination to Service

Catholicism traditionally emphasizes hierarchical authority. But hierarchy becomes toxic when separated from service and accountability. A liberative ecclesiology reframes authority through:

- synodality,
- participation,
- transparency,
- shared leadership,

- listening, and
- horizontal relationships.

a. Christ's Authority Was Kenotic, Not Imperial

Philippians 2 describes Christ's authority as *kenosis*—self-emptying. Jesus emptied Himself of privilege, status, and power, choosing instead solidarity with the poor and confrontation with the elites who oppressed them.

Authority in the Church must reflect this kenotic pattern. Archbishop Desmond Tutu modeled this when he washed the feet of mothers who lost children to apartheid, saying, "The bishop must be where the pain is."

b. Episcopal Authority Must Become Accountable

A prophetic ecclesiology requires:

- term limits or functional accountability for bishops
- transparent selection processes
- lay participation in episcopal evaluations
- oversight mechanisms for financial and pastoral misconduct

Authority without accountability becomes authoritarianism.

John Henry Newman emphasized that the sensus fidelium—the sense of the faithful—is an essential source of truth. African bishops cannot claim ecclesial authority while ignoring the faithful's cry for justice.[33]

8.3 Conscience as the Engine of Prophetic Renewal

A prophetic Church must empower conscience rather than suppress it. Catholics must be taught that:

- conscience is not rebellion
- conscience is not disobedience
- conscience is not pride

---

33. Newman, *On Consulting the Faithful in Matters of Doctrine*.

- conscience is the primary means by which God speaks within the human person

Vatican II affirms:

> "Conscience is the most secret core and sanctuary of the human person."[34]

But African clergy often preach obedience to hierarchy rather than obedience to conscience. This distortion breeds:

- passive clergy
- fearful laity
- uncritical seminaries
- authoritarian ecclesial cultures

A liberative ecclesiology must insist that *conscience is the root of all prophecy*. Without conscience, there can be no Jeremiah, no Elijah, no John the Baptist, no Romero.

8.4 The Preferential Option for the Poor: The Theological Heart of Reform

a. Why the Poor Must Be the Center

The preferential option for the poor is not a pastoral strategy—it is the very identity of the Church. According to Gutiérrez, God's preferential love for the poor is a theological truth rooted in Scripture itself.[35]

African Catholicism must place the poor at the center of:

- theology
- liturgy
- pastoral practice
- resource allocation
- public witness
- ecclesial decision-making

---

34. *Gaudium et Spes,*, §16.
35. Gutiérrez, *A Theology of Liberation*.

A Church that marginalizes the poor will inevitably lose them to Pentecostalism or to despair.

b. Practicing the Option for the Poor

This involves:

- relocating diocesan offices to poor neighborhoods
- celebrating Mass in slums, prisons, and refugee camps
- prioritizing social justice ministries
- investing in schools, hospitals, and cooperatives
- resisting corruption at every level
- forming clergy to live simply
- elevating poor voices in ecclesial governance

This is not "liberal activism"—it is biblical fidelity.

As Pope Francis noted, "The Church is called to be the Church of the poor and for the poor."[36] Africa needs this urgently.

8.5 Liturgical Renewal as Prophetic Formation

The liturgy must become a school of prophecy, not a ritual of passive spectatorship. African liturgy often blends rich cultural expression with sacramental depth, but it sometimes fails to connect worship with justice.

a. Homilies Must Confront Injustice

Homilies should interpret:

- corruption
- state violence
- unemployment
- ethnic conflict
- trauma

---

36. Francis, *Laudato Si'*.

- migration
- ecological degradation

through the lens of Scripture.
The Word of God must become the fire that awakens conscience.

b. The Eucharist as Protest

The Eucharist must be preached as:

- the sacrament of solidarity
- the judgment against systems that exclude the poor
- the nourishment for struggle
- a reminder that Christ was executed for confronting injustice

The Eucharist is not an escape from suffering; it is a commitment to transform suffering.

c. Music and Prayer as Instruments of Liberation

African charisms—song, dance, lamentation, celebration—must be harnessed as vehicles of prophetic identity. Liturgy must empower, not anesthetize.

8.6 Inculturation and Indigenous Wisdom: Toward an African Prophetic Identity

A prophetic African ecclesiology must draw from indigenous wisdom traditions that emphasize:

- community
- ancestral memory
- moral responsibility
- social harmony
- cosmic balance
- the spiritual significance of justice

As Bénézet Bujo argues, African ethics is relational, communal, and life-centered.³⁷ This worldview aligns naturally with liberation theology's insistence on structural justice.

African Christianity becomes prophetic when it reconnects with African anthropology, not when it imitates European clerical culture.

8.7 A Church That Accompanies Social Movements

The Church cannot stand apart from struggles for justice. It must accompany:

- youth movements
- women's rights groups
- anti-corruption campaigns
- environmental justice initiatives
- pro-democracy movements
- peacebuilding networks

This accompaniment must not be symbolic; it must be embodied.

Romero walked with workers. Tutu walked with students. African bishops must walk with the oppressed—not simply issue statements about them.

8.8 A Theology of Memory and Martyrdom

Africa needs new martyrs—prophetic witnesses whose courage rewrites ecclesial history.

The Church must remember the martyrs of justice:

- The Ugandan martyrs
- Christian activists murdered in Congo
- Church leaders imprisoned in South Sudan
- Priests killed in Nigeria
- Catechists martyred across Africa

Their memory must inspire new courage.

---

37. Bujo, *African Christian Morality at the Age of Inculturation*.

As Romero proclaimed:
"If they kill me, I will rise in the people."[38]
Africa needs bishops and priests who speak with such conviction.

9. THE CRY FOR COURAGE: A NEW BIRTH OF PROPHETIC AFRICAN CATHOLICISM

There are moments when history stands still, waiting for someone to speak. Africa is in such a moment now. The continent groans under the weight of cycles of authoritarianism, corruption, violence, poverty, and injustice. The people cry out, not for a Church that manages institutions, but for a Church that *carries their pain, defends their dignity,* and *dares to confront the Pharaohs of this age.* This cry is rising from villages and cities, from youth and elders, from slums and diaspora communities, from refugees and victims of conflict. It is the cry for courage.

The African Catholic Church now stands between two possible futures. One is the path of silence—respectable, cautious, institutional, and safe. The other is the path of prophecy—dangerous, disruptive, liberating, and faithful. History has shown that when the Church chooses silence, the people turn elsewhere. But when the Church chooses prophecy, it becomes the beating heart of social transformation.

This chapter has traced the wounds, failures, and structural sins that have weakened the Church's prophetic voice. It has shown how clericalism, fear, political entanglement, theological distortions, and bureaucratic inertia have prevented the Church from speaking boldly into the crises that define African lives. It has named the exodus of millions of Catholics toward Pentecostalism not as a rejection of faith, but as a search for a spiritual home where courage, empowerment, and truth still flourish.

Yet the story is not over. The very crisis that exposes the Church's failure is also the furnace in which a new prophetic African Catholicism can be forged.

9.1 The Spirit Is Still Calling the Church to Prophetic Fire

Liberation theology teaches that God speaks first in the cry of the poor. If this is true, then Africa is now one of the most sacred spaces in the world, for nowhere is the cry louder. The Church must rediscover that salvation

---

38. Romero, *The Violence of Love.*

is not an abstract doctrine but a *transformative encounter with the God who hears that cry*.

As Gustavo Gutiérrez wrote, "The task of theology is not to speak about liberation but to live liberation."[39] African Catholicism cannot limit itself to intellectual analysis or diplomatic statements; it must become a living sacrament of justice.

Romero's legacy reminds us that the Spirit calls ordinary priests, bishops, catechists, and laypeople to extraordinary courage. Jean-Marc Ela's writings affirm that the Gospel speaks most powerfully when it arises "from below," from the lives of the oppressed.[40] Mveng declares that African theology must confront "the anthropological poverty" created by systems that deny African humanity.[41] These voices form a prophetic chorus urging the Church to rise.

9.2 The Time for Safe Christianity Is Over

A safe Christianity—one that avoids conflict, fears controversy, and seeks harmony with authoritarian rulers—is not the Christianity of Jesus. It is the Christianity of Caiaphas, not of Calvary. Jesus was executed because he confronted structures of power that dehumanized the poor. The African Church cannot claim to follow Him while refusing to take similar risks.

Desmond Tutu said, "There is no neutrality in the face of injustice" (Tutu, 1984). Neutrality is siding with the oppressor. Silence is siding with the murderer. Diplomatic caution is siding with the corrupt. The Church must reject the illusion that prophecy can be exercised without conflict. The Gospel is not polite—it is transformative.

9.3 Youth Are Waiting for a Church Worth Living For

Africa is the youngest continent in the world. Its youth face:

- massive unemployment
- political disenfranchisement
- insecurity

---

39. Gutiérrez, *A Theology of Liberation*, 28.
40. Ela, *African Cry*.
41. Mveng, *African Liberation Theology*.

- social instability
- psychological trauma
- forced migration
- disillusionment with institutions

They yearn for meaning, purpose, and moral clarity.

Pentecostalism offers them courage, empowerment, spiritual warfare, and communal belonging. The Catholic Church must offer the same—not by imitating Pentecostal style, but by rediscovering Catholic substance: sacrament, Scripture, conscience, solidarity, community, and prophetic audacity.

African youth do not want a cautious Church. They want a courageous one.

9.4 Prophetic Renewal Will Begin at the Margins

The rebirth of African Catholic prophecy will not come from episcopal conferences or Vatican councils. It will begin:

- in the slums where priests choose to live among the poor
- in parishes that accompany victims of violence
- in youth communities seeking justice
- in religious orders reclaiming their radical charisms
- in theologians daring to interpret Scripture from the underside of history
- in lay movements that refuse to be silenced
- in diaspora communities building Afro-Catholic spaces of justice and hope

The Spirit always begins at the margins.

9.5 A Prophetic Church Will Be a Persecuted Church

African Catholicism must accept a truth the martyrs always knew:

If the Church is not persecuted, it is not prophetic.

The prophetic Church will lose access to presidents. It will lose government subsidies. It will face media attacks, online harassment, police intimidation, and internal resistance from clergy who prefer comfort. But this is the cost of fidelity.

The early Church paid this cost. The martyrs of Uganda paid it. Romero paid it. Tutu nearly paid it. Many African priests and lay activists have already paid it in silence and obscurity.

To follow Christ is to embrace this cost.

9.6 A Final Word: The Courage That Awaits Us

A new prophetic African Catholicism is not only possible—it is necessary for the survival of the Church itself. Without reform, courage, and a return to the liberative heart of the Gospel, Catholicism risks becoming an empty monument admired from afar but abandoned by those who suffer.

But with courage—with the courage of prophets, martyrs, theologians, catechists, youth, and ordinary faithful—the Church can again become a flame of justice, a refuge for the oppressed, a voice for the voiceless, a witness to Christ in history.

The Spirit is calling Africa to raise a new generation of Romeros, Elas, Mvengs, Tutu-like prophets, and fearless disciples. The call is clear:

Rise. Speak. Dare. Defend. Liberate.

For Africa deserves a Church that bleeds with its people.

A Church that speaks with fire.

A Church that walks into danger armed with nothing but truth.

A Church that believes God is still leading an Exodus today.

The time for silence is over.

Let prophecy begin.

CHAPTER 6

The Collapse of Prophetic Witness: African Church Elites and Political Complicity

A) THE SILENCE OF SHEPHERDS IN A TIME OF BLOOD

1. The Prophetic Wound of an African Church in Crisis

There are moments in human history when silence is not merely an omission but a betrayal. Africa knows this silence intimately. It is the silence that hovered over nations where presidents-for-life rewrote constitutions to entrench themselves; where opposition figures vanished into prison cells or shallow graves; where poverty became endemic not by accident but by design; where corruption hollowed out the state until nothing remained but a predatory shell.

This is the silence that echoes in Catholic cathedrals across the continent: a silence that grows louder with every unchallenged abuse of power, every uncondemned killing, every unspoken truth. It is the silence of shepherds who forgot the smell of the sheep, bishops who embraced safety instead of solidarity, and an ecclesiastical elite who traded the prophetic fire of Scripture for the cold diplomacy of appeasement.

This chapter emerges not from academic neutrality but from theological grief. It grieves a Church that has often chosen the security of palace invitations over the insecurity of prophetic resistance. It grieves a hierarchy that has mistaken cordiality for charity, compliance for communion, and institutional stability for theological fidelity. Such a Church cannot heal Africa's wounds—it deepens them.

Across sub-Saharan Africa, millions of Catholics have drifted away not because they rejected the Gospel but because the institution failed to embody it. They seek a God who sees oppression, hears the cry of the poor, and acts in history—as the God of Exodus did.[1] But instead of finding this God in the Church, many discover Him in Pentecostal gatherings and revival halls where the language of deliverance is spoken not in whispers but in fire.[2]

A spiritual migration is underway. It is not a migration from Christianity, but a migration from cowardice.

Ela observed that "The African Christian is suffocating under a Christianity that does not listen to the cry of the poor."[3] Desmond Tutu, speaking from the heart of South Africa's liberation struggle, warned: "If you are neutral in situations of injustice, you have chosen the side of the oppressor."[4]

Neutrality has become the African Church's gravest heresy.

B) WHEN THE CHURCH SITS AT THE TABLE OF PHARAOH

2. The Seduction of Power and the Domestication of the Church

Postcolonial African leaders learned quickly that to neutralize the Church they needed not to persecute it, but to flatter it. Invitations to state dinners, medals of honor, donations to diocesan projects, and warm greetings at national events became tools of political theology. Propaganda cameras captured images of presidents kneeling before altars, receiving ashes, or standing alongside bishops draped in liturgical splendor.

The visual message was unmistakable:

"The Church is with us. God blesses our rule."

And tragically, the Church often played along.

In Cameroon, Paul Biya—Africa's longest-ruling authoritarian—perfected the art of ecclesial co-optation. He cultivated warm public relationships with bishops, attended liturgical events, and ensured that state support flowed toward Church institutions that remained politically quiet.

---

1. Gutiérrez, *A Theology of Liberation*.
2. Anderson, *An Introduction to Pentecostalism*; Meyer, *Christianity in Africa*.
3. Ela, *African Cry*, 12.
4. Tutu, *Hope and Suffering*, 19.

In the Democratic Republic of Congo, politicians treated the Church both as a threat and a trophy, embracing it when needed, intimidating it when necessary.[5]

Zimbabwean dictator Robert Mugabe positioned himself as a champion of "traditional Christian morality," thereby winning occasional support—or at least silence—from some Church leaders.[6] Nigerian politicians routinely sought Catholic endorsements during elections, not because they loved the Gospel but because they understood the Church's symbolic power.

> Hans Küng foresaw this decades ago:
> "When the Church aligns itself too closely with political power, it loses the freedom to proclaim the Gospel."[7]

The African experience is a case study in Küng's warning.

3. The Theology of Silence: When Piety Becomes Cowardice

African bishops frequently justify their refusal to speak out with three main arguments:

1. "The Church must remain neutral."
2. "Our role is to pray, not to interfere in politics."
3. "Speaking out may provoke violence."

> Yet none of these arguments withstand theological scrutiny.
> The prophets did not consider naming injustice "political."
> Jesus did not consider confronting Herod "imprudent."
> John the Baptist did not consider denouncing adultery "divisive."

Ela lamented that "African Christianity has hidden behind sacristies while the people perish."[8] Silence in a burning house is complicity in arson.

This theology of silence rests on three illusions:

---

5. CENCO. *Déclaration des Evêques...*
6. Gifford, *Christianity and Politics in Doe's Liberia.*
7. Küng, *The Church,* 88.
8. Ela, *African Cry,* 75.

a) The illusion of neutrality

A Church silent in the face of state violence is not neutral—it sides with the oppressor.⁹

b) The illusion of spiritualizing suffering

Priests who preach that poverty or injustice is "your cross to carry" turn Christian discipleship into a weapon against the poor.¹⁰

c) The illusion of prudence

What bishops call "prudence" is often fear: fear of losing political favor, state subsidies, or personal security.

There is nothing prudent about abandoning the oppressed.

4. Why the People Leave: A Church Without Prophecy

African Catholics are not leaving because they reject doctrine or sacraments. They leave because the Church has left them. Pentecostal churches speak directly and boldly to social suffering. They name injustice, confront poverty, cast visions of transformation, and promise divine intervention in the personal and political struggles of everyday life.¹¹

For many Africans, Pentecostalism became the theological home that Catholicism refused to be.

> Ela captured this existential crisis:
> "A religion that does not liberate in this world will not convince Africans that it can liberate in the next."¹²

A Church that will not fight for justice forfeits its right to speak of heaven.

---

9. Romero, *The Violence of Love*.
10. Kä Mana. *Christians and the Social Question in Africa*.
11. Meyer, *Sensational Movies*.
12. Ela, *My Faith as an African*, 33.

C) THE CAMEROONIAN CRISIS: A CHURCH CAPTURED BY THE STATE

If one seeks an example of the collapse of prophetic witness, Cameroon's Anglophone struggle is among the most devastating. Since 2016, thousands have been killed, villages burned, children brutalized, and millions displaced. Yet many Catholic leaders—especially those in positions of national prominence—have remained cautiously silent or politically accommodating.

Two figures have come under particularly intense criticism: Archbishop Andrew Nkea of Bamenda and Bishop Michael Bibi of Buea.

Their actions illustrate the theological and pastoral consequences of ecclesial complicity.

5. Archbishop Andrew Nkea: A Case Study in Pastoral Compromise

Archbishop Andrew Nkea has long been admired for his intelligence and administrative capacity. Yet in the context of the Anglophone struggle, his leadership has raised profound pastoral concerns.

a) Accusations of closeness to Paul Biya

Nkea has been widely criticized for appearing too close to the Biya regime. His attendance at state events, cordial public interactions with high-ranking officials, and acceptance of government gifts have created the perception—fair or not—of a bishop who prefers proximity to power over solidarity with victims.

In a region where the military routinely commits abuses, such perceived alignment is pastorally devastating.

b) The 2025 kidnapping of priests

In late 2025, several priests from the Bamenda Archdiocese were kidnapped. In their recorded statements, the kidnappers accused the Archdiocese of functioning as "a wing of the CPDM," Cameroon's ruling party.

While criminal actions can never be justified, the accusation itself is revealing. It shows how deeply compromised the Church appears to segments of the suffering population.

A Church associated with its people's oppressors loses its sacramental credibility.

c) Failure to denounce state atrocities

At a time when Anglophone civilians face killings, disappearances, military raids, and torture, Archbishop Nkea's statements have been widely viewed as vague, diplomatic, and insufficiently prophetic.

Calls for peace without demands for justice sound like demands for silence.

d) The danger of episcopal legitimacy under authoritarianism

Archbishop Nkea's perceived alignment with the Biya government allows the regime to claim legitimacy through ecclesial association. This dynamic is not new; authoritarian regimes throughout history have used religious leaders to sanitize oppression.[13]

A bishop's credibility is not measured by his relationship with the president, but by his relationship with the crucified.

6. Bishop Michael Bibi: Theological Disaster in Public View

If Archbishop Nkea represents cautious silence, Bishop Michael Bibi of Buea represents a more explicit crisis: the public legitimization of electoral fraud.

In 2025, despite extensive evidence of vote manipulation, ballot-box stuffing, and systemic disenfranchisement, Bishop Bibi publicly declared that Paul Biya won the presidential election.

This statement was not merely politically controversial; it was theologically catastrophic.

a) Contradiction of Catholic Social Teaching

Catholic Social Teaching insists on the people's right to authentic political participation.[14] Supporting fraudulent elections violates this moral principle.

---

13. Chabal and Daloz. *Africa Works.*
14. Vatican II, *Gaudium et Spes.*

b) Betrayal of the oppressed

For a suffering people risking their lives for justice, hearing a bishop validate the dictator's victory is a profound spiritual injury.

c) The loss of moral authority

A bishop who legitimizes falsehood forfeits the trust required to preach the Gospel.

7. A Continent Bleeding: The Pastoral Absence of Prophets

From the Central African Republic to Ethiopia, from Burkina Faso to Mozambique, political violence tears communities apart while many bishops remain silent. Their silence in times of bloodshed contradicts the Church's mission to defend life and dignity.

Ela described this phenomenon as *"the pastoral desert,"* a Church physically present but morally absent.[15]

The pastoral desert is more dangerous than physical deserts, because spiritual abandonment destroys hope.

8. Case Studies of Episcopal Complicity Across Africa

a) Equatorial Guinea

Bishops praised one of the world's most repressive regimes, even as citizens starved under kleptocracy.[16]

b) Zimbabwe

Under Mugabe, Church elites frequently hesitated to confront political violence.

c) DR Congo

While CENCO eventually took bold action, years of hesitation enabled constant manipulation of the population.

d) Cameroon

The silence surrounding the Anglophone struggle remains one of the most painful examples of ecclesial complicity.

---

15. Ela, *African Cry*.
16. Chabal and Daloz. *Africa Works*.

9. Prophetic Exceptions: Signs of Hope

- African Church history is not devoid of prophetic courage.
- Cardinal Monsengwo rejected fraudulent elections and demanded accountability.
- South African bishops under apartheid risked persecution to condemn injustice.
- Kenyan bishops decried political manipulation and violence.

These exceptions prove that prophetic leadership is possible—but not normal.

10. The Structural Roots of Episcopal Silence

The pastoral failures of African bishops cannot be reduced to personal weakness; they are products of structural forces:

- Missionary legacy emphasizing obedience
- Dependence on government funding
- Clerical elitism
- Fear of retaliation
- Vatican preference for diplomacy over confrontation

These structures create bishops more accountable to political rulers than to the people of God.

Mveng called this "anthropological poverty within the Church"—the inability of elites to see or feel the suffering of ordinary people.[17]

11. Witchcraft, Fear, and the Church's Pastoral Abdication

Witchcraft accusations remain among Africa's most devastating social problems. They destroy families, endanger the elderly and mentally ill, and generate cycles of violence and stigma.[18]

Yet bishops rarely denounce these injustices. Silence here is as deadly as silence before political oppression.

17. Mveng, *African Liberation Theology*.
18. Kä Mana. *Christians and the Social Question in Africa*.

12. Economic Capture: How Money Buys Silence

Political elites strategically fund Church building projects, diocesan events, and clerical travel. As Chabal and Daloz argue, African regimes often use "instrumental disorder"—strategic chaos and controlled patronage—to maintain power.[19]

A bishop dependent on state generosity cannot speak freely.

Economic independence is a prerequisite for prophetic mission.

13. Digital Authoritarianism: The New Frontier of Silence

Governments across Africa now deploy digital surveillance, facial recognition, internet shutdowns, and misinformation to suppress dissent.[20] The Church, however, has been slow to recognize the moral implications of such technologies.

Prophetic witness must engage new forms of oppression—not only traditional ones.

14. Toward a Recovered Prophetic Church in Africa

For the Church to recover its credibility, it must:

- Recenter the poor as theological subjects
- Break from political patronage
- Train clergy in social analysis and liberation ethics
- Speak clearly and consistently on injustice
- Learn from the diaspora
- Embrace the risks of prophetic leadership

Romero taught that "a Church that does not risk its life for the poor is not the Church of Jesus Christ."[21]

The African Church will be prophetic or it will die—not institutionally, but morally.

---

19. Chabal and Daloz. *Africa Works*.
20. Zuboff, *The Age of Surveillance Capitalism*.
21. Romero, *The Violence of Love*.

CHAPTER 7

The Crucified Body: Clerical Sexual Abuse as a Systemic Theological Crisis

"Whatever you did to the least of these... you did to me."
(Matthew 25:40, Jerusalem Bible)

INTRODUCTION: WHEN THE BODY OF CHRIST IS VIOLATED

FEW CRISES IN THE history of Christianity have exposed the Church's deepest wounds as starkly as the global clerical sexual abuse scandal. It is not merely a moral failure, nor only a legal crisis, nor simply a public relations catastrophe. It is, fundamentally, a theological rupture—a desecration of what the Church claims to be. Every child violated by a priest, every victim silenced by bishops, every family betrayed by secrecy rends apart the Church's sacramental identity. Abuse within the Church is not just sin; it is *anti-sacrament*—the inversion of grace, the corruption of spiritual authority, and the crucifixion of innocence.

When priests abuse children, the very hands consecrated to bless become instruments of desecration. The same mouth that proclaims "This is my Body" becomes complicit in destroying the bodies of the vulnerable. Victims often describe a feeling of being "spiritually murdered." One survivor told the U.S. bishops' John Jay Commission, "It wasn't just my body he hurt. He killed my soul."[1] These are not merely personal traumas; they are theological earthquakes.

---

1. *John Jay College.*

This chapter confronts the clerical sexual abuse crisis as a global, systemic, institutional sin, not an American or European anomaly. African victims, too long silenced, are beginning to raise their voices. Their testimonies reveal that Africa is not immune but simply *late in reckoning* with an already universal catastrophe. The African Church's prophetic rebirth will require truth-telling, repentance, justice, and a new ecclesiology grounded not in clerical privilege but in liberation, accountability, and healing.

I. ABUSE AS THE ANTI-SACRAMENT: WHEN THE CHURCH BECOMES A SITE OF TRAUMA

1. Sacramentality Turned Upside Down

Catholic theology teaches that a sacrament is "an outward sign of inward grace."
Sexual abuse by clergy is the opposite:

- an outward sign of inward corruption,
- an encounter with evil disguised as holiness,
- a perversion of priestly identity.

Leonardo Boff argued that the Church can either mediate grace or become an "anti-sign" that conceals the face of God.[2] Clerical abuse is precisely such an anti-sign. It obliterates trust, distorts the image of God, and weaponizes sacred authority against the weakest members of Christ's body.

When victims report that they could no longer pray, or that the Eucharist triggered panic, we see how abuse becomes a theological trauma, not only a psychological one.

2. The Priest as Perpetrator: A Spiritual Paradox

The priest stands at the altar *in persona Christi*, representing Christ's love, compassion, and self-giving. When he abuses a child:

- Christ's image is distorted,

---

2. Boff, *Church: Charism and Power*, 31.

- the Gospel is betrayed,
- the Church's credibility is destroyed,
- victims are left with a shattered understanding of God.

Hans Küng wrote that clerical abuse represents a "catastrophic failure of ecclesial structure," not merely individual sin.[3] The offender's sin is compounded by the institutional response that follows.

3. Abuse as a Violation of Sacred Space

Much abuse occurs within:

- sacristies
- confessionals
- rectories
- church offices
- catechism classrooms

Spaces meant for holiness become sites of trauma. Victims often report feeling paralysed because the abuse was committed by "God's representative." This theological confusion deepens the wound.

Scripture says:

> "If anyone should cause one of these little ones to stumble, it would be better for him to be thrown into the sea with a millstone around his neck." Mark 9:42 (Jerusalem Bible)

This is not hyperbole. It is divine outrage.

II. STRUCTURAL SIN AND INSTITUTIONAL CORRUPTION

Sexual abuse is not a random moral failure but the symptom of a deeper pathology: clericalism, secrecy, and institutional self-preservation.

---

3. Küng, *Can the Church Still Be Saved?*, 54.

1. Clericalism: The Root System of Abuse

Pope Francis stated clearly: "Clericalism is a perversion of the Church," one that creates conditions for abuse and cover-up.[4] Clericalism manifests as:

- spiritual elitism
- hierarchical immunity
- the belief that priests are above scrutiny
- fear of criticizing clergy
- protective loyalty among church elites

Jean-Marc Ela warned decades earlier that African clergy risk becoming "new chiefs in cassocks," reproducing colonial structures of domination inside the Church.[5] Abuse is easier in systems where authority is unquestioned.

2. The Culture of Secrecy

For decades, bishops worldwide responded to abuse with:

- silence
- transferring offenders
- intimidation of victims
- threats of excommunication
- manipulation of families
- destruction or hiding of records

This culture is not incidental. It is structural.

The John Jay Report demonstrated that U.S. bishops concealed thousands of cases over half a century.[6] Bishop Accountability reports similar patterns emerging in Latin America, Asia, and Africa.[7]

---

4. Francis, *Address of His Holiness Pope Francis to the Roman Curia.*
5. Ela, *My Faith as an African,* 44.
6. *John Jay Report.*
7. *Bishop Accountability.*

3. Institutional Self-Preservation

When the Church prioritizes:

- reputation over truth,
- hierarchy over justice,
- clergy over victims,
- secrecy over transparency,

the Church becomes complicit.

Gutiérrez wrote: "Sin is not only personal; it is historical, structural, and collective."[8] When bishops hide abusers, they participate in structural sin.

4. Abuse as a Crisis of Ecclesiology

The Church's theology of itself—as holy, apostolic, and indefectible—has often discouraged honest self-examination. Yet the presence of abuse demands a more humble ecclesiology, one that recognizes:

- the Church can commit grave sin
- reform is part of conversion
- holiness requires truth-telling
- authority must be accountable

Karl Rahner argued that the Church must continually repent and rediscover its identity as a "Church of sinners on the way to salvation."[9] This crisis forces us to take Rahner's insight seriously.

III. CASE STUDY: THE U.S. CATHOLIC CRISIS AND EMERGING PARALLELS IN AFRICA

The U.S. Catholic Church became the global epicenter of public scandal, not because abuse was more widespread there, but because exposure came earlier and more thoroughly.

---

8. Gutiérrez, *A Theology of Liberation*, 175.
9. Rahner, *The Church and the Sacraments*, 89.

THE CRUCIFIED BODY 253

1. The 2002 Boston Globe Investigation

In 2002, *The Boston Globe*'s Spotlight team revealed:

- systematic cover-up by the Archdiocese of Boston
- decades-long patterns of transferring offenders
- intimidation of victims
- hidden archives of allegations

This catalyzed the U.S. Church's largest reckoning. Within two years:

- over 4,400 priests were credibly accused
- more than 11,000 victims came forward
- dioceses paid over $1 billion in settlements
- multiple dioceses declared bankruptcy

This was not a phenomenon of "a few bad apples." It was systemic.

2. What Made Accountability Possible in the U.S.?

A free press

- An independent judiciary
- A culture of whistleblowing
- Survivor organizations
- Financial transparency laws
- Public outrage

Most African countries lack such mechanisms—making silence easier and exposure harder.

3. Emerging African Cases

African clergy, bishops, and laypeople have gradually begun reporting abuses:

a. Nigeria

Media investigations reveal increasing reports of:

- abuse of teenage girls in parishes
- seminarians pressured sexually by superiors
- financial extortion linked with exploitation

b. Kenya

Religious sisters reported sexual exploitation by clergy for decades—first documented by NCR journalists in the 1990s, resurfacing in 2018.[10]

c. South Africa

A series of cases in Johannesburg, Cape Town, and Durban reveal patterns nearly identical to the United States: transfer of offenders, sealed records, intimidation of whistleblowers.

d. Ghana and Uganda

Reports of abuse in seminaries and minor seminaries have begun to surface, though still limited by social stigma and ecclesial pressure.

4. Why Africa's Crisis Is Largely Hidden—for Now

Several factors delay exposure:

- intense reverence for clergy
- cultural stigma around sexual topics
- fear of shaming families
- lack of investigative journalism
- weak legal protections for minors
- bishops' solidarity with clergy

---

10. Goodstein, *Nuns Accuse Priests of Sexual Abuse, Prompting Vatican Investigation.*

- social dependence on the Church for education and employment

As one Kenyan survivor told a journalist:

"If I speak, I lose my family, my job, my faith community. Silence is safer."

But silence is not healing. Silence is complicity.

As African societies become more open, and as survivors gain courage, a larger wave of exposure is inevitable.

IV. HIDDEN WOUNDS, AFRICAN SILENCES: CASE STUDIES AND EMERGING VOICES

The African Church has long assumed that the clerical sexual abuse crisis is primarily a "Western problem"—a crisis of Europe and North America, born of secularism, liberalism, and moral decline. This illusion served as a protective shield, allowing bishops and clergy to believe that Africa was still "pure," that African culture itself acted as a safeguard against Western moral corruption. But history has shown that abuse flourishes wherever accountability is weak, and wherever power is unexamined. Africa is no exception.

If anything, the African context—marked by high reverence for priests, cultural silence around sexuality, patriarchal social structures, and minimal institutional transparency—creates *fertile soil* for abuse to remain hidden, often for decades. Victims often have nowhere to report, and even when they do, their allegations may be dismissed as attempts to "destroy the Church."

But slowly, painfully, courageously, the silence is beginning to crack.

1. The New Wave of African Whistleblowers: The George Nchumbonga Lekelefac Revelations

Across Africa, lay Catholics, journalists, former seminarians, and survivors have begun revealing stories that challenge the myth of African clerical innocence. Among the most visible voices is George Nchumbonga Lekelefac, whose work on social media—especially his detailed testimonies and investigative posts on Facebook—has sparked national debate in Cameroon.

Beginning around 2018 and growing more prominent in the early 2020s, George Nchumbonga Lekelefac began publishing accounts of:

- clerical abuses in seminaries
- sexual exploitation of minors and young adults
- financial corruption intertwined with sexual misconduct
- patterns of cover-up within diocesan structures
- intimidation of whistleblowers
- clergy living double lives—heterosexual or homosexual—while publicly preaching celibacy

His posts, often detailed, specific, and accompanied by evidence or testimonies, have forced a reckoning that ecclesial structures in Cameroon had long resisted. While some Church officials dismissed him as a provocateur, many lay Catholics saw in his revelations the first courageous attempt to articulate what they had long suspected: that the Church's internal culture contains deep shadows that must be exposed to the light.

Nchunbong's work shows:

- abuse is not isolated; it is patterned
- silence is maintained by fear of reprisals
- some victims suffered as minors
- others as seminarians under ecclesial authority
- financial corruption and sexual exploitation often coexist
- some episcopal authorities have failed to investigate adequately

These revelations are part of a wider pattern across Africa—Whistleblowers in South Africa, Nigeria, Kenya, and Ghana have begun speaking in similar ways. But in Cameroon, where ecclesiastical authority is traditionally strong and political repression is a persistent threat, Nchunbong's courage represents a new prophetic moment.

2. The Psychological and Spiritual Cost of Speaking Out

In societies where priests are revered as spiritual fathers—sometimes more trusted than biological parents—accusing a priest is seen not merely as a complaint but as an attack on God's anointed. Survivors who speak out risk:

- being ostracized by their families
- losing their place in the parish community
- threats and intimidation
- social media harassment
- accusations of being "agents of Satan"
- internal spiritual collapse

One Cameroonian survivor interviewed anonymously said:
"In my village, the priest is next to God. If I accuse him, it means I am challenging God Himself."

Another, a former seminarian, described being sexually targeted by a superior:
"I thought I was losing my vocation because something was wrong with me. Only later did I realize the problem was not me; it was the structure that protected him."

These testimonies mirror those heard in the United States, Ireland, Chile, and Australia, demonstrating that the psychology of abuse transcends geography. When the abuser is a priest, the spiritual betrayal compounds the trauma tenfold.

Hans Küng calls this the "theological abuse of conscience"—the misuse of sacred authority to manipulate, silence, and control.[11]

3. Why African Abuse Remains Less Visible

There are several systemic reasons:

3.1. Cultural Reverence and Clerical Immunity

African societies often treat clergy with exceptional deference. This sacred status can be exploited to:

- gain access to children
- suppress dissent

---

11. Küng, *Can the Church Still Be Saved?*, 62.

- evade accountability

Jean-Marc Ela (1988) warned that African clergy often inherit the sociological structures of colonial chiefs—where authority is absolute and rarely questioned.

3.2. Weak Investigative Journalism

Unlike the U.S., where *The Boston Globe* sparked national reckoning, most African countries lack robust media independence. Journalists fear:

- political retaliation,
- lawsuits they cannot afford to fight,
- ecclesial pressure,
- community outrage.

Even when journalists investigate, their findings may never see publication.

3.3. The Silence of Women Religious

A neglected dimension of African abuse involves nuns exploited by priests, a scandal first exposed globally by NCR journalists in the 1990s. African sisters—especially in Cameroon, Nigeria, Kenya, and Congo—reported being:

- coerced into sexual relations
- dismissed if pregnant
- pressured into abortions
- silenced by superiors who feared scandal

This is only now coming to light again, particularly through digital testimonies.

3.4. Dependence on the Church

In many African communities, the Church provides:

- schools

- hospitals
- scholarships
- employment
- mediation with government

Families fear that accusing a priest will destroy their future economic security.

4. Emerging Parallels with the U.S. Crisis

The African situation increasingly resembles pre-2002 America:

- patterns of transfer rather than discipline
- secret archives
- bishops protecting priests
- reluctance to report to police
- intimidation of victims
- legal avoidance

The South African Conference of Catholic Bishops acknowledged in 2022 that cases had been mishandled in the past. In Ghana, bishops have quietly removed priests without explaining why. In Nigeria, at least three dioceses have faced credible accusations of sexual exploitation of minors or seminarians, but few public investigations have occurred.

The same institutional dynamics—clericalism, secrecy, self-preservation—are present in Africa just as they were in Boston, Chicago, and Dublin.

What is missing in Africa is not abuse, but exposure.

5. What Makes African Survivors Vulnerable?

5.1. Age and Poverty

Many victims come from families who rely on the Church for:

- tuition
- food assistance

- parish stipends
- employment

Poverty makes resistance difficult.

5.2. Orphaned and Vulnerable Children

In contexts marked by HIV/AIDS, war, and displacement, many children lack parental protection. Priests who run orphanages, youth centers, or boarding schools are sometimes able to exploit structural vulnerabilities.

5.3. Homophobia and the Silencing of Male Victims

African societies often equate male victimhood with homosexuality—immediately silencing male survivors due to stigma. This creates perfect cover for perpetrators.

6. Why Whistleblowers Like Nchunbong Are Theologically Significant

It is not an exaggeration to say that figures like George Nchumbonga Lekelefac are performing a prophetic act. They are:

- naming the sin the Church refuses to confront,
- amplifying the voices of the voiceless,
- calling clergy to accountability,
- demanding structural reform,
- awakening laypeople to their agency.

In the Bible, prophets were rarely priests. They were ordinary people who saw injustice and spoke with courage.

Amos cried:

> "The lion roars—who can but prophesy?" (Amos 3:8, Jerusalem Bible)

The lion of injustice is roaring in Africa. Whistleblowers are responding to that roar.

Leonardo Boff writes:
"Wherever the Church refuses to hear the cry of the oppressed, prophecy arises from outside the institution."[12]

That is precisely what is happening now.

7. The Spiritual Meaning of Exposure

Truth-telling is not an attack on the Church. It is the beginning of the Church's healing.

Rahner insisted that the Church must continually undergo conversion—*metanoia*.[13] Exposure is painful but necessary. It is the only pathway toward:

- justice
- accountability
- structural reform
- restored credibility
- healing for victims
- authentic holiness

The Church cannot claim to be the Body of Christ while remaining indifferent when parts of that Body are destroyed.

V. TOWARD TRUTH, JUSTICE, AND A RESTORATIVE ECCLESIOLOGY

If clerical sexual abuse is the anti-sacrament, then truth-telling becomes the first sacrament of healing. No reform, no justice, no survivor healing, and no renewal of the Church's credibility will occur without a radical commitment to truth. Truth is not the enemy of the Church; truth is Christ Himself. As Jesus says, "The truth will make you free" (John 8:32, Jerusalem Bible). The question is whether the Church is prepared to be freed by the truth—or whether it prefers the chains of institutional denial.

Liberation theology teaches that salvation is not possible without confronting the structures that cause oppression. Likewise, healing in the

---

12. Boff, *Church: Charism and Power*, 49.
13. Rahner, *The Church and the Sacraments*.

Church cannot occur unless the institution confronts the systems that enabled abuse—clericalism, secrecy, patriarchy, hierarchy without accountability, and the misuse of sacramental authority.

A restorative ecclesiology requires more than apologies. It requires:

- Truth-telling
- Justice
- Accountability
- Structural reform
- Survivor-centered pastoral care
- Transparency in governance
- Reimagining priesthood and power

Anything less is cosmetic.

1. Truth as Ecclesial Conversion: The First Step in Healing

1.1. Theological Meaning of Truth-Telling

In Scripture, truth is not merely accurate speech—it is fidelity to God.

The prophet Isaiah denounces leaders who "call evil good and good evil" (Isaiah 5:20).

Jeremiah warns of religious leaders who cry "Peace! Peace!" when there is no peace (Jeremiah 6:14).

When Church leaders reassure the faithful that "all is well" while survivors suffer in silence, they repeat the sins of Israel's corrupt priesthood. Truth-telling is the only antidote to this corruption.

Hans Küng argues that the Church must abandon its "culture of mendacity" if it hopes to regain moral authority.[14] Truth-telling, then, becomes not a public relations strategy, but a spiritual discipline—a form of conversion.

1.2. Institutional Courage and Moral Risk

Speaking truth about abuse risks:

- scandal

---

14. Küng, *Can the Church Still Be Saved?*, 77.

- lawsuits
- financial loss
- reputational damage

Yet hiding abuse destroys trust, the very currency of the Church's mission.

Liberation theologian Ignacio Ellacuría insisted that the Church's task is to "take the crucified people down from the cross." Survivors of clerical abuse are among the crucified of our time; truth-telling is the beginning of taking them down.

1.3. Why Truth Still Terrifies Many African Bishops

Several factors explain episcopal resistance in Africa:

- A belief that exposing abuse will fuel anti-Catholic sentiment in Protestant-majority regions.
- Fear of losing political alliances with authoritarian regimes.
- Confusing "protecting the Church" with protecting clergy.
- Lack of structures for safe reporting.
- Cultural taboos around discussing sexuality publicly.
- The perception that western scandals were caused by secularism and thus irrelevant to Africa.

But as Lekelefac's revelations have shown, the truth will come out whether bishops want it to or not. Transparency is always cheaper—spiritually, financially, and institutionally—than cover-up.

2. Justice: What the Church Owes Its Victims

Justice is not vengeance.
Justice is not a threat to the Church.
Justice is the heart of the Gospel.

Pope Francis declared that "tolerating abuse is itself a form of abuse."[15] A Church that refuses justice becomes complicit.

---

15. Francis, *Address of His Holiness Pope Francis to the Roman Curia.*

2.1. Forms of Justice

A. Canonical Justice

This requires:

- laicizing abusers
- banning from ministry those credibly accused
- holding bishops accountable for cover-ups
- establishing independent review boards

B. Civil Justice

The Church must:

- cooperate fully with law enforcement
- end the practice of "private settlements" that include silence clauses
- report all allegations to civil authorities

  The Church cannot ask victims to "forgive" while refusing justice.

C. Reparative Justice

Meaningful reparations require:

- psychological therapy funded by dioceses
- financial compensation
- public acknowledgment of wrongdoing
- pastoral support for families

D. Liturgical and Communal Justice

The parish community must:

- acknowledge the harm
- lament together
- accompany survivors

Justice must be public, not concealed in chancery archives.

3. Toward a Restorative Ecclesiology

A restorative ecclesiology recognizes that abuse has wounded not only individuals but the entire Body of Christ. If the Church is to heal, it must reimagine itself as:

- a community of the wounded
- a community of truth
- a community of accountability
- a community of liberation
- a community where victims' voices shape reform

This transformation requires changes in theology, structure, formation, and pastoral practice.

4. Restorative Models from Global Contexts

The Church can learn from movements worldwide.

4.1. The Truth and Reconciliation Commissions (TRCs)

Modeled in South Africa after apartheid, TRCs reveal three principles the Church needs:

1. Truth must be public.
2. Victims must be centered.
3. Forgiveness cannot precede justice.

    A Church-run TRC in every diocese—especially in Africa—could:

- invite survivors to speak
- document historical abuse
- recommend reforms
- break the culture of secrecy

4.2. The Irish Model: National Investigations

Ireland's Ryan Report[16] and Murphy Report[17] exposed massive institutional abuse. Though painful, these investigations forced:

- public accountability
- closure of abusive institutions
- rethinking of child protection norms

Africa will eventually need similar national investigations.

4.3. The Chilean Example: When Bishops Resigned

In 2018, after revelations of systemic cover-up, every Chilean bishop submitted his resignation to Pope Francis. Though only some were accepted, the act symbolizes what an entire episcopacy can do when moral failure becomes undeniable.

African episcopacies may someday face a similar reckoning.

5. Preventing Future Abuse: Structural Reforms

5.1. Safeguarding Offices in Every Diocese

These must be:

- independent from bishops
- professionally staffed
- open to lay leadership
- transparent in reporting

5.2. Mandatory Reporting to Civil Authorities

No bishop should adjudicate a criminal act internally. Abuse is not a "sin" alone; it is a crime.

---

16. Ryan Report.
17. Murphy Report.

5.3. Psychological Screening and Formation

Seminary formation must:

- include trauma-informed training
- screen for narcissism and psychosexual immaturity
- cultivate humility and accountability
- train seminarians to recognize power dynamics

5.4. Ending Clerical Privilege

Clericalism must die. As Boff warned, institutional clerical privilege is incompatible with the Gospel.[18]

Priests should:

- live simply
- avoid excessive financial control
- be accountable to parish councils
- receive regular evaluations from laypeople

5.5. Women in Leadership

Women must be included in:

- safeguarding offices
- seminary teaching
- diocesan administration
- decision-making bodies

Abuse flourishes in homosocial, male-dominated environments where power is unchecked.

6. Theology of Priesthood: A Necessary Reimagining

Sexual abuse forces the Church to rethink what priesthood means.

18. Boff, *Church: Charism and Power.*

6.1. *The Priesthood Must Be Disentangled From Power*

The early Church ordained elders, not monarchs.

Priesthood was service, not status.

Ela writes: "A priest who does not smell like his people cannot preach the Gospel."[19] Priests must be configured to Christ the servant, not Christ the ruler.

6.2. *The Myth of Priestly Exceptionalism*

The belief that priests are ontologically superior leads to:

- arrogance
- entitlement
- immunity
- abuse of power

The Church must emphasize the baptismal priesthood of all believers, reducing the distance between clergy and laity.

6.3. *Celibacy and Structural Vulnerability*

Though celibacy is not the cause of abuse, mandatory celibacy—without support systems, psychological formation, or community oversight—can:

- create emotional isolation
- foster dual lives
- conceal unhealthy behavior

The Church must foster healthier community structures for clergy.

7. Restorative Spirituality: Healing the Body of Christ

The Church needs a spirituality that directly addresses abuse.

---

19. Ela, *My Faith as an African*, 66.

7.1. *Liturgy of Lament*

Parishes should hold regular services where survivors:

- are acknowledged
- are prayed for
- tell their stories
- receive communal support

7.2. *The Eucharist Reimagined*

The Eucharist can no longer be celebrated without acknowledging:

- the bodies violated
- the trust betrayed
- the Christ wounded in victims

  The Eucharist must become a site of truth.

7.3. *A Theology of the Wounded Christ*

Christ is present in the wounds of victims. To encounter survivors is to encounter the suffering Christ.
    As Pope Francis said in 2016:
    "The wounds of Christ are still visible in the wounds of victims."[20]

6. Resurrection After the Rupture: Reclaiming Ecclesial Identity After Abuse

The clerical sexual abuse crisis has struck at the very heart of Catholic identity. It has revealed that the Body of Christ—wounded in history—can also be wounded by those entrusted with His ministry. The crisis is therefore not peripheral or accidental; it is ecclesiological, spiritual, and sacramental in nature. The Church cannot simply "move on." It must pass through judgment, repentance, and renewal. It must descend into the tomb of institutional death before rising to new life.

---

20. Francis, *Amoris Laetitia*.

In Africa and the diaspora alike, survivors and whistleblowers have forced the Church to confront the uncomfortable truth that holiness is not automatic, that sacramental power does not guarantee moral integrity, and that the Church must earn credibility not by insisting on its divine mandate, but by embodying the justice and mercy of Christ.

This final section reflects on how the African Church—and the global Church—might reclaim a prophetic identity beyond the scandal.

1. *The African Episcopate and the Moral Imperative of Reform*

African bishops now face a defining moment. Their response will determine whether the Church becomes:

- a refuge for the oppressed
- or a refuge for abusers

The moral imperative is clear.

1.1. Silence Is No Longer Tenable

For decades, many African bishops viewed sexual abuse as a "Western problem," insisting:

- "It does not happen here."
- "African culture protects children."
- "These allegations are attacks on the Church."

But as cases surface—and as whistleblowers like Lekelefac expose patterns of abuse and cover-up—these claims appear increasingly hollow. Silence is not a defense; it is an indictment.

1.2. Why Bishops Must Lead Reform

Bishops possess:

- sacramental authority
- moral influence
- institutional control
- budgetary power
- formation oversight

If they fail to act, the Church will face a catastrophic loss of trust—one already visible in the growing exodus of young Africans to Pentecostal churches.

African Catholicism stands at the threshold of a generational shift. Without accountability, it will lose millions more.

1.3. Episcopal Courage: A Historical Necessity

The Church in Latin America changed when bishops like Óscar Romero, Samuel Ruiz, and Helder Câmara aligned themselves with the oppressed. Africa now needs bishops who will:

- confront abusive clergy
- open diocesan archives
- support survivors publicly
- end patterns of secrecy
- implement lay-led safeguarding structures

This courage will be costly. But it will also be redemptive.

2. *The Role of the Laity: From Spectators to Stewards of Reform*

The laity are not passive recipients of clerical decisions; they are the People of God. Vatican II affirmed that the Spirit speaks not only through hierarchy but through the *sensus fidelium*—the lived faith and wisdom of the baptized.

2.1. Why Lay Leadership Matters

Clericalism thrives in closed systems. But:

- lay parents
- teachers
- psychologists
- judges
- journalists
- theologians
- youth leaders

possess critical expertise and moral clarity essential to confronting abuse.

2.2. Lay-Driven Reform Is Already Happening

Across Africa, lay Catholics have begun:

- organizing survivor support groups
- demanding transparency from bishops
- reporting abusive clergy to civil authorities
- monitoring diocesan finances
- creating digital platforms for raising awareness
- challenging cultural silences around sexuality

In Cameroon, the online witness of George Nchumbonga Lekelefac exemplifies how ordinary Catholics are reclaiming their prophetic responsibility when institutions fail.

2.3. The Laity as Guardians of the Gospel

When bishops remain silent, laypeople must speak.
When clerical privilege suffocates truth, lay conscience must prevail.
When children are endangered, lay action becomes a sacrament of protection.

Ela insisted that the true Church in Africa is often found among the laity, who "live the Gospel in the harsh realities where theological discourse fears to go."[21] This insight has never been more relevant.

3. *The African Diaspora: A Warning and an Opportunity*

African Catholics in Europe and North America confront the abuse crisis more directly because they live in societies where:

- victims speak openly
- institutions are scrutinized
- legal accountability is expected

As a result, many African immigrants have:

---

21. Ela, *African Cry*, 22.

- left the Catholic Church
- joined Pentecostal or African Independent Churches
- created new Afro-Caribbean congregations
- rejected institutional religion entirely

This phenomenon mirrors what is happening in Africa: people seek spiritual homes where leaders are accountable and communities protect their children.

3.1. Diaspora Voices as Prophetic Bridges

African Catholics abroad can serve as:

- cultural interpreters
- advocates for reform
- connectors between global survivor movements and African contexts

Their exposure to Western ecclesial reforms gives them unique insight into what the African Church must eventually face. In many ways, the diaspora is the future of the African Church.

3.2. The Risk of Losing a Generation

Young Africans in the diaspora often reject Catholicism because they see:

- hypocrisy
- unaddressed abuse
- lack of transparency
- authoritarian leadership
- insufficient lay empowerment

If the Church does not reform, an entire generation will be lost—not because they lack faith, but because the Church failed to embody the Gospel.

4. *The Crucified Body and the Hope of Resurrection*

The sexual abuse crisis is a crucifixion of the Church's credibility. But in Christian theology, crucifixion is never the final word. Resurrection does not erase the wounds; it transforms them.

4.1. Bearing the Wounds of Christ

After the Resurrection, Jesus kept His wounds.
He said to Thomas:

> "Put your finger here… do not doubt but believe." John 20:27 (Jerusalem Bible)

This is the model for ecclesial healing:

- not hiding wounds
- not spiritualizing pain
- not denying the past
- but confronting the wounds as sites of encounter

Survivors' voices are the wounds of Christ speaking to the Church.

4.2. Restorative Ecclesiology: A Church That Heals by Being Honest

A resurrected Church will be one that:

- admits its failures
- protects the vulnerable
- welcomes scrutiny
- decentralizes power
- listens to survivors as teachers
- reforms priesthood and governance
- models transparency
- embraces truth as sacrament

Truth becomes a form of grace; justice becomes a form of mercy.

4.3. The Resurrection Begins With the Victims

The path to renewal begins not in chancery offices, but with survivors. Their courage is the new Pentecost.

When victims speak, the Spirit speaks through them.

When the Church listens, it is converted.

When the Church acts, resurrection begins.

5. A Final Theology of Hope

Hope is not optimism. Optimism ignores reality.

Hope confronts reality and insists that God is still at work.

Rahner said that the Church must continually undergo death and resurrection.[22]

Ela (1988) insisted that the African Church must always be "reborn from the suffering of the poor" (p. 51).[23]

Gutiérrez taught that liberation is always a movement from death to life.[24]

The abuse crisis is the Church's descent into the tomb.

Reform is the Church's struggle in Holy Saturday.

Justice is the dawn of Easter morning.

Restoration is the rising of the Son.

But resurrection requires repentance—public, painful, humble repentance.

It requires courage—moral, spiritual, institutional courage.

It requires a new ecclesiology—one built not on clerical privilege but on the crucified and risen Christ.

Africa deserves such a Church.

The diaspora hungers for such a Church.

Survivors cry out for such a Church.

The world waits for such a Church.

Let the Church rise from the tomb it has dug for itself.

Let the victims become the theologians of renewal.

Let the wounds of Christ teach the Church how to love again.

For only a crucified Church can truly be a resurrected Church.

And only a resurrected Church can heal the world.

---

22. Rahner, *Theological Investigations*.
23. Ela, *My Faith as an African*, 51.
24. Gutiérrez, *A Theology of Liberation*.

CHAPTER 8

Christian Nationalism and the Failure of Orthopraxy in the American Church

"Not everyone who says to me, 'Lord, Lord,' shall enter the kingdom of heaven, but only those who do the will of my Father."

—Matthew 7:21 (Jerusalem Bible)

A) INTRODUCTION: WHEN CHRISTIANITY BECOMES A FLAG

In recent decades, the United States has witnessed the emergence of a powerful and troubling phenomenon: Christian nationalism, an ideology that fuses religious identity with political power, Scripture with partisan loyalty, and faith with a mythologized vision of American destiny. Its most visible form appears in what is popularly known as the Make American Great Again (MAGA) movement, but the roots of this ideology predate any single political leader. Christian nationalism emerges from a deeper theological distortion—the belief that God has uniquely chosen the United States as a covenant nation, that political opponents are enemies of God, and that Christianity is validated not by its fidelity to the poor or the oppressed, but by its proximity to state power.

This chapter explores Christian nationalism not as a political critique, but as a theological and moral crisis—a collapse of orthopraxy, the lived practice of faith. Christian nationalism represents a failure of discipleship, a betrayal of the Gospel's preferential love for the poor, and a new form of idolatry in which nation, race, and political ideology replace Christ as the center of Christian identity.

While Christian nationalism is most visible in white evangelical spaces, it has also found resonance among some Catholics, including bishops, priests, and influential lay leaders. This complicity reveals a deeper issue: the Church in the United States has not fully reckoned with its own entanglement in the histories of racism, colonialism, and political power.

The task of theology—especially liberative theology—is to expose false gods, critique unjust structures, and call Christians back to the prophetic, liberating identity of Jesus. This chapter does precisely that.

I. THE MAGA MOVEMENT AND THE DISTORTION OF CHRISTIAN IDENTITY

1.1. Christianity as a Political Identity Marker

In the MAGA universe, Christianity has become less a spiritual path and more a tribal marker—a means of distinguishing "insiders" from "outsiders." Faith is not measured by compassion, humility, justice, or peacemaking, but by political allegiance. Jesus becomes a mascot rather than a master.

Symbols of the movement say everything:

- crosses carried alongside AR-15 rifles
- prayer rallies for political power rather than spiritual repentance
- "Jesus is my Savior, Trump is my President" banners
- pastors preaching "spiritual warfare" against political opponents
- prophetic figures announcing Trump's election as divinely ordained

This is not Christianity. It is political religion—a form of idolatry.

In Scripture, idols are not merely statues; they are systems that replace God with human-made power structures. Christian nationalism is such a system.

1.2. The Theological Error of Covenant Exceptionalism

At the core of Christian nationalism is the myth that America is:

- uniquely chosen by God
- morally superior to other nations
- entitled to divine favor regardless of its actions

This is a modern revival of the Old Testament covenant, but without the demands for justice that accompanied the biblical covenant. The prophets warned Israel repeatedly that God's favor was conditional on ethical living:

> "I hate your festivals… let justice roll like waters." Amos 5:21, 24 (Jerusalem Bible)

Christian nationalists claim the privileges of "chosenness" but reject its responsibilities.

1.3. Authoritarian Temptation: Jesus with a Sword Instead of a Cross

The MAGA movement often portrays Jesus as:

- a warrior
- a nationalist
- a defender of ethnic purity
- a protector of private property
- a punisher of enemies

This is the anti-Gospel. Jesus refused political power (John 6:15), rejected violence (Matthew 26:52), embraced the marginalized, and died at the hands of empire rather than wielding imperial power.

Christian nationalism crucifies Christ anew—this time by weaponizing His name.

II. RACE, POLITICS, AND MORAL INCOHERENCE

Christian nationalism is not simply a political ideology; it is deeply entangled with race, particularly with the myth of white Christian identity.

2.1. The Myth of the White Christian Nation

Historically, whiteness and Christianity became intertwined in the United States:

- slavery was defended from pulpits
- Indigenous genocide was framed as divine mandate
- segregation was justified as Christian morality
- Black liberation movements were condemned as "Marxist"

The MAGA slogan "Make America Great Again" resonates with those who remember a past when white Christians controlled political, economic, and cultural power.

For many white evangelicals, "again" means before the Civil Rights movement.

Christian nationalism thus becomes a way to defend a racial hierarchy under religious cover.

2.2. The Moral Blindness of Partisan Christianity

Christian nationalists often invoke "family values" while supporting policies that:

- separate migrant children from parents
- cut social welfare programs
- oppose universal healthcare
- criminalize poverty
- deny asylum seekers safety
- defend police brutality
- ignore racial injustice

This disconnect reveals a collapse of orthopraxy—ethical action no longer aligns with professed belief.

Jesus says:

> "In so far as you neglected to do this to one of the least of these, you neglected to do it to me." Matthew 25:45 (Jerusalem Bible)

A Christianity that harms the least is not Christian.

2.3. Selective Morality and the Weaponization of Abortion

Christian nationalists often claim that abortion is the single political issue of moral weight. Yet:

- they oppose programs that reduce abortion rates (education, healthcare, childcare)
- they reject economic policies that support mothers
- they ignore other life issues (racism, poverty, guns, capital punishment, immigration)

This selective morality reveals that the real concern is not life, but control, especially control over women's bodies and sexuality.

Liberation theology reminds us that moral issues cannot be separated from social structures. "Life" must be understood holistically—economic life, racial justice, environmental sustainability, and human dignity.

III. EVANGELICAL NATIONALISM AND CATHOLIC COMPLICITY: A CASE STUDY

While Christian nationalism is often associated with white evangelicalism, the crisis extends into Catholicism.

3.1. Evangelical Nationalism: Religion as Ideological Armor

White evangelical churches have become engines of Christian nationalism through:

- political sermons
- prophetic declarations about elections
- spiritual warfare rhetoric
- fear-based narratives about cultural decline
- megachurch propaganda environments
- Christian media ecosystems

The theology preached often emphasizes:

- purity culture
- prosperity gospel
- male headship
- distrust of science
- anti-intellectualism
- suspicion of government (except when conservative)

This creates a closed ideological world where political loyalty becomes a spiritual obligation.

3.2. Catholic Complicity: A Troubling Alignment

Most American Catholics do not embrace Christian nationalism—but a significant minority of leaders do.

Catholic expressions of MAGA alignment include:

- priests preaching partisan homilies
- bishops openly endorsing political candidates
- the "Vote Catholic" movement equating faith with one political party
- the "Church Militant" media ecosystem
- Eucharistic processions framed as political demonstrations
- demonization of political opponents

This alignment contradicts Catholic Social Teaching, which calls for:

- solidarity
- preferential option for the poor
- racial justice
- economic justice
- welcoming the stranger
- peacemaking
- care for creation

3.3. The Theology of Silence: When Bishops Fail to Speak

Many bishops remain silent not out of agreement, but out of fear:

- fear of alienating wealthy donors
- fear of political backlash
- fear of losing conservative Catholics
- fear of being labeled "liberal"
- fear of internal division

Yet silence in the face of injustice is complicity.

Just as African bishops often fail to confront political corruption, U.S. bishops often fail to confront Christian nationalism—especially when clergy are involved.

3.4. The Prophetic Minority

Thankfully, some Catholic leaders speak against nationalism. Pope Francis consistently warns that:

- nationalism contradicts Christian universalism
- xenophobia is incompatible with the Gospel
- hatred of migrants is a denial of Christ
- the Church must resist authoritarian politics

But many American Catholics reject Pope Francis precisely because his teachings challenge their ideology.

This exposes the deeper crisis: political identity has replaced Catholic identity.

IV. A LIBERATIVE CHRISTIAN CITIZENSHIP

Liberation theology offers an alternative vision of Christian political life—one rooted not in domination, but in justice, solidarity, and human dignity.

4.1. Citizenship as Discipleship

A liberative Christian citizenship requires:

- advocating for the marginalized
- resisting authoritarianism
- defending the rights of minorities
- promoting peace
- confronting racism
- protecting the vulnerable
- safeguarding democracy

This is not "left-wing politics." It is the Gospel.

4.2. The Kingdom of God Against the Kingdom of Empire

Christian nationalism confuses nation with kingdom.
But Jesus proclaimed:

> "My kingdom is not of this world." John 18:36 (Jerusalem Bible)

The Kingdom of God:

- lifts the poor
- challenges the powerful
- embraces the stranger
- heals the sick
- proclaims liberty to captives

It stands in perpetual tension with political empires.

4.3. Reclaiming Orthopraxy

Orthopraxy—right action—is the heart of Christian ethics. Without it, orthodoxy becomes dead doctrine.

A liberative orthopraxy requires:

- justice

- mercy
- humility
- truth
- solidarity
- personal conversion
- structural transformation

In short: Christianity without justice is not Christianity.

B) THE DEEP ROOTS OF CHRISTIAN NATIONALISM: HISTORY, SCRIPTURE, AND THE MAKING OF A POLITICAL RELIGION

Christian nationalism did not emerge suddenly with the MAGA movement. It is the latest manifestation of a centuries-long fusion of Christianity, race, and political power in the United States. To understand its theological danger, we must excavate the historical soil from which it grew. Only then can we see why it is fundamentally incompatible with the liberative Gospel.

1. Christian Nationalism as America's "Original Heresy"

1.1. The Puritan Covenant and the Myth of Divine Election

Christian nationalism traces its genealogy to the early English settlers who imagined America as a "New Israel," a nation chosen by God to be a light to the world. John Winthrop's vision of a "city on a hill" was not merely poetic—it was theological exceptionalism, the belief that America possessed a divine mandate.

This myth of chosenness became woven into American identity. It justified:

- westward expansion,
- Native dispossession,
- slavery,
- segregation,

- militarism,
- and global interventionism.

It is the precursor of the modern MAGA ideology, which frames political loyalty as spiritual fidelity.

1.2. Slavery, Segregation, and the Racialization of Christianity

American Christianity was constructed through systems of racial hierarchy.

White churches taught:

- Black inferiority
- Obedience to masters
- Divine sanction of social order

Black churches proclaimed:

- Exodus
- Liberation
- God on the side of the oppressed

The Civil War and Civil Rights movements were not only political conflicts—they were theological battles over the nature of God.

White Christian nationalism maintains the theology of domination; Black liberation theology exposed the God of justice.

1.3. The Cold War and the Fusion of Christianity with Patriotism

In the 1950s, as the United States positioned itself against "godless communism," Christian identity became synonymous with patriotism. This led to:

- "In God We Trust" on currency
- "Under God" added to the Pledge of Allegiance
- Pastors blessing military campaigns
- The rise of the Religious Right

This era cultivated a belief that Christianity and American military power were extensions of one another.

It also reinforced the myth that Christianity requires political dominance, setting the stage for Christian nationalism's modern forms.

2. Scripture in the Hands of Empire: How the Bible Is Misused

Christian nationalism does not quote Scripture to illuminate the Gospel; it quotes Scripture to legitimize power.

2.1. Misuse of Romans 13

Romans 13—"Let everyone be subject to the governing authorities"—is often cited to:

- justify police militarization
- defend family separation policies
- silence protest movements
- sanctify political leaders

But the same Paul who wrote Romans 13 spent much of his ministry in prison for resisting authorities. The prophets routinely denounced kings. Jesus Himself was executed by the state.

Thus, Romans 13 cannot be used to bless authoritarianism. Christians follow God first, not Caesar.

2.2. Old Testament Warrior Narratives

Christian nationalists frequently misuse stories of Joshua, David, and other biblical warriors to justify:

- gun culture
- political aggression
- militarism
- violent rhetoric

But these narratives cannot be extracted from their ethical context: the prophets condemned all violence divorced from justice.

"He will judge between the nations… They will beat their swords into ploughshares." Isaiah 2:4 (Jerusalem Bible)

2.3. Revelation as Apocalyptic Weaponry

Many Christian nationalists interpret Revelation not as a poetic resistance text against empire but as:

- affirmation of their enemies' destruction
- a coded endorsement of contemporary politics
- a prediction of geopolitical events

This politicized reading turns Revelation into a tool of fear rather than hope.

3. January 6, 2021: When Christian Nationalism Became a Sacrilege

The attack on the U.S. Capitol was not only a political crisis—it was a theological moment, a visible expression of American Christian nationalism at its peak.

3.1. Religious Symbols on the Front Lines

During the insurrection, observers saw:

- wooden crosses
- banners stating "Jesus Saves"
- Christian flags
- shofars blowing like in biblical battle narratives
- men kneeling in prayer before storming the building

It was a liturgy of conquest—an unholy marriage of Christian language and political violence.

3.2. The Theology Behind the Violence

Participants believed:

- God had ordained their political leader
- Opponents were demonic
- Violence was justified as spiritual warfare
- Their identity as Christians mandated political takeover

    This is not Christianity; it is theology corrupted by ideology.

3.3. Why Many Churches Could Not Condemn the Attack

Some evangelical pastors and Catholic clergy refused to denounce January 6 because:

- many congregants supported the movement
- leaders feared losing members
- political identity eclipsed Christian ethics
- they themselves had fueled the rhetoric

    This failure of moral clarity reveals the collapse of orthopraxy: The inability to distinguish discipleship from political loyalty.

4. Christian Nationalism's Threat to American Democracy

Christian nationalism is not simply a religious movement; it is a threat to democratic principles.

4.1. Democracy Requires Pluralism

Christian nationalism denies the legitimacy of:

- non-Christian citizens
- non-white citizens
- political opponents
- immigrants

- Muslims
- secular institutions

Democracy cannot survive if only one group is deemed "real Americans."

4.2. The Rise of Authoritarian Christianity

Christian nationalism promotes:

- strongman leaders
- suspicion of elections
- conspiracy ideologies
- hostility to institutions
- glorification of military force
- refusal to accept political defeat

Authoritarianism, once adopted, becomes a theological lens. Political opponents are not merely wrong—they are enemies of God.

4.3. The Erosion of the Common Good

Catholic Social Teaching emphasizes:

- dignity of every person
- solidarity
- subsidiarity
- social justice
- care for the poor

Christian nationalism undermines all of these.

It reduces politics to a cosmic war between "God's people" and "God's enemies," destroying the shared civic values necessary for peaceful coexistence.

5. African Immigrants and the Shock of American Christian Nationalism

African immigrants entering U.S. churches often encounter a theological and political world that is bewildering. Many come seeking:

- community
- stability
- familiar liturgy
- support networks

  Instead, they encounter congregations where:

- politics saturates sermons
- patriotism is conflated with faith
- racial tensions are unspoken but palpable
- social justice is ignored or condemned
- immigrants are viewed with suspicion

5.1. Why African Immigrants Are Vulnerable to Christian Nationalism

Many African Christians:

- already value conservative moral teachings
- see the U.S. as a Christian nation
- are unfamiliar with American racial history
- are taught to respect authority
- may view progressives as anti-religion

  These factors make them susceptible to Christian nationalist rhetoric.

5.2. When African Catholics Feel Betrayed

Some African Catholics report feeling alienated when:

- white Catholics refuse to acknowledge racism

- political ideology replaces the Gospel
- anti-immigrant rhetoric is delivered from the pulpit

One Cameroonian Catholic in Texas said:
"I came to church for Christ. Instead, they gave me a flag."

5.3. Diaspora Theologies of Resistance

African immigrants bring with them:

- lived experience of political corruption
- memory of dictatorships
- suspicion of state manipulation of religion
- a strong sense of spiritual warfare
- liberationist instincts

These resources can help African Catholics recognize Christian nationalism as authoritarianism disguised as faith.

6. Why Liberation Theology Is the Antidote to Christian Nationalism

Liberation theology is not a political ideology—it is a theological corrective to all systems that distort the Gospel for power.

6.1. Liberation Theology Exposes Idolatry

Christian nationalism worships:

- race
- nation
- political leaders
- militarism
- economic privilege

Liberation theology names these idols and dismantles them.

6.2. Liberation Theology Centers the Poor

Christian nationalism centers the powerful.
    Liberation theology centers:

- the poor
- migrants
- the marginalized
- racial minorities
- the oppressed

6.3. Liberation Theology Proclaims the Universal Christ

Christian nationalism proclaims a tribal Christ.
    Liberation theology proclaims a Christ who:

- breaks down dividing walls
- embraces the stranger
- stands with the oppressed
- refuses complicity with empire

C) THE PSYCHOLOGY OF CHRISTIAN NATIONALISM AND THE EROSION OF ORTHOPRAXY

Christian nationalism is not only a historical phenomenon or a political ideology. It is also a psychological and spiritual formation system—a way of seeing the world, interpreting Scripture, understanding identity, and responding to fear. To challenge Christian nationalism, we must understand the psychological forces that sustain it and the ecclesial practices that enable it.

1. The Psychology of Christian Nationalism: Fear, Identity, and Moral Displacement

1.1. Fear as the Fuel of Christian Nationalism

Christian nationalism thrives on fear:

- fear of cultural change
- fear of racial demographic shifts
- fear of economic insecurity
- fear of progressive politics
- fear of secularism
- fear of losing political dominance
- fear of becoming a minority

Fear is not just an emotion; it becomes a theological lens. Political leaders and some clergy frame social trends as existential threats, convincing believers that their faith, family, and nation are under siege.

This fear then requires a rescuer, a messianic leader, or a political savior. The movement becomes emotionally dependent on strongmen promising protection.

This is why political figures are often portrayed as divinely chosen. Fear demands reassurance; reassurance demands myth.

1.2. Identity Crisis: From Faith in Christ to Faith in a Tribe

When Christian identity becomes inseparable from:

- whiteness,
- patriotism,
- political conservatism,
- cultural nostalgia,

faith shifts from being a relationship with God to being a badge of belonging.

In this tribal Christianity:

- orthodoxy becomes ideological purity
- orthopraxy becomes political behavior
- the "other" becomes the enemy
- dissent becomes betrayal

This is why Christian nationalists often treat political disagreement as spiritual rebellion.

1.3. Moral Displacement and Cognitive Dissonance

Christian nationalism creates cognitive dissonance: a conflict between the ethics of Jesus and the politics of the movement.

To resolve this dissonance, the mind rewrites morality:

- compassion becomes "weakness"
- hospitality becomes "danger"
- humility becomes "compromise"
- peacemaking becomes "appeasement"
- justice becomes "Marxism"
- truth becomes "fake news"
- opponents become "demonic"

Moral values are displaced by political loyalty. This is the collapse of orthopraxy—the moral practice of Christianity.

Jesus says:

> "You will know them by their fruits." Matthew 7:16 (Jerusalem Bible)

Christian nationalism changes the fruits.

2. The Ecosystem That Sustains Christian Nationalism: Media, Clergy, and Social Networks

Christian nationalism is not accidental—it is cultivated.

2.1. The Evangelical Media Universe

Millions of Americans consume only Christian nationalist media:

- Christian radio
- televangelists
- YouTube prophets
- social media influencers
- alternative "news" networks

These platforms create an alternative reality:

- conspiracy theories
- apocalyptic warnings
- demonization of political opponents
- claims of prophetic authority
- spiritual warfare rhetoric

This media environment is emotionally addictive and religiously legitimized. It substitutes catechesis with propaganda.

2.2. The Pastoral Pipeline: Clergy Who Preach Politics as Gospel

Some conservative pastors have reshaped sermons into political indoctrination:

- biblical texts are used to justify policy positions
- political events are explained as divine signs
- partisan allegiance is treated as obedience to God
- voting becomes a sacrament
- political leaders become God's instrument

When the pulpit becomes a political platform, faith becomes ideology.

2.3. Social Reinforcement: Belonging as a Barrier to Exit

Christian nationalism thrives in:

- tight-knit congregations
- family networks
- online communities
- cultural enclaves

  Leaving the ideology often means:

- losing social belonging
- losing family approval
- losing pastoral support
- losing one's sense of identity

Many remain in the movement not because they believe, but because they fear isolation.

This is religious captivity—faith held hostage by community pressure.

3. Catholic Complicity: Why Some Catholics Align with Christian Nationalism

Though Catholic teaching explicitly rejects nationalism, Catholic complicity persists.

3.1. The Appeal of Authoritarianism

Some Catholics admire strongman leaders who:

- oppose abortion
- defend "traditional values"
- resist secularism
- challenge liberal policies

Authoritarianism appears to offer moral clarity in a world of complexity. But it is a counterfeit morality—order without justice.

3.2. The Lure of Moral Simplicity

For many Catholics, Christian nationalism offers:

- simple answers
- clear enemies
- rigid moral codes
- a sense of purpose
- emotional validation

But simplicity often comes at the cost of the Gospel's radical demands for justice, mercy, and humility.

3.3. The Echoes of Pre-Vatican II Catholicism

Some Catholics long for:

- hierarchical certainty
- clerical dominance
- confessional states
- cultural homogeneity

Christian nationalism appears to restore these imagined certainties. But this nostalgia distorts Church history and ignores Vatican II's insistence on human dignity and religious freedom.

3.4. Anti-Francis Sentiment and the Global Right

Pope Francis's focus on refugees, the poor, climate justice, and anti-authoritarianism threatens Christian nationalist ideologies.
Thus:

- some bishops oppose Francis
- some media outlets attack him
- some Catholics treat him as illegitimate

This reveals that political ideology has eclipsed magisterial teaching.

4. Catholic Resistance: Prophetic Minority Voices

Despite widespread complicity, a prophetic minority resists Christian nationalism.

4.1. Pope Francis as a Theological Counterweight

Pope Francis consistently warns against:

- xenophobia
- nationalism
- hatred of migrants
- political idolatry
- the distortion of the Gospel

He teaches that:

- the poor are central to Christian identity
- mercy outweighs judgment
- dialogue outweighs domination
- peace outweighs violence
- the Church must resist empire

This directly contradicts Christian nationalism's core values.

Francis represents a *global Church* refusing to be absorbed by American political ideology.

4.2. Catholic Theologians and Pastors Speaking Out

Some Catholic scholars and clergy challenge the nationalist drift:

- they preach the social Gospel
- they engage in anti-racist work
- they critique partisan manipulation
- they teach authentic Catholic Social Teaching
- they call for prophetic citizenship

These voices are often attacked from within—but they are essential.

4.3. Latino, African, and Asian Catholics as Corrective Witnesses

Immigrant Catholics often recognize Christian nationalism as:

- a betrayal of hospitality
- a distortion of faith
- an expression of xenophobia
- a threat to democracy

Their lived experience challenges white nationalist interpretations of Christianity.

African immigrants, in particular, whose nations suffered under authoritarian regimes, recognize the dangerous fusion of political power and religion. Their presence in the Church is a theological corrective to American exceptionalism.

5. The Collapse of Orthopraxy: When Faith No Longer Shapes Action

The deepest theological crisis of Christian nationalism is the collapse of orthopraxy—right action.

5.1. Orthodoxy Without Orthopraxy Is Dead Faith

James 2:17 says:

> "Faith without works is dead."

Christian nationalism proclaims "right belief" while committing injustices:

- racism
- xenophobia
- anti-Muslim hatred
- cruelty to migrants
- economic greed

- environmental neglect
- political violence

This is dead faith—faith severed from love.

5.2. The Discipleship Test: Would Jesus Recognize This Christianity?

If Jesus walked into many Christian nationalist churches today, would He recognize Himself?
Would He recognize:

- His Sermon on the Mount?
- His call to love enemies?
- His preferential option for the poor?
- His embrace of the foreigner?
- His rejection of violence?
- His love for the marginalized?

Christian nationalism preaches Jesus but practices Caesar.

5.3. The Church's Witness Has Been Compromised

The world sees:

- pastors blessing violence
- Christians chanting racist slogans
- religious leaders excusing cruelty
- churches rejecting refugees
- Catholics defending authoritarian politicians

This undermines the credibility of the Gospel.

6. Liberation Theology's Challenge to U.S. Christianity

Liberation theology confronts Christian nationalism by asking:

- Who benefits from this theology?

- Who is harmed?
- Where is the poor Christ in this ideology?
- Does this movement align with the God of the Exodus or the Pharaohs?
- Does it practice the Beatitudes or deny them?

Liberation theology reveals Christian nationalism as a theology of domination, not liberation.

It calls Christians to:

- reject idols
- protect the oppressed
- resist authoritarianism
- live the Gospel with integrity

It calls Christians back to Jesus.

D) A LIBERATIVE CHRISTIAN CITIZENSHIP: RECLAIMING THE GOSPEL FROM IDEOLOGY

Christian nationalism represents a profound distortion of the Gospel—a collapse of prophetic imagination, moral discernment, and Christian orthopraxy. But theology cannot stop at critique. The task of liberative theology is to proclaim an alternative: a transformative vision of Christian citizenship rooted in justice, solidarity, humility, and the universal love of God.

In this final section, we outline a constructive pathway toward liberative Christian citizenship, one that can counteract the idolatry of nationalism and reclaim the Gospel as a force for emancipation rather than domination.

1. Reclaiming Christian Citizenship: The Gospel Before the Flag

1.1. *The Kingdom of God as the First Allegiance*

Jesus proclaimed:

> "Seek first the kingdom of God and his righteousness." Matthew 6:33 (Jerusalem Bible)

The Kingdom of God is not a place but a moral orientation, a way of ordering society according to:

- justice,
- mercy,
- reconciliation,
- radical hospitality,
- and solidarity with the oppressed.

Christian nationalism reverses this command, seeking first the nation—and only then using God as an ornament.

Liberative Christian citizenship insists that:

- loyalty to Christ supersedes all political identities,
- discipleship cannot be subordinated to partisanship,
- and national narratives must be critiqued by the Gospel, not the reverse.

1.2. *The Danger of Conflating Nation and Gospel*

Every time Christians merge God with nation, faith becomes a tool of political power. This is the pattern of:

- Constantine's imperial Christianity
- medieval crusader ideology
- colonial missionary domination
- European fascist movements
- apartheid theology
- contemporary nationalism

The Kingdom of God stands in permanent tension with empire. Christian nationalism collapses that tension, producing a faith without crucifixion and a discipleship without risk.

1.3. A Post-National Christian Identity

The early Church introduced a revolutionary idea: Christians belonged to a community *beyond political borders*. Paul writes:

> "There is no longer Jew or Greek… for you are all one in Christ Jesus." Galatians 3:28 (Jerusalem Bible)

For liberation theology, this universal identity is not abstract but concrete. It demands:

- solidarity with migrants,
- dismantling racial hierarchies,
- resisting xenophobia,
- advocating for the poor and excluded.

> Christian nationalism asks, "Who belongs to the nation?"
> The Gospel asks, "Who belongs to Christ?"
> The answers differ.

2. The Liberative Model: What Christian Citizenship Should Look Like

2.1. A Christianity That Protects the Vulnerable

Jesus identifies Himself directly with the marginalized:

> "In so far as you did this to the least of these, you did it to me." Matthew 25:40 (Jerusalem Bible)

A Christian citizen, therefore:

- defends the dignity of immigrants
- works for racial justice
- advocates for the poor
- protects children
- supports the marginalized
- resists policies that harm the vulnerable

Christian nationalism does the opposite. It scapegoats the weak and aligns with the powerful.

Liberative Christian citizenship makes care for the vulnerable the center, not the periphery, of public life.

2.2. A Christianity That Seeks Justice, Not Domination

Micah 6:8 summarizes the prophetic ethic:

> "Act justly, love tenderly, and walk humbly with your God."

Justice is not ideological. It is not partisan. It is not optional.
Justice is the essence of discipleship.
This means Christians cannot:

- support racist policies
- remain indifferent to inequality
- justify violence
- normalize dishonesty
- participate in xenophobia

A liberative Christian citizenship measures political action by the well-being of the oppressed, not the comfort of the powerful.

2.3. A Christianity That Rejects Violence

Christian nationalism often embraces violent rhetoric and imagery:

- "spiritual warfare"
- militarized masculinity
- apocalyptic conflict
- "fighting for the soul of America"

But Jesus rejects violence:

> "Put your sword back… for all who take the sword shall perish by the sword." Matthew 26:52 (Jerusalem Bible)

A liberative Christian citizen is committed to:

- peacemaking
- nonviolence

- dialogue
- reconciliation

Peace is not weakness—it is the strength of Christ.

2.4. A Christianity That Embraces Truth

Christian nationalism thrives on conspiracy, misinformation, and selective facts.
But the Gospel teaches:

> "The truth will make you free." John 8:32 (Jerusalem Bible)

Truth must be:

- empirical,
- historical,
- theological,
- and moral.

A Christian citizen does not manipulate truth for political convenience.

3. Lessons From African and Latin American Liberation Traditions

American Christianity can be renewed by listening to voices outside its borders—especially from the Global South.

3.1. Africa's Experience with Authoritarianism

Africans understand the danger of fusing political power with religious legitimacy. Many post-colonial regimes used religious rhetoric to justify oppression.
Thus, African Christians know that when:

- leaders become messiahs,
- dissenters become enemies,
- and the nation becomes sacred,

oppression is near.

African diaspora Catholics in the U.S. often recognize Christian nationalism as a sign of authoritarian drift. Their experience is a prophetic warning.

3.2. Latin America's Theology of Liberation

Gustavo Gutiérrez, Leonardo Boff, Jon Sobrino, and others teach that:

- God sides with the poor
- faith requires political transformation
- structural sin must be named
- Christian discipleship demands solidarity with the oppressed

This theological lens exposes Christian nationalism as:

- a theology of privilege
- a spirituality of domination
- a political idolatry
- a betrayal of the Cross

Liberation theology provides the tools to reclaim the Gospel from nationalism.

3.3. Pope Francis: The Global Pastor Against Nationalism

Pope Francis embodies the liberative tradition:

- he condemns xenophobia
- he critiques populist authoritarianism
- he defends migrants
- he rejects political Christianity
- he warns against "ideological colonization"
- he re-centers the Gospel of mercy

His teaching directly challenges American Christian nationalism. This is why nationalist Catholics often oppose him.

Francis insists that the Church must be:

- a field hospital
- a home for all
- a defender of the poor
- a servant of peace

Not a political faction.

4. Prophetic Discipleship: The Church's Role in Healing the Nation

The Church can help heal the United States if it embraces a prophetic, rather than partisan, vocation.

4.1. Prophetic Preaching

Preachers must proclaim the Gospel boldly:

- condemning racism
- rejecting xenophobia
- denouncing authoritarianism
- advocating for the poor
- exposing lies
- defending human dignity

Prophecy will cost something.
It always has.

4.2. Prophetic Formation: Teaching the Social Gospel

Catholic Social Teaching must be restored to the center of catechesis:

- the dignity of every person
- the common good
- solidarity
- subsidiarity

- economic justice
- care for creation
- peacebuilding

American Catholics are often unaware of this tradition. Its teaching can dismantle nationalist ideologies.

4.3. Prophetic Community: Parishes as Sanctuaries of Truth

Parishes must become places where:

- immigrants are defended
- racial justice is discussed
- political idolatry is challenged
- the Beatitudes guide action
- diverse communities worship together

This creates an alternative to the nationalist imaginary.

4.4. Prophetic Citizenship: Christian Action in Society

Christian citizenship rooted in liberation includes:

- voting for policies that protect the vulnerable
- resisting anti-democratic rhetoric
- joining movements for justice
- supporting labor rights
- advocating for healthcare access
- resisting racism and xenophobia
- protecting creation

This is not partisan.
It is Gospel.

5. Theological Synthesis: Christianity Beyond Nationalism

The final task is theological: to articulate a vision of Christian identity beyond nationalism.

5.1. The Crucified Christ Against Empire

Christian nationalism wants a victorious, imperial Christ.

The Gospel gives us a crucified Christ—condemned by empire, rejected by religious elites, standing with the oppressed.

This Christ cannot be used to justify domination.

5.2. The Resurrection as a New Politics of Hope

Resurrection is not triumphalism.
It is the vindication of:

- justice
- mercy
- peace
- truth

Christian nationalism promises victory.
The Gospel promises transformation.

5.3. Pentecost as the Anti-Nationalist Event

At Pentecost:

- many languages
- many cultures
- many nations

were united by the Spirit—not by assimilation, but by mutual recognition.

Pentecost is the undoing of nationalism, a celebration of diversity grounded in divine love.

5.4. *The Universal Church as a Sign of God's Reign*

The Catholic Church is global by definition.
    It cannot be domesticated by any nation.
    A properly Catholic Church:

- transcends borders
- refuses tribal identity
- embraces global solidarity
- stands with the oppressed everywhere

    Christian nationalism shrinks the Church to a tribe.
    Liberation theology expands it to the world.

6. Final Exhortation: A Call to Liberative Christian Citizenship

The American Church stands at a crossroads.
It can:

- continue down the path of Christian nationalism, sacrificing the Gospel to ideology,
- or
- embrace a liberative Christian citizenship that embodies Christ's justice and compassion.

    The choice is theological, moral, and spiritual.
    Liberative Christian citizenship means:

- Christ before country
- the poor before privilege
- justice before ideology
- truth before propaganda
- mercy before domination
- solidarity before tribalism
- the Kingdom of God before all kingdoms of this world

    This is the path of discipleship.
    This is the path of liberation.

This is the path that leads away from the idols of nationalism and back to the living Christ—who is neither American nor nationalist, but the crucified and risen Lord of all creation.

CHAPTER 9

Theology of Institutions: Why Churches Drift Into Self-Preservation

Sociological and Theological Analysis • Sinful Structures and Moral Blindness • Reform, Transparency, Democratization • Case Studies: The Vatican, Megachurches, African Dioceses

A) INTRODUCTION: WHEN THE CHURCH BECOMES ITS OWN MISSION

Institutions are paradoxical realities. They protect, stabilize, transmit, and embody the wisdom, memory, and rituals of communities. Without institutions, the Christian faith would never have survived the fragmentation of the early Church, the persecutions of empire, or the turbulence of history. Yet the same institutions that preserve the Gospel can also betray it. They can become rigid, defensive, opaque, and ultimately more invested in their own survival than in the mission they exist to serve.

This chapter examines a fundamental theological question:

Why do churches—communities founded on the Gospel of vulnerability, truth, justice, and service—so often become closed, fearful, bureaucratic, and self-protective institutions?

This phenomenon is not unique to Catholicism, nor to Africa, nor to the United States. It is global. It affects:

- the Roman Curia and national episcopal conferences,
- mainline Protestant denominations declining in membership,

- American megachurches built on personality-driven leadership,
- African dioceses navigating postcolonial identity, poverty, and state pressure,
- Pentecostal ministries managing rapid expansion and charisma-based authority.

The drift toward self-preservation is not simply a sociological accident. It is rooted in deeper theological and spiritual pathologies: distortions of power, misreadings of authority, and a failure to practice the kenosis—the self-emptying—modeled by Christ (Philippians 2:6–11).

This chapter draws on sociology, ecclesiology, liberation theology, psychology, and African contextual analysis to argue that institutional sin arises when the Church forgets *who it is* and *for whom it exists*.

The Church is the Body of Christ, ut too often, it behaves like a corporation, a monarchy, or a fortified enclave.

Understanding this drift is essential for any program of reform.

B) THE SOCIOLOGICAL DYNAMICS OF INSTITUTIONAL DRIFT

1. Institutions Naturally Gravitate Toward Survival

Sociologists such as Max Weber, Robert Michels, and Peter Berger long observed that all institutions—religious or secular—tend toward bureaucratization. This is known as the "iron law of oligarchy":[1]
Power concentrates. Decision-making narrows. Leaders become insulated. Structures prioritize continuity over change.

For churches, this means:

- safeguarding reputation over truth,
- protecting clergy over the vulnerable,
- maintaining hierarchy over participation,
- resisting reform even when reform is morally imperative.

No institution is immune—not even one founded by a crucified Messiah.

---

1. Michels, *Political Parties*.

2. The Drift from Charism to Bureaucracy

Weber noted that movements start with charisma—a prophetic founding spirit—but eventually must institutionalize to survive. Christianity began with a Galilean teacher proclaiming the Reign of God. But as communities grew:

- roles were formalized,
- offices were created,
- authority structures emerged,
- practices standardized,
- doctrines codified.

This is not inherently negative. Without such institutionalization, the Church would dissolve into fragmentation. But the danger arises when bureaucracy suffocates charisma, when the Spirit's creativity is subordinated to administrative caution.

Liberation theologian Leonardo Boff argued that power—left unchecked—tends to distort the ecclesial community from within, leading to clericalism and spiritual stagnation.[2]

3. Risk Aversion and Fear of Scandal

Institutions fear scandal more than sin.
This reversal is spiritually catastrophic.

As we saw in Chapter 7, fear of public embarrassment led to the concealment of sexual abuse worldwide. In Africa, the same logic explains silence around corruption, ethnic bias in appointments, and the misuse of church funds.

Fear-driven institutions:

- suppress truth,
- discipline whistleblowers,
- reward conformity,
- close ranks against outsiders,
- spiritualize obedience to avoid accountability.

---

2. Boff, *Church: Charism and Power.*

The Gospel becomes not a liberating fire, but a veil behind which power hides.

C) THE THEOLOGICAL ROOTS OF INSTITUTIONAL SELF-PRESERVATION

1. Misunderstanding the Nature of Authority

Catholic theology distinguishes between power (potestas) and authority (auctoritas).
Power controls.
Authority *draws, persuades, illuminates.*

Jesus exercised authority, not domination:

> "He taught them with authority, and not as their scribes." Matthew 7:29 (Jerusalem Bible)

But over centuries, ecclesial power became conflated with Christ's authority. This theological confusion led to:

- clerical superiority over the laity,
- episcopal immunity to scrutiny,
- hierarchical distance,
- spiritualization of obedience,
- justification of secrecy.

Self-preservation became a theological virtue—misidentified as "defending the Church."

2. Spiritualizing Sin (and Minimizing Its Consequences)

The Church sometimes treats institutional failure as merely a "spiritual" matter—confessible, forgivable, forgettable. But institutional sin is not ethereal; it is concrete and structural.

Gutiérrez and Mveng both emphasize that *sin embedded in structures* harms real people.[3] When bishops cover up abuse, when church leaders support dictators, when dioceses refuse transparency, the sin is not just personal—it is systemic and theological.

---

3. Gutiérrez, *A Theology of Liberation*; Mveng, *African Liberation Theology*.

3. The Myth of Sacred Immunity

Many church leaders unconsciously believe the Church is immune from critique because it is divinely founded. This leads to:

- defensiveness,
- self-righteousness,
- theological exceptionalism,
- refusal to admit wrongdoing,
- minimizing the need for reform.

But in the Bible, God regularly judges His own people—Israel and the Church—not outsiders.

The prophetic tradition teaches that the people of God are held more, not less, accountable.

4. The Loss of Kenosis

Kenosis—Christ's self-emptying—is the structural opposite of self-preservation.

> "He emptied himself, taking the form of a slave… becoming obedient unto death." Philippians 2:7–8 (Jerusalem Bible)

Institutions forget kenosis when they become obsessed with:

- image,
- prestige,
- status,
- authority,
- material success.

The institutional Church often prefers *glory* over *Golgotha*, *power* over *poverty*, *safety* over *truth*.

D) SINFUL STRUCTURES AND MORAL BLINDNESS

1. When Good People Uphold Unjust Systems

One of the tragedies of institutional sin is that most individuals within the Church are not malicious. They are often:

- well-meaning priests,
- hardworking lay staff,
- devout parishioners,
- bishops formed in inherited systems.

But good people can uphold harmful structures when:

- obedience overrides conscience,
- loyalty overrides truth,
- culture overrides morality,
- fear overrides justice.

African liberation theologian Jean-Marc Ela wrote that the Church in Africa often becomes "a fortress of silence," preferring institutional harmony to genuine conversion.[4]

2. Clericalism as a Cultural Pathology

Pope Francis repeatedly identifies clericalism as the root of ecclesial rot.
Clericalism is:

- the elevation of clergy above laity,
- the belief that priests are quasi-sacred,
- the assumption that bishops are beyond criticism,
- the infantilization of the faithful.

Clericalism is not a moral failure; it is a cultural disease.
And diseases infect institutions.
Clericalism produces moral blindness because:

- leaders believe they cannot err,

---

4. Ela, *My Faith as an African*.

- victims are disbelieved,
- reformers are punished,
- power becomes opaque and unaccountable.

3. The Theology of Silence

Silence becomes a theological strategy. It is justified as:

- "avoiding scandal,"
- "defending the Church,"
- "respecting authority,"
- "maintaining unity."

But silence is never neutral.
It always protects the powerful and harms the vulnerable.
The theology of silence is one of the most pervasive forms of institutional sin in Africa, the Vatican, and megachurch cultures alike.

E) CASE STUDIES: THE VATICAN, MEGACHURCHES, AND AFRICAN DIOCESES

I now turn to three institutional contexts as illustrations—not as condemnations, but as signs of a universal ecclesial pathology.

Case Study 1 — The Vatican: Centralization and the Weight of History

The Vatican is a complex spiritual, cultural, administrative, and political institution. Its strengths include:

- continuity,
- global unity,
- historical memory,
- doctrinal coherence.

But its weaknesses are equally real:

- centralized decision-making,
- bureaucratic inefficiency,
- resistance to transparency,
- internal factions,
- diplomacy over prophecy.

Pope Francis's attempts at reform—financial transparency, curial restructuring, empowering episcopal conferences—demonstrate how difficult institutional change is when centuries of culture must be confronted.

Case Study 2 — Megachurches: Charisma Without Accountability

American megachurches display the opposite pathology:

- decentralized governance,
- personality-driven leadership,
- entrepreneurial structures,
- emotional worship culture,
- financial opacity,
- lack of external oversight.

When scandals erupt—sexual misconduct, financial impropriety, abuse of power—there is often no effective accountability mechanism.

The institution collapses into crisis because its foundation was charisma, not community.

Case Study 3 — African Dioceses: Colonial Legacy, Patronage, and Ethnicity

African dioceses face unique pressures:

- postcolonial political entanglements,
- ethnic favoritism in appointments,
- clerical lifestyles disconnected from the poor,
- silence in the face of authoritarian regimes.

Some bishops live like aristocrats.

Some dioceses mirror governmental corruption.
Some priests engage in ethnic partisanship that divides communities.
These are not isolated moral failures; they are structural distortions.
But Africa also possesses tremendous resources for reform:

- vibrant laity,
- strong women's Catholic organizations,
- youth movements,
- diaspora voices,
- prophetic theologians (Ela, Mveng, Orobator),
- Pope Francis's influence on a younger generation of clergy.

The future of African Catholicism will depend on whether these reforming energies can overcome institutional inertia.

F) REFORM, TRANSPARENCY, AND DEMOCRATIZATION

1. Reform Must Be Structural, Not Symbolic

Reform cannot rely on:

- speeches,
- apologies,
- episcopal letters,
- committees.

True reform requires:

- accountability,
- independent oversight,
- financial transparency,
- lay participation in governance,
- clear reporting mechanisms,
- protections for whistleblowers.

2. Transparency as a Spiritual Discipline

Transparency is not a bureaucratic requirement. It is a theological virtue rooted in:

- truth,
- humility,
- justice,
- kenosis.

> Opaque systems hide sin.
> Transparent systems expose it.

3. Democratization of Ecclesial Governance

This does NOT mean turning the Church into a secular democracy. It means:

- involving laity in decision-making,
- listening to women's voices,
- empowering parish councils,
- consulting the faithful in episcopal appointments,
- encouraging synodality (as Francis emphasizes).

Synodality is the antidote to self-preservation because it decentralizes power and opens space for the Spirit.

G) CONCLUSION: THE CHURCH MUST CHOOSE BETWEEN CONTROL AND CONVERSION

In this chapter, we have seen that institutional self-preservation is a universal temptation. It is not the failure of a few "bad leaders" but a structural distortion rooted in:

- fear,
- clericalism,
- historical patterns of hierarchy,

- misinterpretations of authority,
- lack of transparency,
- loss of kenosis.

The Church must choose:

Either to protect itself through secrecy, hierarchy, and fear—and slowly lose credibility, vitality, and moral authority,

Or to reform itself through transparency, humility, participation, and prophetic courage.

Self-preservation is the way of empire.

Self-emptying is the way of Christ.

The Church cannot follow both.

PART III: LIBERATION, JUSTICE, AND THE OPPRESSED

Part III examines the realities of social sin in the public sphere through the lens of Critical-Liberative Theology (CLT). It explores how political oppression, fear, economic injustice, and forced migration deform human dignity, and how theology must respond with prophetic clarity and structural analysis.

Chapter 10 applies liberation theology to the Ambazonia struggle in Cameroon, arguing that genuine self-determination emerges from the moral imperatives of justice, human rights, and the dignity of oppressed peoples. Drawing comparisons with Eritrea, South Sudan, and East Timor, the chapter reveals how the Church has often remained silent or complicit in state violence. It proposes a theology of national emancipation rooted in peace, restorative justice, and the preferential option for peoples denied political voice.

Chapter 11 investigates the destructive role of fear in African communities where witchcraft accusations disproportionately target women, children, the elderly, and the poor. These accusations serve as forms of social violence that mask economic tensions, mental-health crises, and communal breakdown. Case studies from Ghana, Nigeria, and Cameroon expose witchcraft discourse as a theological distortion that dehumanizes the vulnerable. CLT proposes a liberative anthropology grounded in reason, dignity, and pastoral accompaniment.

Chapter 12 analyzes poverty as structural violence. It critiques global capitalism, exploitative labor systems, and widening inequalities that marginalize workers, migrants, and informal-economy participants. Through CLT and Catholic Social Teaching, the chapter redefines economic justice as a theological imperative and calls for transformative policies, ethical supply chains, and global solidarity.

Chapter 13 turns to migration and forced displacement, reading refugees as "modern crucified peoples." Through biblical paradigms of exile and prophetic hospitality, and case studies from Syria to Central America and African migration routes, it proposes a theology of borders grounded in compassion, protection, and human flourishing.

Together, these chapters argue that liberation theology must confront not only personal sin but structural, political, economic, and transnational forms of oppression.

CHAPTER 10

Liberation Theology and the Ambazonia Struggle: Justice, Peace, and Moral Legitimacy

A) INTRODUCTION: WHEN A PEOPLE BECOME "CRUCIFIED"

Liberation theology begins with a simple but demanding conviction: GOD IS FOUND IN the cry of the oppressed. To do theology is to listen to that cry, interpret its meaning, and discern God's call to justice within it. Nowhere in contemporary Africa is that cry more desperate, more prolonged, or more misunderstood than in the ongoing Ambazonia conflict in Cameroon.

For decades, the people of the English-speaking regions of Cameroon—Southern Cameroonians, also known as Ambazonians—have endured structural discrimination, political marginalization, cultural repression, and state-sponsored violence. What began as peaceful protests in 2016 escalated into a brutal conflict that has cost thousands of lives, displaced millions, destroyed villages, and fractured families and communities. It is, in every theological sense, a crucifixion of a people.

This chapter is not a political manifesto. It is a theological interrogation:

Is the Ambazonian struggle morally legitimate? How does liberation theology interpret this conflict? What responsibilities do churches have in such contexts? And what does a theology of national emancipation look like?

To answer these questions, we will examine:

- the moral grounds for self-determination,
- the silence or failure of Church leadership,
- historical analogues (Eritrea, South Sudan, East Timor),
- and a constructive proposal for a liberation theology of national emancipation.

This is not an abstract reflection. It is a reading of history and suffering through the lens of the Gospel—an attempt, however modest, to give theological voice to a people whose wounds are too often ignored.

B) THE MORAL GROUNDS FOR SELF-DETERMINATION

1. Liberation Theology and the Right to Exist

Liberation theology understands political oppression not merely as a political crime, but as a sin against human dignity. Gustavo Gutiérrez writes that liberation has three inseparable dimensions:
(1) social and political liberation, (2) the affirmation of human dignity, and (3) communion with God.[1]

The Ambazonian crisis is a textbook case of a people denied these three dimensions simultaneously. Their:

- linguistic identity,
- legal traditions,
- educational system,
- economic opportunities,
- and cultural autonomy

have all been systematically violated. In liberation theology, such oppression creates a moral mandate for resistance—not for violence per se, but for the assertion of dignity and justice.

Self-determination is not only a political principle; it is a theological one.

---

1. Gutiérrez, *A Theology of Liberation*.

2. Biblical Foundations for National Self-Determination

The Bible is filled with narratives of peoples seeking liberation from oppressive systems:

- Israel under Pharaoh (Exodus 1–15),
- the exiles in Babylon (Psalm 137),
- the Maccabean struggle (1 Maccabees),
- Jesus proclaiming liberation in Nazareth (Luke 4:18–19).

The God of Scripture is consistently portrayed as siding with oppressed peoples seeking historical and political freedom.

> "I have seen the misery of my people… and I mean to deliver them." Exodus 3:7–8 (Jerusalem Bible)

In this paradigm, a people's cry for freedom is not merely political—it is theological.

3. International Law and the Theological Argument for Self-Determination

Self-determination is recognized under:

- the UN Charter,
- the International Covenant on Civil and Political Rights (ICCPR),
- the African Charter on Human and Peoples' Rights.

But liberation theology goes further:
Self-determination becomes morally grounded when a people's survival, dignity, or cultural identity is systematically undermined.

Under this criterion, the Ambazonian struggle embodies the moral conditions for legitimate self-determination:

a. Historical autonomy repeatedly denied

> Southern Cameroons existed as a distinct political entity under German, British, and League of Nations/UN Trusteeship.

b. Forced political union without genuine consent

> The 1961 plebiscite did *not* offer independence as an option. This undermines any claim of free association.

c. Violation of federal guarantees

The destruction of the federal constitution in 1972 dissolved the terms under which Southern Cameroons joined the union, making the arrangement morally void.

d. Persistent structural injustice

For decades, Anglophones have faced systemic exclusion in:

- government,
- education,
- infrastructure allocation,
- judiciary systems,
- security structures.

e. State violence and human rights abuses

When peaceful protests were met with military brutality in 2016–2017, the moral calculus shifted decisively from reform to survival.

4. The Limits of Moral Resistance: When Does Struggle Become Justified?

Liberation theology does not romanticize armed struggle. Rather, it follows the logic of Catholic Just War theory and the broader tradition of Christian nonviolent resistance.

The criteria that make resistance morally legitimate include:

- grave and lasting injustice,
- exhaustion of peaceful avenues,
- proportionality,
- aim toward peace,
- protection of noncombatants,
- restorative—not vengeful—goals.

By these criteria, the Ambazonian struggle is morally understandable, even if its execution—like all conflicts—contains moral ambiguities and failures. Liberation theology insists that the oppressed always retain the right to seek justice, but that their methods must continue to reflect human dignity.

In short:
Self-determination for Ambazonia is not only historically grounded but morally justified.

C) THE CHURCH'S FAILURE TO SUPPORT JUSTICE

The Ambazonian conflict represents not only a political and humanitarian catastrophe but also a profound ecclesial crisis. The Church—called to be the moral conscience of society—has struggled, hesitated, and often failed to offer prophetic clarity. While individual priests, pastors, and lay leaders have shown tremendous courage, the institutional Church in Cameroon and its global counterparts have largely remained cautious, divided, or silent.

This section examines why.

1. The Ambiguous Voice of the Catholic Hierarchy in Cameroon

1.1. Official Statements: Rhetoric Without Prophetic Power

Since 2016, the Catholic Bishops' Conference of Cameroon (CENC) has issued several statements calling for peace, dialogue, and reconciliation. These documents express concern but avoid naming the historical injustices, political structures, or state violence at the root of the conflict.

They speak of:

- "misunderstandings,"
- "the need for unity,"
- "excesses on both sides,"
- "our beloved nation Cameroon."

But liberation theology teaches that false neutrality in situations of oppression becomes complicity.

When a house is burning, to say "everyone should stop the fire" without naming the arsonist is a theological failure.

1.2. Fear of Retaliation and the Weight of Authoritarianism

Cameroon is a state where dissent is dangerous. Bishops know that:

- churches can be targeted,
- clergy can be arrested or expelled,
- resources can be restricted,
- Catholic media can be censored,
- diocesan projects can be obstructed.

And so many bishops choose caution.
But prophetic courage is never convenient.
Oscar Romero, who challenged El Salvador's military repression and was assassinated in 1980, wrote:

> "A Church that does not provoke any crises, that does not unsettle, is a Church that has betrayed Christ."[2]

1.3. The Pull of National Unity Ideology

Some church leaders—particularly those from Francophone regions—adhere to the postcolonial nationalist narrative that Cameroon's unity is sacred. But "unity" without justice becomes theological idolatry.

True unity is built on:

- truth,
- recognition of historical grievances,
- structural reform,
- mutual dignity.

Unity enforced through violence is not unity but domination.

2. The Scandal of Silence: How Institutions Become Complicit

2.1. When Silence Protects the Oppressor

Liberation theologians insist that silence in the face of injustice is itself an act of violence. To fail to speak is to abandon the oppressed to their fate.

Jean-Marc Ela criticized the African Church for being "too close to the throne, too far from the village."

The Ambazonian conflict confirms Ela's insight.

---

2. Romero, *The Violence of Love*.

2.2. Pastoral Abandonment of Suffering Communities

Within the Anglophone regions:

- villages have been burned,
- schools closed,
- civilians brutalized,
- women raped,
- youths executed or disappeared,
- priests kidnapped,
- churches used as military bases.

Yet many parishes report feeling abandoned by the institutional Church:

- Some bishops refused to visit conflict zones.
- Priests were discouraged from speaking publicly.
- Lay leaders received no diocesan support.
- Victims and displaced families received little coordinated pastoral care.

For many Anglophone Catholics, this silence was a spiritual wound deeper than political oppression.

3. The Internal Divisions of the Church: Francophone–Anglophone Tensions

The Church in Cameroon mirrors the divisions of the nation:

- Some Francophone clergy view Anglophone grievances as "exaggerated."
- Some Anglophone clergy feel treated as junior partners in a bilingual Church.
- Seminarians report unequal treatment in some formation houses.
- Bishops differ sharply in their diagnosis of the crisis.

    The Church thus suffers from the same fractures it should be healing.

This is not merely a pastoral problem but a theological scandal, because it contradicts the Church's claim to be a sacrament of unity.

4. Protestant and Pentecostal Churches: Between Prophecy and Cooptation

4.1. Historically Prophetic Churches That Grew Cautious

Historically, the Presbyterian Church in Cameroon (PCC) and Baptist communities were more outspoken about social injustice. But state pressure and internal fear have muted many voices.

Exceptions exist—some PCC leaders courageously condemned repression—but institutional bodies often hesitated.

4.2. Pentecostal Churches: From Prophetic Potential to Political Fragility

Pentecostal churches could have been a grassroots prophetic force.
Instead:

- some pastors aligned themselves with state officials,
- others spiritualized the conflict ("a demonic attack on Cameroon"),
- many avoided political issues to protect their ministries,
- some exploited displaced people with false prophecies.

The result is moral confusion among congregants.

5. Diaspora Churches: Courageous Voices and Emerging Tensions

The Cameroonian diaspora—especially in Europe and North America—has been vocally engaged in advocating for Ambazonian rights.

5.1. Why Diaspora Clergy Speak More Freely

Diaspora clergy face:

- less state surveillance,
- more exposure to justice-oriented Christian traditions,

- greater international awareness,
- congregations that expect moral clarity.

Thus some diaspora priests and pastors have become prophetic voices.

5.2. The Price of Prophecy

Some have faced:

- threats from pro-regime actors abroad,
- denunciations to their bishops,
- pressure to "avoid political matters,"
- suspensions or punitive transfers.

Their experiences reveal the global reach of authoritarian fear, even within the Church.

6. Comparative Case Studies: When Churches Failed Elsewhere

6.1. Eritrea: The Church That Chose Silence

During Eritrea's independence struggle, most church leaders refused to condemn atrocities. After independence, the government persecuted churches, proving that silence does not guarantee safety.

6.2. South Sudan: When Ethnic Divisions Weakened the Church

Churches in South Sudan often mirrored ethnic divides, weakening their ability to advocate for justice during the conflict. Today, they struggle to rebuild unity.

6.3. East Timor: A Model of Prophetic Courage

In contrast, Bishop Carlos Belo and the Catholic Church in East Timor courageously spoke against Indonesian occupation. Their boldness:

- galvanized global support,

- protected civilians,
- contributed directly to independence.

The lesson is stark:
Prophetic courage changes history. Silence prolongs suffering.

7. Why the Church's Failure Matters Theologically

7.1. The Credibility of the Gospel Is at Stake

When the Church fails to stand with the oppressed, it distorts the image of Christ.

7.2. Sacraments Lose Moral Force

The Eucharist proclaims communion—but what communion exists when a people's suffering is ignored?

7.3. The Church Ceases to Be a Sign of the Kingdom

A Church that aligns with power becomes a chaplain of empire, not the Body of Christ.

D) TOWARD A THEOLOGY OF NATIONAL EMANCIPATION

If liberation theology demands fidelity to the oppressed and the crucified peoples of history, then it must also articulate a theological framework for national emancipation—the moral, spiritual, and communal process by which oppressed peoples reclaim agency, dignity, and political identity. The Ambazonian case is one such struggle, but its implications reach far beyond Cameroon. It raises fundamental questions about the relationship between God, peoplehood, justice, and political autonomy.

This section outlines the principles of a Critical-Liberative Theology (CLT) of national emancipation.

1. Theological Foundations for National Emancipation

1.1. The God Who Liberates Peoples, Not Just Individuals

The biblical narrative is consistently communal. Liberation is not primarily about individual salvation. It is about a people:

- enslaved under Pharaoh,
- exiled under Babylon,
- subjugated under empire,
- crying out together.

In Exodus, God does not simply save Moses. God liberates Israel as a political entity (Exodus 3:7–10). Political liberation precedes spiritual renewal.

This establishes a moral principle:
Oppressed peoples have a God-given right to reclaim their dignity and shape their destiny.

1.2. Jesus and National Freedom: A Misunderstood Narrative

Jesus did not lead a nationalist revolt, but His proclamation of the Kingdom was profoundly political. It challenged:

- Roman imperial claims,
- religious collaboration with empire,
- economic exploitation,
- social exclusion.

Jesus' mission is not nationalistic, but it is radically anti-oppression.
He reveals a God who sides with crushed communities (Luke 4:18–19).
National emancipation, therefore, is not idolatry when:

- it resists systemic injustice,
- upholds human dignity,
- promotes the common good,
- and seeks peace rooted in justice.

1.3. Catholic Social Teaching and the Right of Peoples

The Church's social doctrine affirms that all peoples have the right to:

- culture,
- language,
- political participation,
- equitable development,
- non-domination (Compendium of the Social Doctrine of the Church, §§157–160).

Pope John Paul II, during the fall of communism, repeatedly insisted that the rights of peoples are foundational to peace (JPII, *Centesimus Annus*, 1991).

Where these rights are systematically denied, claims to self-determination become morally legitimate.

2. Conditions That Justify National Emancipation

Drawing from liberation theology, just war principles, Catholic social teaching, and postcolonial theory, we can identify the moral conditions under which national emancipation becomes justified.

2.1. Long-Term Systemic Injustice Against a Distinct People

A group becomes a "people" when they share:

- history,
- culture,
- language,
- institutions,
- legal traditions,
- political identity.

Ambazonia clearly meets these criteria.

Persistent injustice against such a people—across decades—creates the moral foundation for emancipation.

2.2. The Violation of Foundational Agreements

The union between Southern Cameroons and La République du Cameroun was:

- historically conditional,
- rooted in a federal structure,
- established through international oversight.

The dismantling of the federation in 1972 nullified the moral legitimacy of the union.
If a marriage's terms are violated, the covenant dissolves.
The same holds politically.

2.3. Failure of All Peaceful Mechanisms

Before any form of resistance becomes morally justifiable, peaceful pathways must be exhausted.
Ambazonians pursued:

- petitions (1950s–1990s),
- constitutional conferences (1990s),
- legal appeals,
- civil society mobilization,
- nonviolent protests (2016).

These were consistently ignored or violently suppressed.

2.4. Protection of Human Dignity and Survival

When a people face:

- military violence,
- cultural assimilation,
- political disenfranchisement,
- economic marginalization,
- existential threat,

resistance becomes not merely justified but necessary for survival.

3. Comparative Lessons from Eritrea, South Sudan, and East Timor

3.1. Eritrea: The Costly Path to Legitimate Emancipation

Eritrea fought a 30-year struggle against Ethiopian domination. Despite internal divisions, international neglect, and immense suffering, Eritreans eventually secured independence in 1993.

The theological insight:

When a people demonstrates sustained commitment to self-determination, global indifference does not erase moral legitimacy.

3.2. South Sudan: Emancipation Compromised by Internal Fragmentation

South Sudan's long liberation struggle culminated in independence in 2011. But internal ethnic fractures and weak institutions created new conflicts.

Lesson:

Liberation without reconciliation risks reproducing oppression.
National emancipation must be rooted in justice *and* unity.

3.3. East Timor: The Power of Prophetic Church Leadership

The Catholic Church—especially Bishop Carlos Belo's prophetic witness—played a crucial role in East Timor's liberation from Indonesian occupation. His fearless denunciations internationalized the crisis and protected civilians.

Lesson:

When Church leaders embrace prophetic courage, liberation becomes possible without descending into moral chaos.

This comparison exposes Cameroon's ecclesial failure.

4. A Constructive Proposal: A Theology of National Emancipation

4.1. Emancipation Must Serve Life, Not Vengeance

National liberation must aim at:

- justice,
- accountability,
- truth,
- healing,
- institutional reform,
- peace rooted in dignity.

If liberation becomes revenge or domination, it loses theological legitimacy.

4.2. Nations Are Not Idols—They Are Communities of Moral Purpose

Liberation theology rejects nationalism when it becomes:

- xenophobic,
- ethnic supremacist,
- violent regardless of justice.

But it affirms emancipation when it:

- restores crushed peoples,
- promotes coexistence,
- protects cultural identity,
- centers the poor and marginalized.

4.3. Emancipation as a Path Toward God

Liberation is not just political. It is:

- spiritual (restoring hope),
- social (rebuilding community),

- moral (pursuing truth),
- sacramental (healing the body politic).

A people reclaiming their dignity participates in God's liberating work.

5. The Role of the Church in Emancipation

5.1. *The Church Must Be a Midwife of Justice*

The Church should accompany oppressed peoples by:

- naming injustice,
- advocating peace,
- defending victims,
- condemning state abuses,
- supporting reconciliation,
- forming conscience,
- offering sanctuary.

5.2. *The Church Must Refuse Political Cooptation*

Church leaders must resist:

- government intimidation,
- financial incentives,
- ethnopolitical alliances,
- fear of losing status.

> Silence is not neutrality.
> Silence is betrayal.

5.3. *The Church Must Prepare the Ground for Peace*

Not all clergy must become political activists.
    But all must be witnesses to truth.

The Church can:

- teach nonviolence,
- promote dialogue,
- support trauma healing,
- advocate international intervention,
- document abuses,
- defend displaced people.

5.4. The Church Must Be Ready for a Post-Liberation Future

If Ambazonia achieves autonomy or independence, the Church must ensure:

- human rights protections,
- avoidance of ethnic revenge,
- building inclusive institutions,
- resisting clerical dominance in politics,
- prioritizing the poorest.

Emancipation is not the end; it is the beginning of building a just society.

E) CONCLUSION: THE CROSS AND RESURRECTION OF A PEOPLE

Liberation theology insists that history is the arena of God's saving action. Oppression is never the final word, and the cry of a suffering people is always a theological event. The Ambazonian crisis—its wounds, resilience, failures, and hopes—must therefore be interpreted not merely as a geopolitical conflict but as a profound theo-historical struggle in which a people confront the forces that deny their humanity.

In this final section, we bring together the themes explored in the chapter to articulate a theological vision for the Ambazonian struggle: a vision rooted in justice, tempered by peace, purified by truth, and sustained by hope.

1. The Cross: Naming the Suffering of a People

Every crucifixion in history has a face, and the Ambazonian struggle is marked by thousands:

- families fleeing burned villages,
- schoolchildren traumatized,
- mothers mourning disappeared sons,
- clergy forced into impossible moral dilemmas,
- youths caught between state violence and armed groups,
- displaced persons searching for dignity,
- communal identity cracked but unbroken.

The cross is not only a symbol; it is a social reality, where the powerful nail the vulnerable onto structures of domination. Ambazonia is a crucified people.

For liberation theology, naming this suffering is the first act of truth. There is no peace without truth, no reconciliation without justice, no healing without acknowledgement.

2. Holy Saturday: The Ambiguity of Struggle

Between crucifixion and resurrection lies Holy Saturday—a day of waiting, uncertainty, fragmentation, and silence.
Ambazonia currently inhabits this liminal space:

- political stagnation,
- humanitarian disaster,
- leadership disputes within the movement,
- international indifference,
- ecclesial hesitation,
- societal exhaustion.

Holy Saturday is a time when God seems silent, yet is mysteriously present. It is the time when faith must be reimagined, and hope must be disciplined.

A theology of national emancipation must speak to this moment:

Truth will rise, but it must be guarded by perseverance, humility, and moral clarity.

3. Resurrection: Envisioning a Liberated Future

Liberation is not only resistance to injustice; it is the construction of a new social reality. Resurrection in this context means:

3.1. *The restoration of human dignity*

A society where people are not defined by fear, violence, or marginalization.

3.2. *Justice as the foundation of peace*

Peace cannot be built on silence; it must be built on transformation of structures.

3.3. *Reconciliation rooted in truth*

Forgiveness is impossible without exposing oppression.
   Reconciliation is impossible without accountability.

3.4. *Institutions rebuilt in transparency and participation*

New political structures must:

- protect minorities,
- resist authoritarianism,
- decentralize power,
- prioritize the poor,
- uphold human rights.

3.5. *A Church reborn as prophetic companion*

A post-liberation Church must embody:

- kenosis rather than clericalism,
- solidarity rather than silence,
- prophetic courage rather than political caution.

4. A Warning: Liberation Without Ethics is Not Liberation

The tragic experiences of Eritrea, South Sudan, and other nations reveal that freedom can decay into oppression if emancipation is not grounded in:

- the common good,
- inclusive governance,
- accountability,
- respect for diversity,
- nonviolence,
- humility.

Liberation theology, therefore, must guide not only the struggle for freedom but also the crafting of its aftermath.

Ambazonia—or any oppressed people—must ensure that their liberation does not become the oppression of another group.

The oppressed must not become the new oppressors.

5. The Church's Ongoing Vocation: From Silence to Prophetic Witness

The Church cannot merely accompany liberation from the sidelines. She must become:

- the conscience of society,
- the defender of human dignity,
- the prophetic critic of unjust structures,
- the healer of wounds,
- the educator of conscience,
- the midwife of peace,

- the custodian of truth.

  Silence is no longer an option.
  Neutrality is not possible.
  Prophecy is not optional—it is the essence of the Gospel.
  A Church that stands with the crucified becomes the Church of the Resurrection.

6. The Theological Heart of the Ambazonian Struggle

In summary, a Critical-Liberative Theology of national emancipation affirms:

- The struggle for Ambazonian dignity is morally legitimate.
- Self-determination is rooted in human rights and divine justice.
- Oppressed peoples have a theological right to reclaim their identity.
- The Church must stand with the oppressed, not the powerful.
- Liberation must be ethical, inclusive, and peace-oriented.
- Resurrection follows crucifixion, but only through truth and justice.

Ultimately, Ambazonia's story is a chapter in the larger history of God acting through suffering peoples.

It is a reminder that liberation is not only a political aspiration but a spiritual vocation, a participation in the divine movement from crucifixion toward resurrection.

The final word of history is not oppression.
The final word is life, justice, and hope.

CHAPTER 11

Witchcraft, Fear, and the Demonization of the Poor in Africa

A Critical-Liberative Reassessment of Superstition, Social Violence, and Human Dignity

A) WITCHCRAFT: IGNORANCE, FEAR, AND ANACHRONISTIC BELIEFS

1. Introduction: When Faith Becomes Fear

Across the African continent, belief in witchcraft remains one of the most enduring and destructive forces shaping social relationships, communal life, and religious practice. It cuts across ethnic, religious, and national boundaries—found in Ghanaian villages, Nigerian megacities, Cameroonian towns, Congolese churches, and even in African diaspora communities in Europe and America. Despite tremendous advances in education, technology, medicine, and theology, the fear of witchcraft continues to haunt personal and communal imagination, shaping how people understand misfortune, sickness, death, conflict, and even success.

This chapter argues that witchcraft belief is irrational, unscientific, theologically inconsistent, and morally devastating. It has no empirical basis, no theological necessity, and no place in a liberationist Christian vision of human dignity. More importantly, witchcraft accusations function as a social mechanism of exclusion, scapegoating, and violence—especially against the poor, the elderly, widows, children, people with disabilities, and those suffering from mental illness.

The fear of witchcraft persists in Africa not because witchcraft is real but because:

1. Critical thinking is underdeveloped in many educational systems.[1]
2. Scientific literacy is limited, and modern medicine is often mistrusted.[2]
3. Pentecostal deliverance ministries exploit fear for financial gain and influence.[3]
4. The Catholic Church has not always offered strong rational or theological guidance, and some clergy now imitate Pentecostal practices.
5. Structural poverty and social stress amplify irrational explanations.[4]

The goal of this chapter is therefore threefold:

- To expose witchcraft belief as a form of social and theological violence, not a spiritual reality.
- To critique the rise of exorcism culture within African Christianity—especially Pentecostalism but increasingly within Catholic circles.
- To articulate a liberative theology of human dignity that dismantles superstition and empowers communities through reason, faith, and justice.

Liberation theology, properly understood, must liberate not only from political and economic oppression but also from epistemological oppression—the captivity of the human mind by fear, irrationality, and superstition.

2. The Lingering Shadow of Medieval Theology

Belief in witchcraft flourished in Europe during the Middle Ages, especially between the 14th and 17th centuries, culminating in witch hunts

---

1. Wiredu, *Cultural Universals and Particulars.*
2. Okeja, *Philosophy and the Postcolonial.*
3. Gifford, *Christianity and Politics in Doe's Liberia.*
4. Comaroff and Comaroff. *Occult Economies and the Violence of Abstraction.*

that resulted in the death of tens of thousands of people—primarily women.[5] What fueled these atrocities were:

- Scientific ignorance
- Political instability
- Religious conflict
- Literalist biblical interpretation
- Theological confusion about Satan and demons
- Social anxieties projected onto vulnerable persons

When the Enlightenment emerged and scientific knowledge expanded, witchcraft belief rapidly declined in Western societies. By the 18th century, the Catholic Church and Protestant churches alike began abandoning witch hunts, driven by advances in:

- Medicine
- Psychology
- Physics
- Astronomy
- Social sciences
- Biblical criticism

Today, in Europe and North America, witchcraft belief is marginal, often relegated to fringe spiritualities or entertainment media. No bishop, priest, or credible theologian in the West believes that witches cause infertility, academic failure, road accidents, cancer, or poverty.

But in Africa, these beliefs continue to flourish—not because Africa is "culturally primitive," but because Africa's scientific revolution has not kept pace with its technological adoption. Mobile phones are widespread; critical rationality is not. People use smartphones built on quantum mechanics yet explain sickness using cosmological categories from centuries before Christ.

This contradiction reveals the epistemological crisis at the heart of African Christianity: a pre-scientific worldview operating within a technologically modern environment.

---

5. Levack, *The Witch-Hunt in Early Modern Europe*.

3. Pentecostalism, Fear, and the Rise of Deliverance Economies

Pentecostalism in Africa has grown explosively over the past 40 years. While Pentecostal communities offer vibrant worship and real spiritual energy, many popular strands are built on an unhealthy obsession with:

- witchcraft,
- curses,
- demons,
- ancestral spirits, and
- exorcism rituals.

These churches often frame Christianity as a cosmic war with malevolent forces allegedly responsible for every misfortune. They encourage believers to attribute:

- business failure,
- unemployment,
- infertility,
- marital conflict,
- miscarriage,
- academic failure,
- and even natural death

  to the actions of witches or demons.
  Deliverance ministries charge for:

- prophetic consultations,
- healing sessions,
- exorcisms,
- "breaking ancestral covenants,"
- "unlocking destinies,"
- "neutralizing witches."

As Gifford argues, African Pentecostalism has become a spiritualized neoliberalism: every problem is an invisible attack; every solution is a product to be purchased.[6] This is not Christianity—it is fear-based capitalism in religious disguise.

The Catholic Church, witnessing the massive appeal of such ministries, faces enormous pressure. Some priests have begun performing exorcisms regularly, offering deliverances, or blessing anointed oils—adopting Pentecostal methods under the false assumption that this is "good pastoral care."

It is not.

It is theological regression.

Liberation theology must call the Church back to reason, justice, human dignity, and the Gospel—not superstition.

4. Witchcraft and the Scapegoating of the Vulnerable

In Africa, witchcraft accusations often target:

- widows,
- childless women,
- elderly persons,
- stepchildren,
- orphans,
- persons with albinism,
- people with epilepsy, autism, or schizophrenia,
- socially awkward individuals,
- the mentally ill.

This pattern is not accidental. It reflects the dynamics of social marginalization. Where structural injustice exists, societies search for convenient scapegoats.

Witchcraft belief therefore functions as:

- a psychological weapon,
- a social control mechanism,
- a justification for violence,
- a mask for patriarchy,

---

6. Gifford, *Christianity and Politics in Doe's Liberia*.

- a rationalization for poverty,
- a form of epistemic violence.

It is no different from the scapegoating of Jews in medieval Europe, or the Salem witch trials, or the racialization of Black people in America. The oppressed are blamed for the very suffering imposed upon them.

In this sense, witchcraft belief is not merely irrational; it is structurally sinful.

5. Why the Church Must Reject Exorcism Practices

a. Exorcism is based on outdated cosmology

While the Church historically practiced exorcisms, these rituals emerged before the modern understanding of:

- psychology,
- neurology,
- trauma,
- infectious disease,
- genetics.

Today, conditions once attributed to demons are known to be medical or psychological. Therefore, continuing exorcism culture—especially in Africa—actually perpetuates suffering by delaying access to medical or psychological care.

b. Jesus' exorcisms were symbolic confrontations with oppression

New Testament scholarship widely affirms that Jesus' exorcisms symbolically addressed:

- social exclusion,
- trauma,
- systemic marginalization—
- not literal demons flying around.

c. The Church must be a center of reason, not superstition

The Catholic tradition has always emphasized faith and reason.[7] The rise of pseudo-exorcists contradicts this theological heritage.

The Church does not need exorcists.

It needs:

- counselors,
- social workers,
- mental health ministers,
- scientists,
- pastoral caregivers grounded in critical thinking.

A 21st-century Church performing medieval rituals is abandoning its intellectual mission.

B) THE PSYCHOLOGY OF FEAR AND THE ROOTS OF WITCHCRAFT BELIEF

1. Understanding Fear in a Pre-Scientific Environment

Anthropologists consistently show that witchcraft belief flourishes most strongly in contexts where individuals experience low control over their environment.[8] In Africa, the daily experience of uncertainty—economic instability, corrupt governance, lack of healthcare, high child mortality, unpredictable weather patterns, limited job opportunities—creates fertile ground for fear-based explanations.

When misfortune strikes, individuals instinctively reach for supernatural causation. This is not because Africans are inherently superstitious, but because structural conditions reward non-rational explanations and offer few scientific alternatives. As Okeja notes, where institutions fail to offer rational order, society fills the gap with "moralized cosmology."[9]

In such contexts:

- Illness becomes "spiritual attack."

---

7. John Paul II, *Fides et Ratio*.

8. Douglas, *Purity and Danger*; Evans-Pritchard, *Witchcraft, Oracles, and Magic Among the Azande*.

9. Okeja, *Philosophy and the Postcolonial*.

- Failure becomes "curses."
- Death becomes "witchcraft."
- Mental illness becomes "possession."
- Poverty becomes "ancestral bondage."
- Social conflict becomes "evil manipulation."

The supernatural explanation is emotionally satisfying because it offers:

1. A culprit,
2. An intelligible narrative,
3. A potential solution (through ritual),
4. A sense of regained control.

Modern psychology calls this compensatory control theory—people invent patterns and agentic causes when reality feels chaotic.[10]

Thus, witchcraft belief in Africa functions as a psychological coping mechanism, not a theological truth.

2. The Cognitive Dimension: Pattern-Seeking Minds in a Low-Rationality Context

Human beings are "pattern-seeking creatures."[11] When confronted with complex events, our brains search for "agents"—someone or something intentionally causing the outcome. This leads to what psychologists call "hyperactive agency detection."

In a highly educated society, rational inquiry checks this impulse. But in a society without widespread scientific reasoning, the cognitive gap is filled by supernatural agency.

Thus:

- A child dies → "someone must have done it."
- Business collapses → "a jealous neighbor bewitched me."
- Woman miscarries → "evil spirits attacked the womb."
- Student fails exam → "teacher spiritually blocked me."

10. Kay et al., *Compensatory Control*.
11. Shermer, *The Believing Brain*.

The "witchcraft hypothesis" becomes a default explanatory model because it requires no empirical testing and aligns with communal narratives.

The tragedy is that this cognitive shortcut becomes a moral weapon when combined with fear.

3. Fear of Ambiguity and the Need for Simple Explanations

African societies often operate under high uncertainty: political volatility, economic precarity, communal conflict, and weak social safety nets. In these conditions, ambiguity is perceived as existentially threatening.

Witchcraft belief offers:

- certainty,
- predictability,
- moral clarity, in an unpredictable world.

Unlike scientific explanations—which can be complex, tentative, or counterintuitive—witchcraft explanations are simple and emotionally compelling:

- "This person harmed you."
- "This ritual will protect you."
- "Your misfortune has a spiritual cause."

This simplicity, however, is intellectually dishonest and morally corrosive. It prevents critical inquiry, discourages structural analysis, and masks the real sources of suffering (inequality, corruption, disease, lack of education).

4. Fear, Social Envy, and the Psychology of Resentment

Another driver of witchcraft belief is envy—a universal human emotion. In many African communities, visible success is often interpreted with suspicion:

- "How did he get rich so fast?"
- "How did she build a house without a sugar daddy?"

- "How is that child doing so well in school?"

In contexts of economic scarcity, one person's progress is perceived as another's loss. Witchcraft accusations become a way of policing success and reinforcing communal conformity.

The psychological function is clear:

- Envious individuals externalize their frustration.
- Communities punish those perceived as disruptive.
- Social tensions are projected onto convenient targets.

Instead of confronting inequality, nepotism, or lack of opportunity, African societies fall back on spiritual moralizing.

Witchcraft belief therefore functions as social envy spiritualized.

5. The Social Psychology of Witchcraft Rumors

Rumors spread rapidly in environments where:

- institutions are weak,
- information systems are unreliable,
- education levels vary,
- mistrust is high.

Witchcraft rumors follow predictable psychological patterns:

a. Rumors provide communal cohesion

Believing the same rumor reinforces group identity.

b. Rumors simplify social complexity

Witchcraft turns complicated socioeconomic issues into personal dramas.

c. Rumors protect power structures

Blaming "witches" diverts attention from:

- corrupt leaders,
- unjust systems,
- failed policies,
- institutional neglect.

d. Rumors maintain hierarchy

Accusations are rarely made against chiefs, politicians, clergy, or wealthy elites.

They target the vulnerable.

Thus, witchcraft belief is a political psychology, not merely a spiritual fear.

6. Witchcraft as a Social Script for Misfortune

In many African communities, witchcraft belief is not optional; it is a social script—a culturally encoded narrative forced upon individuals regardless of personal belief.

For example:

- If your child dies unexpectedly, others *will* accuse someone of witchcraft.
- If a business collapses, family members *will* search for the "enemy."
- If sickness persists, neighbors *will* propose spiritual explanations.

This forces even educated individuals into a social ritual they privately reject.

Thus, witchcraft belief survives not because people wholeheartedly believe it, but because the community demands conformity.

Social belonging outweighs individual dissent.

But liberation theology insists that truth must challenge destructive communal norms.

7. The Role of Religion in Amplifying Psychological Fear

Pentecostalism has amplified witchcraft belief by framing Christianity as spiritual warfare. While classical Pentecostalism in the early 20th century emphasized holiness and communal empowerment, African neo-Pentecostalism emphasizes:

- demons everywhere,
- curses inherited over generations,
- spiritual monitoring spirits,

- destiny blockers,
- "marine spirits,"
- spiritual marriages,
- prophetic diagnoses of witches.

This religious worldview replaces structural analysis with spiritual paranoia.

Instead of addressing:

- poverty,
- unemployment,
- disease,
- government corruption,
- domestic violence,
- illiteracy,

Africans are taught to fight invisible enemies.

This produces a population trapped in fear, endlessly seeking spiritual solutions to material problems.

8. Catholic Temptation and the Risk of Regressing into Magical Thinking

Historically, the Catholic Church has championed reason, science, and philosophy. But in many African dioceses today, some clergy—fascinated by the spectacular success of Pentecostal churches—have begun adopting:

- exorcisms during Mass,
- "healing lines,"
- deliverance sessions,
- anti-witchcraft prayers,
- anointing oils,
- holy water rituals resembling Pentecostal performances.

This trend is dangerous because:

1. It undermines Catholic intellectual tradition.
2. It indirectly legitimizes witchcraft belief.
3. It turns priests into spiritual performers.
4. It weakens sacramental theology.
5. It fuels fear rather than faith.

The Church does not need exorcists.
It needs prophets of truth, ministers of reason, and teachers of critical faith.

If the Church fails to confront witchcraft belief theologically and rationally, it risks becoming complicit in the cycles of violence it ought to heal.

9. The Theological Insufficiency of Witchcraft Explanations

From a theological perspective, witchcraft belief is fundamentally flawed:

- It attributes godlike power to humans.
- It contradicts divine sovereignty.
- It undermines trust in God's providence.
- It turns neighbors into enemies.
- It reduces sin to magical causation instead of moral responsibility.
- It contradicts the Incarnation, which teaches that God entered history to liberate from fear and ignorance.

Liberation theology cannot coexist with witchcraft cosmology.
One is based on reason, justice, and the dignity of the human person; the other on superstition and fear.

C) WITCHCRAFT ACCUSATIONS AS SOCIAL VIOLENCE

Witchcraft accusations in Africa do not exist in a vacuum. They function as a form of social violence, operating through cultural scripts, patriarchal structures, communal anxieties, and economic pressures. This section examines how these accusations unfold in real contexts, using examples from Ghana, Nigeria, and Cameroon. These case studies reveal a consistent pattern: witchcraft discourse disproportionately targets the poor and marginalized, legitimizes violence, and erodes human dignity.

Belief in witchcraft may appear to be a harmless cultural tradition, but its consequences are deadly. As Amnesty International and Human Rights Watch show, thousands of Africans are beaten, expelled, imprisoned, tortured, or killed each year due to accusations based on non-scientific superstition.[12] Liberation theology must reckon with this reality as a form of sin—not individual sin, but structural and epistemic sin.

1. Ghana: The Tragedy of the "Witch Camps"

Ghana provides one of the most vivid examples of how witchcraft belief becomes institutionalized as social violence. In the northern regions—particularly Gushegu, Yendi, and Gambaga—so-called "witch camps" have existed for nearly a century. These are settlements where mostly elderly women accused of witchcraft are exiled for safety.

Who Are the Accused?

Over 90% of residents are:

- elderly,
- widowed,
- childless,
- mentally or physically frail,
- socially isolated.

Thus, the accused reflect existing social vulnerabilities. Accusations are often triggered by:

- unexplained illness in the family,
- sudden death,
- economic hardship,
- jealousy,
- tension around inheritance,

---

12. Amnesty International, *Africa*; Amnesty International, *Ghana*; Human Rights Watch, *Nigeria*.

- mental health symptoms (e.g., dementia, schizophrenia).

Instead of seeking medical or scientific explanations, communities resort to witchcraft allegations because these narratives offer socially convenient scapegoats.

The Religious Dimension

Traditional priests, Pentecostal pastors, and sometimes even local catechists claim to "discern witches" through rituals or visions. Their pronouncements carry enormous social power because questioning them appears irreligious.

Theological Analysis

In Ghana, witchcraft accusation serves as:

- a punishment for vulnerability,
- a displacement of structural injustice (poverty, lack of healthcare),
- a misogynistic mechanism that targets widows,
- a denial of human dignity.

This is fundamentally incompatible with the Gospel's emphasis on protecting the vulnerable (Matt 25:40). No Catholic, Anglican, or Pentecostal theology rooted in the dignity of the human person can justify such systemic violence.

2. Nigeria: The Rise of Child-Witch Accusations and the Economies of Deliverance

Nigeria presents a different but equally troubling phenomenon: the explosion of child-witch accusations, particularly in Akwa Ibom and Cross River States. Beginning in the 1990s and intensifying in the 2000s, thousands of children—some as young as two—were accused of witchcraft by Pentecostal "prophets."

How It Happens

Common triggers for accusations include:

- bedwetting,
- nightmares,
- stubborn behavior,
- developmental delays,
- epilepsy,
- autism,
- poor academic performance.

Pastors, claiming supernatural insight, identify the child as a "witch" causing harm to the family. Parents—terrified, poorly educated, and influenced by the pastor's spiritual authority—respond with:

- beatings,
- starvation,
- abandonment,
- forced exorcisms involving torture.

Numerous NGOs (such as Stepping Stones Nigeria, and Child's Rights and Rehabilitation Network) have documented brutal cases in which children were:

- burned,
- poisoned,
- buried alive,
- or permanently disfigured.

The Role of Nollywood

Nigerian films have normalized witchcraft fear. Movies portray children transforming into animals, killing relatives with spells, or performing supernatural feats. These narratives reinforce belief in child witches, embedding superstition in popular culture.

The Deliverance Economy

Pastors profit enormously by:

- selling deliverance sessions,
- conducting "family cleansing rituals,"
- demanding offerings to "break curses,"
- establishing reputations as demon-slayers.

This transforms fear into income. As Gifford and Marshall-Fratani argue, Pentecostalism in Nigeria has evolved into a religious marketplace, where spiritual insecurity fuels financial exploitation.[13]

Theological Analysis

Accusing children of witchcraft violates every principle of Christian ethics:

- dignity of the child,
- protection of the vulnerable,
- truthfulness,
- justice,
- scientific reason,
- the preferential option for the poor.

> Moreover, Jesus explicitly condemned harming children: "Anyone who causes one of these little ones to stumble would be better thrown into the sea with a millstone around his neck" (Jerusalem Bible, Mark 9:42)

A Church or pastor who blesses or tolerates child-witch accusations contradicts Christ Himself.

---

13. Gifford, *Christianity, Development, and Modernity in Africa*; Marshall-Fratani, *Mediating the Global and Local in Nigerian Pentecostalism*.

3. Cameroon: The Everyday Tyranny of Witchcraft Suspicion

Cameroon, like much of Central Africa, is permeated by witchcraft discourse at every social level—from villages to elite circles. Cameroon is not unique, but its witchcraft features a unique blend of:

- traditional religion,
- Catholic sacramentalism,
- Pentecostal deliverance,
- political manipulation,
- fear of jealousy ("bad heart"),
- cultural fatalism.

Everyday Misfortune Interpreted as Witchcraft

In Cameroon:

- failing an exam,
- losing a job,
- infertility,
- business collapse,
- headaches,
- marital conflict,

are frequently attributed to witchcraft.
Instead of addressing real causes—poor schooling, bad governance, stress, health problems—people turn to supernatural explanations.

The Role of Catholic Clergy in Spreading Belief in Witchcraft

Belief in witchcraft remains pervasive across many African societies, shaping interpretations of misfortune, illness, conflict, and social disruption. Rather than diminishing under Christianity, these beliefs have often been reinforced by Catholic clergy themselves. In Cameroon, this dynamic is especially visible: witchcraft discourse circulates openly within pastoral practice, and many priests—and even bishops—publicly affirm the reality of witchcraft as a central explanatory category of life. This stands in tension with Catholic doctrine, which rejects superstition and warns against attributing spiritual causality without discernment.[14] Yet the lived religious experience in much of Africa demonstrates how pastoral leadership can unintentionally perpetuate precisely the fears the Church aims to dispel.

High-ranking prelates have made statements that implicitly validate witchcraft as a real causal force. For example, Archbishop Andrew Nkea of Bamenda publicly described LGBTQ inclusion as "witchcraft," a rhetorical move that both demonizes sexual minorities and confirms for ordinary Catholics that witchcraft is an operative, malevolent reality in contemporary society. Similarly, the former Bishop of Bertoua, a Polish missionary bishop, stated in *L'Effort Camerounais* that witchcraft makes sense and that people in his native country also believe in it.[15] Statements like these, coming from episcopal leaders, carry enormous interpretive weight; they blur the line between cultural belief and Church teaching.

Individual priests also contribute to this normalization. One priest, Fr. George Nkeze, asserted in conversation that "to question the belief in witchcraft is to doubt the existence of evil." Such reasoning collapses metaphysics into folklore, equating cultural narratives of witchcraft with Christian doctrine on moral evil. Another influential voice, Fr. Humphrey Tatah Mbuy, has published numerous articles and books on witchcraft, including *Encountering Witches and Wizards in Africa*.[16] As a seminarian, questioning him on the epistemological basis for such claims revealed the theological and philosophical fragility beneath these assertions. Nonetheless, these writings shaped clergy formation in the 1990s and continue to influence pastoral imagination.

The broader context amplifies this trend. Historically, Catholics in Africa did not practice Pentecostal-style deliverance. Exorcism was rare, tightly regulated, and grounded in sacramental theology. However, the spread of Pentecostalism and the rise of the Catholic Charismatic Renewal have transformed pastoral expectations. Deliverance rituals—once marginal—are now widespread. Practices such as prayer rooms, healing Masses, family liberation Masses, midnight deliverance services, and rituals aimed at breaking ancestral curses have become mainstream in Cameroon and across Africa (Kalu, 2008). These developments shift Catholic

---

14. *Catechism of the Catholic Church*, 2110–17.
15. *L'Effort Camerounais*.
16. Mbuy, *Encountering Witches and Wizards in Africa*.

spirituality from sacramental depth toward a quasi-magical worldview in which spiritual power is measured by its ability to neutralize occult harm.

Parishioners now expect priests to protect them from witches, identify hidden enemies, and "break" curses. Young clergy, pressured by these expectations and inspired by the popularity of charismatic priests, often perform deliverance rituals despite lacking theological grounding or canonical mandate. In doing so, they inadvertently legitimize witchcraft belief as an operative moral and social framework.

The result is a pastoral landscape where fear, suspicion, and supernatural explanations dominate religious life. Instead of liberating believers from the anxieties associated with witchcraft, the Church—often unintentionally—reinforces a worldview in which witchcraft is omnipresent, powerful, and determinative of human destiny. This represents not theological depth but a regression into Christianized magical thinking, where spiritual authority is measured less by sacramental integrity than by perceived power over invisible forces.

Witchcraft and the Politics of Fear

Political elites in Cameroon often weaponize witchcraft rhetoric:

- opponents are accused of occultism,
- deaths are blamed on mystical attacks,
- fear becomes a tool of control.

Jean-Marc Ela argued that African rulers exploit religious fear to maintain domination. Witchcraft discourse becomes a substitute for political accountability.[17]

The Paradox: Success is Feared, Not Celebrated

In Cameroon, as in much of Africa, social success invites suspicion. Prosperous individuals are rumored to be:

- members of *nyongo*, a illusive group whose members "eat people spiritually,"
- sacrificing relatives,

---

17. Ela, *My Faith as an African*.

- using "*juju* to get rich,"
- working with demons.

Thus, witchcraft belief punishes achievement. This creates:

- intellectual stagnation,
- fear of ambition,
- communal envy,
- resistance to innovation.

A society that interprets excellence as witchcraft can never progress scientifically or economically.

4. Witchcraft as Structural and Gendered Violence

Across Africa, witchcraft accusations function as tools of gendered oppression. Women—especially widows—are disproportionately targeted. With the death of a husband, a woman often loses social protection. Accusing her of witchcraft becomes a convenient mechanism to:

- seize property,
- expel her from the home,
- justify violence.

Similarly, accusations against children reflect systemic child rights violations and lack of mental health services.

Witchcraft belief is therefore not "African culture." It is a form of:

- patriarchal violence,
- epistemic injustice,
- social exclusion,
- moral corruption,
- communal trauma.

5. Why Witchcraft Accusation Is Theologically Illegitimate

From the perspective of liberation theology, any practice that targets the vulnerable and absolves the powerful is structurally sinful. Witchcraft accusation:

- blames victims instead of systems,
- reinforces oppressive hierarchies,
- creates moral panic,
- destroys community trust,
- contradicts biblical teachings,
- distracts from real causes of suffering,
- denies the dignity of the human person.

It is therefore incompatible with:

- Catholic Social Teaching,
- the theology of creation,
- the incarnation,
- the command to love neighbor,
- the Gospel preferential option for the poor.

Liberation theology must categorically reject witchcraft belief as a theological, ethical, and rational error.

D) A LIBERATIVE THEOLOGY OF HUMAN DIGNITY

Liberation theology is fundamentally concerned with the dignity of the human person and the structures—spiritual, psychological, social, and political—that either uphold or violate that dignity. To confront witchcraft belief in Africa, liberation theology must offer more than critique; it must articulate a positive theological alternative grounded in reason, justice, the Gospel, and human flourishing.

The goal is not simply to condemn superstition but to replace it with a liberating theological anthropology—one that empowers individuals, strengthens communities, and dismantles the social and epistemic structures that allow witchcraft fear to thrive.

1. Human Beings Are Not Witches: A Theological Anthropology

Christian theology affirms that every human person is created imago Dei—in the image of God (Genesis 1:27, Jerusalem Bible). This is the foundation of all Catholic social teaching and liberation theology. Witchcraft belief fundamentally contradicts this doctrine in several ways:

a. It attributes intrinsic malice to individuals

Witchcraft accusations assume that certain people possess a supernatural predisposition to harm others. This implies a dual-creation theology where some individuals are created by God but endowed with demonic power.

No Christian anthropology supports such a view.

b. It presupposes magical determinism

In witchcraft cosmology, a person's moral value is determined by invisible forces rather than by free will, conscience, or character. This negates the Christian understanding of moral responsibility and freedom.

c. It denies grace

If a person is labeled a witch from birth or by inheritance, then:

- Christ's redemptive power becomes irrelevant.
- Baptism, sacraments, and conversion lose meaning.
- The Gospel's assurance that "nothing can separate us from the love of God" (Romans 8:38) is contradicted.

d. It dehumanizes the vulnerable

Witchcraft belief almost always targets:

- women,
- children,
- the elderly,

- the disabled,
- the mentally ill,
- the socially marginalized.

This makes witchcraft accusation a form of systemic dehumanization, not spirituality.

A liberative theology must assert unequivocally:

There are no witches—only human beings endowed with dignity, freedom, and reason.

2. Evil Is Structural, Not Magical: Reframing the Theology of Evil

Witchcraft belief proposes that evil comes from "witches" who harm others spiritually. Liberation theology offers a superior framework: evil is structural, historical, and social.

a. Poverty is evil
Not because witches cause it, but because unjust economic systems produce it.

b. Corruption is evil
Not because ancestors curse a nation, but because leaders abuse power.

c. Disease is evil
Not because demons attack individuals, but because healthcare systems fail.

d. Domestic violence is evil
Not because spiritual spouses torment women, but because patriarchy remains unchallenged.

e. Child mortality is evil
Not because "children are witches," but because access to medicine is inadequate.

This reframing aligns with what Gutiérrez calls "the social roots of sin"[18] and what Jean-Marc Ela terms "the cry of the African poor."[19]

Witchcraft belief obscures true evil by redirecting moral outrage toward imaginary enemies.

Liberative theology exposes these illusions and redirects attention to structural transformation.

18. Gutiérrez, *A Theology of Liberation*.
19. Ela, *My Faith as an African*.

3. The Church as an Agent of Reason, Not Superstition

The Church's vocation is not to perpetuate medieval enchantments but to form:

- Reasonable believers,
- scientifically literate citizens,
- critically engaged disciples,
- agents of justice and liberation.

a. Rejecting exorcism culture

Exorcisms belong to a pre-scientific worldview. While retained in Catholic ritual books, the Church in the West rarely uses them—and even then only after psychological evaluation. African contexts, however, have resurrected and commercialized them.

A liberative Church must:

- discourage exorcism practices,
- reject collaboration with Pentecostal deliverance theology,
- avoid blessing oils and objects used for "witch-hunting,"
- teach the faithful that human problems have natural causes and natural solutions.

b. Promoting science and critical inquiry

The Church must champion:

- science education,
- psychology,
- sociology,
- anthropology,
- medicine,
- empirical reasoning.

Catholic universities, seminaries, and parishes must become centers of intellectual liberation.

As Pope Francis repeatedly insists, "faith and science must walk together."[20]

c. Forming clergy in mental health and social analysis

Most African clergy are not trained in:

- mental health,
- trauma counseling,
- psychology,
- scientific worldview,
- community development.

Thus they default to spiritual explanations.

Liberation theology requires that clergy become pastoral agents of truth, not facilitators of superstition.

4. A Liberationist Reinterpretation of Spiritual Warfare

African Christianity is saturated with the language of spiritual warfare. Liberation theology must reinterpret this symbolically rather than literally.

a. The "demons" we must fight are structural injustices

unemployment,

- corruption,
- gender inequality,
- inadequate healthcare,
- domestic violence,
- dictatorship.

---

20. Francis, *Laudato Si'*.

These are the true "principalities and powers" (Ephesians 6:12)—not witches hiding in families.

b. Evil is psychological, relational, and social

trauma,

- resentment,
- envy,
- fear,
- ignorance,
- addiction,
- communal conflict.

These are real spiritual struggles requiring pastoral care—not exorcism rituals.

c. Christ liberates from fear, not through fear

Jesus repeatedly told His followers:
"Do not be afraid."
Not once did He command them to hunt witches.
Liberative theology must reclaim Jesus as:

- healer of trauma,
- liberator of the oppressed,
- critic of unjust systems,
- teacher of wisdom and reason.

This model excludes superstition.

5. Deconstructing the Witchcraft Narrative in African Christianity

Liberation theology must challenge the three pillars that allow witchcraft belief to survive:

a. Epistemic authority

Pastors claim supernatural knowledge: "I see in the spirit."
 Liberation theology insists on discernment, evidence, and rational inquiry.

b. Communal conformity

Communities pressure individuals to accept witchcraft explanations.
 Liberation theology empowers conscience over communal fear.

c. Political manipulation

Leaders use witchcraft rumors to distract from their failures.
 Liberation theology unmasks this deception.
 Witchcraft belief is therefore not merely false; it is a tool of oppression, sustained by power dynamics.

6. A Positive, Rational, and Liberative Theology for Africa

Liberative theology must proclaim:

  a. God is not the author of fear

   Fear-based religion is anti-Gospel.

  b. Human beings are rational and capable

   Reason is not Western—it is human.

  c. The Church must defend the oppressed, not accuse them

   Standing with victims of witchcraft accusation is a theological mandate.

  d. Scientific explanations honor God's creation

   Understanding natural causes is a form of reverence.

  e. Education is liberation

   Superstition flourishes where critical thinking is absent.

  f. Faith must confront social and structural evil

   The spiritualization of suffering is a form of complicity.

E) CONCLUSION: TOWARD AN AFRICA FREED FROM FEAR

Witchcraft belief is not merely an intellectual error. It is a *social system*, a moral economy, a psychological refuge in times of uncertainty, and a political tool used to reinforce power hierarchies and maintain social control. In Africa, it has become one of the greatest obstacles to human development, rational inquiry, scientific progress, and genuine Christian discipleship. It is a captivity of the mind that reproduces captivity in society.

This chapter has demonstrated that witchcraft fear persists not because witches exist, but because fear exists—fear intensified by poverty, weak institutions, psychological stress, patriarchal norms, and religious leaders who exploit insecurity rather than dismantle it.

It is therefore imperative that a liberation theologian confronts witchcraft belief not as a cultural given but as a form of epistemic, structural, and theological violence.

1. Naming the Real Enemy: Ignorance, Not Witches

In modern societies with strong educational systems, belief in witchcraft has become marginal. Not because Western people are spiritually superior, but because scientific literacy displaced supernatural explanations. Diseases once blamed on demons are now known to be caused by viruses or genetics. Success and failure are now explained by economic and educational factors, not "spiritual attacks." Misfortune is understood in terms of probability, not malevolent intention.

Africa is not yet free from witchcraft belief because Africa is not yet free from:

- poor education systems,
- political corruption,
- social inequality,
- inadequate healthcare,
- patriarchal social structures,
- religious manipulation.

These are the real "demons," not imaginary witches.

Ignorance, not supernatural malice, is the true adversary.

Liberation theology must therefore become an instrument of intellectual liberation.

2. The Church's Prophetic Task: To Break the Chains of Superstition

The Church cannot remain silent. Silence is complicity. Witchcraft accusations destroy lives, especially the lives of:

- children,
- widows,
- the disabled,
- the mentally ill,
- the socially marginalized.

A Church that tolerates witchcraft discourse betrays the Gospel. The Church must:

a. Publicly denounce witchcraft accusations

Not ambiguously, not timidly—explicitly.
No baptized Christian should believe in or participate in witch-hunting.

b. Reject exorcism practices and deliverance theatrics

These rituals belong to antiquity, not a rational, sacramental, and liberation-oriented Church. They reinforce fear and legitimize superstition.

c. Promote scientific and psychological explanations for misfortune

Priests and pastors must be trained to understand mental health, developmental disorders, trauma, and medical conditions that are often mistaken for possession or witchcraft.

d. Stand with victims

The Church must defend the accused, offering:

- sanctuary,
- legal support,

- counseling,
- public advocacy.

  e. Challenge Pentecostal exploitation

    A Church rooted in reason cannot imitate ministries that enrich themselves through fear.

  f. Teach a theology of liberation, not bondage

    A Gospel that liberates from fear is the only authentic Gospel.

    Pope Francis has often warned against "spiritual worldliness" and "religious exploitation." In Africa, this warning must be applied to witchcraft narratives that turn Christianity into a marketplace of fear.

3. Embracing a Biblical Theology of Freedom

The Bible's message is consistently one of liberation from fear, not enslavement to it. Throughout Scripture (Jerusalem Bible):

- "Do not be afraid" (Isaiah 41:10).
- "Perfect love casts out fear" (1 John 4:18).
- "God gave us a spirit not of fear, but of power and love and self-control" (2 Timothy 1:7).
- "If the Son sets you free, you will indeed be free" (John 8:36).

Jesus never taught His disciples to fear witches. He never instructed them to accuse their neighbors. He never said illness came from family curses. Instead, He healed the sick, confronted injustice, condemned hypocrisy, and liberated people from psychological and social oppression.

A liberation theology of witchcraft must reclaim Jesus as a healer of trauma, teacher of reason, and liberator of oppressed minds, not as a divine exorcist fighting imaginary magical enemies.

4. The Way Forward: Toward a Rational and Liberated African Christianity

To dismantle witchcraft belief, Africa needs a multidimensional strategy:

a. Educational Reform

Critical thinking, scientific literacy, and social analysis must be integrated into basic education and catechesis.

b. Pastoral Training

Clergy must be educated in mental health, social sciences, and rational theology—not just spiritual warfare rhetoric.

c. Public Policy

Governments must criminalize harmful witchcraft accusations and protect vulnerable populations.

d. Media Responsibility

Nollywood and other African film industries must stop perpetuating harmful stereotypes.

e. Interfaith Collaboration

Christian, Muslim, and traditional leaders must unite to protect victims and dismantle harmful beliefs.

f. A New Theological Narrative

Liberation theology must articulate a narrative that:
- affirms human dignity,
- celebrates reason,
- confronts structural injustice,
- rejects magical determinism,
- empowers communities to control their destinies.

5. Final Word: Liberation Begins in the Mind

Africa cannot be politically or economically liberated until it is epistemologically liberated.

The struggle against witchcraft belief is not a war against culture; it is a war against fear, superstition, violence, and the demonization of the vulnerable.

True liberation does not require exorcists.
It requires:

- teachers,
- scientists,
- theologians,
- courageous clergy,
- critical thinkers,
- human rights defenders,
- communities committed to truth.

As long as Africans believe that witches—not systems—cause suffering, political and economic liberation will remain elusive. Witchcraft belief keeps people blaming each other rather than confronting injustice.

The task of liberation theology is clear:
Free the African mind from fear.
Free African society from superstition.
Free the Church from medieval bondage.
Free the poor from violence in the name of God.
Only then can Africa rise into the future God intends—
a future of dignity, reason, justice, and hope.

CHAPTER 12

Economic Oppression and the Theology of Structural Sin

A Critical-Liberative Theology of Poverty, Global Capital, and Human Dignity

A) INTRODUCTION: WHEN POVERTY BECOMES VIOLENCE

POVERTY IS NOT SIMPLY a misfortune. It is not an accident of nature, a moral failing, or a divine punishment. Poverty—especially mass, persistent, and preventable poverty—is a form of violence. It destroys lives just as surely as bullets and bombs. It shortens life expectancy, exposes people to disease, reduces educational opportunities, degrades human dignity, and fractures communities. As Paul Farmer famously argued, such suffering is not random but produced by historical and structural forces—what he called structural violence.[1]

Liberation theology has long insisted that poverty is the result of sinful structures—economic, political, and social systems that benefit the few at the expense of the many.[2] These structures are sustained not only by explicit injustice but also by global economic arrangements, corporate power, weak governance, corruption, extractive capitalism, and ideological narratives that mask inequality. In this sense, poverty is not merely a social condition; it is a theological problem, demanding a theological response.

---

1. Farmer, *Pathologies of Power*.
2. Gutiérrez, *A Theology of Liberation*; Sobrino, *Christology at the Crossroads*.

The African context reveals this structural violence with devastating clarity. Across sub-Saharan Africa, millions survive through informal markets, precarious labor, small-scale agriculture, or low-wage service economies. These workers are the backbone of African societies—yet they live without adequate wages, legal protection, healthcare, safe working conditions, or opportunities for upward mobility. Migrants, women, and young people bear the heaviest burdens. The informal economy—far from being a marginal sector—accounts for 80–90% of jobs in countries like Cameroon, Nigeria, Tanzania, and the Democratic Republic of Congo.[3] Yet these workers remain invisible in national policy and unprotected in global supply chains.

Meanwhile, global corporations extract resources, cheap labor, and market access from Africa, while offering minimal investment, exploitative working conditions, and little tax revenue. The benefits of global capitalism flow upward and outward, following the contours of a world economy designed to enrich those who already possess wealth and power. As Pope Francis warns, "an economy that kills" is not simply unjust; it is morally indefensible.[4]

This chapter argues that economic oppression is a contemporary form of structural sin—a sin embedded not in individual hearts but in institutions, markets, legal codes, international trade systems, and political ideologies. A liberationist interpretation of Catholic Social Teaching must therefore expand beyond charity and development models toward a Critical-Liberative Theology (CLT) that confronts the root causes of exploitation and reimagines economic life as a sphere of justice, solidarity, and dignity.

B) POVERTY AS VIOLENCE: A LIBERATIVE INTERPRETATION

1. Poverty as the Denial of Human Flourishing

The traditional Christian view has sometimes framed poverty as a spiritual ideal, citing Jesus' preferential love for the poor or the beatitudes' blessing of the lowly. Yet liberation theologians like Gutiérrez and Boff have demonstrated that biblical references to "the poor" refer not to

---

3. ILO, *Women and Men in the Informal Economy*.
4. Francis, *Fratelli Tutti*.

voluntary poverty but to those who suffer unjust deprivation.[5] Poverty is not holy; it is a violation of the divine intention for human life.

People die early because they are poor.
They suffer preventable diseases because they are poor.
Their children lack schooling because they are poor.
This is not fate. It is violence.

If an unjust action is morally sinful, then the preservation of unjust structures is *structurally sinful*.

2. Poverty as Slow, Silent, Social Death

The World Health Organization estimates that millions die annually from causes that are entirely preventable with proper health systems, nutrition, sanitation, and infrastructure—systems denied to the poor by global inequity.[6] Liberation theology identifies this as slow violence, a phrase anthropologist Rob Nixon[7] uses to describe harms that unfold gradually yet destroy lives.

Economic injustice kills:

- through malnutrition,
- inadequate housing,
- lack of clean water,
- inaccessible healthcare,
- exploitative labor practices,
- environmental degradation,
- educational exclusion.

Violence is not always visible. A collapsed mine, a toxic dump, a polluted river, a garment factory fire, or a child forced into dangerous labor is also violence.

---

5. Gutiérrez, *A Theology of Liberation*; Boff, *Church: Charism and Power*.
6. WHO, *World Health Statistics 2022*.
7. Nixon, *Slow Violence and the Environmentalism of the Poor*.

3. The Myth of Meritocracy

Neo-liberal capitalism maintains a moral narrative that wealth is earned and poverty is the result of laziness or incompetence. Such narratives ignore:

- colonial history,
- structural adjustment programs,
- unfair trade systems,
- institutional corruption,
- resource extraction,
- wage suppression,
- systemic racism.

Catholic Social Teaching rejects this myth. From Rerum Novarum[8] to Laudato Si'[9] and Fratelli Tutti,[10] the Church insists that economic structures must serve human dignity—not the other way around.

It is structurally sinful to design, sustain, or profit from systems in which millions cannot meet basic needs while a minority accumulates unlimited wealth.

C) GLOBAL ECONOMIC INJUSTICE

1. The Postcolonial Economic Order: Independence Without Liberation

African nations emerged from colonial rule politically independent but economically dependent. Colonial borders, resource flows, extractive infrastructures, and foreign-oriented trade systems persisted. Postcolonial elites inherited state machinery built for exploitation, not development.

The global economy still treats Africa primarily as a site for:

- raw materials,
- cheap labor,
- land acquisition,

---

8. Leo XIII, *Rerum Novarum*.
9. Francis, *Laudato Si'*.
10. Francis, *Fratelli Tutti*.

- mineral extraction,
- agribusiness,
- dumping of substandard goods.

Corporations profit from this arrangement; African workers do not.

2. Debt, Austerity, and Structural Adjustment

In the 1980s and 1990s, the IMF and World Bank imposed Structural Adjustment Programs (SAPs) across Africa. These reforms mandated:

- privatization of public services,
- reduction in social spending,
- removal of trade protections,
- currency devaluation.

SAPs devastated social sectors—healthcare, education, and public employment—pushing millions deeper into poverty.[11]

Economic "reform" became another form of violence.

3. Global Supply Chains and the New Colonialism

Today's global supply chains replicate colonial dynamics:

- African miners extract cobalt for Western tech giants (Amnesty International, 2016).
- Garment workers labor in dangerous conditions for multinational brands.
- Fruit and cocoa plantations exploit migrant laborers.
- Fisherfolk are displaced by industrial trawlers.

The Global North enjoys cheap products; the Global South bears the human cost.

Catholic Social Teaching, especially *Fratelli Tutti*,[12] condemns these inequities and calls for solidarity, yet many corporations continue to operate with near-total impunity.

---

11. Mkandawire and Soludo, *Our Continent, Our Future*.
12. Francis, *Fratelli Tutti*.

D) WORKERS, MIGRANTS, AND THE VIOLENCE OF EXPLOITATIVE CAPITALISM

1. Workers as Disposable

In many African economies, workers lack:

- contracts,
- health insurance,
- living wages,
- legal protections,
- union rights.

They are treated as replaceable units of labor rather than human beings.
This is not simply an economic injustice; it is a theological affront.
Catholic Social Teaching asserts the inherent dignity of work and the worker.[13]
When capitalism devalues workers, it devalues God's image.

2. Migrants as the New Crucified of History

African migrants—within Africa and abroad—are frequently:

- exploited,
- underpaid,
- abused,
- trafficked,
- detained,
- deported,
- racially profiled.

Pope Francis calls migrants "the crucified people of our time."[14]
Their suffering is not accidental but the result of:

- restrictive immigration policies,

---

13. John Paul II, *Laborem Exercens*.
14. Francis, *Message for the World Day of Migrants and Refugees*.

- labor exploitation,
- xenophobia,
- global inequality.

Liberation theology must affirm:
Borders cannot function as moral justifications for human suffering.

3. The Informal Economy: Survival Without Protection

The informal economy includes:

- street vendors,
- carpenters,
- taxi drivers,
- seamstresses,
- masons,
- hairdressers,
- market traders.

These workers sustain national economies—but they are denied:

- legal protection,
- social security,
- healthcare,
- fair wages.

Their poverty is not the result of laziness but of structural exclusion.

E) CASE STUDY: THE AFRICAN INFORMAL ECONOMY AND GLOBAL SUPPLY CHAINS

1. Informal Work as Institutionalized Insecurity

In much of Africa, formal employment is limited to small sectors: government, banking, oil, telecommunications. Everyone else survives in the informal economy. Workers must navigate:

- police harassment,
- bribe demands,
- lack of capital,
- market instability,
- unsafe conditions.

This is structural sin: society benefits from their labor while denying them stability or upward mobility.

2. Global Corporations and Resource Extraction

Examples include:

- cobalt mining in DRC under dangerous conditions,[15]
- cocoa plantations in Ghana and Ivory Coast using child labor,[16]
- large-scale land grabs displacing poor farmers.[17]

These abuses occur because global supply chains prioritize efficiency and profit over human dignity.

Corporate violence is sanitized through language—"outsourcing," "cost management," "competitive advantage"—but its consequences remain brutal.

3. The Theology of Structural Sin

Structural sin arises when:

- economic systems degrade human dignity,
- political elites collude with corporations,
- profits outweigh ethics,
- the poor bear costs while others reap benefits.

---

15. Amnesty International, *Africa*.
16. ILO, *Child Labour in Cocoa Supply Chains*.
17. Zoomers, *Globalisation and the Foreignisation of Space*.

This concept, developed by Sobrino[18] and expanded by African theologians like Ela[19] and Magesa,[20] holds that sin can be embedded in systems, not merely individual choices.

In a globalized world, structural sin is the primary form of evil.

D) CATHOLIC SOCIAL TEACHING THROUGH A CRITICAL-LIBERATIVE LENS

1. From Charity to Structural Transformation

Classical Catholic Social Teaching (CST) emphasizes:

- human dignity,
- solidarity,
- subsidiarity,
- rights of workers,
- universal destination of goods,
- preferential option for the poor.

But many African churches treat CST as a moral ideal rather than a political and economic imperative. CLT pushes CST to confront:

- exploitative capitalism,
- political corruption,
- unjust trade systems,
- oppressive economic policies.

Justice, not charity, is the goal.

2. Rediscovering the Radical Economic Message of the Gospel

Jesus' ministry consistently centers the poor (Luke 4:18). His teachings condemn:

---

18. Sobrino, *Christology at the Crossroads*.
19. Ela, *My Faith as an African*.
20. Magesa, *African Religion*.

- exploitation,
- hoarding,
- indifference to suffering,
- oppressive wealth systems (Matt 25:31–46).

The Acts community shared goods so "there was not a needy person among them" (Acts 4:34).

CST must recover this radical communal vision.

3. Toward a Liberationist Economics

CLT proposes:

- living wages,
- workers' cooperatives,
- ethical trade policies,
- public accountability,
- anti-corruption structures,
- environmental justice,
- protection of migrants,
- universal access to healthcare and education.

Economic arrangements must be judged by one criterion:
Do they promote human dignity and liberation?
If not, they are sinful structures requiring transformation.

CHAPTER 13

Migration, Exile, and the Theology of Forced Displacement

A Critical-Liberative Reading of Borders, Belonging, and the God of Migrants

A) INTRODUCTION: THE AGE OF DISPLACEMENT

We live in an age of unprecedented human displacement. More people are forcibly uprooted today than at any moment since the Second World War. According to UNHCR (2023), more than 110 million people worldwide are refugees, asylum seekers, internally displaced persons, or stateless. Their journeys—by foot, by sea, across deserts, through forests, and into detention centers—form one of the greatest moral crises of our time.

Migration is not merely a political issue; it is a theological one. Forced displacement raises fundamental questions about human dignity, moral responsibility, borders, solidarity, and the meaning of belonging. Liberation theology insists that the modern displaced person is a crucified figure, bearing the wounds of unjust global structures: war, political repression, climate change, economic marginalization, and the failures of both states and churches.

The Christian scriptures themselves are a story of migration and exile. Abraham migrates at God's command (Gen 12). Israel becomes a migrant people through famine (Gen 46), forced labor (Exod 1), exodus (Exod 12), exile (2 Kgs 24), and diaspora. Jesus is born under the shadow of a census and flees as a refugee to Egypt (Matt 2:13–15, Jerusalem Bible). The early Christian communities were often migrants—both voluntary and forced—scattered across the Roman Empire. The Bible's preferential concern for the "stranger," the "sojourner," and the "resident alien" is not incidental; it is central to its vision of justice.

Migration, then, is not a marginal theme of scripture. It is a theological paradigm.

Today, however, migrants experience hostility, fear, and rejection. Borders become instruments of exclusion; immigration systems criminalize the vulnerable; refugee policies prioritize national security over human security. Despite its own identity as a pilgrim people, the global Church has often struggled to respond with clarity, courage, or prophetic solidarity. While Pope Francis has spoken with remarkable force—calling migrants "the crucified of our age"[1]—many local churches remain timid or indifferent.

This chapter argues that forced displacement must be understood as a contemporary site of structural sin, and that Catholic Social Teaching—expanded through Critical-Liberative Theology (CLT)—demands a radical rethinking of borders, belonging, and hospitality. A liberative theology of migration must insist that:

- No human being is illegal.
- Borders cannot supersede human dignity.
- Refugees are moral claimants, not burdens.
- Receiving migrants is not optional charity but Christian duty.

Forced migration is not an accident; it is the predictable outcome of global inequalities, war economies, climate injustice, and political repression. As such, a theology of migration must confront its causes, not merely its symptoms.

B) BIBLICAL MIGRATIONS AND EXILE: A THEOLOGY OF THE JOURNEY

1. Abraham: Migration as Vocation

Abraham's journey begins with a divine command: "Leave your country, your kindred and your father's house for a country which I will show you" (Gen 12:1, Jerusalem Bible). Migration here is not a fall from stability; it

---

1. Francis, *Message for the World Day of Migrants and Refugees*.

is the beginning of God's covenant. The biblical imagination treats migration not as anomaly but as the normal condition of faith.

Abraham becomes the archetype of those who must leave in order to live.

2. Israel in Egypt: Migration, Famine, and Survival

Migration emerges again when famine drives Jacob's sons to Egypt. What begins as a survival strategy becomes the root of both refuge and oppression (Gen 46; Exod 1). The Israelites become forced laborers, illustrating how migrants are often welcomed when economically useful and persecuted when politically inconvenient (Exod 1:8–14).

Scripture reveals a profound psychological truth:

Migrants are vulnerable because their presence exposes the moral weakness of host nations.

3. Exodus: Liberation as Migration

The Exodus is the defining narrative of Israel's faith—a story of forced labor, divine liberation, and the search for a homeland. God identifies with a migrant people and defeats the imperial structures that enslave them. The Exodus reveals:

- God takes the side of the displaced.
- Liberation begins with movement.
- Migration can be a journey toward promise.

The migrant community becomes God's chosen people.

4. Exile: Theology Born Out of Homelessness

The Babylonian Exile (587 BCE) is a catastrophic displacement. Jerusalem falls, the temple is destroyed, and elites are deported. Yet in this devastation, Israel discovers a deeper faith. Prophets reinterpret exile not as divine abandonment but as a site of purification, solidarity, and renewed hope (Jer 29:4–14).

Exile becomes a theological teacher.

5. Jesus the Refugee

Matthew's Gospel narrates the Holy Family's flight from Herod: "Joseph got up, took the child and his mother by night and left for Egypt" (Matt 2:14, Jerusalem Bible). Jesus' first experience is not adoration but danger; his first identity is not citizen but refugee.

The Incarnation sanctifies the displaced human body.
God enters history as a migrant child.

6. Early Christianity: Diaspora and Mission

The earliest Christian communities were migrant networks—traders, artisans, slaves, and converts dispersed across cities from Antioch to Rome. Persecution forced many into exile. Migration became the engine of evangelization.

Christian faith grows not in imperial centers but on the roads, among the uprooted.

C) REFUGEES AS THE MODERN CRUCIFIED PEOPLES

Liberation theology describes the oppressed as the crucified people—those who suffer unjustly from the sins of the powerful.[2] Today, refugees and migrants embody this reality.

1. Structural Causes of Forced Migration

People flee because of:

- war and political violence,
- climate change disasters,
- economic collapse,
- persecution,
- corruption,
- gender-based violence,
- ethnic cleansing,

---

2. Sobrino, *Christology at the Crossroads*.

- state failure.

These are not random misfortunes; they are consequences of structural sin.

2. Vulnerability on the Journey

Forced migrants endure:

- extortion by smugglers,
- rape and human trafficking,
- dehydration in deserts,
- drowning at sea,
- torture in detention centers,
- xenophobia at borders.

The Mediterranean, the Sahara, and the Darién Gap have become contemporary Calvaries—geographies of death created by political choices.

3. The Moral Failure of Nations

Wealthy nations respond with:

- border militarization,
- indefinite detention,
- criminalization of asylum seekers,
- deportations,
- refusal to share responsibility.

This is not prudential policy; it is a rejection of human brotherhood, condemned in *Fratelli Tutti*.[3]

---

3. Francis, *Fratelli Tutti*.

4. The Silence of the Churches

Many churches fear alienating politicians or wealthy parishioners. Others adopt nationalist ideologies that justify exclusion. African churches often remain silent about migrant abuses in Libya, the Mediterranean, or domestic xenophobia. American churches are frequently divided along political lines. European churches struggle to resist rising populism.

Meanwhile, migrants suffer.

Pope Francis stands almost alone among global Christian leaders in consistently defending refugees—calling for welcome, protection, promotion, and integration.[4] But rhetoric has not yet transformed practice.

Migrants remain the contemporary crucified.

D) CASE STUDIES: SYRIA, AFRICAN MIGRANTS, AND CENTRAL AMERICA

1. Syria: The Destruction of a People

The Syrian civil war created one of the largest refugee crises in modern history. Millions fled to Lebanon, Jordan, Turkey, and Europe. Families were separated; entire cities destroyed. Many drowned in the Mediterranean.

International powers intervened militarily but failed morally.

The Church, though active in humanitarian aid, rarely confronted the geopolitical structures fueling the war. Liberation theology demands not only charity but prophetic denunciation of the powers perpetuating conflict.

2. African Migrants: Libya, the Mediterranean, and the New Slave Markets

African migrants fleeing economic deprivation, conflict, or authoritarianism face horrific abuses:

- enslavement in Libyan detention camps,[5]
- drowning in the Mediterranean,

---

4. Francis, *Address of His Holiness Pope Francis to the Roman Curia*.
5. UNHCR, *Desperate Journeys*.

- extortion,
- racism in transit countries,
- rejection upon arrival.

Many of these migrants are young people from West and Central Africa—Cameroon, Nigeria, Eritrea, Sudan—risking death for the possibility of life.

African states largely ignore their suffering. Many African churches rarely speak out.

3. Central America: Violence, Cartels, and the Exodus North

Migrants from Honduras, Guatemala, and El Salvador flee gang violence, economic collapse, and political corruption. Their journey northward through Mexico is marked by extortion, assault, rape, kidnapping, and death.

American immigration policies increasingly criminalize asylum seekers, separating families and detaining children. Some U.S. churches resist; others align with nationalist ideologies.

Liberation theology reveals this crisis as an indictment of both sending and receiving nations.

E) TOWARD A THEOLOGY OF HOSPITALITY AND BORDERS

1. Hospitality as a Divine Command

Scripture repeatedly commands hospitality toward strangers:

- "You must not molest the stranger or oppress him, for you yourselves were once strangers in Egypt" (Exod 22:21, JB).
- Jesus identifies himself with the migrant: "I was a stranger and you made me welcome" (Matt 25:35, JB).

Hospitality is not optional; it is a criterion for salvation.

2. Rethinking Borders

Borders are human constructs, not divine mandates. They can serve the common good, but they often function as moral barriers that exclude the vulnerable.

A CLT perspective argues:

- Borders must serve human dignity.
- They cannot justify death, exclusion, or exploitation.
- National security cannot override moral responsibility.

3. Migrants as Gifts, Not Threats

Migration enriches receiving societies economically, culturally, and spiritually. Migrants bring resilience, creativity, faith, and labor. The fear-based narrative surrounding migrants is often politically manufactured.

4. From Charity to Justice

The Church must move beyond:

- food drives,
- clothing distributions,
- short-term aid.

It must embrace:

- advocacy for humane migration laws,
- resistance to xenophobia,
- accompaniment ministries,
- political pressure on unjust systems.

5. Building a Theology of Encounter

Pope Francis' theology of encounter emphasizes:

- face-to-face relationships,

- mutual recognition,
- rejection of fear,
- affirmation of shared humanity.

Hospitality is not giving from power but meeting as equals.

PART IV — FAITH, GENDER, AND THE BODY: TOWARD A LIBERATIVE ANTHROPOLOGY

Part IV develops the anthropological foundations of Critical-Liberative Theology (CLT), arguing that any authentic liberation must begin with a renewed understanding of the human person—embodied, dignified, relational, and free. Chapter 14 constructs a theological anthropology in which the body is not a site of suspicion but a sacramental locus of God's presence. Drawing from feminist, African, and liberationist perspectives, it affirms gender, sexuality, and moral agency as dimensions of human dignity rather than threats to doctrine. African philosophies of personhood—such as *ubuntu*—enrich this anthropology by emphasizing relationality, communal flourishing, and embodied humanity.

Chapter 15 exposes the exclusion of women from ecclesial leadership as a form of structural sin rooted in patriarchy. Through feminist-liberative critique and African women theologians—such as Oduyoye, Kanyoro, and Nadar—the chapter shows how ecclesial patriarchy distorts the Gospel and impedes the Church's mission. Contemporary debates in the global Synod reveal both resistance and hope for structural reform.

Chapter 16 revisits Bernard Häring's moral theology, applying CLT to issues of contraception and women's health. Reproductive justice is framed not as rebellion against doctrine but as an affirmation of life, autonomy, and maternal dignity—particularly urgent in contexts like Africa, where maternal mortality remains a theological scandal.

Chapter 17 critiques mandatory priestly celibacy as a structural injustice that restricts vocation, burdens clergy, and perpetuates psychological harm. Case studies from Africa and Latin America illuminate how celibacy contributes to priest shortages and pastoral failure, suggesting a need for historic reform.

Chapter 18 argues that LGBTQ+ inclusion is a Christological imperative grounded in Jesus' ministry of mercy, healing, and boundary-breaking love. The chapter examines persecution in Africa, pastoral challenges in the U.S., and the emerging call for sacramental inclusion rooted in justice and dignity.

Together, these chapters assert that liberation must be embodied, gendered, relational, and radically inclusive.

CHAPTER 14

The Human Person in Critical-Liberative Theology: Body, Embodiment, Freedom, and Moral Agency

A Foundational Theological Anthropology for Liberation

A) INTRODUCTION: WHY ANTHROPOLOGY IS THE HEART OF LIBERATION THEOLOGY

Every theology rests on an anthropology. The question *Who is the human being?* determines how we understand God, salvation, the Church, morality, and justice. When anthropology is distorted, theology becomes oppressive. When anthropology is truthful, theology becomes liberative.

Critical-Liberative Theology (CLT) insists that any serious theology of justice must begin with a renewed understanding of the human person as:

- embodied,
- relational,
- free,
- historically situated,
- creative,
- and morally responsible.

This chapter proposes a theological anthropology grounded in *imago Dei*—the belief that every human person bears the image of God (Gen 1:27, Jerusalem Bible). But unlike classical interpretations that equate divine image with rationality, spiritual capacity, or masculine authority, CLT expands *imago Dei* to include the entirety of human existence, especially the body, sexuality, relationality, and moral agency.

Imago Dei, expanded through CLT

CLT argues that human dignity derives not from abstract spiritual traits but from the concrete, lived, embodied reality of persons. To bear the image of God means:

- the body is sacred,
- freedom is essential,
- sexuality is dignified,
- autonomy is morally meaningful,
- relationship is constitutive,
- diversity reflects divine creativity,
- liberation is the expression of God's justice in history.

This broader understanding of *imago Dei* challenges patriarchal theologies that restrict moral agency, limit gender roles, demonize sexuality, or silence marginalized groups.

The Consequence of Anthropology in the Church

The Church's historical suspicion of the body and restrictive sexual ethics come from a flawed anthropology that:

- idealized celibacy over embodiment;
- cast women as sources of temptation;
- treated LGBTQ+ persons as defective or disordered;
- reduced sexuality to procreation;
- interpreted the body through dualistic, Platonic frameworks.

Liberation theology exposes the harm produced by these distortions—not only spiritual but psychological, political, and ecclesial.

Anthropology and Structural Sin

Oppression begins with false anthropology:

- Racism rests on the lie that some bodies are inferior.
- Patriarchy rests on the lie that women cannot lead.
- Homophobia rests on the lie that LGBTQ+ bodies contradict creation.
- Clericalism rests on the lie that priests possess higher spiritual dignity.
- Colonialism rests on the lie that Africans are less human.

These lies violate *imago Dei* and diminish the sacredness of *ntu*—the African life-force that constitutes human existence.

This chapter argues that liberation begins with reclaiming embodied dignity as the ground of theology.

B) THEOLOGICAL ANTHROPOLOGY IN CLT: PERSONHOOD, FREEDOM, AND DIGNITY

1. Personhood as Imago Dei: Beyond Rationality

Christian theology traditionally identified the divine image with intellect, soul, or rationality—traits associated with male, educated, Western bodies. CLT rejects such reduction. The divine image is not partial, but holistic:

- body,
- mind,
- emotion,
- history,
- sexuality,
- relationality,
- freedom.

To be human is to participate in divine dignity simply by existing. The human body—Black, African, female, disabled, queer, wounded—is a site of revelation.

2. Freedom as the Condition of Moral Agency

Karl Rahner argues that human persons are "hearers of the Word," beings whose freedom opens them to divine transcendence (Rahner, 1966). Freedom is not the luxury of elites but the core of humanity. CLT extends this: the oppressed possess full moral agency, even when institutions deny it.

To deny freedom—women's autonomy, LGBTQ+ personhood, the conscience of laypeople—is to deny *imago Dei*.

3. Sin as the Violation of Dignity

In classical theology, sin is often understood as voluntary wrongdoing by individuals. CLT reframes sin as:

- the distortion of personhood,
- the suppression of freedom,
- the violation of embodied dignity,
- the reduction of persons to objects,
- the collective and systemic violence embedded in structures.

Structural sin prevents human beings from flourishing as images of God. Liberation is therefore anthropological healing.

C) THE BODY AS SACRAMENTAL: A CLT RESPONSE TO BODY-SUSPICIOUS THEOLOGIES

1. Incarnation and the Affirmation of Embodiment

"The Word became flesh" (John 1:14). God's self-revelation is not abstract; it is bodily. Jesus heals, touches, embraces. Salvation unfolds through bodies: crucified, risen, feeding, suffering, rejoicing. The sacraments are embodied signs—bread, wine, water, oil, touch.

Any theology that fears the body contradicts the very heart of Christianity.

2. Sexuality as Relational Goodness

CLT rejects moral frameworks that treat sexuality primarily as danger, temptation, or impurity. Sexual desire is:

- relational,
- communicative,
- a form of vulnerability,
- a site of mutuality and self-gift,
- a dimension of divine creativity.

Ethics must center consent, equality, justice, and mutual flourishing, not fear or control.

3. Gender as Sacred Diversity

Gender is not a hierarchy but a prism of divine creativity. Patriarchal anthropologies that restrict leadership to men violate the inclusive vision of Galatians 3:28 and suppress the Spirit's gifts in women and gender-diverse persons.

CLT affirms:

- women's full moral and ecclesial agency,
- LGBTQ+ dignity,
- gender diversity as part of creation's multiplicity.

D) AFRICAN THEOLOGICAL ANTHROPOLOGY: UBUNTU, NTU, AND ANTHROPOLOGICAL PAUPERIZATION

African conceptions of personhood enrich CLT by offering relational, embodied, and holistic anthropologies capable of resisting Western dualism and ecclesial patriarchy.

1. Ubuntu and the Communal Self

Ubuntu ("I am because we are") asserts that personhood is constitutive, not individualistic.[1] Dignity arises from:

- mutual recognition,
- solidarity,
- shared flourishing,
- communal identity.

Oppression tears communities apart and dehumanizes persons.

2. Engelbert Mveng and Anthropological Pauperization

Mveng identifies three forms of colonial and postcolonial oppression:

- material pauperization,
- cultural pauperization,
- anthropological pauperization—the deepest form.

Anthropological pauperization is the theft of humanity itself. It reduces Africans to objects of exploitation, strips cultural meaning, and destroys the ability to imagine oneself as a dignified, free subject of history.[2]

Liberation, therefore, must restore humanity, not just resources.

3. *Ntu*: The African Metaphysics of Life-Force

The Bantu concept *Ntu*—as articulated by V.Y. Mudimbe, Tempels, and Kibangou—describes the vital energy, relational force, and unity of spirit-body-community in African anthropology.

Ntu affirms:

- embodiment as sacred,
- sexuality as vitality,
- community as ontology,

---

1. Mbiti, *African Religions and Philosophy*.
2. Mveng, *L'Afrique dans L'Église*.

- diversity as life,
- relational autonomy as freedom.

Oppression is metaphysical violence because it diminishes *ntu*.

4. African Holism Against Dualism

African anthropology rejects body-soul dualism. Personhood is unity. Thus, any theology that denigrates the body, condemns sexuality, or restricts gendered embodiment violates African personhood and diminishes *ntu*.

E) THEOLOGY OF THE BODY (TOB) AND CLT: POINTS OF CONVERGENCE AND CONFLICT

1. What Theology of the Body Gets Right

John Paul II's Theology of the Body (TOB) affirms:

- the goodness of the body,
- the dignity of sexuality,
- the nuptial meaning of self-gift,
- embodiment as revelation.

These insights align with CLT's affirmation of embodiment. TOB is a corrective to earlier Catholic suspicion of the body, and CLT acknowledges its strengths.

2. Where TOB Falls Short

Despite its beauty, TOB operates within a narrow anthropology shaped by:

- heteronormativity,
- patriarchal complementarity,
- biologism,
- Eurocentric cultural assumptions,

- normative idealization of celibacy,
- moral suspicion of non-procreative sexuality.

a. Gender Complementarity

TOB treats men and women as essentially different in ways that justify gender hierarchy. CLT rejects this because:

- complementarity reduces women's freedom;
- it excludes women from leadership;
- it ignores gender diversity;
- it is culturally Western, not universal.

b. Sexuality as Exclusively Heterosexual and Procreative

TOB cannot make sense of:

- LGBTQ+ identities,
- non-procreative sexual love,
- embodied relationality beyond marriage.

  CLT views this as an anthropological deficiency.

c. Idealization of Celibacy

TOB continues a tradition that glorifies celibacy as superior. CLT counters:

- celibacy is a discipline, not a divine ontology,
- celibacy often produces unhealthy repression,
- forced celibacy contributes to abuse crises,
- embodied sexuality is not inferior.

d. The Absence of Structural Analysis

TOB individualizes sexuality without addressing:

- patriarchy,
- colonialism,
- racism,
- economic oppression,
- anthropological pauperization.

A theology of the body that ignores structural sin cannot be liberative.

3. CLT as a Liberative Theology of the Body

CLT offers a more expansive vision:

- the body as site of revelation and resistance;
- sexuality as relational justice;
- gender as diverse expression of *imago Dei*;
- liberation as restoration of vitality (*ntu*);
- embodiment as political and spiritual.

Where TOB idealizes, CLT historicizes. Where TOB moralizes, CLT liberates.

F) CONCLUSION: TOWARD A LIBERATIVE THEOLOGICAL ANTHROPOLOGY

Oppression begins with false anthropologies; liberation begins with reclaiming the sacredness of embodied human life. CLT proposes that every person—woman, man, queer, African, migrant, disabled, impoverished—is a living sacrament of God's liberating presence.

This anthropology grounds:

- women's full equality (Ch. 14),
- reproductive justice (Ch. 15),
- celibacy reform (Ch. 16),
- LGBTQ+ inclusion (Ch. 17).

To deny any person's dignity is to deny *imago Dei*, destroy *ntu*, and perpetuate anthropological pauperization.

Liberation begins with the human body—because God's love became flesh.

CHAPTER 15

Women, Power, and the Structural Sin of Ecclesial Exclusion

A Critical-Liberative Theology of Gender, Sacramentality, and Equal Vocation

I. INTRODUCTION: NAMING THE STRUCTURAL SIN OF PATRIARCHY

THE EXCLUSION OF WOMEN from ordained ministry, from positions of juridical authority, and from meaningful participation in ecclesial decision-making is not an unfortunate accident of history; it is a persistent pattern of structural sin embedded within the institutional life of the Roman Catholic Church. As liberation theologians have long insisted, sin is not confined to personal moral failure. It is woven into unjust systems, institutional arrangements, cultural assumptions, and patterns of domination that distort the dignity of God's people. Gustavo Gutiérrez described structural sin as "the crystallization of injustice within social, political, and religious arrangements that perpetuate marginalization."[1] When applied internally to the Church, the charge is unavoidable: patriarchy functions as a structural sin that contradicts the Gospel's demands of justice, equality, and human flourishing.

The Church proclaims a God who liberates the oppressed, yet internally maintains structures that deny women's full equality. It teaches that every baptized person shares equally in the dignity of the *Imago Dei* (Genesis 1:27, Jerusalem Bible), yet restricts sacramental and juridical

---

1. Gutiérrez, *A Theology of Liberation*.

authority to men. It condemns misogyny in society but upholds ecclesial practices rooted in androcentric anthropology and medieval legal categories. This contradiction is not merely theoretical; it has material, spiritual, and pastoral consequences for the global Church, especially in communities where women sustain the ecclesial mission through catechesis, healthcare, education, and social service.

This chapter offers a systematic liberation-theological critique of ecclesial patriarchy as structural sin. It argues for the full inclusion of women in all ministries and offices of the Church—not merely as a concession to contemporary culture, but as a requirement of Gospel fidelity. The arguments used to exclude women from ordained ministry are shown to be theologically weak, philosophically incoherent, historically inaccurate, and pastorally harmful. Furthermore, the chapter situates the struggle for women's equality within global feminist, womanist, and African theological movements, integrating insights from Mercy Amba Oduyoye, Teresa Okure, Elisabeth Schüssler Fiorenza, and others.

While affirming the dignity of unborn life and opposing abortion as a tragic violation of human flourishing, the chapter rejects the ideological use of abortion debates to marginalize women within the Church or deny them leadership, sacramental authority, or vocational legitimacy. A liberationist ethic insists that protecting unborn life must go hand in hand with dismantling all structures that deny the dignity, agency, and full humanity of women.

The goal of this chapter is not to propose minor reforms, but to articulate the theological foundations of a radical structural conversion: a Church in which women and men share fully and equally in sacramental ministry, governance, theological authority, and every dimension of Christian life.

II. THEOLOGICAL ANTHROPOLOGY AND THE IMAGO DEI

2.1. Imago Dei as the Ground of Equality

The foundational error in patriarchal ecclesiology is anthropological. A distorted understanding of the human person has shaped ecclesial structures, sacramental theology, and canon law. The biblical witness begins not with hierarchy but with the equal dignity of all persons created in the image of God: "God created man in the image of himself, in the image of God he created him, male and female he created them" (Genesis 1:27, Jerusalem Bible). There is no hierarchy in the text: male and female together constitute the image of God. No sex more fully represents God; no gender is more capable of mediating grace.

Liberation theology interprets the *Imago Dei* relationally and communally. Human beings reflect God not through biological attributes but through capacity for freedom, love, justice, and solidarity. Rahner famously argued that the human person is "the event of God's self-communication," a reality that transcends gender.[2] If God's self-communication is universal and unrestricted by biology, then the capacity to symbolize Christ in sacramental ministry cannot be limited to male physicality.

2.2. Embodiment and the Sacramentality of the Human Body

Catholic theology rightly affirms the sacramentality of the body, yet it has often reduced sacramental representation to male anatomy. This reductionism contradicts the Church's own theological framework. If the body is sacramental because it reveals God, then the bodies of women—not only men—are icons of divine grace. Women's bodies do not diminish the image of Christ; they expand it.

The overemphasis on male embodiment reflects not divine intention but historical patriarchy. As Schüssler Fiorenza argues, early Church leadership was shaped by Greco-Roman public norms, in which women were barred from public authority.[3] These cultural constraints were absorbed into Christian practice, later misinterpreted as divine law.

2.3. African Anthropologies: Ubuntu, *Ntu*, and the Communion of Dignity

African theological anthropology strengthens the liberationist critique. African philosophies such as *ubuntu* ("I am because we are") and *ntu*,[4] a Bantu metaphysical category describing the relational interconnectedness

---

2. Rahner, *Foundations of Christian Faith*.
3. Fiorenza, *In Memory of Her*.
4. Kibangou, *The Mvengian Vision of Anthropological Pauperization*; Kibangou, *La Philosophie Bantoue de L'être*.

of all existence, emphasize the communal and relational nature of personhood. Dignity flows from belonging, not hierarchy; from participation, not exclusion.

Engelbert Mveng's concept of anthropological pauperization further clarifies the stakes.[5] He argues that colonialism and ongoing global injustices have stripped African peoples of cultural, spiritual, and anthropological identity. The exclusion of women from full ecclesial participation is another form of anthropological pauperization—this time inflicted not by colonial powers but by the Church itself. When women are denied sacramental authority, their full personhood is diminished in the ecclesial sphere, perpetuating a spiritual poverty that mirrors social and economic marginalization.

2.4. Liberation Anthropology: Equal Call, Equal Dignity

A liberationist theological anthropology insists:

- All persons are equal in dignity.
- All vocations originate from the Holy Spirit.
- Embodiment is not a basis for exclusion.
- Patriarchal hierarchy distorts the image of God.

This anthropology is incompatible with restricting ordained ministry to men.

III. THE HISTORICAL CONSTRUCTION OF PATRIARCHY IN THE CHURCH

3.1. Patriarchy as a Historical—Not Divine—Inheritance

To expose patriarchal exclusion as structural sin, it is essential to disentangle divine revelation from the historical, cultural, and political systems that shaped the early Church. Too often, arguments against women's ordination rely on the presumption that the Church's current

---

5. Mveng, *L'Afrique dans L'Église*.

patriarchal system flows directly from Jesus rather than from Greco-Roman patriarchy, Roman law, medieval canon structures, or post-Tridentine clericalism.

Elisabeth Schüssler Fiorenza argues convincingly that Christianity emerged within a profoundly patriarchal culture in which women were legally minors, excluded from public authority, and restricted to domestic roles.[6] These constraints deeply influenced early Christian practices. When the Church later codified structures of ministry, it absorbed these cultural norms, treating them as normative rather than historically contingent.

The result is a form of "sanctified patriarchy," where unjust structures are retroactively presented as divine will. Liberation theology calls this what it is: a theological distortion that turns cultural bias into supposed revelation.

3.2. Greco-Roman Legal Categories and the Exclusion of Women

The Roman Empire prohibited women from holding public office, governing male subjects, or representing others in legal matters. These restrictions had nothing to do with theology—they were civil laws grounded in patriarchal assumptions about reason, authority, and public virtue.

When the early Church developed its ministries, it relied heavily on Roman administrative models, especially as it grew after Constantine. Roman patriarchal norms became ecclesial norms. Later theologians constructed post hoc theological justifications for practices that had originally been matters of secular law, not divine command.

This explains why historical evidence of women deacons and prominent women leaders could later be suppressed or reinterpreted. The shift was political and cultural, not theological.

3.3. Augustine, Aquinas, and the Ambiguities of Tradition

Augustine's anthropology contains both liberative and restrictive elements. While he affirmed that women are created equally in God's image *spiritually*, he adopted Neo-Platonic assumptions that aligned femininity with weakness and concupiscence. Aquinas, shaped by Aristotle's

---

6. Fiorenza, *In Memory of Her*.

biological claims, explicitly called woman "misbegotten,"[7] reflecting the scientific views of his time rather than revelation.

It is unjust and theologically incoherent to bind the Church permanently to the scientific errors or patriarchal assumptions of medieval Europe. Rahner warned that theology must distinguish between historically conditioned expressions and the timeless truth of revelation.[8] The Church's current stance fails this distinction.

3.4. Medieval Canon Law and the Consolidation of Male-Only Power

Canon law systematically codified male supremacy in ordained ministry:

- Only men could hold jurisdictional power.
- Women were legally barred from liturgical roles.
- Monasteries of women were placed under male control.
- Mystical women were revered but denied governance.

The law was organized around the assumption that women were unfit for public, juridical, or sacramental authority. This was not theology—it was medieval sociology turned into canon law.

3.5. Erasure of Women in the Early Church

Multiple historical sources—inscriptions, letters, liturgical manuals—show evidence of:

- Women deacons (*diakonoi*)
- Women presbyters (*presbytides*)
- Women apostles (Junia; cf. Romans 16:7, JB)
- Women who presided over house churches
- Women performing liturgical and pastoral leadership

The later erasure of these roles is one of the most severe distortions of tradition. As Fiorenza notes, the tradition that excludes women is not

---

7. Aquinas, *Summa Theologica* I, q. 92, a. 1.
8. Rahner, *Foundations of Christian Faith*.

apostolic but androcentric—constructed by later male leaders who reinterpreted early evidence through patriarchal lenses.[9]

3.6. Patriarchy and the Political Economy of Power

Leonardo Boff argues that clericalism is always tied to the preservation of institutional power.[10] The exclusion of women must therefore be interpreted through the lens of political economy:

- Male priesthood concentrated control over sacraments, resources, and governance.
- Excluding women prevented challenges to male authority.
- Patriarchy preserved institutional stability but contradicted Gospel justice.

This is structural sin: injustice embedded not merely in individuals but in the very architecture of the Church.

IV. CRITIQUING THE THEOLOGICAL ARGUMENTS AGAINST WOMEN'S ORDINATION

The Church's refusal to ordain women rests primarily on three arguments:

1. Apostolic precedent — Jesus chose only male apostles.
2. In persona Christi — Priests must resemble Christ in maleness.
3. Unbroken Tradition — The Church has "always done this."

Liberation theology evaluates these not as isolated claims but as ideological structures serving patriarchy.

4.1. *Ordinatio Sacerdotalis* (1994): A Critical Analysis

Pope John Paul II's *Ordinatio Sacerdotalis* is the most frequently cited document defending the exclusion of women from priesthood. It claims

---

9. Fiorenza, *In Memory of Her*.
10. Boff, *Church: Charism and Power*.

the Church has "no authority whatsoever" to ordain women and that this judgment must be considered "definitive."

However, a closer analysis reveals several theological, historical, and ecclesiological flaws:

4.1.1. Ordinatio Sacerdotalis is not an infallible ex cathedra statement

The Congregation for the Doctrine of the Faith attempted to interpret O.S. as infallible, but this interpretation was rejected by numerous theologians, canonists, and bishops. Even Pope Francis has stated that the matter is still under theological examination.

Canon law[11] states that no teaching is presumed infallible unless clearly so defined. O.S. lacks:

- The intent to define ex cathedra
- A conciliar affirmation
- Reception by the sensus fidelium

Therefore, it cannot bind the Church irreversibly.

4.1.2. Historical error: the claim of unbroken male-only ministry

Modern scholarship—including discovered inscriptions, liturgical texts, and archaeological evidence—contradicts the claim that the Church has *always* excluded women. Women served as deacons, leaders, and prominent ministers.

4.1.3. The Christological reductionism of "male resemblance"

To claim that Christ's maleness is essential for sacramental representation is to deny the universality of redemption. It contradicts Galatians 3:28: "There is neither male nor female; for you are all one in Christ Jesus" (JB).

It also makes male anatomy a sacramental category—a theological move with no grounding in Scripture or tradition.

---

11. CIC 749 §3.

4.1.4. The document declines to engage the development of doctrine

Newman insisted that doctrine develops organically in response to new contexts.[12] O.S. freezes the tradition in a selective historical moment, ignoring centuries of doctrinal evolution.

4.1.5. Liberation critique: O.S. upholds patriarchy rather than Gospel justice

Liberation theology measures truth by its fruits (Matthew 7:16) and by whether a teaching promotes justice. O.S., by perpetuating institutional misogyny, fails this criterion.

4.2. In Persona Christi: The Major Theological Error

This argument claims a priest must be male because Christ was male. Liberationists identify multiple errors:

1. It reduces Christ's salvific role to biology.
2. It contradicts Christological universality.
3. It ignores that sacraments are effective by grace, not resemblance.
4. It is rooted in patriarchal symbolism, not divine revelation.

Christ's ability to represent humanity before God is based on His humanity—not His male sex. To require maleness for sacramental representation would imply:

- Christ can only represent men
- Women are ontologically dissimilar to Christ
- Male physical traits are spiritually superior

This borders on heresy. The Council of Chalcedon affirmed Christ's full humanity—not male-specific anatomy—as the basis of salvation.

4.3. Apostolic Precedent: A Misreading of Scripture

The argument that Jesus chose only male apostles ignores essential facts:

---

12. Newman, *An Essay on the Development of Christian Doctrine*.

- Jesus also had women disciples (Luke 8:1–3).
- Women were the first witnesses of the Resurrection (Luke 24:1–10).
- The early house churches were led by women (e.g., Lydia, Priscilla).
- Paul names Junia "prominent among the apostles" (Romans 16:7, JB).

The selection of twelve men reflects symbolic continuity with the twelve tribes, not a normative rule for ministry.

4.4. "Unbroken Tradition": A Theological Fiction

Tradition is not static; it is interpretive. Evidence of women's leadership has been minimized or erased. The claim of an unbroken tradition of male-only ministry is historically unsustainable.

V. STRUCTURAL SIN AND VOCATIONAL INJUSTICE

5.1. Patriarchy as Institutionalized Violence Against Women's Vocations

Liberation theology names injustice where it occurs—not simply in the secular sphere, but inside ecclesial structures. The exclusion of women from ordained ministry is not merely a disciplinary mistake or a prudential decision. It is a form of institutional violence against vocation. It is structural sin because it:

- Distorts the emergence of the Spirit's gifts
- Maims the ecclesial Body by amputating half its potential
- Creates spiritual insecurity, shame, and diminished belonging
- Contradicts the very nature of Church as communion

The Church teaches that the Holy Spirit calls whom God wills (1 Corinthians 12:11). Yet it simultaneously restricts the discernment of vocation to male bodies—a contradiction that cannot be reconciled theologically. Sin always wounds; in this case, it wounds both the women whose calls are stifled and the Church deprived of their leadership.

5.2. The Theology of "Silence" and Its Consequences

The refusal to question unjust structures is itself a manifestation of sin. Silence becomes complicity. African bishops, European clergy, Latin American episcopal conferences, and Vatican dicasteries routinely avoid public discussion of women's ordination—not because the theological debate is settled, but because patriarchal norms dominate ecclesial culture.

This silence has several consequences:

- It suppresses the discernment of women whose vocation is authentic.
- It teaches the faithful that God's grace is limited by gender.
- It delegitimizes feminist, womanist, and mujerista contributions.
- It weakens confidence in synodality and ecclesial reform.

5.3. Economic Exploitation of Women Religious

Women religious sustain Catholic schools, hospitals, catechetical programs, orphanages, humanitarian agencies, and spiritual retreats around the world. They often do so while living in economic precarity, receiving minimal support from diocesan structures that rely on their unpaid or underpaid labor.[13] Male clergy benefit from their work while retaining all jurisdiction, sacramental authority, and financial control.

This is a structural echo of global capitalism, where women provide foundational labor but are denied leadership and compensation. Liberation theology calls this by its proper name: sinful exploitation.

5.4. Clericalism and the Culture of Male Spiritual Superiority

Pope Francis has warned repeatedly about clericalism as "a perversion of the priesthood."[14] Yet clericalism is inseparable from patriarchy. Clericalism thrives because it is linked to male privilege, justified through theological language.

When ordination is reserved for men:

- Men become the sole arbiters of orthodoxy.

---

13. Guglielmi, *The Crisis of Vocation*.
14. Francis, *Address of His Holiness Pope Francis to the Roman Curia*.

- Men control sacramental access.
- Men dominate all ecclesial governance.
- Women become perpetual dependents, spiritually and institutionally.

This asymmetry corrupts the ecclesial vision of the People of God and reinforces the sin of domination.

VI. JESUS AND THE DIGNITY OF WOMEN: A COUNTERCULTURAL WITNESS

6.1. Women and Inferiority in First-Century Judaism

To understand the revolutionary nature of Jesus' actions, one must appreciate the deeply patriarchal context of first-century Judaism:

- Women could not testify legally in court.
- Women were often considered ritually impure.
- Women were excluded from key religious functions.
- Rabbinic literature sometimes portrayed women as intellectually inferior.
- A pious Jewish man recited a prayer thanking God "for not making me a woman."

This cultural system did not come from Torah but from post-exilic patriarchy, Greco-Roman influences, and rabbinic interpretation. In this world, a woman was socially and religiously subordinate. The Church often relies on this historical context to justify modern exclusion, forgetting that Jesus did not affirm these hierarchies—He subverted them.

6.2. Christ's Liberative Encounter: "Woman, neither do I condemn you"

In the story of the woman caught in adultery (John 8:1–11), Jesus does not simply forgive sin. He challenges structural injustice. According to Jewish law, both parties in adultery should be stoned (Deuteronomy 22:22), but only the woman was brought forward—an act revealing misogynistic double standards.

Jesus intervenes prophetically. After disarming her accusers, he turns to her and says:

> "Woman, where are they? Has no one condemned you?"
> "No one, sir," she replied.
> "Neither do I condemn you," said Jesus. "Go away, and from this moment sin no more." *(John 8:10–11, Jerusalem Bible)*

This is not leniency. It is liberation. It is a public rejection of women's legal inferiority and a refusal to allow patriarchy to masquerade as divine justice.

6.3. The Samaritan Woman as Theologian and Evangelist

In John 4, Jesus speaks with a Samaritan woman in public—violating social norms. She becomes:

- The first recorded theologian of Christology ("Come see a man…").
- The first evangelist to Samaria.
- A symbol of cross-cultural, gender-transcending mission.

Jesus does not silence her. He commissions her.

6.4. Mary Magdalene: Apostle to the Apostles

Jesus gives Mary Magdalene the first Resurrection proclamation:

> "Go and tell my brothers…" *(John 20:17, JB)*

In a culture where women could not testify legally, Jesus entrusts the foundational Christian truth—the Resurrection—to a woman. This is deliberate theological disruption. It means:

- God entrusts authority to women.
- Women's witness is valid and foundational.
- The Resurrection itself inaugurates a new anthropology.

The Church's refusal to ordain women contradicts the very logic of Christ's ministry.

VII. AFRICAN WOMEN THEOLOGIANS AND THE GLOBAL STRUGGLE FOR JUSTICE

7.1. Mercy Amba Oduyoye and the Theology of Full Humanity

Oduyoye argues that African culture and the Church both marginalize women, creating a "double jeopardy." Liberation must occur in both spheres. She insists that salvation in Christ must include full humanity for women, not partial inclusion.

Her critique makes two essential claims:

1. Culture is not static, and harmful elements must be transformed.
2. The Church has no moral authority to challenge societal patriarchy while maintaining it internally.

7.2. Teresa Okure: Christology Without Patriarchy

Okure emphasizes that Jesus' maleness is *functionally incidental* to His salvific mission. Redemption flows from His humanity and divinity—not gender. Therefore, limiting sacramental representation to males contradicts both Christology and anthropology.

7.3. Musimbi Kanyoro: Cultural Hermeneutics and Women's Agency

Kanyoro's "cultural hermeneutics" critiques how African culture and Church teachings align to constrain women. She emphasizes the need to reinterpret cultural symbols in ways that promote liberation.

7.4. Womanist and Mujerista Parallels

Womanist theologians (e.g., Jacquelyn Grant, Delores Williams) highlight the intersection of racism and sexism.

- Mujerista theologians (Ada María Isasi-Díaz) highlight the daily oppression of Latina women.

Both strands contribute to a global liberationist understanding of women's marginalization within Christianity.

VIII. A LIBERATIVE CATHOLIC ETHIC ON ABORTION

8.1. Affirming the Dignity of Unborn Life

Critical-Liberative Theology affirms the sanctity of life. Abortion represents a tragic rupture in the continuum of human dignity. The unborn, like the poor and the oppressed, deserve protection. However, CLT refuses to weaponize this truth against women.

8.2. Structural Conditions That Lead to Abortion

Abortion often arises from:

- Poverty
- Gender-based violence
- Lack of access to healthcare
- Abandonment by male partners
- Cultural shame
- Clerical silence on women's struggles

Thus, abortion is not merely a personal moral failure; it is often the outcome of economic and social injustice.

8.3. Rejecting Misogynistic Framings

To oppose abortion is not to blame or condemn women. It is:

- To address structural violence
- To create social and ecclesial support
- To accompany rather than moralize

Any moral teaching that condemns women while ignoring structural injustice is distorted and un-Catholic.

8.4. Abortion Opposition Does Not Justify Excluding Women from Ordination

Some ecclesial voices use abortion as a rhetorical tool to delegitimize feminist theology or portray women as morally unreliable. Liberation theology rejects this manipulation. A woman's moral agency does not diminish her ability to represent Christ, lead communities, or exercise sacramental ministry.

IX. TOWARD STRUCTURAL CONVERSION: PATHWAYS OF REFORM FOR AN EGALITARIAN CHURCH

If patriarchy within the Catholic Church is a form of structural sin, then liberation requires not cosmetic adjustment but structural conversion—a transformation of the very architecture of ecclesial life. Liberation theology demands action in history; it rejects all theoretical solutions that do not concretely transform unjust conditions. In this spirit, the following reforms are not optional: they are the necessary steps toward restoring Gospel authenticity.

9.1. Restoring the Female Diaconate: A Non-Negotiable First Step

9.1.1. Historical Evidence

The existence of women deacons in the early Church is beyond serious scholarly dispute. Inscriptions (e.g., the tomb of Deaconess Sophia), patristic writings (e.g., Canon 19 of Nicaea), and liturgical manuals demonstrate that women:

- Assisted in baptisms
- Performed anointings
- Distributed communion
- Led communities
- Engaged in pastoral care
- Handled women's confessions in some regions

The argument that their role was merely "disciplinary" or "non-sacramental" collapses under historical scrutiny.

9.1.2. *Theological Necessity*

Restoring the female diaconate would:

- Affirm women's sacramental capacity
- Break the symbolic monopoly of male liturgical presence
- Provide real pastoral support in communities
- Signal a move away from patriarchal structures

Most importantly, it would confront the false anthropology that denies women sacramental representation.

9.2. Opening the Priesthood and Episcopacy to Women

9.2.1. *Priesthood as a Charism, Not a Gendered Privilege*

The priesthood is not a biological entitlement but a charism of service. It makes no theological sense to argue that a woman's body—created in the Imago Dei, redeemed in Christ, filled with the Spirit—is incapable of sacramental representation.

9.2.2. *Arguments Against Women Priests Are Theologically and Philosophically Weak*

Philosophically: Representation is symbolic, not anatomical.

- Biblically: Christ chose women as primary witnesses.
- Anthropologically: Women have equal moral and spiritual agency.
- Historically: Early Christian communities were far more diverse.
- Doctrinally: No dogma defines priesthood as male-only.

Ordinatio Sacerdotalis (1994) does not settle the debate because:

- It is not infallible.
- It rests on historically incorrect claims.
- It lacks engagement with theological development.
- It contradicts Gospel liberation and the sensus fidelium.

9.2.3. *The Pastoral Crisis Demands Women's Leadership*

Around the world:

- Parishes close due to priest shortages.
- Women already function as de facto pastors in many rural missions.
- The sacramental starvation of communities contradicts pastoral charity.

The refusal to ordain women is no longer merely unjust—it is pastorally destructive.

9.3. Decoupling Jurisdiction from Ordination

9.3.1. *Jurisdiction Is Not Intrinsic to Holy Orders*

Canon law currently ties governance (jurisdiction) to ordination, effectively placing all major decision-making in the hands of ordained men. Yet history shows:

- Medieval abbesses exercised jurisdiction.
- Lay cardinals existed in the early Church.
- Bishops once relied heavily on elected lay councils.

Jurisdiction is an administrative function, not a sacramental one.

9.3.2. *Structural Reform: Shared and Decentralized Governance*

The Church must:

- Allow women (and lay men) to lead diocesan curias
- Permit women to serve as chancellors, tribunal judges, vicars general
- Create genuinely authoritative parish and diocesan councils
- Require bishops to share financial and personnel decisions

This is not optional; without shared governance, synodality becomes theatrics.

9.4. Liturgical and Linguistic Reform: De-Patriarchalizing Worship

9.4.1. God-Language Must Reflect the Fullness of Revelation

To refer to God exclusively with masculine titles is both theologically inaccurate and spiritually harmful. Although Scripture uses male metaphors, it also describes God:

- As a mother (Isaiah 49:15; 66:13)
- As a woman in labor (Isaiah 42:14)
- As a hen gathering her chicks (Matthew 23:37)

Liturgical language must reflect this scriptural diversity. If God-language remains patriarchal, the imagination of the faithful will continue to equate holiness with maleness.

9.4.2. Marian Devotion Must Be Liberative, Not Submissive

Liberation theology reclaims Mary as:

- Prophet of justice (Magnificat)
- Voice of the poor
- Disrupter of oppressive systems

Not as a model of passive obedience.
The Church often uses Mary to keep women silent. The true Mary—bold, prophetic, revolutionary—breaks this mold.

9.5. Economic Justice for Women Religious

Reform must include:

- Just wages
- Direct control over finances
- Representation on all Church governing boards
- Accountability for exploitation
- Transparent resource allocation

Justice begins where money is—because money reveals power.

9.6. Formation and Education: Dismantling Patriarchal Theologies

Seminaries must teach:

- Feminist theology
- Womanist theology
- African women's theology
- Historical-critical analysis of patriarchy
- Anthropological critiques of ecclesial culture

Without intellectual conversion, no structural conversion can succeed.

X. CONCLUSION: THE FUTURE CHURCH AND THE FULLNESS OF THE GOSPEL

The exclusion of women from ordained ministry and governance is not a matter of preference, tradition, or cultural sensitivity. It is a crisis of theological integrity, a contradiction at the heart of the Church's self-definition as sacrament of justice, liberation, and communion.

10.1. The Church Cannot Evangelize While Oppressing Its Own Members

If the Church hopes to challenge:

- Dictatorship
- Capitalist exploitation
- Racism
- Ecological destruction
- Colonial legacies
- Violence against the poor

It must dismantle its own internal structures of inequality. The Church loses moral credibility when it opposes injustice externally but maintains it internally.

10.2. Women's Liberation Is Ecclesial Liberation

To ordain women is not to capitulate to modernity. It is:

- To follow the liberating example of Christ
- To restore early Christian diversity
- To embody the radical equality of the Gospel
- To honor the Spirit's gifts in all people
- To dismantle the structural sin of patriarchy

The liberation of women is inseparable from the liberation of the Church itself.

10.3. The Spirit Is Speaking Through the *Sensus Fidelium*

The global Synod revealed an overwhelming desire for women to share in:

- Preaching
- Governance
- Diaconal ministry
- Sacramental life

When the faithful speak with such unity—across continents, cultures, and generations—the Spirit is at work.

10.4. The Church Will Either Change or Become Irrelevant

The refusal to ordain women is a refusal to listen to the Spirit, a refusal to honor the equality of the *Imago Dei*, and a refusal to follow Christ's liberative example.

A Church that excludes half of humanity cannot fully reveal the God who created all in Love. A Church that silences women cannot speak with prophetic truth. A Church that denies women sacramental agency cannot embody the inclusive Body of Christ.

The future belongs to a Church that welcomes women fully—at the altar, in the pulpit, in the episcopate, in the papal conclave. Anything less compromises the Gospel.

CHAPTER 16

Contraception, Women's Health, and Moral Freedom

THE QUESTION OF CONTRACEPTION sits at one of the most contested crossroads in Catholic moral theology. It touches the intimate space of marital love, the concrete realities of women's bodies, and the structural conditions of poverty, health, and gender power. It has also become a fault-line between official doctrine and the lived experience of many Catholic families, particularly in the Global South, where women bear disproportionate burdens of maternal mortality, economic precarity, and social expectation.

In this chapter, I revisit the debate on non-abortive contraception through the lens of Critical-Liberative Theology (CLT), in dialogue with the moral method of Bernard Häring. While I remain firmly opposed to abortion as the deliberate destruction of nascent life, I argue that non-abortive contraceptive methods can be morally permissible—and in many cases morally urgent—when evaluated in light of women's health, human dignity, and structural justice.

Bernard Häring's personalist and proportionalist ethics provide a way to move beyond a purely legalistic reading of *Humanae Vitae* toward a more integrated discernment that takes seriously intention, consequences, and social context.[1] Liberation theology presses that method further, insisting that theological ethics must begin from the cry of the poor and the oppressed—in this case, the cry of women whose bodies and futures are at stake.[2]

---

1. Häring, *The Law of Christ*.
2. Gutiérrez, *A Theology of Liberation*; Boff and Boff, *Introducing Liberation Theology*.

The argument unfolds in six steps: first, a brief sketch of Häring's moral framework; second, the integration of CLT and reproductive justice; third, comparative religious perspectives on non-abortive contraception; fourth, a focused look at women's health and maternal mortality in Africa; fifth, an ethical synthesis; and finally, pastoral and ecclesial implications.

1. BERNARD HÄRING'S MORAL METHOD: PERSONALISM AND PROPORTIONALITY

Bernard Häring was one of the most influential Catholic moral theologians of the twentieth century. His work helped move Catholic ethics away from a narrow, act-centered legalism toward a personalist, Christocentric, and scriptural approach. Rather than starting from abstract prohibitions, Häring insists that moral discernment engages the whole person in relationship—with God, with others, and within concrete historical circumstances.[3]

At the heart of his method lies the classical tripartite analysis of human acts:

1. The object of the act (what is done)
2. The intention of the agent (why it is done)
3. The circumstances surrounding the act (how, when, to whom, and with what effects)

Häring does not deny that some acts may be intrinsically disordered, yet he insists that many moral questions require careful evaluation of intention and circumstances. Moral evaluation is not a mechanical application of rules but a discerning search for fidelity to Christ in concrete situations.

In matters of sexuality and family life, Häring maintains the traditional Catholic conviction that marital intercourse has both unitive and procreative meanings. However, he resists reducing these meanings to physical biology alone. They must be understood in the context of the couple's vocation, the health of the spouses, the well-being of children, and the demands of justice in their environment. Here his method creates

---

3. Häring, *The Law of Christ*.

space for deeper reflection on non-abortive contraception—methods that prevent conception without destroying nascent life.

Within such a framework, non-abortive contraception cannot simply be dismissed by an a priori label. It must be evaluated in light of:

- the couple's intention (e.g., responsible parenthood, protection of health),
- the foreseeable consequences (e.g., avoidance of grave harm, reduction of maternal mortality),
- the broader circumstances (e.g., poverty, lack of medical care, social expectations on women).

This is precisely where Critical-Liberative Theology becomes indispensable.

2. CRITICAL-LIBERATIVE THEOLOGY AND REPRODUCTIVE JUSTICE

Liberation theology insists that moral theology begins not from a neutral, abstract vantage point, but from the underside of history—from the perspective of those who suffer structural injustice.[4] Ethics that ignore the lived realities of the poor, of women, of marginalized communities, risk becoming complicit with oppression.

Applied to contraception, a CLT perspective asks probing questions:

- Who suffers when non-abortive contraception is prohibited or stigmatized?
- Whose bodies are exposed to repeated high-risk pregnancies without adequate care?
- Who bears the burden of raising many children in poverty when reproductive autonomy is denied?
- How do cultural patriarchy and ecclesial patriarchy intersect to restrict women's moral agency?

In many African, Asian, and Latin American contexts, women already carry the weight of unpaid care work, domestic labor, and informal economic activity. They are often denied equal access to education and

---

4. Gutiérrez, *A Theology of Liberation*; Boff and Boff, *Introducing Liberation Theology*.

formal employment. When religious authorities then insist on strict rejection of all non-abortive contraception, without regard to circumstances, the result can be a double oppression: cultural and ecclesial, material and spiritual.

CLT insists that any moral norm must be evaluated in light of its real effects on the poor. A teaching that leads to preventable maternal deaths, heightened vulnerability, and entrenched gender inequality requires serious re-examination. To say this is not to capitulate to secularism; it is to take seriously the Gospel's own criteria: "By their fruits you will know them" (Matthew 7:16, Jerusalem Bible).

Häring's proportionalism offers a way to integrate these concerns. If morality involves weighing the proportion between good and evil effects of an action, then policies that foreseeably produce grave harm for women and children must be questioned, even if they are justified by appealing to the "objective structure" of the marital act. CLT presses that question urgently, in the name of the preferential option for the poor—here, concretely, the preferential option for women whose bodies are not abstractions but sites of risk, suffering, and hope.

3. NON-ABORTIVE CONTRACEPTION: MORAL DISTINCTIONS AND POSSIBILITIES

Non-abortive contraception includes methods that prevent conception without destroying an already fertilized egg. These methods range from barrier methods (condoms, diaphragms) and hormonal pills that inhibit ovulation, to copper or hormonal intrauterine devices and morally sound forms of natural family planning. They are distinct from abortifacient methods, which terminate pregnancy or prevent implantation after fertilization.[5]

Within a CLT-inspired rereading of Häring, three key points emerge:

1. Avoidance of abortion remains non-negotiable. The direct taking of nascent human life is morally unacceptable and incompatible with Christian reverence for the vulnerable.

2. Non-abortive contraception does not share this intrinsic moral structure. Its moral evaluation therefore depends heavily on intention and circumstances, not only on its physical mechanism.

---

5. Steinberg, *Contraception and Moral Theology*.

3. When intended to protect health, promote responsible parenthood, and prevent grave harm to women and children, non-abortive contraception can be a morally responsible choice.

Consider the intention of a woman in rural Cameroon, Nigeria, or South Sudan, whose health has been severely weakened by multiple pregnancies, poor nutrition, and lack of obstetric care. Another pregnancy may pose a significant risk to her life. Non-abortive contraception in such a case is not a selfish refusal of life but a rational act of care for life—her own life and the lives of her existing children.

Häring's framework allows us to see that moral discernment in this case is not about individual disobedience to abstract rules, but about the call to preserve life, steward limited resources, and act responsibly in a context of structural vulnerability.[6]

4. COMPARATIVE RELIGIOUS PERSPECTIVES ON CONTRACEPTION

The Catholic prohibition of "artificial" contraception is not universally shared even among Christian traditions, nor among other monotheistic religions. A comparative glance helps situate the Catholic debate within a wider moral horizon.

4.1. Protestant Traditions

Many mainline Protestant churches, such as the Evangelical Lutheran Church in America (ELCA) and the United Methodist Church, regard non-abortive contraception as morally legitimate and often as positively responsible. Couples are encouraged to plan their families with an eye to health, economic stability, and the well-being of children.[7]

From a liberation perspective, this approach recognizes that unregulated fertility in contexts of poverty can perpetuate suffering and limit children's access to education, nutrition, and healthcare. Contraception, in such settings, becomes part of a broader ethic of justice and stewardship.

---

6. Häring, *The Law of Christ*.
7. Fletcher, *Ethics and Human Reproduction in Protestant Thought*.

4.2. Eastern Orthodoxy

The Orthodox churches, while emphasizing the sacredness of marriage and the value of children, often adopt a pastorally flexible stance. Non-abortive contraception may be permitted under spiritual guidance when it serves the welfare of the family, protects maternal health, or responds to serious economic and social conditions.[8]

The key is not legalistic prohibition but discernment, carried out in dialogue with spiritual mentors. This pastoral model resonates with CLT by taking context seriously and by recognizing that strict norms, applied without prudence, can become oppressive.

4.3. Islamic Bioethics

In Islamic jurisprudence, many scholars permit non-abortive contraception as long as it does not involve permanent sterilization, is based on mutual consent of spouses, and is justified by legitimate reasons such as maternal health, economic constraints, or the need to care for existing children.[9]

Here, too, we find an ethic that seeks to balance reverence for life with prudential concern for health, justice, and the common good. For many Muslim women in poor contexts, contraception is understood as a means of preserving life and dignity, not as a rejection of motherhood.

4.4. Ethical Convergence and Catholic Re-Engagement

This brief comparison shows that across traditions, there is considerable convergence around three principles:

- Clear opposition to abortion as the direct destruction of nascent life
- Acceptance of non-abortive contraception as morally legitimate in many circumstances
- Serious concern for women's health, family welfare, and social justice

---

8. Papadopoulos, *Contraception in the Orthodox Christian Tradition*.

9. Esposito, *What Everyone Needs to Know About Islam*; Rahman, *Health and Reproduction in Islamic Jurisprudence*.

Catholic moral theology, especially in light of Häring's method, can learn from this convergence. While remaining faithful to the core conviction that life is sacred from conception, it can still recognize that non-abortive contraception may be a necessary means of protecting life and dignity in our world of structural inequality.

5. WOMEN'S HEALTH AND MATERNAL MORTALITY: A CASE STUDY FROM AFRICA

Nowhere is the intersection of contraception, women's health, and structural injustice clearer than in the realities of maternal mortality in Africa. Sub-Saharan Africa bears a disproportionate share of the world's maternal deaths. Many of these deaths are preventable and are linked to:

- closely spaced pregnancies,
- high parity (many births),
- lack of access to skilled obstetric care,
- anemia and malnutrition,
- unsafe abortions resulting from unwanted pregnancies.[10]

From a CLT perspective, these are not just statistics; they are faces—mothers, daughters, sisters, friends—whose lives end prematurely because structures of health care, economics, gender, and religion intersect to deprive them of basic means of protection.

Non-abortive contraception is one of the most effective tools for reducing maternal mortality:

- Spacing births by at least two years significantly reduces the risk of maternal and infant death.[11]
- Access to contraception reduces the number of high-risk pregnancies among very young women and older mothers.
- Family-planning services reduce recourse to unsafe abortion by preventing unwanted pregnancies.[12]

---

10. WHO, *Family Planning/Contraception*; Sedgh et al., *Unmet Need for Contraception in Developing Countries*.
11. WHO, *Short Birth Intervals and Child Mortality*.
12. Sedgh et al., *Unmet Need for Contraception in Developing Countries*.

For a woman in rural Africa, the lack of access to contraception is not an abstract moral issue; it is a question of survival. To insist, in such a context, that the only licit means of birth regulation is periodic abstinence—without considering the realities of gender power, male behavior, cultural expectations, and poverty—is morally naïve at best and structurally violent at worst.

Liberation theology insists that structural violence is sin. If ecclesial teachings or pastoral practices contribute to preventable deaths by refusing to engage the ethical legitimacy of non-abortive contraception, they must be subjected to prophetic critique.

6. WOMEN'S RIGHTS, AUTONOMY, AND SOCIAL JUSTICE

Contraception is not only about health; it is also about agency. Women's ability to decide when and how often to bear children is fundamental to their participation in:

- education,
- economic life,
- public leadership,
- political processes.

International human-rights instruments, such as CEDAW, recognize reproductive self-determination as integral to women's dignity and equality. When religious teachings are interpreted and enforced in ways that deny women meaningful control over their fertility, they reinforce patriarchal structures that treat women's bodies as reproductive instruments for family, culture, or Church.[13]

From a CLT perspective, moral theology must expose and resist such structures. The option for the poor includes an option for women—poor women especially—who suffer when reproductive decisions are made over their heads by husbands, elders, priests, or bishops.

Häring's personalist ethics is fundamentally compatible with this concern. His focus on the human person as the subject of moral responsibility implies that women, no less than men, must be treated as moral agents capable of discerning God's will in their lives. Blanket prohibitions

---

13. Shaw, *Women, Religion, and Reproductive Rights.*

that functionally strip women of that agency contradict the very personalism they claim to uphold.

7. ETHICAL SYNTHESIS: PROPORTIONALISM AND LIBERATION PRAXIS

Bringing together Häring's method and CLT, we can outline a coherent ethical synthesis regarding non-abortive contraception:

1. Abortion remains morally unacceptable. This chapter does not advocate for abortion. It affirms the Church's consistent teaching that the direct destruction of nascent life is incompatible with Christian ethics.

2. Non-abortive contraception stands in a different moral category. It regulates fertility but does not destroy an already existing human life. Its morality cannot be determined solely by abstract natural-law claims; it must be evaluated through intention, circumstances, and consequences.

3. Proportionalist discernment highlights contexts where non-abortive contraception is morally justified—even morally required. When repeated high-risk pregnancies threaten a woman's life, when poverty makes it impossible to care for many children, when contraceptive use avoids unsafe abortion and protects the well-being of existing children, non-abortive contraception can be an act of responsible love.[14]

4. Liberation praxis adds a structural dimension. The refusal to acknowledge this moral space in practice—especially in poor communities—perpetuates structural injustice and gender inequality. Prohibiting non-abortive contraception in such settings becomes an act of complicity with systems that kill and oppress women.[15]

5. Women's voices and experiences must be central. Any moral teaching that affects women's bodies and futures must actively incorporate their perspectives. To formulate reproductive ethics without listening to women is itself a moral failure.

14. Häring, *The Law of Christ*; Sedgh et al., *Unmet Need for Contraception in Developing Countries*.
15. Gutiérrez, *A Theology of Liberation*; Boff and Boff, *Introducing Liberation Theology*.

In this light, non-abortive contraception can be seen not as a rejection of life but as a strategy of life-affirmation, particularly in contexts of structural vulnerability.

8. PASTORAL AND ECCLESIAL IMPLICATIONS

If CLT and Häring's ethics support the moral legitimacy of non-abortive contraception under many real-world conditions, what follows for pastoral practice and ecclesial life?

1. Pastoral accompaniment, not condemnation. Priests, catechists, and pastoral workers should accompany couples and women in discerning responsible ways of living marital love, taking seriously health, economic conditions, and family needs. Simplistic condemnation of all contraception, without nuance, contradicts both pastoral charity and moral intelligence.

2. Truthful education. Catholic health institutions and pastoral programs should provide accurate information about non-abortive methods, their moral status, and their health effects. Deliberate ignorance is not holiness.

3. Advocacy in public policy. The Church should lend its considerable social influence to promoting women's health, ensuring access to non-abortive contraceptive services in public health systems, especially in rural and poor communities. This can be done while maintaining clear opposition to abortion.

4. Integration into a broader vision of justice. Contraception cannot be isolated from other struggles: for girls' education, for economic justice, for an end to gender-based violence. A liberationist ethic integrates all these dimensions into a holistic vision of human flourishing.

5. Theologians and bishops must reopen serious discussion. Rather than treating *Humanae Vitae* as the final word on all aspects of contraception, the Church must allow moral theologians, women's voices, and empirical data to inform a renewed discernment. To refuse such discussion in the face of global maternal suffering is pastorally irresponsible and theologically fragile.

9. CONCLUSION: TOWARD A LIBERATIVE CATHOLIC SEXUAL ETHIC

In revisiting Bernard Häring through the lens of Critical-Liberative Theology, this chapter has argued that non-abortive contraception can be morally permissible and even morally necessary in many contexts, especially where women's health and family survival are at stake. This position does not dilute Catholic reverence for life; it deepens it by insisting that ethical reflection must attend to all the lives involved, especially the most vulnerable.

A liberationist Catholic sexual ethic will therefore:

- uphold the sacredness of nascent life,
- defend women's right to health, dignity, and moral agency,
- confront structural injustice in health systems and gender relations,
- support non-abortive contraception as one tool among many for promoting integral human development.

In this way, the Church can witness to a God who is not the enemy of women's bodies, but their ally; a God who desires "life, and life to the full" (John 10:10, JB) for every woman, man, and child.

CHAPTER 17

Celibacy as Structural Injustice: Vocation, Freedom, and Reform

1. INTRODUCTION: A DISCIPLINE TURNED INTO A TEST OF ORTHODOXY

PRIESTLY CELIBACY IN THE Latin Catholic Church is officially described as a *discipline*, not a dogma. Historically, it emerged gradually rather than descending fully formed from apostolic times. Married clergy were normal in the first millennium, and even popes were married; obligatory celibacy for diocesan priests in the West was consolidated only from the 11th–12th centuries, amid concerns about property, clerical "purity," and reform.[1]

Yet in contemporary Catholicism, celibacy is often treated as if it were near-dogmatic: a non-negotiable badge of priestly identity and obedience. To question it is frequently perceived as disloyalty. This absolutization of a contingent discipline has created a profound tension between official ideals and lived realities—especially in contexts, like much of Africa, where cultural expectations around marriage and fertility sharply clash with enforced lifelong celibacy.[2]

From the standpoint of Critical-Liberative Theology (CLT), the question of celibacy is not merely internal Church housekeeping; it is about structural justice, human flourishing, and the credibility of the Gospel. When a discipline systematically generates double lives, sexual

---

1. Cozzens, *The Changing Face of the Priesthood*; Sipe, *Celibacy in Crisis*.
2. Doyle, *Clericalism*; Rahner, *Theological Investigations*.

exploitation, and pastoral hypocrisy—while also contributing to priest shortages and pastoral deserts—it becomes more than a "spiritual counsel." It becomes a *structural sin*.[3]

This chapter argues that mandatory celibacy in its current Latin form is a serious obstacle to vocational justice and ecclesial integrity, particularly in the African context. It draws on sociological research, liberation theology, and my own personal journey—from a celibacy-embracing seminarian to a theologian who now regards compulsory celibacy as pastorally destructive and morally indefensible.

2. MY STORY: FROM IDEALIZED CELIBACY TO DISILLUSIONMENT

From childhood I wanted to be a priest. Knowing the celibacy requirement, I embraced it with youthful seriousness. I remained a virgin all through my formative years and into the seminary, believing that total sexual renunciation was a necessary sacrifice for serving Christ and the Church.

In the seminary, the official discourse on celibacy was lofty: we were told that celibacy freed us for "undivided devotion to the Lord" (cf. 1 Cor 7:32–35, Jerusalem Bible) and made us a powerful "sign" of the Kingdom. In class, we discussed Augustine, Aquinas, and later Rahner's reflections on ministry and availability.[4] I internalized the idea that marriage, though holy, was somehow a "lesser" path for those unable to embrace perfect continence.

Then I began to see how different reality was.

Already in the seminary, stories circulated about priests—sometimes our own formators—who had mistresses, and in at least one case, a child. Some of these were whispered rumors; others were widely known facts everyone pretended not to know. A devout Christian once described the presbytery in his town as "a brothel," a comment I initially dismissed as bitterness but later recognized as painfully close to the truth in some places.

I myself, despite my firm commitment to celibacy, experienced how difficult it was in African cultural contexts where a man without a wife and children is often regarded as incomplete or even suspicious. In

---

3. Gutiérrez, *A Theology of Liberation*.
4. Rahner, *Theological Investigations*.

such an environment, the priest's status and prestige make him a *highly desirable* partner. I remember being courted by women while still a seminarian—sometimes gently, sometimes very directly. The combination of cultural pressure, male ego, and clerical power made it easy for some seminarians and priests simply to give in.

With time, the pattern became undeniable: in many African settings, mandatory celibacy was less a shining sign of the Kingdom and more a breeding ground for double lives—secret relationships, unofficial "wives," and children kept in the shadows. The gap between official rhetoric and lived practice became intolerable to me.

I did not lose faith in God, but I lost confidence in a system that demanded public vows it had little realistic intention—or capacity—to enforce with integrity. For many ordinary Christians who were themselves living faithful marriages, this hypocrisy was scandalous. Some began drifting to Pentecostal communities where pastors were married and where moral demands, however strict in other ways, did not include the denial of such a basic aspect of human life.[5]

Those experiences profoundly shaped my conviction that, especially in Africa, the current form of universal, mandatory celibacy has largely *failed*—spiritually, psychologically, and pastorally. From a CLT perspective, it must be named and confronted as structural injustice.

3. HISTORICAL AND THEOLOGICAL CONTEXT: CELIBACY AS CONTINGENT DISCIPLINE

3.1. A Late and Uneven Emergence

Historical research clearly shows that married clergy were widespread in the early Church, and that clerical celibacy became obligatory in the Latin West only centuries later. Married priests, and even married bishops, were not anomalous; the last married pope, Adrian II, reigned in the 9th century.[6] Beginning in late antiquity and culminating in the Gregorian Reform era (11th–12th centuries), new legislation increasingly restricted clerical marriage. Motivations were complex: concerns about cultic

---

5. Cozzens, *The Changing Face of the Priesthood*.
6. Cozzens, *The Changing Face of the Priesthood*, 19–21.

purity, influence from monastic ideals, and very concrete anxieties about ecclesiastical property being inherited by priests' children.[7]

By the 12th century, celibacy had become normative for Latin priests, though local resistance persisted for centuries.[8] Even today, the Eastern Catholic Churches and the Orthodox Churches retain a different discipline: they ordain married men to the priesthood while selecting bishops from monastic celibates.[9] This demonstrates conclusively that priestly celibacy is not an ontological requirement of the sacrament of Orders, but a disciplinary practice tied to a particular ecclesial and cultural history.

3.2. Official Ideals and Their Limits

The Latin Church's modern justification for celibacy emphasizes a closer conformity to Christ's own unmarried life, an eschatological sign of the Kingdom where "they neither marry nor are given in marriage" (Mt 22:30, JB), and a practical freedom for pastoral service. These themes are present in *Presbyterorum Ordinis* and subsequent magisterial teaching, as well as in the 1993 Roman document on celibacy and inculturation.[10]

From a CLT perspective, none of these motivations is without value. Voluntary celibacy can be a beautiful and prophetic vocation for some, a charism that speaks of eschatological hope and radical availability.[11] Liberation theology does not reject celibacy *per se*; it critiques structures that impose it universally regardless of cultural context, personal maturity, or psychological readiness, and then enforce it through secrecy and repression rather than honest discernment.[12]

---

7. Sipe, *Celibacy in Crisis*, 31–52.

8. Sipe, *Celibacy in Crisis*.

9. Rahner, *Theological Investigations*; Vatican Congregation for the Clergy, *Directory on the Ministry and Life of Priests*.

10. Vatican Congregation for the Clergy, *Directory on the Ministry and Life of Priests*.

11. Rahner, *Theological Investigations*.

12. Gutiérrez, *A Theology of Liberation*.

4. CELIBACY, SECRECY, AND SEXUAL DYSFUNCTION

4.1. The "Secret World" of Celibacy

Extensive sociological research has documented the gap between official celibate ideals and clerical practice. In his landmark study *Celibacy in Crisis: A Secret World Revisited*, A. W. Richard Sipe, drawing on 25 years of confidential interviews with over 1,500 priests, former priests, and partners, concluded that only a minority of priests live sustained lifelong celibacy as officially defined. He estimated that at any given time, roughly half are not observing celibacy in the strict sense.[13]

Sipe argues that the seminary system, shaped by a culture of secrecy and unrealistic expectations, is structurally incapable of forming large numbers of men into sexually integrated, emotionally mature celibates.[14] Instead, it often produces environments where sexual experimentation is hidden, homosexual and heterosexual relationships are tacitly tolerated so long as they remain invisible, and honest discussion of desire is repressed. Donald Cozzens, in *The Changing Face of the Priesthood*, reaches similar conclusions, describing the priesthood as a vocation in crisis, marked by loneliness, unresolved sexuality, and deep identity conflicts.[15]

4.2. Celibacy, Clericalism, and Abuse

While celibacy itself does not *cause* sexual abuse, a growing body of research links the *system* of enforced celibacy and clericalism to patterns of abuse and cover-up. Thomas Doyle argues that the abuse crisis cannot be explained by "a few bad apples" but must be seen as the product of a hierarchical culture that idealizes priests, isolates them from normal accountability, and demands secrecy around sexuality.[16]

Recent national and diocesan reports in the United States, Ireland, Germany, and elsewhere confirm that clericalism—understood as the elevation of clergy above laypeople, combined with a culture of deference and silence—creates environments where abusive behavior can flourish and victims are disbelieved or intimidated.[17] Pope Francis, in his *Letter*

---

13. Sipe, *Celibacy in Crisis*, 62–64.
14. Sipe, *Celibacy in Crisis*.
15. Cozzens, *Changing Face*.
16. Doyle, *Clericalism*.
17. Doyle, *Clericalism*; Sipe, *Celibacy in Crisis*.

to the People of God on abuse, identified clericalism as a key structural factor and insisted that saying "no" to abuse requires an emphatic "no" to all forms of clericalism.[18]

Mandatory celibacy, when enforced in a clerical culture that discourages transparency, can thus contribute to unhealthy sexual repression, double lives, and patterns of boundary violation. CLT names this not as an individual failure alone but as a *structural sin*—a sinful pattern embedded in institutional norms and protected by power.[19]

5. THE AFRICAN CONTEXT: CULTURE, MASCULINITY, AND THE FAILURE OF CELIBACY

5.1. Celibacy in a Culture of Marriage

In many African societies, adulthood is closely tied to marriage and children. A man without a wife and offspring is often viewed as incomplete, immature, or even morally suspect.[20] In such a cultural context, a universal discipline of lifelong celibacy for priests is not simply countercultural in a prophetic sense; it is often *socially unintelligible*.

This creates intense pressure on seminarians and priests. Their public status as "men of God" gives them prestige, access, and emotional dependence from parishioners—especially women. For many women, a relationship with a priest can promise spiritual intimacy, social status, and material support. The result is a combustible mixture of loneliness, cultural expectation, and opportunity.

My own experience confirms what sociological snapshots suggest: in many African dioceses, the doctrine of celibacy is widely proclaimed but quietly undermined by pervasive, sometimes institutionalized, sexual relationships. From mistresses housed near rectories to "parish wives" who are known but never named, the reality is an open secret. Priests with children are not rare, even if the children are never officially acknowledged.

---

18. Francis, *Address of His Holiness Pope Francis to the Roman Curia*.
19. Boff, *Church: Charism and Power*; Gutiérrez, *A Theology of Liberation*.
20. Ela, *African Cry*.

5.2. Hypocrisy and Scandal for the Faithful

Ordinary Catholics, many of whom live faithful, sacramental marriages under difficult economic conditions, are not naïve. They see the double lives of some priests; they observe the gap between homily and habit. For many, this has become a profound scandal, feeding disillusionment and religious migration. Studies of religious affiliation in sub-Saharan Africa note a significant movement of Catholics into Pentecostal and charismatic churches, where pastors are married and where at least this dimension of life is not hidden.[21]

In Cameroon and other African countries, I have seen increasing numbers of Catholics drawn to Pentecostal and independent churches where pastors are married and where, at least in this regard, there is no requirement to hide one's sexual and emotional life. Of course, these communities have their own problems—authoritarian leaders, prosperity preaching, and sometimes exploitative "deliverance" ministries.[22] But the simple fact of marital transparency often feels more honest to the faithful than Catholic structures in which celibacy is preached but widely violated.

From a CLT viewpoint, this hemorrhaging of trust is itself an instance of injustice. The poor, who often give sacrificially to support the parish and its priest, have a right to leaders whose public commitments are lived with integrity—or whose structures are reformed when integrity becomes impossible.[23]

5.3. My Own Disillusionment

It was against this backdrop that my personal disillusionment deepened. Having kept my own commitment to celibacy seriously, I came to feel that the institution was asking of me—and of others—something it neither truly supported nor honestly evaluated.

The presbytery that one Christian in my circle called "a brothel" was not an isolated caricature; it symbolized a broader pattern. When seminary formators themselves are rumored or known to have relationships and even children, the formation process is compromised at its

---

21. Pew Research Center, *Tolerance and Tension*.
22. Kalu, *African Pentecostalism*.
23. Gutiérrez, *A Theology of Liberation*.

root. Young seminarians quickly learn that the real rule is not chastity but secrecy; not holiness but "not getting caught."

At that point, celibacy ceases to be a charism and becomes a school of duplicity. For a theology committed to liberation, this is intolerable. Structures that train people to lie about their deepest human realities cannot be justified as "sacred tradition."[24]

6. CELIBACY, STRUCTURAL SIN, AND THE CRISIS OF VOCATIONS

6.1. A Global Manpower Crisis

The Catholic Church today faces an acute priest shortage in many regions. Globally, the number of Catholics has grown significantly since 1970, while the total number of priests has stagnated or slightly declined. Vatican statistics show that as of 2023 there were about 407,000 priests worldwide, a slight decrease even as the Catholic population continues to expand, raising the ratio of Catholics per priest above 3,000 in many regions.[25] Independent analyses in major media similarly note that while the global Catholic population has roughly doubled since 1970, priest numbers have dipped or remained flat, forcing parish closures and reliance on aging or foreign clergy.[26]

Europe sees especially sharp declines. In France, for example, the number of priests has plummeted from around 65,000 in the 1960s to about 12,000 today, with only a fraction still active.[27] In Ireland and parts of Germany, new priestly vocations have dropped to historically low levels.

While multiple factors drive this crisis—secularization, abuse scandals, loss of trust—mandatory celibacy is consistently named by both scholars and ordinary Catholics as a major deterrent for otherwise qualified men who feel called to ministry but not to lifelong sexual abstinence.[28]

---

24. Sipe, *Celibacy in Crisis*.

25. Vatican News, *New Church Statistics Reveal Growing Catholic Population, Fewer Priests*.

26. Wall Street Journal, *The Catholic Church Has a Manpower Problem*.

27. Wall Street Journal, *The Catholic Church Has a Manpower Problem*.

28. Cozzens, *The Changing Face of the Priesthood*; Sipe, *Celibacy in Crisis*.

6.2. Optional Celibacy as Structural Justice

From a CLT perspective, the question is not simply whether optional celibacy would yield more priests. It is whether a discipline that has become a major structural barrier to pastoral care and vocational flourishing can still be morally justified.

In regions where parishes go without Eucharist for months because there is no priest—and where mature, proven married men (*viri probati*) could be ordained without theological contradiction—the maintenance of mandatory celibacy looks less like fidelity to Christ and more like fidelity to a particular clerical culture.[29] It is the poor who suffer most from this sacramental deprivation.

At the same time, Eastern Catholic and Orthodox Churches show that married priesthood is perfectly compatible with sacramental validity and ecclesial identity.[30] Their example, along with the existence of married former Anglican clergy serving as Catholic priests today, is empirical proof that ordained ministry and marriage are not mutually exclusive.

CLT therefore regards the continued universal imposition of celibacy in the Latin Church as a form of structural sin:

- it systematically excludes many potential vocations;
- it contributes to unhealthy sexual cultures and secrecy;
- it burdens poor communities with priest shortages;
- it reinforces clericalism by treating a non-essential discipline as a quasi-dogma.[31]

Justice demands its reform.

7. TOWARD A LIBERATIVE REFORM OF CELIBACY

From within the Catholic tradition itself, change is possible without doctrinal rupture. The goal is not to abolish celibacy but to *liberate* it—so that those who choose it do so as a genuine charism, not under systemic pressure or cultural unreality.

---

29. Rahner, *Theological Investigations*.

30. Vatican Congregation for the Clergy, *Directory on the Ministry and Life of Priests*.

31. Boff, *Church: Charism and Power*; Gutiérrez, *A Theology of Liberation*.

7.1. Recognizing Celibacy as Charism, Not Condition

CLT proposes a simple but radical reorientation: celibacy should be a charism freely chosen, not a requirement for ordination. Candidates for priesthood should be discerned primarily on their pastoral gifts, moral integrity, and commitment to justice, not on their willingness to renounce marriage.[32]

This would bring the Latin Church more in line with the plural practice of the universal Church and with its own earlier history.[33]

7.2. Inculturation in Africa

In Africa, where social structures and conceptions of masculinity are deeply tied to family life, a liberative reform would include:

- ordaining married men who are already recognized community leaders;
- creating pathways for existing priests who fall in love and wish to marry to transition into a married clergy state without being forced to abandon ministry;
- offering formation that integrates sexuality, affectivity, and cultural realities rather than repressing them.[34]

Such steps would not only reduce hypocrisy; they would also affirm African cultures in a positive way, rejecting colonial-era assumptions that equate holiness with a disembodied European ideal of celibate maleness.

7.3. Structural Transparency and Accountability

Reform of celibacy discipline must be accompanied by structural changes:

- ending the culture of secrecy around priests' relationships and children;
- establishing transparent mechanisms for acknowledging and supporting priests' children who already exist;

---

32. Rahner, *Theological Investigations*.
33. Cozzens, *The Changing Face of the Priesthood*; Vatican Congregation for the Clergy, *Directory on the Ministry and Life of Priests*.
34. Ela, *African Cry*.

- linking any remaining practice of celibacy to robust psychological evaluation and ongoing accompaniment, rather than naive assumptions of automatic virtue.[35]

Only such measures can begin to dismantle the pattern whereby celibacy becomes a mask behind which exploitation and abuse hide.[36]

8. CONCLUSION: CELIBACY, TRUTH, AND THE CREDIBILITY OF THE GOSPEL

From the vantage point of Critical-Liberative Theology, celibacy must be judged by its fruits. Where it is freely chosen and truthfully lived, it can be a powerful sign of eschatological hope and radical availability. Where it is imposed regardless of cultural reality, maturity, or psychological health—and then enforced through secrecy and clerical privilege—it becomes a structure of sin.

My own journey—from an idealistic seminarian who embraced celibacy with reverence, through the shock of discovering widespread promiscuity and hypocrisy, to a theologian convinced of the need for structural reform—is not unique. It echoes the experience of many who have loved the Church enough to see its wounds and to refuse comforting illusions.

The Church of the poor and the marginalized, which CLT envisions, cannot be built on a foundation of double lives and structural dishonesty. It requires leaders whose sexuality is integrated, whose commitments are realistic, and whose celibacy or marriage is lived in the light, not in the shadows.

Reform of mandatory celibacy will not solve all ecclesial problems, nor will it eliminate sin. But it is a necessary step toward a more truthful, just, and credible Church—a Church where pastoral ministry is not reserved to those willing to inhabit an unrealistic ideal, but opened to all whom the Spirit calls, in the concrete conditions of their humanity.

To cling to the current discipline as untouchable is, in effect, to sacrifice both truth and justice to institutional habit. To reform it is to align discipline once more with the Gospel's liberating purpose: that God's people "may have life, and have it to the full" (Jn 10:10, JB).

---

35. Cozzens, *The Changing Face of the Priesthood;* Sipe, *Celibacy in Crisis.*
36. Doyle, *Clericalism.*

CHAPTER 18

Neither Do I Condemn You: LGBTQ+ Inclusion as a Christological Imperative

> "Woman, where are they? Has no one condemned you? ... Neither do I condemn you. Go away, and from this moment sin no more."
>
> (John 8:10–11, Jerusalem Bible)

1. INTRODUCTION: FROM CRISIS OF CONDEMNATION TO RADICAL HOSPITALITY

1.1. The Contemporary Context and Ecclesial Rift

THE RELATIONSHIP BETWEEN CHRISTIAN faith and LGBTQ+ identity remains one of the most fraught and divisive ethical issues in contemporary theology. It is not a marginal pastoral dilemma but a crisis of conscience that exposes a deep ecclesial rift. For decades, non-affirming interpretations of Scripture and Natural Law have been marshaled to justify exclusion, discrimination, and psychological harm, contributing to heightened rates of suicide, homelessness, and spiritual trauma among LGBTQ+ Christians.[1]

Within Catholicism, the Magisterium's classification of same-sex acts as "intrinsically disordered" and homosexual inclination as "objectively

---

[1]. American Psychological Association, *Resolution on Appropriate Affirmative Responses to Sexual Orientation and Distress*; Meyer, *Prejudice, Social Stress, and Mental Health in Lesbian, Gay, and Bisexual Populations*; Asongu, *Holistic Resilience*; Asongu, *Hidden Selves*.

disordered"[2] places an unbearable spiritual burden on millions of faithful Catholics. They are forced into an agonizing split between their authentic sense of self and their relationship with the Church. LGBTQ+ Catholics are, in practice, asked either to fragment themselves or to leave.

The tragedy is amplified by the widely acknowledged yet seldom honestly discussed reality that a significant number of Catholic clergy—including priests and bishops—are themselves gay. Many serve faithfully and sacrificially even while publicly sustaining a doctrinal system that names their own deepest affective orientation as "disordered." The resulting culture of secrecy and double standards creates systemic hypocrisy, fosters clerical closets, and weaponizes silence. The Church simultaneously depends on the ministry of gay priests while denying the moral legitimacy of their capacity for love, intimacy, and covenantal partnership. This contradiction itself is a form of structural spiritual violence.

Yet, as many biblical scholars and theologians argue, the dominant condemnatory interpretations reflect cultural bias and an incomplete understanding of human nature and divine intent.[3] The crisis is therefore not merely social or political; it is doctrinal, pastoral, and Christological. It tests the Church's claim to be a universal sacrament of salvation and love.

1.2. Methodological Approach: A Catholic Hermeneutic of Liberation

This chapter offers a systematic theological defense of LGBTQ+ inclusion grounded explicitly in a Catholic hermeneutic and a Critical Liberation Theology (CLT) framework. This approach engages three interrelated pillars:

1. Scripture. Following *Divino Afflante Spiritu* and *Dei Verbum*, we employ historical-critical exegesis to discern the *sensus literalis* of key texts and then interpret them through a Christocentric lens,

---

2. Congregation for the Doctrine of the Faith [CDF], *Letter to the Bishops of the Catholic Church on the Pastoral Care of Homosexual Persons*; CDF, *Catechism of the Catholic Church*; Catechism of the Catholic Church, §§2357–2359.

3. Boswell, *Christianity, Social Tolerance, and Homosexuality*; Brownson, *Bible, Gender, Sexuality*; Gushee, *Changing Our Mind*.

recognizing Christ as the fullness of revelation and the normative rule of Christian ethics.[4]

2. Tradition. We engage Magisterial teaching critically, using the Catholic principles of Development of Doctrine[5] and the hierarchy of truths, and we contrast a reductive physicalist Natural Law with a personalist and relational Natural Law model.[6]

3. Reason and Experience. We give theological weight to the lived experience of LGBTQ+ Catholics, current scientific and psychological research, and the *sensus fidelium* as authentic *loci* of the Spirit's ongoing guidance.[7] Empirical data on mental health consequences of stigma, and the testimonies of LGBTQ+ believers themselves, must be considered in moral discernment.[8]

1.3. Thesis: From Boundary Enforcement to Radical Communion

The central claim is non-negotiable: The gospel of Jesus Christ calls the Church to unconditional agape and justice, and these principles are the ultimate interpretive lens for all claims about sexuality (Gal 5:14; Rom 13:10). The moral trajectory of the New Covenant moves from boundary enforcement, purity codes, and legalism toward radical inclusion, mercy, and communion.

Exclusion from full ecclesial and sacramental life on the basis of sexual orientation or gender identity thus constitutes a theological and ethical failure to embody Christ's mission. It is incompatible with the Christ who refused to condemn the woman caught in adultery, stood in the dust beside her, and disarmed her accusers: "Neither do I condemn you" (John 8:11).

The chapter unfolds in four major movements:

---

4. Brownson, Bible, Gender, Sexuality; Hays, *The Moral Vision of the New Testament*.
5. Newman, *An Essay on the Development of Christian Doctrine*.
6. Farley, *Just Love*; Finnis, *Natural Law and Natural Rights*.
7. Gutiérrez, *A Theology of Liberation*; Cone, For My People.
8. American Psychological Association, *Resolution on Appropriate Affirmative Responses to Sexual Orientation and Distress*; Meyer, *Prejudice, Social Stress, and Mental Health in Lesbian, Gay, and Bisexual Populations*; Asongu, *Holistic Resilience*; Asongu, *Hidden Selves*.

1. The ontological dignity of the *imago Dei* and the anthropological grounding of moral equality.
2. A definitional and scientific clarification of LGBTQ+ identities and the harm of fragmentation.
3. A Christocentric re-reading of Scripture, including the "clobber texts."
4. The ecclesial and sacramental imperative for full inclusion, with particular attention to hypocrisy, structural sin, and the call to reform.

2. IMAGO DEI AND THE ONTOLOGICAL FOUNDATION OF MORAL EQUALITY

2.1. Imago Dei as Ontological Vocation

Any theology of LGBTQ+ inclusion must begin where Christian anthropology begins: Genesis 1:26–27. Humanity is created in the image and likeness of God—the *imago Dei*—prior to any mention of sexual differentiation or procreative function. This image is ontological: given simply by existing as human, not earned by conforming to a set of gendered or sexual norms.

In the Catholic tradition, Thomas Aquinas locates the *imago Dei* primarily in the rational and spiritual capacities of the human person—the ability to know and love God.[9] The image is primarily a matter of intellect, will, and relational capacity, not of genital structure or reproductive potential. Put differently, the capacity for covenantal love, knowledge, and self-gift is the center of the divine image, not heterosexual functioning.

From this perspective, a person's sexual orientation or gender identity, when experienced as a stable, non-chosen dimension of selfhood affirmed by psychological and scientific research as non-pathological,[10] cannot nullify their participation in the *imago Dei*. To suggest that an

---

9. Aquinas, Summa Theologiae I.93.4.

10. American Psychological Association, *Resolution on Appropriate Affirmative Responses to Sexual Orientation and Distress*; Drescher, *Out of DSM: Depathologizing Homosexuality*; Pan American Health Organization/World Health Organization, *LGBT Health Sees Progress and Challenges 15 Years After Homosexuality Ceased Being Classified as a Mental Disorder*; World Health Organization, *Moving One Step Closer to Better Health and Rights for Transgender People*.

LGBTQ+ person's authentic expression of love or gender somehow cancels their reflection of God is to impose a condition on the imago that neither Scripture nor Tradition warrants.

2.2. Integrity of Body and Soul: Against Dualistic Condemnation

Contemporary Catholic personalism, influenced by figures like Karol Wojtyła (John Paul II), insists that the human person is a psychosomatic unity. The *imago Dei* is impressed upon the whole person—body, psyche, and spirit—not only upon an abstract "soul." Any theology that praises the "soul" of the LGBTQ+ person while condemning their embodied capacity for love and intimacy reintroduces a dualism the Incarnation itself rejects.[11]

If an LGBTQ+ person's orientation or identity is a deep, enduring aspect of self, then their moral vocation is not perpetual suppression but integrated holiness: to live love, fidelity, and justice through their actual, embodied reality. To demand that they permanently deny or "convert" this core dimension of selfhood is a form of spiritual violence, undermining integrity (*integritas*) and fostering the identity fragmentation described later as Triple Masking.

2.3. Relational Imago and the Trinitarian Analogy

The divine "Let us make humankind in our image" (Gen 1:26) hints at an inherently relational image. The triune God is an eternal communion of persons; thus, the *imago Dei* is not only rational capacity, but relational capacity—to give and receive love, to form covenant, to create community.[12]

Diversity of human embodiment, culture, affection, and gender expression can therefore be understood as an outflow of the infinite creativity of the Trinity rather than as a threat to divine order. When loving, faithful same-sex or gender-diverse relationships mirror covenantal self-giving, they participate in this relational *imago* and therefore deserve theological recognition, not condemnation.

---

11. McFague, *The Body of God*; Rogers, *Sexuality and the Christian Body*.
12. McFague, *The Body of God*; Cone, *For My People*.

2.4. The Ethical Implication: Justice and Oppression

James Cone argues that any theology that functions to marginalize or dehumanize a group becomes a theology of oppression.[13] When Church discourse and discipline construct LGBTQ+ identity as morally defective or "disordered," they effectively deny the full *imago Dei* and facilitate structures of injustice—familial rejection, social exclusion, criminalization, and internalized shame.

To affirm LGBTQ+ persons, then, is not "permissive liberalism" but fidelity to ontological truth: God has already declared creation "very good" (Gen 1:31). The Church's calling is to align its doctrine and practice with that divine affirmation.

3. DEFINING THE COMMUNITY: THE LANDSCAPE OF LGBTQ+ IDENTITIES

A credible theology cannot speak about "LGBTQ+ people" in the abstract without definitional clarity.

- Lesbian, gay, bisexual (LGB) describe patterns of enduring emotional, romantic, and sexual attraction.
- Transgender (T) refers to a person whose gender identity differs from the sex assigned at birth.
- Queer (Q) functions both as an umbrella identity and a critique of rigid categories.
- Intersex (I) names natural variations in sex characteristics that destabilize simplistic binary models.
- Asexual and aromantic (A) describe people whose capacity for sexual or romantic attraction is minimal or absent.
- The "+" recognizes non-binary, pansexual, genderfluid, and other identities.

A key distinction: sexual orientation concerns who one is drawn to; gender identity concerns who one is. Both are dimensions of personhood empirically recognized as non-pathological variations of human experience.[14]

---

13. Cone, *For My People*.
14. American Psychological Association. Resolution on Appropriate Affirmative

To collapse these distinctions—or to treat them all as moral defects—is to refuse the patient, incarnational task of theology, which is to listen carefully to real bodies and lives.

4. SCIENTIFIC ANTHROPOLOGY AND THE STRUCTURAL SIN OF FRAGMENTATION

Liberation theology insists that truth is discerned in history and that the "signs of the times" include scientific insight.[15] Modern medicine and psychology have decisively depathologized sexual and gender diversity.[16] To cling to outdated assumptions that homosexuality or transgender identity are illnesses is to turn theology into an anti-scientific ideology.

4.1. Triple Masking: The Psychology of Survival

Within non-affirming religious environments, many LGBTQ+ believers survive by engaging in Triple Masking:

1. Identity Masking: Concealing orientation or gender identity to avoid rejection.

2. Minority Stress Masking: Hiding chronic anxiety, hypervigilance, and trauma produced by discrimination.[17]

3. Faith Masking: Suppressing genuine spiritual desires and vocations to remain acceptable within hostile religious settings.

The result is identity fragmentation—a split between the self God created and the self the Church will tolerate. Clinical research correlates this fragmentation and chronic stress with increased depression, suicidality, and substance abuse among LGBTQ+ youth and adults.[18] When

---

Responses to Sexual Orientation and Distress; WHO, Moving One Step Closer to Better Health and Rights for Transgender People.

15. Gutiérrez, A Theology of Liberation; Boff and Boff, Introducing Liberation Theology.

16. Drescher, Out of DSM: Depathologizing Homosexuality; Pan American Health Organization/World Health Organization. "LGBT Health Sees Progress and Challenges 15 Years After Homosexuality Ceased Being Classified as a Mental Disorder; WHO, Moving One Step Closer to Better Health and Rights for Transgender People.

17. Meyer, Prejudice, Social Stress, and Mental Health in Lesbian, Gay, and Bisexual Populations.

18. American Psychological Association, Resolution on Appropriate Affirmative

Church doctrine and pastoral practice are primary drivers of this fragmentation, they become mechanisms of structural sin.

4.2. Holistic Resilience: Integration as Grace

The counter-concept is Holistic Resilience: the capacity to live as a unified self—psychologically, spiritually, and relationally. Integration is fostered when communities affirm LGBTQ+ identities, bless covenanted relationships, and provide safe spaces for ministry and leadership. Theologically, this integration resonates with Jesus' promise of life "in abundance" (John 10:10).

An ethic that systematically prevents such integration and flourishing for LGBTQ+ believers cannot be reconciled with the Spirit of life.

5. RE-EXAMINING THE "CLOBBER TEXTS": HERMENEUTICS OF CONTEXT AND LIBERATION

A handful of biblical passages—Genesis 19; Leviticus 18:22 and 20:13; Romans 1:26-27; 1 Corinthians 6:9; and 1 Timothy 1:10—are often deployed as weapons against LGBTQ+ Christians. Catholic biblical theology, however, requires historical-critical exegesis and Christocentric interpretation.[19]

5.1. Sodom and the Sin Against Justice (Genesis 19)

Genesis 19 describes an attempted gang rape—a violent assertion of dominance over vulnerable strangers. The Hebrew verb *yāda'* ("to know") can have sexual connotations, but the prophetic tradition clarifies the meaning: Sodom's sin was arrogance, neglect of the poor, and injustice (Ezek 16:49–50; Isa 1:10–17). Jesus himself links Sodom's fate to inhospitality toward God's messengers (Luke 10:10–12).

Responses to Sexual Orientation and Distress; Meyer, *Prejudice, Social Stress, and Mental Health in Lesbian, Gay, and Bisexual Populations*.

19. Brownson, *Bible, Gender, Sexuality*; Hays, *The Moral Vision of the New Testament*; Loader, *The New Testament on Sexuality*.

To use this narrative to condemn consensual, loving same-sex relationships is a hermeneutical distortion.[20] The text addresses violent exploitation, not mutual affection.

5.2. Levitical Holiness Codes (Leviticus 18:22; 20:13)

The Levitical prohibitions must be read within the matrix of Israel's ritual-purity system and its separation from surrounding cultures. The term *to'evah* ("abomination") often refers to cultic or ritual transgressions—such as eating shellfish, wearing mixed fabrics, or charging interest—not to universal moral evils.[21]

The New Testament decisively relativizes such purity codes (Mark 7:19; Acts 10). To selectively resurrect these verses against LGBTQ+ persons while ignoring parallel prohibitions is a theologically inconsistent and culturally driven choice.

5.3. Romans 1: Idolatry, Excess, and "Against Nature"

Romans 1:26–27 is often read as a blanket condemnation of same-sex intimacy. Yet Paul's primary concern is idolatry—the exchange of the Creator for created things. The sexual acts he describes are symptoms of this deeper distortion, not its essence.[22]

The term *para physin* ("against nature") is ambiguous. In ancient usage, it could mean "against one's own customary nature" or "contrary to expected social pattern," not necessarily contrary to universal moral law.[23] Many scholars argue that Paul is describing exploitative, excessive, or idolatrous practices, likely within a context of pederasty and imperial excess, not loving, mutual, lifelong same-sex relationships.[24]

---

20. Boswell, *Christianity, Social Tolerance, and Homosexuality*; Brownson, *Bible, Gender, Sexuality*.
21. Wright, *How God Became King*.
22. Brownson, *Bible, Gender, Sexuality*; Loader, *The New Testament on Sexuality*.
23. Boswell, *Christianity, Social Tolerance, and Homosexuality*.
24. Brownson, *Bible, Gender, Sexuality*; Loader, *The New Testament on Sexuality*.

5.4. 1 Corinthians 6:9 and 1 Timothy 1:10: Translation and Exploitation

The infamous terms *malakoi* and *arsenokoitai* have been mistranslated as "homosexuals" in some modern Bibles. Historically:

- *Malakoi* ("soft") referred broadly to moral weakness or effeminacy, often stigmatizing men who failed to perform expected masculinity, and in some contexts the passive partners in exploitative relations.
- *Arsenokoitai* is rare, but likely refers to sexual exploiters, pederasts, or men who use others sexually or economically.[25]

Neither term can responsibly be equated with a loving, egalitarian, committed same-sex relationship. Paul condemns abusive, exploitative patterns, not the gift of mutual, covenantal love.

6. CHRISTOCENTRIC ETHICS: LOVE, JUSTICE, AND THE NEW COVENANT

Exegesis alone is not enough. Catholic moral theology locates the final authority in the person of Jesus Christ, who fulfills and reinterprets the Law (Matt 5:17; Rom 10:4).

6.1. Agape as the Criterion

Agape—self-giving, other-seeking love—is the supreme norm: "Love is the fulfillment of the law" (Rom 13:10; Gal 5:14). Richard Hays and Margaret Farley argue that New Testament ethics are fundamentally relational and justice-oriented.[26] Any doctrine that reliably produces shame, despair, and self-hatred in LGBTQ+ believers fails this agape criterion.

6.2. "Neither Do I Condemn You": Mercy as Revelation

In John 8, Jesus refuses to join the law-enforcers, even though they possess textual warrant for stoning. He disrupts the lethal application of the Law with a new hermeneutic: self-critique, mercy, and restoration. His

---

25. Scroggs, *The New Testament and Homosexuality*; Brownson, *Bible, Gender, Sexuality*.
26. Hays, *The Moral Vision of the New Testament*; Farley, *Just Love*.

first word is not a moral lecture but a refusal to condemn: "Neither do I condemn you" (John 8:11).

This story becomes paradigmatic for any group placed in the center of the circle of stones by religious authorities—including LGBTQ+ people. If the Church stands with the stone-throwers rather than with Christ in the dust, it betrays its Lord.

6.3. Relationship-Centered Morality

Farley proposes a relationship-centered sexual ethic structured around justice, mutuality, fidelity, and non-violence.[27] Same-sex relationships that embody these virtues are, by definition, morally good and conducive to holiness. Conversely, heterosexually configured relationships that lack these virtues are morally deficient.

The criterion is not *who* is loved in terms of gender, but how love is enacted. This is the Christocentric shift from act-centered to relationship-centered morality.

7. TRADITION, DEVELOPMENT, AND THE HYPOCRISY OF THE CLOSET

7.1. Non-Infallible Teaching and Development of Doctrine

The Church's current teaching on homosexuality is authoritative but non-infallible. It belongs to the realm of moral doctrine, which can—and historically has—undergone development and reform.[28] The Church has reversed or radically revised prior stances on slavery, usury, and religious liberty in light of deeper insight into the Gospel and human dignity.

Given new scientific knowledge and the catastrophic pastoral fruits of the current teaching, the classification of same-sex acts as "intrinsically disordered" is best understood as a reformable judgment, not a permanent dogma.

---

27. Farley, *Just Love*.

28. *Lumen Gentium* 25; Newman, *An Essay on the Development of Christian Doctrine*.

7.2. Natural Law and Personalist Revision

A reductive Natural Law focused almost exclusively on procreation cannot carry the full weight of Catholic sexual ethics. A personalist Natural Law considers the basic goods of relationship, community, and mutual flourishing.[29] Since the Church blesses marriages that are non-procreative (due to age or infertility), it implicitly recognizes that the unitive, covenantal good of the spouses is central to the sacrament.

By this logic, covenanted same-sex unions that embody fidelity, mutual care, and openness to generativity (through parenting, mentoring, hospitality, or service) participate in the goods marriage is meant to serve and deserve sacramental recognition.

7.3. The Closet and Institutional Hypocrisy

The existence of a large number of gay priests and bishops—some celibate, some not—renders the current regime of condemnation morally and spiritually untenable. The Church:

- relies heavily on the gifted ministry of gay clergy,
- demands public adherence to a doctrine that stigmatizes their very orientation,
- tolerates a culture of secrecy and double lives,
- and then projects moral panic onto lay LGBTQ+ people whose only "fault" is to seek honest, covenanted love.

This is institutional hypocrisy. It burdens consciences, warps formation, and undermines the Church's credibility in teaching on sexuality. Authentic reform requires not only changing official language but dismantling the closet culture that forces many priests to divide their inner truth from their public persona.

7.4. *Sensus Fidelium* and Emerging Consensus

The growing number of Catholics—including theologians, parents, and pastoral ministers—who affirm LGBTQ+ inclusion reflects not mere capitulation to secular culture, but an emerging *sensus fidelium*. Their lived,

---

29. Farley, *Just Love*; Finnis, *Natural Law and Natural Rights*.

prayerful discernment, often born of walking with LGBTQ+ loved ones, is a privileged locus of the Spirit's work.[30]

8. STRUCTURAL VIOLENCE, GLOBAL CRIMINALIZATION, AND THE PREFERENTIAL OPTION

Liberation theology identifies structural sin in systems and laws that crush the poor and marginalized.[31] Today, criminalization of LGBTQ+ people in many countries—including draconian laws in parts of Africa and Asia—is often supported by Christian rhetoric and sometimes explicitly by Church leaders (Amnesty International, 2024).

Many of these laws are colonial imports from 19th-century European penal codes, not indigenous traditions. When churches defend such laws as "protecting culture," they unwittingly protect colonial residues while placing LGBTQ+ persons in mortal danger.

The preferential option for the poor today must explicitly include those rendered "poor" by sexuality and gender—those who risk imprisonment, torture, or death simply for existing. To remain silent, or worse, to encourage such policies, is to stand not with Christ crucified, but with the powers that crucify.

9. "NEITHER DO I CONDEMN YOU": TOWARD FULL SACRAMENTAL INCLUSION

9.1. The Efficacy of Baptism and Koinonia

Through baptism, every Christian is incorporated into Christ's Body and marked with an indelible dignity. Sexual orientation or gender identity cannot erase this character (Gal 3:27–28). When the Church denies LGBTQ+ people access to:

- marriage,
- leadership,
- ordination,
- or fully acknowledged ministry,

---

30. *Lumen Gentium* 12; Gushee, *Changing Our Mind*.
31. Gutiérrez, *A Theology of Liberation*; Cone, *For My People*.

it creates a two-tiered membership that contradicts its own ecclesiology as "universal sacrament of salvation."[32]

9.2. Marriage as Sign, Not Biology

The sacrament of marriage is a visible sign of Christ's covenant with the Church. Its sacramental essence lies in enduring, faithful, mutual self-gift, not in genital complementarity per se.[33] Where same-sex couples manifest these covenantal qualities, the Church is called to discern not deviance but grace.

9.3. *Fiducia Supplicans*: A Beginning, Not an Endpoint

The 2023 declaration *Fiducia Supplicans* authorizing certain non-liturgical blessings for couples in "irregular situations"—including same-sex couples—signals an important shift.[34] The Church acknowledges that God's grace can be at work in these relationships. From a CLT perspective, this is not the endpoint but the beginning: if grace is present, the logical conclusion is that such relationships deserve full sacramental recognition and ecclesial integration.

10. CONCLUSION: THE CHRISTOLOGICAL IMPERATIVE OF INTEGRATION

At the heart of Christianity stands the rejected, crucified, and vindicated body of Jesus. LGBTQ+ persons—condemned, shamed, driven out of homes and churches, and subjected to violence and criminalization—bear, in their own bodies, the contemporary stigmata of this rejection.

The Church now faces a decisive choice:

- to side with systems of exclusion, sustaining doctrinal formulations and disciplinary structures that generate suicide, despair, and hypocrisy,

or

---

32. *Lumen Gentium* 1.
33. Farley, *Just Love*.
34. Dicastery for the Doctrine of the Faith, *Fiducia Supplicans*.

- to stand with Christ in the dust, saying with integrity to LGBTQ+ persons: "Neither do I condemn you", and then walking with them into lives of covenantal love, ministry, and holiness.

Full inclusion—in teaching, law, and sacramental practice—is not a luxury or an optional pastoral strategy; it is the Christological imperative of our time. It is what fidelity to the Gospel looks like when the condemned are LGBTQ+ believers.

In affirming the lives, loves, and vocations of LGBTQ+ people, the Church does not betray its Lord; it finally begins to resemble him.

PART V — COSMIC LIBERATION: ECOLOGY, TECHNOLOGY, AND THE FUTURE OF HUMANITY

Part V comprises two chapters that extend liberation theology into the ecological and technological horizons shaping the destiny of humanity and the planet.

Chapter 19 — Cosmic Liberation: Ecology, African Cosmology, And Intergenerational Justice. This chapter offers a unified vision of liberation that moves beyond social and political structures to embrace the Earth itself, ancestral landscapes, and future generations. Drawing on *Laudato Si'* and global eco-theology, it argues that environmental devastation—climate change, pollution, deforestation, extractive capitalism—is a form of structural sin inseparable from the suffering of the poor. Case studies from the Amazon Basin, the Bakweri land struggle, the Niger Delta, and Mount Cameroon conservation illustrate how ecological destruction disproportionately burdens Indigenous and marginalized communities while eroding cultural identity and spiritual memory.

The chapter then shifts to a cosmic and intergenerational horizon. Future generations are treated as genuine theological subjects whose flourishing is imperiled by present-day ecological irresponsibility. Environmental degradation becomes a form of intergenerational violence that violates both justice and covenant. Eschatology is reimagined not as an escape from the world but as a hopeful vision of creation's healing and renewal. The chapter culminates in a spirituality of cosmic solidarity, in which humans, Earth, and the wider cosmos participate together in God's ongoing work of liberation.

Chapter 20 — AI, Technology, and Digital Oppression: A New Frontier of Liberation Theology. This chapter turns to the digital sphere as an emerging site of oppression and potential liberation. It examines surveillance capitalism, algorithmic bias, and digital colonialism as structures that reproduce inequality and disproportionately harm the poor and the Global South. Through case studies—including African digital ID systems, automated decision-making, and global patterns of AI discrimination—the chapter shows how technological infrastructures can entrench new forms of structural injustice. It concludes by proposing a liberative technological ethic grounded in transparency, dignity, equity, and the preferential option for the poor, positioning AI as one of the decisive frontiers for 21st-century liberation theology

CHAPTER 19

Cosmic Liberation: Ecology, African Cosmology, and Intergenerational Justice

I — INTRODUCTION, THEOLOGICAL FOUNDATIONS, AND LAUDATO SI'

Introduction: The Expanding Horizon of Liberation

LIBERATION THEOLOGY HAS HISTORICALLY centered its prophetic critique on the human social order—capitalism, racism, sexism, colonialism, and political structures that marginalize the poor. Yet the present ecological crisis forces theology to widen its horizon. Environmental destruction now constitutes one of the most pervasive and lethal forms of structural sin in the world. Climate change, biodiversity loss, extreme weather events, pollution, and extractive capitalism devastate millions of lives, particularly among the poor, the Indigenous, and the Global South.[1]

This chapter advances a theological argument that liberation must become cosmic. The Christian tradition has long proclaimed that salvation encompasses all creation—"that God may be all in all" (1 Cor 15:28). Yet theological reflection has often privileged human beings, treating the Earth as background rather than protagonist. The present moment demands that liberation theology rediscover its cosmic vocation: creation itself groans under oppression, awaiting redemption (Rom 8:19–22).

---

1. Boff, *Cry of the Earth, Cry of the Poor*; Francis, *Laudato Si'*.

To speak of "cosmic liberation" is not to abstract theology into mysticism but to recognize that ecological harm is inflicted through human systems of domination. These systems—colonialism, hyper-capitalism, technological exploitation—degrade both ecosystems and the communities that depend on them. Ecological destruction is, therefore, a theological wound. The cry of the Earth and the cry of the poor cannot be separated.[2]

This chapter integrates four dimensions—eco-theology, African cosmology, intergenerational justice, and CSR metaphysics—to articulate a theological vision in which Earth, humanity, ancestors, and future generations participate in God's unfolding work of liberation.

2. Theological Foundations: CSR, Revelation, and the Ontology of Creation

2.1. CSR's Metaphysical Grounding for Ecology

Critical Synthetic Realism (CSR), presented earlier in this work, provides the metaphysical scaffolding for a cosmic ecological theology. CSR insists that truth is discovered at the intersection of:

1. Revelation (God's self-disclosure in Scripture and creation),
2. Reason (scientific knowledge, philosophical clarity),
3. Experience (the lived testimony of communities),
4. Ethical Responsibility (commitment to liberation and justice).

To ignore scientific ecology is to reject reason; to ignore Indigenous testimony is to reject experience; to ignore the cry of the Earth is to reject ethics; and to ignore biblical revelation about the goodness of creation is to reject Scripture (Gen 1:31; Ps 104). CSR therefore positions creation care not as optional but as essential to theological truth.

CSR emphasizes relational ontology: everything exists in interconnected networks. This reflects both the biblical view (Col 1:15–20) and ecological science, which sees ecosystems as interdependent systems where harm to one part reverberates through the whole. CSR thereby affirms that liberation must embrace the entire web of life.

---

2. Francis, *Laudato Si'*, §49.

2.2. Biblical Foundations: Creation as Covenant Partner

Christian ecological theology begins not with *Laudato Si'* but with Genesis. The creation narratives reveal:

- Intrinsic goodness of creation (Gen 1:31)
- Humanity's vocation as guardians ("till and keep" the Earth) (Gen 2:15)
- Land as belonging to God, not humans (Lev 25:23)
- Sabbath for land and workers (Exod 23:10–12)

Land is not a commodity; it is a covenant partner. Scripture repeatedly condemns those who exploit land for unjust gain (Isa 5:8; Mic 2:2; Hos 4:1–3). Ecological injustice is presented as a moral transgression with cosmic consequences—"the land mourns" (Hos 4:3).

Paul's cosmic Christology reinforces this:

- All things were created in Christ and for Christ (Col 1:16)
- In Christ, creation is reconciled (Col 1:20)
- Creation groans, awaiting liberation (Rom 8:22)

Liberation is not solely anthropocentric; it is cosmic redemption. The incarnation, in which God takes on material existence, confirms the sacredness of matter itself (John 1:14).

2.3. Liberation Theology's Turn Toward the Earth

Liberation theologians, especially Leonardo Boff and Sallie McFague, argue that the ecological crisis must be interpreted as structural sin. Just as racism or economic exploitation wounds human dignity, environmental exploitation wounds the integrity of creation.[3] Boff insists that ecology and poverty are intertwined: "To defend the Earth is to defend the poor."[4]

This chapter applies this insight to African contexts, where ecological violence—land dispossession, pollution, soil degradation—intersects directly with colonial and postcolonial oppression.

---

3. Boff, *Introducing Liberation Theology*; McFague, *The Body of God*.
4. Boff, *Cry of the Earth, Cry of the Poor*, 24.

3. LAUDATO SI' AND THE ECCLESIAL MANDATE FOR ECOLOGICAL LIBERATION

3.1. The Revolutionary Contribution of Laudato Si'

Pope Francis's *Laudato Si'* marks a doctrinal shift that situates ecological care at the heart of Christian discipleship. The document affirms, first, that the ecological crisis is a result of human sin—"the consequences of our collective actions."[5] Second, the encyclical insists that environmental degradation disproportionately harms the poor, making ecology a matter of justice.[6] Third, it condemns the technocratic paradigm—an uncontested faith in technological mastery that disregards human dignity or ecological limits.[7]

Francis thus establishes an ecclesial mandate: Christians are morally obligated to resist ecological destruction.

3.2. Integral Ecology: A Theological Synthesis

Integral ecology, the core concept of *Laudato Si'*, rejects the artificial separation between human and non-human life. It asserts that:

- ecological health,
- social justice,
- cultural identity,
- economic structures, and
- spirituality

are inseparably linked. Harm to one dimension inevitably harms the others. This is a profoundly African insight, as African cosmology also grounds identity and spirituality in land, ancestors, and ecological interdependence.

---

5. Francis, *Laudato Si'*, §3.
6. Francis, *Laudato Si'*, §48.
7. Francis, *Laudato Si'*, §101.

3.3. Structural Sin and the Throwaway Culture

Francis's critique of the "throwaway culture" is not merely moralistic but structural: modern society continually sacrifices both people and ecosystems in pursuit of profit. Plastic pollution, deforestation for export crops, toxic waste dumping, and excessive consumption are symptoms of a deeper condition: the commodification of creation.

CSR identifies this as a failure in metaphysical perception—seeing the world as objects rather than as sacred relations. When creation is reduced to a resource, exploitation becomes naturalized, and the cry of the Earth is silenced.

3.4. Ecological Conversion as Theological Imperative

Francis calls for "ecological conversion":[8] a transformation in how Christians perceive and relate to the world. This mirrors CSR's emphasis on the reformation of consciousness. Ecological conversion requires:

- humility toward creation,
- reverence for life,
- solidarity with ecological victims,
- repentance for ecological sins, and
- active participation in environmental justice movements.

This chapter argues that ecological conversion is not peripheral but essential for authentic Christian discipleship in the twenty-first century.

4. Global Ecological Crisis as a Sign of the Times

4.1. Climate Change and the Global Poor

Climate change disproportionately impacts the poorest regions of the world: Africa, South Asia, Latin America, and island nations. Rising temperatures reduce crop yields, increase droughts, trigger conflict over resources, and force migration. Francis (2015) warns that climate injustice is a new form of global colonialism.

---

8. Francis, *Laudato Si'*, §216.

4.2. Extractive Capitalism and Sacrifice Zones

Modern capitalism designates certain regions "sacrifice zones"—areas where ecological destruction is deemed acceptable for economic gains. These zones almost always coincide with communities that lack political power. Examples include:

- the Niger Delta,
- the Amazon Basin,
- the copperbelt of Zambia and DRC,
- the tar sands of Alberta,
- mining regions of Madagascar.

The Earth is sacrificed along with its poorest inhabitants.

4.3. The Human Cost of Ecological Violence

Ecological devastation produces:

- respiratory illness,
- cancers,
- infertility,
- water scarcity,
- food insecurity,
- cultural trauma,
- loss of ancestral identity.

Theological reflection must name this violence. Ecological harm is a violation of the commandment: "You shall not kill."

CSR insists that truth emerges through empirical evidence; thus, ecological theology must integrate climate science, public health data, and environmental research. The facts testify: ecological collapse threatens the very possibility of human flourishing.

II — CASE STUDIES IN ECO-SIN AND STRUCTURAL ECOLOGICAL INJUSTICE

5. Case Studies in Eco-Sin: When Creation Becomes a Victim

To understand ecological destruction as structural sin, theology must descend from abstraction into lived reality. Liberation theology is empirical; it begins with the concrete suffering of people and places.[9] Ecological sin becomes visible in devastated rivers, poisoned air, deforested lands, displaced peoples, and communities sacrificed for economic gain.

The following case studies—Amazon Basin, Niger Delta, the Bakweri land struggle, and Mount Cameroon—illustrate how ecological destruction functions as a continuation of colonial patterns of domination. They also demonstrate that the cry of the Earth is inseparable from cultural trauma, spiritual violation, and economic marginalization.

6. The Amazon Basin: The Lungs of the Planet Under Siege

6.1. Ecological and Spiritual Devastation

The Amazon rainforest, often referred to as the "lungs of the planet," absorbs enormous quantities of carbon dioxide and produces a significant share of the world's oxygen. Yet it is rapidly being destroyed by industrial agriculture, mining, logging, and hydroelectric projects.

This ecological devastation has profound human consequences. Indigenous communities suffer loss of land, cultural disintegration, and violence from land-grabbers supported by global corporations and corrupt political structures. The Amazon has become a paradigmatic "sacrifice zone," where ecosystems and Indigenous lives are deemed expendable for economic profit.

The Amazon Synod (2019) affirmed that the struggle for the forest is a struggle for the survival of its peoples, spirituality, and cosmology. Francis called the region "a theological locus," meaning that God's revelation is mediated through the suffering of the forest and its peoples. This is a profound extension of liberation theology: creation itself becomes a site of divine manifestation.

---

9. Gutiérrez, *A Theology of Liberation*.

6.2. Colonial Continuities

The exploitation of the Amazon is rooted in colonial logic: the idea that land without European-style ownership is "empty" and therefore available for extraction. But Indigenous cosmologies see the forest as animate, spiritual, and relational. Extractive industries violate not only ecosystems but also entire spiritual worlds.

CSR detects here a collapse of relational ontology. When creation is objectified, the metaphysical truth of interdependence is lost. This cognitive distortion produces ecological sin on a massive scale.

7. The Niger Delta: Ecological Apartheid in the Era of Oil

7.1. A Region of Ecological Horror

For more than six decades, the Niger Delta has suffered catastrophic environmental degradation due to oil extraction by multinational corporations.[10] Gas flaring, oil spills, and toxic waste dumping have poisoned water sources, destroyed fisheries, and undermined agriculture.

Villages that once survived through fishing now face widespread infertility, cancer, and respiratory disease. The Delta exemplifies ecological apartheid: the poor bear the ecological burdens, while wealth flows outward to corporations and political elites.

7.2. The Theology of Ecological Martyrdom

Ken Saro-Wiwa, executed in 1995 for protesting environmental destruction, is an ecological martyr. His death reveals how ecological sin is protected by political violence. The people of the Niger Delta continue to experience what Boff calls "the crucifixion of Earth communities."[11]

The moral weight of this crisis demands theological confrontation. The Catechism condemns actions that cause "harm to the environment and the common good." The Niger Delta shows that these sins are not incidental; they are systemic, ongoing, and the result of deliberate policy choices driven by greed.

---

10. Okonta and Douglas, *Where Vultures Feast*.
11. Boff, *Cry of the Earth, Cry of the Poor*.

7.3. CSR and the Critique of Technocratic Power

CSR identifies the technocratic paradigm as a metaphysical disorder: the illusion that human mastery over nature is limitless. Oil extraction in the Niger Delta demonstrates the destructive consequences of this mentality:

- land reduced to commodity,
- rivers reduced to industrial waste channels,
- communities reduced to labor reserves,
- ecosystems denied intrinsic value.

This is not simply injustice; it is metaphysical blindness—a refusal to see creation as a sacred relational field sustained by divine presence.

8. The Bakweri Land Struggle: Ecological Justice and Ancestral Identity

8.1. Land as Sacred Trust in Bakweri Cosmology

Among the Bakweri people of Cameroon, land is not an economic asset but a sacred inheritance. The land contains ancestral graves, cultural identity, and spiritual meaning. British colonial occupation in the late 19th century seized vast stretches of Bakweri land for plantations. This dispossession continued post-independence under state control.

To the Bakweri, losing land was not merely an economic injury but a spiritual and ontological rupture. As Ngangi demonstrates, the Bakweri struggle for land rights is also a struggle for cultural survival, ancestral continuity, and environmental stewardship.[12]

8.2. Ecological and Cultural Consequences of Dispossession

Colonial plantations introduced monoculture farming, soil exhaustion, and chemical pollution. Traditional ecological knowledge was dismissed, replaced by extractive agricultural models. The land became a site of exploitation rather than reciprocity.

CSR interprets this as a dual alienation:

- alienation of people from land, and

12. Ngangi, *The Bakweri Land Problem*.

- alienation of land from its sacred purpose.

This mirrors the biblical vision: land belongs to God and must not be permanently alienated (Lev 25:23). The Bakweri struggle is thus not only political but theological—an insistence on restoring right relationship with creation.

8.3. Theological Lessons from the Bakweri Experience

Three theological insights emerge:

1. Ecological sin is inseparable from colonial sin.
2. The Earth suffers where people suffer.
3. Land has sacramental significance.
4. It bears memory, identity, and ancestral presence.
5. Restitution and reparation are ecological imperatives.
6. Justice requires returning land or ensuring Indigenous stewardship.

This aligns with the Christian mandate to restore creation and repair relationships broken by historical injustice.

9. Mount Cameroon: Conservation, Culture, and Cosmic Symbolism

9.1. Mount Cameroon as Sacred Geography

Mount Cameroon, known as *Mongo ma Ndemi*, is central in Bakweri cosmology. It is seen as a living presence inhabited by ancestral and spiritual forces. As such, it is a site where geography and theology intersect.

Modern conservation efforts, while environmentally necessary, often disregard Indigenous spiritual relationships with the land. Policies restricting traditional access—hunting, rituals, medicinal harvesting—have marginalized Bakweri communities and created tensions between Western conservation science and Indigenous ecological spirituality.

9.2. Colonial Patterns in Conservation

Conservation has often adopted a "fortress model" that treats humans—especially Indigenous peoples—as threats to nature. This reproduces colonial structures of exclusion. Ecological protection must not become ecological colonialism.

CSR emphasizes that genuine ecological stewardship must integrate:

- scientific knowledge,
- Indigenous ecological wisdom,
- spiritual cosmology,
- community participation.

9.3. Cosmic Symbolism and Theological Meaning

Mount Cameroon is also a cosmic symbol. Its towering presence evokes transcendence and interconnection. Mountains in biblical tradition signify divine encounter—Sinai, Tabor, the Mount of Beatitudes. To desacralize such spaces is to desacralize creation itself.

A cosmic theology sees Mount Cameroon not merely as geological structure but as a revelation of divine grandeur and a call to ecological responsibility.

10. Eco-Sin as Structural and Cosmic Sin

10.1. Defining Eco-Sin

Eco-sin is the violation of relationships that constitute creation. It is sin against:

- God (disrespecting divine creation),
- neighbor (harm to the poor),
- future generations (intergenerational injustice),
- Earth (damage to ecosystems),
- self (alienation from ecological identity).

Eco-sin is structural because it is embedded in systems—economic, political, technological—that perpetuate environmental harm.

10.2. CSR and the Moral Epistemology of Eco-Sin

CSR holds that sin is not merely moral failure but epistemic failure—distorted perception of reality. Eco-sin results from:

- reductionism (seeing ecosystems as objects),
- individualism (ignoring communal and intergenerational responsibility),
- anthropocentrism (denying intrinsic value of non-human life),
- economic absolutism (treating profit as ultimate).

True epistemic clarity requires ecological awareness.

10.3. Ecological Conversion as Liberation

Ecological conversion involves:

- recovering awe before creation,
- acknowledging ecological complicity,
- adopting sustainable lifestyles,
- supporting ecological justice movements,
- healing relationships with land and creation.

This is not optional for Christians; it is intrinsic to discipleship.

III — AFRICAN COSMOLOGY, CSR METAPHYSICS, AND INTERGENERATIONAL JUSTICE

11. African Cosmology and the Sacred Web of Life

11.1. The African Vision of Reality as Relational and Holistic

African cosmologies consistently present the universe as a relational field, not a collection of atomized entities. The universe is an intricate web in which human beings, animals, rivers, forests, mountains, ancestors, spirits, and God form a single, interconnected community.[13]

---

13. Mbiti, *African Religions and Philosophy*.

African thought resists dualisms—body/soul, human/nature, sacred/secular—that characterize much Western metaphysics. Instead, the African worldview affirms cosmic unity:

- The spiritual permeates the material.
- The ancestors inhabit the land.
- Rivers and forests possess spiritual agency.
- Human flourishing depends on harmonious relationships with the natural world.

This worldview aligns naturally with contemporary ecological science, which emphasizes systems theory, interdependence, and ecological balance. African cosmology thus provides fertile ground for an ecological theology rooted in place, community, and sacred relationality.

11.2. Personhood as Ecological Identity

In many African cultures, personhood (*ubuntu, umuntu ngumuntu ngabantu*) is defined through relationships. One becomes a person through participation in community. This includes not only the human community but also the natural world.

Ecological destruction, therefore, is not only material harm—it is ontological harm. When forests are destroyed, rivers polluted, or sacred land desecrated, the community's identity is wounded. Ecological devastation erodes relational personhood.

CSR aligns with this insight by asserting that truth and identity are formed through networks of relations. The ecological crisis is thus not merely environmental but existential—a distortion of the relational structures that constitute human and non-human being.

11.3. African Spirituality and the Sacramentality of Land

African cosmologies see land as the seat of ancestors, the keeper of memory, and the context of divine-human encounter. The land is not merely physical; it is spiritual geography.

To desecrate land is to violate the spiritual order and to rupture relationships with ancestors. This resonates deeply with the biblical understanding in which land is gifted by God, belongs primarily to God, and must not be abused (Lev 25:23).

African spiritual traditions, therefore, offer a sacramental view of creation: the Earth mediates divine presence and ancestral wisdom. A Christian ecological theology must recognize this: the land is sacred space, not merely resource.

12. CSR Metaphysics and the Cosmic Dimension of Liberation

12.1. Creation as Emergent Relational Field

CSR asserts that reality is emergent: complex systems arise from simpler ones through relational interaction. This ecological insight mirrors the metaphysical structure of creation. The cosmos is not static but dynamic, evolving, and relational.

This metaphysical vision reinforces the theological insight that creation participates in God's continuous creativity. Every ecosystem, species, and organism expresses God's relational intention.

Mapping CSR to ecological science yields three insights:

1. Creation is a dynamic, evolving reality—God continually sustains being.
2. All beings are interconnected—ecological harm reverberates cosmically.
3. Liberation must be systemic—healing cannot be isolated to human structures alone.

CSR thus demands a cosmic scope for liberation: oppression of ecosystems interrupts the metaphysical harmony of creation.

12.2. Sin as Disruption of Cosmic Order

Traditional theology understands sin as disordering the relationship between God, self, and neighbor. CSR deepens this by identifying sin as epistemic distortion—a failure to perceive reality truthfully.

Eco-sin emerges when humanity:

- denies ecological limits,
- reduces creation to commodity,

- treats ecosystems as disposable,
- centers profit over planetary health,
- separates human destiny from ecological destiny.

These distortions produce structural injustice and cosmic disharmony.

Liberation, therefore, requires not only political revolution but metaphysical conversion—a transformation of consciousness that recognizes creation as sacred relationality.

12.3. Cosmic Christology and Ecological Redemption

Paul's cosmic Christology (Col 1:15–20) asserts that:

- Christ is the mediator of creation,
- Christ sustains creation, and
- Christ reconciles all creation.

Redemption is universal in scope. The crucified and risen Christ gathers every dimension of creation into divine life. Ecological destruction, therefore, becomes a crucifixion of creation.

A cosmic liberation theology interprets ecological restoration as participation in Christ's reconciling work. Reforestation, conservation, restoration of rivers, and protection of species become sacramental acts that manifest the reign of God.

CSR amplifies this: ecological healing enhances the relational structure that allows truth, beauty, and being to flourish.

13. Intergenerational Justice: A Theology of the Future

13.1. The Future as Theological Subject

The moral weight of ecological destruction becomes clearest when viewed through the lens of intergenerational justice. Decisions made today shape the conditions of life for those who have no voice—future generations.

Catholic theology has always understood covenant in intergenerational terms:

- God's promise to Abraham extends to descendants.

- Israel's ethical obligations safeguard future communities.
- Prophetic warnings condemn failure to protect future well-being.

The future is, therefore, a theological subject, not an abstraction.

13.2. Intergenerational Harm as Moral Violation

Current ecological policies and practices—unchecked carbon emissions, deforestation, overfishing, mining, toxic waste production—place catastrophic burdens on future generations:

- food scarcity,
- water crisis,
- mass extinction,
- climate refugees,
- economic instability.

This is a form of intergenerational violence. To leave a scorched Earth to the next generation violates the Christian ethical principle of the universal destination of goods—creation belongs not only to the present but to the future.

CSR interprets intergenerational harm as a breakdown of moral imagination. Ethics must expand temporally to include the entire horizon of human and cosmic flourishing.

13.3. African Communal Ethics and Future Generations

African ethics strongly emphasizes continuity: the community includes ancestors, the living, and the unborn. Decisions must honor all three. This triadic anthropology directly challenges modern ecological irresponsibility.

The proverb *"We borrow the Earth from our children"* reflects a deeply African and profoundly theological truth. Stewardship is not optional; it is ancestral obligation.

13.4. Biblical Eschatology and Ecological Hope

Christian eschatology does not envision escape from creation but its transformation:

- Isaiah envisions a renewed Earth (Isa 65:17).
- Paul anticipates creation liberated from bondage (Rom 8:21).
- Revelation promises "a new heaven and a new Earth" (Rev 21:1).

Intergenerational justice becomes an eschatological vocation: Work today for the world God promises tomorrow.

The ecological crisis demands a spirituality oriented toward future flourishing. This is not naïve optimism but theological hope grounded in divine fidelity.

14. CSR, Ecology, and the Ethics of Time

CSR provides a philosophical basis for intergenerational ethics by emphasizing that truth unfolds across time. Reality is developmental—scientifically, morally, spiritually. Thus:

- ecological decisions must consider long-term consequences,
- ethics must extend beyond immediate benefits,
- liberation must include those not yet born,
- moral imagination must expand cosmically.

Ecological irresponsibility becomes an epistemic injustice toward the future—a refusal to recognize future communities as bearers of dignity and moral value.

IV — ESCHATOLOGY, COSMIC SACRAMENTALITY, AND CONCLUSION

15. Eschatology as Ecological Hope

15.1. Rejecting Escapist Theologies

A significant obstacle to ecological responsibility within Christianity has been the persistence of escapist eschatologies—interpretations of the faith that treat the Earth as disposable and salvation as an escape from material creation. Such frameworks distort Scripture and undermine moral responsibility. They also contradict the Catholic doctrine of the resurrection of the body and the renewal of creation (Rom 8:19–23; Rev 21:1–5).

Creation is not a temporary stage to be discarded but a beloved participant in God's plan. Destruction of ecosystems, therefore, cannot be justified by claims that "this world will pass away." The theology of cosmic liberation rejects any eschatology that encourages ecological apathy or moral detachment.

Instead, it affirms the biblical vision of a transfigured creation, where God's redemptive purposes include Earth's healing and flourishing.

15.2. The New Creation as Ecological Renewal

The prophetic tradition consistently speaks of renewal:

- "The desert shall bloom" (Isa 35:1).
- "I create new heavens and a new Earth" (Isa 65:17).
- "Creation itself will be set free from bondage" (Rom 8:21).

These texts present eschatology not as annihilation but as transformation. The Earth is not destroyed but liberated.

CSR interprets this as a metaphysical affirmation: the cosmos is oriented toward greater relational harmony, not entropy. The divine intention for creation is flourishing, integration, and communion. Human participation in ecological restoration anticipates this eschatological fulfillment.

15.3. Eschatology, Ethics, and Urgency

The eschaton—God's future—is not a passive hope but an ethical mandate. Christians are called to live as people of the new creation, embodying future justice in present structures. This requires:

- resisting ecological destruction,
- advocating for environmental justice,
- protecting endangered species,

- reducing carbon footprints,
- restructuring economies around sustainability,
- supporting Indigenous ecological leadership.

Eschatological hope becomes a transformative praxis, not escapism. Christians act not because the world will end but because the world is sacred and destined for transfiguration.

16. Cosmic Sacramentality: The Earth as Revelation

16.1. Creation as Sacrament

Catholic theology affirms the sacramentality of creation: the material world mediates divine presence. Theologians such as McFague describe the world as "the body of God"—a metaphor pointing to creation's participation in divine life.[14]

This does not imply pantheism; rather, it affirms that God communicates grace through material reality. Rivers, mountains, forests, and oceans become signs of God's beauty, wisdom, and generosity.

CSR intensifies this claim by asserting that creation reveals metaphysical truth:

- relationality,
- interdependence,
- emergent complexity,
- unity in diversity.

To harm creation is thus to obscure divine revelation.

16.2. Sacramentality in African Thought

African cosmology naturally aligns with cosmic sacramentality. Sacred forests, ancestral mountains, holy rivers, and ritual landscapes function as spiritual centers. They mediate ancestors, divine beings, communal identity, and ecological responsibility.

For instance:

---

14. McFague, *The Body of God*.

- Mount Cameroon is a sacred meeting place between the living and the ancestral world.
- The Congo River is seen as a channel of life and cosmological force.
- Sacred groves in Ghana and Nigeria serve as ecological sanctuaries.

In African spirituality, ecological degradation is both ecological and spiritual desecration. This insight enriches Christian theology, offering a culturally grounded sacramental ecology.

16.3. Cosmic Sacramentality and the Church's Mission

The Church's sacramental worldview calls believers to protect creation as part of their liturgical and moral identity. The Eucharist, which celebrates the transformation of bread and wine—fruits of the Earth—into Christ's body and blood, binds ecological stewardship to Christian worship.

Every Eucharist is an ecological event:

- it affirms creation's goodness,
- reveals creation's capacity for divine presence,
- demands gratitude and responsibility.

A cosmic sacramental theology insists that ecological destruction is an attack on the very elements through which God sanctifies the world.

17. The Preferential Option for the Earth

17.1. Extending the Preferential Option for the Poor

Liberation theology's foundational principle—the preferential option for the poor—must be extended to include the Earth itself. Because the Earth is exploited in ways that parallel and support human oppression, ecology becomes a locus for the same divine preference.

This is not anthropomorphic sentimentality; it reflects a theological truth:

The God who sides with the oppressed also sides with oppressed creation.

17.2. Ecological Hermeneutics of Liberation

Reading Scripture through an ecological lens reveals biblical themes that have been overlooked:

- the Earth as witness (Deut 32:1),
- the land as teacher (Job 12:7–10),
- the Earth as mourning (Jer 4:28),
- creatures praising God (Ps 148).

CSR reinforces that ecological liberation is necessary for epistemic clarity. Distorted ecological relationships distort our perception of God, the world, and ourselves.

18. Toward an Ecological Ethic of Cosmic Solidarity

18.1. Solidarity as Relational Participation

Cosmic solidarity expands the moral imagination. It affirms that Christians must stand with:

- oppressed peoples,
- endangered species,
- wounded ecosystems,
- disappearing cultures,
- future generations,
- the unborn Earth.

Solidarity becomes a cosmic posture of participation in the flourishing of all beings.

18.2. Ecological Virtues

Three ecological virtues emerge from this spirituality:

1. Humility — acknowledging humanity's dependence on creation.
2. Sobriety — resisting consumerism and unnecessary consumption.
3. Reverence — cultivating awe before the sacredness of life.

These virtues mirror *Laudato Si'*'s vision of ecological conversion.

18.3. Structures that Support Cosmic Solidarity

Ecological liberation requires systemic transformation:

- renewable energy adoption,
- communal land rights,
- ecological reparations for colonial harms,
- preservation of Indigenous ecological knowledge,
- reforestation programs,
- environmental protection laws with enforcement teeth.

The Church must advocate for ecological justice not only spiritually but institutionally.

19. Cosmic Liberation as the Future of Theology

19.1. Theological Synthesis

This chapter synthesizes eco-theology, African cosmology, CSR metaphysics, and intergenerational ethics to present a new horizon for liberation theology. It argues:

- ecological destruction is structural sin,
- land is spiritual inheritance,
- future generations are theological subjects,
- eschatology demands ecological responsibility,
- creation is sacramental,
- liberation must be cosmic.

19.2. Implications for Theology and Ministry

Theology must:

- integrate ecological science,

- critique extractive capitalism,
- defend Indigenous ecological rights,
- cultivate ecological spirituality,
- teach intergenerational ethics.

Ministry must:

- incorporate ecological liturgies,
- support environmental movements,
- promote sustainable parish practices,
- educate communities about ecological justice.

19.3. Cosmic Liberation and the Mission of the Church

The Church's mission in the 21st century is inseparable from ecological liberation. To proclaim the Gospel while ignoring ecological collapse is a contradiction. The Church must become:

- protector of creation,
- advocate for ecological justice,
- voice for future generations,
- partner of Indigenous ecological movements,
- witness to hope amid ecological despair.

Cosmic liberation is not an optional theological theme. It is the horizon toward which all creation groans and toward which Christian hope must strive.

20. Conclusion: Creation's Hope and Humanity's Responsibility

The ecological crisis is the defining moral and theological challenge of our era. The Earth is crying out—along with the poor, the marginalized, and future generations. Theological reflection that fails to address ecological destruction is incomplete. The cosmic Christ calls humanity to participate in the redemption and renewal of creation.

Cosmic liberation declares:

- Creation is sacred.
- Justice must be ecological.
- The future must be protected.
- God's love encompasses all beings.

In this vision, humanity becomes truly human—guardian of creation, keeper of ancestral memory, and co-creator of ecological justice.

This is the vocation of the Church, the demand of the Gospel, and the movement of God's Spirit in the world today.

CHAPTER 20

AI, Technology, and Digital Oppression: A New Frontier of Liberation Theology

1. INTRODUCTION: TECHNOLOGY AS A NEW ARENA OF THEOLOGICAL STRUGGLE

ARTIFICIAL INTELLIGENCE HAS EMERGED as one of the defining forces of the twenty-first century, shaping global economies, political systems, social interactions, and human identity. Yet despite its promise, AI is neither morally neutral nor universally beneficial. It is embedded within economic structures, political ideologies, and cultural assumptions that determine who benefits and who is harmed. As Shoshana Zuboff argues, AI participates in an unprecedented regime of surveillance capitalism that extracts human experience for profit.[1] As Ruha Benjamin shows, AI often reinforces preexisting racial and economic inequalities.[2] From the perspective of liberation theology, these dynamics expose AI as a new site of oppression requiring rigorous moral scrutiny.

Classical liberation theology emerged from the cries of the oppressed—peasants, workers, racial minorities, and colonized peoples.[3] Today a new cry emerges: those marginalized by digital systems, excluded by algorithms, surveilled by corporations, displaced by automation, and burdened by the ecological footprint of technology. This chapter argues that AI represents a profound theological challenge, requiring an

1. Zuboff, *The Age of Surveillance Capitalism*.
2. Benjamin, *Race After Technology*.
3. Gutiérrez, *A Theology of Liberation*.

expansion of liberation theology and Catholic social teaching into the digital sphere. The question is no longer whether technology influences human dignity but whether it reshapes the moral landscape of creation itself.

Critical Synthetic Realism (CSR) affirms that moral reality is objective, relational, and participatory; human dignity derives from the metaphysical structure of creation. Any system that fragments the person, reduces them to data, or amplifies structural sin violates this ontological order. Thus, AI is not simply a tool—it is a moral force that must be judged according to the Gospel's command to uphold justice, dignity, and the preferential option for the poor.[4]

2. SURVEILLANCE CAPITALISM: THE ANTI-SACRAMENT OF THE DIGITAL AGE

2.1. The Mechanisms of Digital Extraction

Surveillance capitalism, a term coined by Zuboff, describes the economic logic in which companies capture human behavioral data—search histories, biometrics, location information, emotional patterns—and monetize them without informed consent.[5] The digital infrastructures that enable AI rely on the constant extraction of lived experience. AI models require vast datasets, meaning that human life becomes "training material" for corporate profit.

This extraction contradicts fundamental principles of Catholic anthropology. According to the doctrine of the imago Dei, every person possesses intrinsic dignity and mystery. St. Augustine taught that the human person is a depth known fully only to God; St. Thomas Aquinas emphasized the rational and spiritual capacities that ground human dignity. Surveillance capitalism dissolves this interiority, treating persons as transparent objects. It becomes, in effect, an anti-sacrament—a structure not of grace but of exposure, commodification, and control.

---

4. John Paul II, *Centesimus Annus*; Francis, *Laudato Si'*.
5. Zuboff, *The Age of Surveillance Capitalism*.

2.2. Surveillance as Structural Sin

Poor and marginalized communities endure disproportionate digital surveillance. Predictive policing targets Black and Brown neighborhoods.[6] Welfare recipients face algorithmic monitoring. Migrants are tracked through facial recognition and biometric systems that they cannot refuse. Students in under-resourced schools are subjected to online proctoring systems that often misidentify darker-skinned faces.[7]

Liberation theology defines structural sin as injustice embedded in systems rather than individual choices.[8] Surveillance capitalism is precisely such a system. It constructs a digital panopticon in which the poor are hyper-visible to power yet invisible in terms of political representation and algorithmic fairness.

2.3. CSR and the Moral Disorder of Surveillance

CSR teaches that authentic knowledge emerges from respectful encounter, not domination. Knowledge that violates freedom is morally disordered. AI systems that track, predict, and manipulate behavior generate false knowledge—knowledge without relationship, consent, or reciprocity. Such knowledge is contrary to the moral structure of reality because it treats the person not as a subject but as an object.

3. ALGORITHMIC BIAS, STRUCTURAL RACISM, AND DIGITAL COLONIALISM

3.1. Algorithmic Bias as a Continuation of Oppression

AI systems learn from historical data, which reflects centuries of racial injustice, colonial domination, and economic inequality. Thus:

- Facial recognition misidentifies Black people at alarming rates.[9]
- Hiring algorithms downgrade résumés associated with women or African American names.

---

6. Benjamin, *Race After Technology*.
7. Buolamwini and Gebru, *Gender Shades*.
8. Gutiérrez, *A Theology of Liberation*.
9. Buolamwini and Gebru, *Gender Shades*.

- Healthcare algorithms systematically underestimate the needs of Black patients.
- Predictive policing tools target already criminalized communities.[10]

Safiya Noble (2018) calls this "algorithmic oppression"—structural racism encoded into digital systems. AI does not merely reflect injustice; it amplifies it.

3.2. Digital Colonialism: Extraction Without Representation

Nick Couldry and Ulises Mejías describe digital colonialism as the appropriation of human life through data extraction.[11] In Africa, Asia, and Latin America, Big Tech firms gather personal data at massive scale, using the Global South as a testing ground for experimental technologies such as facial recognition, biometric ID systems, and automated credit scoring.

This mirrors classical colonialism: the Global South provides the resource—data—while the Global North retains the benefits—capital, political power, and technological sovereignty. Data extraction without democratic oversight is a form of technological domination that violates both justice and dignity.

3.3. Theological Response: Sin Against the Imago Dei

Catholic theology insists that social structures must uphold human dignity. Systems that misclassify, dehumanize, or erase entire populations commit a sin against the Creator. As Francis writes in *Laudato Si'*, "technological products are not neutral."[12] They embody "an undifferentiated and one-dimensional paradigm" that disconnects knowledge from ethics.[13]

For liberation theology, algorithmic bias is not a technical issue; it is a soteriological issue, affecting the salvation and flourishing of human beings within history.

---

10. O'Neil, *Weapons of Math Destruction*.
11. Couldry and Mejías, *The Costs of Connection*.
12. Francis, *Laudato Si'*.
13. Francis, *Laudato Si'*, §106.

4. AUTOMATION, LABOR DISPLACEMENT, AND DIGITAL EXCLUSION

4.1. The Poor and the Precarity of Work

AI-driven automation threatens millions of jobs worldwide. Unlike previous waves of technological change, AI threatens not only manual labor but cognitive labor—placing clerical workers, drivers, retail employees, and even middle-skill positions at risk. The poor and working class bear the brunt of this displacement.

Taylor shows historical continuities between discriminatory housing and financial policies and present economic vulnerability.[14] Automation deepens these vulnerabilities by creating a class of digitally "surplus" people.

4.2. The Digital Divide as a New Class System

Digital exclusion intensifies social inequality:

- Rural areas lack broadband infrastructure.
- Poor households cannot afford laptops or AI-powered educational tools.
- Migrants and linguistic minorities face barriers in digital systems.
- Older adults struggle to access digital government services.

Thus the poor experience a double exclusion: excluded from the digital economy and targeted by digital surveillance.

4.3. Catholic Social Teaching and the Right to Participate

Catholic social teaching emphasizes the right to participate in economic and social life. Technological systems that exclude vast populations deny this right. As John Paul II notes, any system that undermines human dignity or restricts participation violates justice.[15]

CSR expands this by arguing that participation is ontological, not optional. To be human is to participate in truth, community, and the

---

14. Taylor, *Race for Profit*.
15. John Paul II, *Centesimus Annus*.

common good. AI systems that deny meaningful participation contradict the moral structure of creation.

5. AI INFRASTRUCTURE, ELECTRICITY CONSUMPTION, AND ENVIRONMENTAL INJUSTICE

5.1. The Hidden Materiality of AI

Contrary to popular perception, AI is not immaterial. It is built on vast physical infrastructures: energy-intensive data centers, water-consuming cooling systems, and supply chains dependent on mining rare-earth metals. Jones documents the enormous carbon footprint of advanced AI models,[16] while Hodge and Morales show how demand from data centers strains electrical grids.[17]

5.2. Rising Electricity Costs and the Disproportionate Impact on the Poor

Across the United States, utilities have raised electricity rates in states hosting large AI data centers—Virginia, Texas, Georgia, Arizona, and others. These costs fall hardest on low-income households, many of whom do not use AI technologies yet must pay higher energy bills.

This parallels the logic of regressive taxation: the poor subsidize technological innovation that benefits wealthier populations.

5.3. Environmental Racism and Digital Energy Demand

AI-driven electricity demand often requires utilities to reactivate or expand fossil fuel plants. Because these plants are disproportionately located in Black, Brown, and low-income communities,[18] AI expansion increases:

- pollution
- respiratory disease

---

16. Jones, *How Big Is AI's Carbon Footprint?*
17. Hodge and Morales, *AI Demand Stresses U.S. Power Grid Amid Rising Electricity Costs.*
18. Bullard, *Dumping in Dixie.*

- groundwater contamination
- ecological degradation

Thus digital injustice merges with ecological injustice.

5.4. Theological Interpretation: Sin Against the Poor and Against Creation

Laudato Si' condemns systems that cause ecological harm while enriching the powerful.[19] AI-driven energy injustice represents a threefold sin:

1. Against the poor, who pay higher prices.
2. Against creation, which absorbs pollution.
3. Against intergenerational justice, violating the rights of future generations.

In CSR metaphysics, this represents a fragmentation of cosmic harmony—technology should support the flourishing of creation, not burden it.

6. CASE STUDIES: AI HARMS IN GLOBAL PERSPECTIVE

6.1. African Digital ID Systems

Robinson and Yu document how biometric digital ID systems across Africa—Kenya's Huduma Namba, Nigeria's NIN, South Africa's Home Affairs systems—often exclude the very people they claim to include:[20]

- fingerprint errors for manual laborers
- unreliable electricity in rural regions
- women lacking birth documentation
- minor data mismatches blocking access to healthcare or schooling

In theological terms, these systems create *digital lepers*—persons rendered unclean or invalid by technological misclassification.

---

19. Francis, *Laudato Si'*.
20. Robinson and Yu, *Digital Identity Systems and Human Rights*.

6.2. Global AI Bias and Machine-Scale Discrimination

AI models built in the Global North are often deployed globally, carrying their biases with them:

- immigration algorithms disproportionately flag travelers from the Global South
- loan algorithms penalize African and Latin American applicants
- healthcare algorithms misdiagnose non-white patients
- AI tutoring underperforms for accented English speakers

O'Neil calls such systems "Weapons of Math Destruction"—tools that scale injustice under a veneer of objectivity.[21]

7. TOWARD A LIBERATIVE TECHNOLOGICAL ETHICS

A theology of AI must move beyond critique toward constructive ethical guidance. A liberative technological ethic requires at least five principles:

7.1. Transparency

Systems must be explainable and auditable. Hidden algorithms producing public consequences contradict both justice and synodality.

7.2. Dignity

No human should be reduced to a data profile. Technologies must honor the imago Dei.

7.3. Equity

AI must reduce—not widen—inequality. This includes algorithmic fairness and equitable access to digital tools.

---

21. O'Neil, *Weapons of Math Destruction*.

7.4. Preferential Option for the Poor

The moral value of any AI system is determined by its impact on the most vulnerable.[22] Catholic ethics demands prioritizing those at risk of exclusion.

7.5. CSR Contribution: Reality as Relational and Moral

CSR emphasizes that knowledge, power, and ethics must be integrated. AI that operates without moral grounding produces epistemological violence—false knowledge that harms real people.

8. ESCHATOLOGY, HOPE, AND THE TECHNOLOGICAL FUTURE

Christian eschatology envisions a redeemed creation, not an escape from history. Technology must participate in this redemptive arc. The Book of Revelation imagines a city where "the nations walk by its light" (Rev. 21:24)—a symbol of human creativity transfigured by justice.

AI can serve this eschatological hope if oriented toward:

- healing community
- protecting creation
- expanding access to knowledge
- uplifting the marginalized
- reducing global inequality

But if oriented toward profit, domination, and surveillance, it becomes an idol—what Pope Benedict XVI described as "the dictatorship of relativism," in which truth is subordinated to power.

9. CONCLUSION: AI MUST CHOOSE BETWEEN PHARAOH AND THE KINGDOM

AI is not destiny. It is a site of contestation between liberation and domination. Like the Exodus, the question is whether AI serves

---

22. Gutiérrez, *A Theology of Liberation*.

Pharaoh—extractive capitalism, digital surveillance, ecological exploitation—or whether it serves the Kingdom—justice, dignity, and the flourishing of the poor.

A liberative theology of AI demands:

- justice over efficiency
- dignity over data extraction
- participation over exclusion
- ecological integrity over technological consumption
- truth over algorithmic distortion
- solidarity over surveillance

In the end, the Gospel judges every system, digital or otherwise, by whether it brings life or death. AI must therefore be reclaimed for liberation, ensuring that technology becomes not a new machinery of oppression but a frontier of justice, equity, and the sacredness of human dignity.

CONCLUSION

Beyond Doctrine: A Manifesto for a Church of the Poor and the Planet

1. INTRODUCTION: THE KAIROS MOMENT OF THE 21ST-CENTURY CHURCH

EVERY AGE OF THE Church has been confronted with a question that forced it beyond doctrinal repetition into moral imagination. The fourth century faced the crisis of Trinitarian identity. The medieval Church confronted Eucharistic doctrine and the nature of sacramental grace. Vatican II confronted modernity, religious freedom, and ecclesial reform. Our present moment is no less decisive.

We stand in an era marked by ecological collapse, structural injustice, global inequality, forced migration, resurgent fascism, and new digital empires that shape consciousness itself. The Church cannot simply restate moral conclusions drawn from a pre-digital, pre-industrial, pre-pluralistic world. Instead, it must undergo what Pope Francis calls an "ecological conversion,"[1] and what liberation theologians insist is a "conversion to the poor."[2]

This Critical-Liberative Theology (CLT) seeks to synthesize:

- Critical Synthetic Realism (CSR) — affirming the moral structure of reality, the dignity of all persons, and the unity of truth.

---

1. Francis, *Laudato Si'*, §217.
2. Gutiérrez, *A Theology of Liberation*.

- Liberation theology — centering the cries of the poor, the oppressed, and the planet.
- Catholic social teaching — insisting that faith is public, political, and relational.
- Christocentric ethics — placing Jesus's radical solidarity and boundary-breaking love at the heart of Christian praxis.

This conclusion presents a prophetic and academic manifesto, calling the Church beyond doctrinal defensiveness into transformative fidelity. As theologian James Cone argued regarding racism, "If the Church is not speaking for the oppressed, it is not the Church of Jesus Christ."[3]

Today the oppressed include:

- the economically dispossessed
- colonized and racialized peoples
- LGBTQ+ persons
- migrants and refugees
- the ecologically devastated
- future generations
- and those rendered invisible by digital injustice

The Church's mission cannot be confined to sacramental administration and moral caution. It must become a catalyst of cosmic liberation, proclaiming that God's preferential love extends to all who suffer under structures of sin—human, ecological, digital, economic, and epistemic.

This manifesto proposes four movements:

1. Ten principles of Critical-Liberative Theology
2. A practical program for ecclesial reform
3. Pastoral commitments for a liberative church
4. A spirituality of emancipation and cosmic solidarity

This is not merely a conclusion—it is an invitation to conversion.

---

3. Cone, *For My People*.

2. THE TEN PRINCIPLES OF CRITICAL-LIBERATIVE THEOLOGY

These ten principles synthesize CSR metaphysics, liberationist ethics, and Catholic tradition into a coherent framework for 21st-century theology.

Principle One: Ontological Dignity Is Universal and Non-Negotiable

The imago Dei is foundational. Every human person—LGBTQ+, Indigenous, immigrant, disabled, imprisoned, digitally marginalized—bears ontological dignity that cannot be annulled by doctrine, law, or cultural tradition.[4] Any theology that permits exclusion violates creation itself.

Principle Two: Sin Is Structural Before It Is Personal

Scripture and liberation theology affirm that sin operates in systems of domination—economic, ecological, racial, digital, patriarchal.[5] Structural sin is not an abstract concept; it is lived in polluted neighborhoods, algorithmic bias, criminalized sexualities, impoverished schools, AI-driven energy burdens,[6] and extractive capitalism.

A Church that does not confront structural sin becomes complicit in it.

Principle Three: The Poor and the Planet Are One Struggle

Ecological devastation and human oppression share a common logic: exploitation, dispossession, and commodification.[7] Climate collapse is not separate from racism, colonialism, or patriarchy. It is their cumulative historical outcome.

The cry of the Earth and the cry of the poor are the same cry because both emerge from systems that sacrifice life for profit.

---

4. Aquinas, *ST* I.93.
5. Gutiérrez, *A Theology of Liberation*; Cone, *For My People*.
6. Hodge and Morales, *AI Demand Stresses U.S. Power Grid Amid Rising Electricity Costs*.
7. Francis, *Laudato Si'*.

Principle Four: Liberation Is Cosmic, Not Merely Social

CSR insists that reality is relational, synthetic, and morally structured. Liberation therefore extends beyond human rights to include:

- ecosystems
- ancestral lands
- future generations
- technological infrastructures
- cultural memory

Salvation is not escape from creation but its healing (Rom 8:22).

Principle Five: Experience Is a Locus of Revelation

Dei Verbum affirms tradition, Scripture, and the Magisterium, but the sensus fidelium—the lived experience of God's people—is a genuine source of theological truth.[8]

This includes the testimonies of:

- queer believers
- African Indigenous communities
- migrants
- women resisting patriarchal exclusion
- the digitally oppressed

Their experience is not anecdotal—it is revelatory.

Principle Six: Doctrine Develops Through Liberation

Following Newman, doctrine grows as the Church deepens its understanding of revelation. Such development is never abstract but emerges through crises that expose injustice. As with slavery, usury, and religious liberty, teachings on gender, sexuality, ecology, and digital ethics must evolve.

Liberation is the condition for doctrinal maturation.

---

8. Vatican II, *Gaudium et Spes*.

Principle Seven: Love Is the Final Hermeneutic

Augustine declared, "If a scriptural interpretation does not build love of God and neighbor, it must be rejected."[9]
Any doctrine, policy, or practice that produces:

- shame
- exclusion
- ecological harm
- violence
- or despair

fails the test of love and cannot represent the Gospel.

Principle Eight: Technology Is a Moral and Theological Arena

AI, data systems, energy infrastructures, and digital economies are not neutral tools but structures that shape human destiny.[10]
Liberation theology must confront:

- surveillance capitalism
- algorithmic bias
- digital colonialism
- ecological costs of AI
- energy injustice
- the commodification of identity

Technology must be governed by ethics, not profit.

Principle Nine: The Church Exists for the Flourishing of the Oppressed

Karl Rahner foresaw a Church that would become "the Church of the poor" or lose credibility.[11] Today this includes:

---

9. Augustine, *De Doctrina Christiana*, I.36.
10. Zuboff, *The Age of Surveillance Capitalism*; Noble, *Algorithms of Oppression*.
11. Rahner, *The Church and the Poor*.

- LGBTQ+ Catholics denied sacraments
- Indigenous communities displaced by extractivism
- African societies burdened by digital colonialism
- victims of climate collapse
- low-income families harmed by rising energy costs driven by AI expansion

The Church must stand not above history, but inside the wounds of the world.

Principle Ten: Eschatology Requires Hope as Resistance

Hope is not naïve optimism but what Moltmann calls "the protest against suffering."[12] Eschatology is not passive waiting but active transformation. The Kingdom of God is not a future consolation—it is a present call to justice.

Hope is resistance against despair, domination, and fatalism.

3. A PRACTICAL PROGRAM OF ECCLESIAL REFORM

If the Church is to embody these principles, reform must be concrete, not rhetorical. A prophetic Church requires structural transformation.

3.1. Reforming Moral Theology

A. Replace punitive moralism with relational ethics

Moral theology must center dignity, justice, and flourishing rather than rule enforcement. As Pope Francis insists, "Realities are more important than ideas."[13]

B. Integrate ecological, racial, economic, and digital ethics

These issues cannot be siloed. They are interwoven dimensions of the same moral crisis.

---

12. Moltmann, *Theology of Hope*.
13. Francis, *Evangelii Gaudium*, §231.

C. Recognize LGBTQ+ dignity and full sacramental participation

This includes:

- recognition of same-sex marriages
- ordination of qualified LGBTQ+ persons
- rejection of language like "intrinsically disordered"
- lifting ecclesial bans rooted in obsolete anthropology

  This is a matter not of social concession but theological truth.

3.2. Reforming Ecclesial Governance

A. Synodality as permanent ecclesial structure

A synodal Church is one where all voices—especially marginalized ones—shape teaching and mission.

B. Decentralization of power

Colonial ecclesial structures obscure the voices of the Global South. Local churches must have authority to respond to local contexts.

C. Accountability for ecological and digital harm

Dioceses must treat ecological destruction and digital injustice as sins requiring penance, education, and active repair.

3.3. Reforming Pastoral Ministry

A. Pastors must become agents of liberation

They must be trained in:

- ecology
- trauma-informed care
- racial justice
- digital ethics
- LGBTQ+ inclusion

B. Parishes must become places of refuge

They must offer:

- legal aid for migrants
- digital literacy training
- ecological solidarity communities
- support groups for LGBTQ+ youth
- climate resilience hubs for vulnerable communities

C. Sacramental life must reflect justice

The Eucharist is not merely ritual but resistance—a communal act proclaiming that domination has no future.

4. PASTORAL COMMITMENTS OF A LIBERATIVE CHURCH

This section articulates concrete commitments that every diocese, parish, and Catholic institution should adopt.

Commitment One: Stand with the Poor

This requires public opposition to economic systems that exploit labor, deny housing, criminalize poverty, or destroy the Earth.

Commitment Two: Honor the Dignity of LGBTQ+ Persons

This includes full ministry, sacramental inclusion, and public reparation for historical and doctrinal harm.

Commitment Three: Defend the Earth as a Sacred Trust

Inspired by *Laudato Si'*, parishes must reduce emissions, preserve biodiversity, support Indigenous land rights, and oppose extractive industries.

Commitment Four: Resist Digital Oppression

The Church must advocate for:

- transparent algorithms
- privacy protections
- equitable access to technology
- ethical limits on AI
- digital sovereignty for the Global South

Commitment Five: Protect Future Generations

Intergenerational justice demands climate action, technological restraint, and a moral economy that does not sacrifice tomorrow for today.

Commitment Six: Practice Reparative Justice

The Church must engage in reparations for colonialism, racism, patriarchy, and ecological harm.

Commitment Seven: Cultivate Communities of Solidarity

Parishes must become centers of spiritual and political empowerment, not passive spectators of injustice.

Commitment Eight: Teach Theology of Liberation as Core Curriculum

Seminaries must integrate:

- liberation theology
- African and Indigenous cosmologies
- feminist and queer theology
- environmental theology
- digital ethics

This is not optional—it is essential for ministerial competence.

Commitment Nine: Promote Economic Democracy

Catholic institutions should support cooperatives, ethical investing, universal basic services, and justice-centered economic reforms.

Commitment Ten: Proclaim the Gospel as Liberation

The Gospel is not doctrine alone; it is a call to transform history. Jesus proclaimed release to captives, good news to the poor, and freedom for the oppressed (Lk 4:18). The Church must proclaim the same.

5. A SPIRITUALITY OF EMANCIPATION

Liberation theology is not merely political; it is mystical. It springs from contemplative awareness of God's presence in wounded creation. A spirituality of emancipation includes five dimensions:

5.1. Contemplation as Resistance

Contemplation unveils truth. As Merton argued, contemplation strips away illusions of power. It reveals the poor not as objects but as sacramental presences of Christ (Matt 25:40).

5.2. Solidarity as Conversion

Solidarity is not charity; it is transformation of consciousness. As Cone taught, solidarity with the oppressed is the only path to authentic Christian identity.[14] One cannot encounter the crucified peoples of history without undergoing conversion.

---

14. Cone, *For My People*.

5.3. Hope as Prophetic Defiance

Hope is not optimism. It is a weapon against despair. It says to empire, "You do not have the final word." It says to ecological collapse, "Creation groans, but God is not finished." It says to LGBTQ+ youth, "Your life is holy."

5.4. Cosmic Belonging

CSR and ecological theology converge to affirm that humans are not isolated moral agents but participants in a cosmic web of relationality. Spirituality must awaken consciousness to:

- the sacredness of rivers and mountains
- the wisdom of Indigenous cosmologies
- the dignity of future generations
- the mystery within every creature

    This is not pantheism; it is sacramental realism.

5.5. Eucharistic Politics

The Eucharist forms a counter-world. It creates a community not of hierarchy but of mutual gift. It enacts an economy of grace, not extraction. It is the weekly rehearsal of liberation, a pledge that domination will not triumph.

6. FINAL PROPHETIC DECLARATION: THE CHURCH WE MUST BECOME

The Church stands at a crossroads. It can cling to outdated paradigms shaped by fear, control, and doctrinal rigidity, or it can embrace the Spirit's call to become the Church of the Poor and the Planet—a prophetic community attuned to the groaning of creation (Rom 8:22), the cries of the oppressed, and the emerging structures of injustice that define our age.

This manifesto declares:

- No more neutrality in the face of ecological collapse.
- No more silence regarding LGBTQ+ dignity.
- No more complicity in racial, digital, or economic oppression.
- No more evasion of structural sin.
- No more theology divorced from the real suffering of the world.

Instead, we proclaim a Church that:

- liberates rather than restrains,
- heals rather than wounds,
- listens rather than polices,
- accompanies rather than excludes,
- protects the Earth rather than destroys it,
- stands with the oppressed rather than the powerful,
- and seeks justice rather than maintaining institutional comfort.

This is the Church to which the Holy Spirit is calling us.
This is the Church that history demands.
This is the Church that the Gospel requires.
And this, finally, is the Church that Christ himself founded—
the Church of radical mercy, courageous truth, and cosmic liberation.
Amen.

Bibliography

Afolayan, Adeshina, and Toyin Falola, eds. *The Palgrave Handbook of African Philosophy*. New York: Palgrave Macmillan, 2017.

Ahn, Byung-Mu. *Jesus and the Minjung*. Maryknoll, NY: Orbis Books, 1993.

Akoko, Robert Mbe, and Piet Konings. *From Africa to America: Ambazonia and the Unmaking of Cameroon*. Bamenda, Cameroon: Langaa Research & Publishing, 2018.

Alison, James. "Catholic Priest and Theologian James Alison: 'Conscience Is About Being Children of God.'" *Outreach*, May 26, 2023.

American Psychological Association. *Resolution on Appropriate Affirmative Responses to Sexual Orientation and Distress*. Washington, DC: APA, 2011.

Amnesty International. *Africa: Barrage of Discriminatory Laws Stoking Hate Against LGBTI Persons*. London: Amnesty International Publications, 2024.

———. *Ghana: Women Branded as Witches Banished to Camps*. London: Amnesty International Publications, 2017.

———. *This Is What We Die For: Human Rights Abuses in the Democratic Republic of the Congo Power the Global Trade in Cobalt*. London: Amnesty International Publications, 2016.

Anderson, Allan. *An Introduction to Pentecostalism: Global Charismatic Christianity*. 2nd ed. Cambridge: Cambridge University Press, 2014.

Aquinas, Thomas. *Summa Theologica*. Translated by Fathers of the English Dominican Province. New York: Benziger Bros., 1947.

Asongu, Januarius. *War, Politics and Business: A Critique of the Global War on Terror*. Frederick, MD: American Star Books, 2007.

———. *Cybersecurity & Emerging Technologies: A Pocket Dictionary for Students and Professionals*. Townsend, DE: Saint Monica University Press, 2025.

———. *Cybersecurity Governance, Risk, and Compliance: Foundations for Secure and Resilient Organizations*. Townsend, DE: Saint Monica University Press, 2025.

———. *Effective Communication in the Modern World: Academic, Workplace, and Digital Skills*. Townsend, DE: Saint Monica University Press, 2025.

———. *Forced Unity: A Critical Appraisal of the Ambazonia Struggle for Emancipation and Self-Determination*. Townsend, DE: Saint Monica University Press, 2025.

———. *Hidden Selves: Triple Masking and the Mental Health Crisis in the Church*. Townsend, DE: Saint Monica University Press, 2025.

———. *Holistic Resilience: Counseling at the Intersection of Faith, Family, and Identity*. Townsend, DE: Saint Monica University Press, 2025.

———. *Strategic Corporate Social Responsibility in Practice: Institutions, Strategy, Innovation, Marketing, and Global Legitimacy*. 2nd ed. Townsend, DE: Saint Monica University Press, 2025.

———. *The Graduate Research Companion: A Step-by-Step Handbook for Thesis Writers*. Townsend, DE: Saint Monica University Press, 2025.

———. *The Human Firewall: How Organizational Culture Shapes Cybersecurity Behavior*. Townsend, DE: Saint Monica University Press, 2025.

———. *The Modern MBA: Core Concepts and Strategies for Global Business Leaders*. Townsend, DE: Saint Monica University Press, 2025.

Asongu, Januarius, and Dana Lundell (Eds.) *Technology in Education and Business*. Lawrence, GA: Greenview Publishing, 2007.

Asongu, Januarius, and Daryl-Palma Asongu Nguatem. *Global Logistics & Supply Chain Management*. Townsend, DE: Saint Monica University Press, 2025.

Asongu, Januarius, and George Alberto Gonzalez. *Unpacking the Mind*. Townsend, DE: Saint Monica University Press, 2025.

Asongu, Januarius, and Nicholas Asongu Jingwa. *Educational Psychology*. Townsend, DE: Saint Monica University Press, 2025.

Asongu, Januarius, and Nkeng Fobellah. *Public Health Foundations and Practice*. Townsend, DE: Saint Monica University Press, 2025.

Asongu, Januarius, and Wilson Taza. *Industrial Engineering Essentials*. Townsend, DE: Saint Monica University Press, 2025.

Asongu, Januarius, C'Lamt Ho, and Marvee Marr (Eds.) *Doing Business Abroad*. Lawrence, GA: Greenview Publishing, 2007.

Augustine. *Confessions*. Translated by Henry Chadwick. Oxford: Oxford University Press, 1998. First published ca. 400.

———. *On Christian Doctrine*. Translated by D. W. Robertson Jr. Upper Saddle River, NJ: Prentice Hall, 1995. First published 397.

Avila, Wanda. "The Diary of a Country Priest: The Transcendent on Film." *Journal of Religion and Film* 10 (October 2006). http://www.unomaha.edu/jrf/Vol10No2/Avila_CountryPriest.htm.

Bebbington, David W. *Evangelicalism in Modern Britain: A History from the 1730s to the 1980s*. London: Routledge, 1989.

Benjamin, Ruha. *Race After Technology: Abolitionist Tools for the New Jim Code*. Cambridge: Polity Press, 2019.

Berger, Peter L., and Thomas Luckmann. *The Social Construction of Reality: A Treatise in the Sociology of Knowledge*. Garden City, NY: Anchor Books, 1966.

Berinyuy, Valentine. "Understanding the Anglophone Crisis in Cameroon: Historical and Socio-Political Perspectives." *African Studies Review* 63, no. 4 (2020): 812–32. https://doi.org/10.1017/asr.2020.19.

Berryman, Phillip. *Liberation Theology: Essential Facts About the Revolutionary Movement in Latin America and Beyond*. New York: Pantheon, 1987.

Boff, Clodovis. *Introducing Liberation Theology*. Maryknoll, NY: Orbis Books, 1987.

Boff, Leonardo. *Church: Charism and Power: Liberation Theology and the Institutional Church*. Translated by John W. Diercksmeier. Eugene, OR: Wipf & Stock, 1985. First published 1981.

———. *Cry of the Earth, Cry of the Poor*. Maryknoll, NY: Orbis Books, 1997.

———. *Ecclesiogenesis: The Base Communities Reinvent the Church*. 2nd ed. Maryknoll, NY: Orbis Books, 1988.

———. *Passion of Christ, Passion of the World.* Maryknoll, NY: Orbis Books, 1987.
Boswell, John. *Christianity, Social Tolerance, and Homosexuality.* Chicago: University of Chicago Press, 1980.
Brennan, Deirdre. *The Irish Church and Child Abuse: Government Inquiries and Catholic Teaching.* Dublin: Gill & Macmillan, 2012.
Brown, Raymond E. *An Introduction to the New Testament.* New Haven: Yale University Press, 1997.
Brownson, James V. *Bible, Gender, Sexuality: Reframing the Church's Debate on Same-Sex Relationships.* Grand Rapids: Eerdmans, 2013.
Brueggemann, Walter. *The Prophetic Imagination.* Minneapolis: Fortress Press, 1978.
———. *The Prophetic Imagination.* 2nd ed. Minneapolis: Fortress Press, 2001.
Bujo, Bénézet. *African Christian Morality at the Age of Inculturation.* Translated by John O. Ekore. Nairobi: Pauline Publications Africa, 1992.
Buolamwini, Joy, and Timnit Gebru. "Gender Shades: Intersectional Accuracy Disparities in Commercial Gender Classification." *Proceedings of Machine Learning Research* 81 (2018): 1–15.
Bullard, Robert D. *Dumping in Dixie: Race, Class, and Environmental Quality.* 3rd ed. Boulder, CO: Westview Press, 2000.
Bureau of Justice Statistics. *Sexual Abuse Reporting Patterns: An International Comparative Analysis.* Washington, DC: United States Department of Justice, 2020.
Carter, J. H. *The End of White Christian America?* Louisville, KY: Westminster John Knox Press, 2020.
Catechism of the Catholic Church. Vatican City: Libreria Editrice Vaticana, 1994.
Cassidy, Sheila. *Audacity to Believe: An Autobiography.* London: Collins, 1985.
CENCO (Conférence Épiscopale Nationale du Congo). *Déclaration des Evêques de la CENCO sur les Résultats Provisoires des Elections Présidentielles.* Kinshasa: CENCO, 2018.
Chabal, Patrick, and Jean-Pascal Daloz. *Africa Works: Disorder as Political Instrument.* Oxford: James Currey, 1999.
Cleland, John, et al. "Family Planning: The Unfinished Agenda." *The Lancet* 380, no. 9837 (2012): 181–93.
Comaroff, Jean, and John L. Comaroff. "Occult Economies and the Violence of Abstraction: Notes from the South African Postcolony." *American Ethnologist* 26, no. 2 (1999): 279–303.
Comblin, José. *The Church and the National Security State.* Maryknoll, NY: Orbis Books, 1979.
Cone, James H. *A Black Theology of Liberation.* Philadelphia: Lippincott, 1970.
———. *For My People: Black Theology and the Black Church.* Maryknoll, NY: Orbis Books, 1984.
———. *God of the Oppressed.* Maryknoll, NY: Orbis Books, 1975.
Congregation for the Doctrine of the Faith. *Catechism of the Catholic Church.* 2nd ed. Vatican City: Libreria Editrice Vaticana, 1997.
———. *Letter to the Bishops of the Catholic Church on the Pastoral Care of Homosexual Persons.* Vatican City: Congregation for the Doctrine of the Faith, 1986.
Couldry, Nick, and Ulises A. Mejías. *The Costs of Connection: How Data Is Colonizing Human Life and Appropriating It for Capitalism.* Stanford, CA: Stanford University Press, 2019.

Cozzens, Donald B. *The Changing Face of the Priesthood: A Reflection on the Priest's Crisis of Soul*. Collegeville, MN: Liturgical Press, 2000.
Crawford, David. "Clericalism and Power: Structural Factors in the Concealment of Abuse." *Journal of Catholic Social Thought* 15, no. 2 (2018): 221–43.
Crawford, Gordon. "Self-Determination and Secession in Africa: The Ambazonian Question in Comparative Perspective." *Journal of Modern African Studies* 59, no. 2 (2021): 179–202. https://doi.org/10.1017/S0022278X21000105.
Daly, Mary. *Beyond God the Father*. Boston: Beacon Press, 1985.
Daniel, Elijah T., and Januarius Asongu. *Advanced Microbiology and Parasitology*. Townsend, DE: Saint Monica University Press, 2025.
Dicastery for the Doctrine of the Faith. *Fiducia Supplicans: On the Pastoral Meaning of Blessings*. Vatican City: Dicastery for the Doctrine of the Faith, 2023.
Douglas, Mary. *Purity and Danger: An Analysis of Concepts of Pollution and Taboo*. London: Routledge, 1966.
Doyle, Thomas P. "Clericalism: Enabler of Clergy Sexual Abuse." *Pastoral Psychology* 54, no. 3 (2006): 189–213.
Drescher, Jack. "Out of DSM: Depathologizing Homosexuality." *Behavioral Sciences* 5, no. 4 (2015): 565–75.
Du Mez, Kristin Kobes. *Jesus and John Wayne: How White Evangelicals Corrupted a Faith and Fractured a Nation*. New York: Liveright, 2020.
Ela, Jean-Marc. *African Cry*. Translated by Mary L. O'Connell. Maryknoll, NY: Orbis Books, 1986.
———. *My Faith as an African*. Translated by John Pairman Brown and Susan Perry. Maryknoll, NY: Orbis Books, 1988.
Ellacuría, Ignacio. *Freedom Made Flesh: The Mission of Christ and the Church*. Maryknoll, NY: Orbis Books, 1993.
Emerson, Michael O., and Christian Smith. *Divided by Faith: Evangelical Religion and the Problem of Race in America*. Oxford: Oxford University Press, 2000.
Englund, Harri, ed. *Christianity and Public Culture in Africa*. Athens: Ohio University Press, 2007.
Esposito, John L. *What Everyone Needs to Know About Islam*. 2nd ed. Oxford: Oxford University Press, 2011.
Evans-Pritchard, E. E. *Witchcraft, Oracles, and Magic Among the Azande*. Oxford: Clarendon Press, 1937.
Farley, Margaret A. *Just Love: A Framework for Christian Sexual Ethics*. New York: Continuum, 2006.
Farmer, Paul. *Pathologies of Power: Health, Human Rights, and the New War on the Poor*. Berkeley: University of California Press, 2005.
Finnis, John. *Natural Law and Natural Rights*. 2nd ed. Oxford: Oxford University Press, 2011.
Fiorenza, Elisabeth Schüssler. *In Memory of Her*. New York: Crossroad, 2011.
———. *Transforming Vision*. Minneapolis: Fortress Press, 2011.
Fletcher, Catherine. *Ethics and Human Reproduction in Protestant Thought*. Cambridge: Cambridge University Press, 2009.
Francis, Pope. *Address of His Holiness Pope Francis to the Roman Curia*. Vatican City: Libreria Editrice Vaticana, 2018.
———. *Amoris Laetitia: The Joy of Love*. Vatican City: Vatican Press, 2016.
———. *Evangelii Gaudium: The Joy of the Gospel*. Vatican City: Vatican Press, 2013.

———. *Fratelli Tutti: On Fraternity and Social Friendship*. Vatican City: Vatican Press, 2020.

———. *Laudato Si': On Care for Our Common Home*. Vatican City: Vatican Press, 2015.

———. *Let Us Dream: The Path to a Better Future*. Edited by Austen Ivereigh. New York: Simon & Schuster, 2021.

———. *Letter of His Holiness Pope Francis to the People of God*. Vatican City: Libreria Editrice Vaticana, 2018.

———. *Message for the World Day of Migrants and Refugees*. Vatican City: Vatican Press, 2014.

———. *Welcoming, Protecting, Promoting, and Integrating Migrants and Refugees: Message for the World Day of Migrants and Refugees*. Vatican City: Vatican Press, 2018.

Gifford, Paul. *Christianity and Politics in Doe's Liberia*. Cambridge: Cambridge University Press, 1995.

———. *Christianity, Development, and Modernity in Africa*. London: Hurst & Company, 2016.

———. *Ghana's New Christianity: Pentecostalism in a Globalizing African Economy*. Bloomington: Indiana University Press, 2004.

Goodstein, Laurie. "Nuns Accuse Priests of Sexual Abuse, Prompting Vatican Investigation." *The New York Times*, February 6, 2018. https://www.nytimes.com/2018/02/06/world/europe/vatican-sexual-abuse-nuns.html.

Gorski, Philip S., and Samuel L. Perry. *The Flag and the Cross: White Christian Nationalism and the Threat to American Democracy*. Oxford: Oxford University Press, 2022.

Guglielmi, Francesco L. "The Crisis of Vocation." *Theological Studies Quarterly* 79, no. 4 (2021): 541–60.

Gushee, David P. *Changing Our Mind*. 3rd ed. Canton, MI: Read the Spirit Books, 2017.

Gutiérrez, Gustavo. *On Job: God-Talk and the Suffering of the Innocent*. Maryknoll, NY: Orbis Books, 1988.

———. *A Theology of Liberation: History, Politics, and Salvation*. Maryknoll, NY: Orbis Books, 1973.

———. *A Theology of Liberation: History, Politics, and Salvation*. Rev. ed. Translated by Caridad Inda and John Eagleson. Maryknoll, NY: Orbis Books, 1988. First published 1971.

———. *We Drink from Our Own Wells: The Spiritual Journey of a People*. Maryknoll, NY: Orbis Books, 1984.

Häring, Bernard. *The Law of Christ: Moral Theology for Priests and Laity*. New York: Herder & Herder, 1979.

Hays, Richard B. *The Moral Vision of the New Testament: A Contemporary Introduction to New Testament Ethics*. San Francisco: HarperOne, 1996.

Hedges, Chris. *American Fascists: The Christian Right and the War on America*. New York: Free Press, 2006.

Heschel, Abraham Joshua. *The Prophets*. New York: Harper & Row, 1962.

Hodge, Brian, and Carlos Morales. "AI Demand Stresses U.S. Power Grid Amid Rising Electricity Costs." *Energy Policy Journal* 52 (2024): 88–104.

Human Rights Watch. *Nigeria: Witchcraft Accusations Against Children*. New York: Human Rights Watch Publications, 2014.

Hyun Kyung, Chung. *Struggle to Be the Sun Again: Introducing Asian Women's Theology.* Maryknoll, NY: Orbis Books, 1990.
International Crisis Group. *Cameroon's Anglophone Crisis: How to Get to Talks?* ICG Africa Report No. 272. Brussels: International Crisis Group, 2019.
International Labour Organization. *Child Labour in Cocoa Supply Chains: A Review of Evidence.* Geneva: ILO Publications, 2020.
———. *Women and Men in the Informal Economy: A Statistical Brief.* Geneva: ILO Publications, 2021.
The Jerusalem Bible. Edited by Alexander Jones. Garden City, NY: Doubleday, 1966.
John Jay College of Criminal Justice. *The Nature and Scope of Sexual Abuse of Minors by Catholic Priests in the United States, 1950-2002.* Washington, DC: United States Conference of Catholic Bishops, 2004.
John Paul II, Pope. *Centesimus Annus.* Vatican City: Vatican Press, 1991.
———. *Fides et Ratio: On the Relationship Between Faith and Reason.* Vatican City: Vatican Press, 1998.
———. *Laborem Exercens: On Human Work.* Vatican City: Vatican Press, 1981.
———. *Ordinatio Sacerdotalis.* Vatican City: Vatican Press, 1994.
———. *Theology of the Body* (General Audiences). Vatican City: Libreria Editrice Vaticana, 1981–1984.
Jones, Nate. "How Big Is AI's Carbon Footprint?" *Nature* 623 (2023): 24–27.
Jones, Robert P. *The End of White Christian America.* New York: Simon & Schuster, 2016.
———. *White Too Long: The Legacy of White Supremacy in American Christianity.* New York: Simon & Schuster, 2021.
Kä Mana. *Christians and the Social Question in Africa: Toward a New Social Ethics.* Nairobi: Paulines Publications Africa, 2002.
Kairos Theologians. *The Kairos Document.* Johannesburg: Kairos Theologians, 1985.
Kalu, Ogbu. *African Pentecostalism: An Introduction.* Oxford: Oxford University Press, 2008.
Kamerun National Archives. *Documents on the 1961 Plebiscite and the Federation Debate.* Yaoundé: Government of Cameroon Historical Bureau, 2017.
Kanyoro, Musimbi R. A. *Cultural Hermeneutics and Women's Empowerment.* Maryknoll, NY: Orbis Books, 2001.
Kaufman, Peter. "Clericalism and Its Theological Roots: A Structural Analysis." *Theological Studies* 80, no. 4 (2019): 827–49. https://doi.org/10.1177/0040563919877504.
Kay, Aaron C., et al. "Compensatory Control: Achieving Order Through the Mind, Our Institutions, and the Heavens." *Current Directions in Psychological Science* 17, no. 5 (2008): 264–68.
Keenan, Marie. *Child Sexual Abuse and the Catholic Church: Gender, Power, and Organizational Culture.* Oxford: Oxford University Press, 2012.
Keller, Timothy. *Generous Justice: How God's Grace Makes Us Just.* New York: Penguin, 2012.
Kibangou, Hermann-Habib. *The Mvengian Vision of Anthropological Pauperization: A Path for Philosophical Reflection on Ntu?* Eugene, OR: Wipf & Stock, 2022.
Kibangou, René. *La Philosophie Bantoue de L'être: Ntu et la Métaphysique Africaine.* Paris: Éditions Présence Africaine, 1999.
Kirkpatrick, Andrew. *Taking America Back for God: Christian Nationalism in the United States.* 2nd ed. Oxford: Oxford University Press, 2021.

Konings, Piet, and Francis B. Nyamnjoh. *Negotiating an Anglophone Identity: A Study of the Politics of Recognition and Representation in Cameroon*. Leiden: Brill, 2003.
Küng, Hans. *Can the Church Still Be Saved?* Translated by Robert and Rita Kimber. Eugene, OR: Wipf & Stock, 2011.
———. *The Church*. London: Sheed and Ward, 1971.
———. *Infallible? An Inquiry*. London: Collins, 1971.
———. *On Being a Christian*. Garden City, NY: Doubleday, 1976.
Küster, Volker. *Global Perspectives on Liberation Theology*. Eugene, OR: Wipf & Stock, 2010.
Laity for Justice in Africa. *Sexual Abuse and Silence in African Catholicism: A Preliminary Report*. Nairobi: Nairobi Press, 2021.
Lendman, Stephen, and Januarius Asongu. *The Iraq Quagmire*. Lawrence, GA: Greenview Publishing, 2007.
Levack, Brian P. *The Witch-Hunt in Early Modern Europe*. London: Longman, 1987.
Loader, William. *The New Testament on Sexuality*. Grand Rapids: Eerdmans, 2013.
Magesa, Laurenti. *African Religion: The Moral Traditions of Abundant Life*. Maryknoll, NY: Paulines Publications Africa, 1997.
———. *African Religion: The Moral Traditions of Abundant Life*. Maryknoll, NY: Orbis Books, 2002.
Marshall-Fratani, Ruth. "Mediating the Global and Local in Nigerian Pentecostalism." *Journal of Religion in Africa* 28, no. 3 (1998): 278–315.
Martí, Gerardo. *American Secularism and the Crisis of Faith*. New York: Routledge, 2020.
Martinez, Juan. *Migrant Faith and American Politics: A Theological Reading*. Maryknoll, NY: Orbis Books, 2018.
Massingale, Bryan N. *Racial Justice and the Catholic Church*. Maryknoll, NY: Orbis Books, 2010.
Massey, Douglas S., and Nancy A. Denton. *American Apartheid: Segregation and the Making of the Underclass*. Cambridge, MA: Harvard University Press, 1993.
Mbiti, John S. *African Religions and Philosophy*. London: Heinemann, 1969.
Mbuy, Humphrey Tatah. *Encountering Witches and Wizards in Africa*. Buea: Bishop Rogan College, 1989.
McFague, Sallie. *The Body of God: An Ecological Theology*. Minneapolis: Fortress Press, 1993.
McQuillan, Dan. *Resisting AI: An Anti-Fascist Approach to Artificial Intelligence*. Manchester: Manchester University Press, 2022.
Metz, Johann Baptist. *Faith in History and Society*. New York: Seabury Press, 1980.
Meyer, Birgit. "Christianity in Africa: From African Independent to Pentecostal-Charismatic Churches." *Annual Review of Anthropology* 33 (2004): 447–74.
———. *Sensational Movies: Video, Vision, and Christianity in Ghana*. Berkeley: University of California Press, 2015.
Meyer, Ilan H. "Prejudice, Social Stress, and Mental Health in Lesbian, Gay, and Bisexual Populations: Conceptual Issues and Research Evidence." *Psychological Bulletin* 129, no. 5 (2003): 674–97.
Michels, Robert. *Political Parties: A Sociological Study of the Oligarchical Tendencies of Modern Democracy*. Translated by Eden Paul and Cedar Paul. New York: Free Press, 1911.

Miller, Steven. "Christian Nationalism and the January 6 Insurrection." *Sociology of Religion* 82, no. 4 (2021): 403–27. https://doi.org/10.1093/socrel/srab039.

Mkandawire, Thandika, and Charles C. Soludo. *Our Continent, Our Future: African Perspectives on Structural Adjustment*. Dakar: Council for the Development of Social Science Research in Africa, 1999.

Moltmann, Jürgen. *The Crucified God*. New York: Harper & Row, 1974.

———. *Theology of Hope*. New York: Harper & Row, 1967.

Mveng, Engelbert. *L'Afrique dans L'Église: Paroles d'un Croyant*. Yaoundé: Éditions Clé, 1985.

———. *African Liberation Theology*. In *A Reader in African Christian Theology*, edited by John Parratt, 177–88. London: SPCK, 1988.

———. "Anthropological Poverty and the Mission of the Church in Africa." In *Impoverishment and Liberation: Toward a Theology of Liberation for Africa*, edited by Engelbert Mveng, 15–40. Maryknoll, NY: Orbis Books, 1988.

———. *Impoverishment and Liberation: Toward a Theology of Liberation for Africa*. Translated by David Smith. Maryknoll, NY: Orbis Books, 1988.

Ngangi, N. *The Bakweri Land Problem: Cultural Identity and Land Rights in Cameroon*. Buea: University of Buea Press, 2007.

Newman, John Henry. *An Essay on the Development of Christian Doctrine*. London: Longmans, Green, and Co., 1845.

———. *Letter to the Duke of Norfolk*. London: Longmans, Green & Co., 1875.

———. *On Consulting the Faithful in Matters of Doctrine*. London: Burns & Oates, 1859.

Ngoh, Victor Julius. *History of Cameroon Since 1800*. Limbe, Cameroon: Presbook, 1996.

Nirmal, Arvind P. *Heuristic Explorations in Dalit Theology*. Chennai: Library of Dalit Theology, 1990.

Nixon, Rob. *Slow Violence and the Environmentalism of the Poor*. Cambridge, MA: Harvard University Press, 2011.

Nkrumah, Kwame. *Neo-Colonialism: The Last Stage of Imperialism*. London: Thomas Nelson & Sons, 1965.

Noble, Safiya Umoja. *Algorithms of Oppression: How Search Engines Reinforce Racism*. New York: NYU Press, 2018.

Noll, Mark A. *The Civil War as a Theological Crisis*. Chapel Hill: University of North Carolina Press, 2006.

———. *The New Shape of World Christianity: How American Experience Reflects Global Faith*. Downers Grove, IL: InterVarsity Press, 2010.

O'Neil, Cathy. *Weapons of Math Destruction: How Big Data Increases Inequality and Threatens Democracy*. New York: Crown, 2016.

Oduyoye, Mercy Amba. *Introducing African Women's Theology*. Sheffield: Sheffield Academic Press, 2001.

Okeja, Uchenna. *Philosophy and the Postcolonial: Perspectives from Africa*. Cham: Springer, 2018.

Okonta, Ike, and Oronto Douglas. *Where Vultures Feast: Shell, Human Rights, and Oil in the Niger Delta*. San Francisco: Sierra Club Books, 2001.

Okure, Teresa. *Jesus and the Woman Question*. Nairobi: Paulines Publications Africa, 1990.

Orobator, Agbonkhianmeghe E. *Theology Brewed in an African Pot*. 2nd ed. Maryknoll, NY: Orbis Books, 2018.

Pan American Health Organization/World Health Organization. "LGBT Health Sees Progress and Challenges 15 Years After Homosexuality Ceased Being Classified as a Mental Disorder." Press release, May 15, 2015.
Papadopoulos, George. "Contraception in the Orthodox Christian Tradition: Pastoral and Theological Considerations." *Journal of Orthodox Theology* 4, no. 2 (2012): 115–34.
Paul VI, Pope. *Humanae Vitae: On the Regulation of Birth*. Vatican City: Vatican Press, 1968.
Pew Research Center. *Tolerance and Tension: Islam and Christianity in Sub-Saharan Africa*. Washington, DC: Pew Research Center, 2010.
Phan, Peter C. *Culture and Liberation: East Asian Liberation Theology*. Maryknoll, NY: Orbis Books, 1996.
Phillips, Kevin. *American Theocracy: The Peril and Politics of Radical Religion, Oil, and Borrowed Money in the 21st Century*. New York: Penguin, 2006.
Popper, Karl. *The Logic of Scientific Discovery*. London: Hutchinson, 1959.
———. *The Open Society and Its Enemies*. London: Routledge, 1945.
Pope, Robert. "Institutional Blindness and the Theology of Accountability: Lessons from the Vatican Reforms." *Journal of Catholic Social Thought* 17, no. 3 (2020): 511–34.
———. "Nationalism, Idolatry, and the American Church: A Catholic Critique." *Theological Studies* 83, no. 3 (2022): 512–34.
Posner, Eric A., and Alan O. Sykes. *Economic Rights of Nations: A Legal and Moral Analysis*. Oxford: Oxford University Press, 2019.
Rahman, Fazlur. *Health and Reproduction in Islamic Jurisprudence*. London: Routledge, 2018.
Rahner, Karl. *The Church and the Poor*. New York: Seabury Press, 1974.
———. *The Church and the Sacraments*. Translated by William Dych. New York: Herder & Herder, 1967.
———. *Foundations of Christian Faith: An Introduction to the Idea of Christianity*. Translated by William V. Dych. New York: Crossroad, 1978. First published 1976.
———. *Hearers of the Word*. Translated by William D. Dych. New York: Herder & Herder, 1966.
———. *Theological Investigations*. Vol. 20. New York: Crossroad, 1971.
Robinson, Paul, and Edward Yu. "Digital Identity Systems and Human Rights: A Critical Review of Biometric Governance in Africa." *Information Technology for Development* 27, no. 4 (2021): 678–95.
Rogers, Eugene F. *Sexuality and the Christian Body: Their Way into the Triune God*. Oxford: Wiley-Blackwell, 1999.
Romero, Óscar A. *The Violence of Love*. Edited by James R. Brockman. Maryknoll, NY: Orbis Books, 1980.
Sant'Egidio Community. Various publications.
Scroggs, Robin. *The New Testament and Homosexuality*. Philadelphia: Fortress Press, 1983.
Second Vatican Council. *Dei Verbum: Dogmatic Constitution on Divine Revelation*. Vatican City: Vatican Press, 1965.
———. *Gaudium et Spes: Pastoral Constitution on the Church in the Modern World*. Vatican City: Vatican Press, 1965.

———. *Lumen Gentium: Dogmatic Constitution on the Church*. Vatican City: Vatican Press, 1964.

Sedgh, Gilda, et al. "Unmet Need for Contraception in Developing Countries: Examining Causes and Consequences." *Studies in Family Planning* 47, no. 1 (2016): 3–14.

Segundo, Juan Luis. *Theology for the Art of Living*. 5 vols. Maryknoll, NY: Orbis Books, 1976–1982.

Shaw, Mary. "Women, Religion, and Reproductive Rights." *Journal of Gender Studies* 24, no. 5 (2015): 555–69.

Shermer, Michael. *The Believing Brain: From Ghosts and Gods to Politics and Conspiracies—How We Construct Beliefs and Reinforce Them as Truths*. New York: Times Books, 2011.

Sipe, A. W. Richard. *Celibacy in Crisis: A Secret World Revisited*. New York: Brunner-Routledge, 2003.

Sobrino, Jon. *Christology at the Crossroads*. Maryknoll, NY: Orbis Books, 1994.

———. *Jesus the Liberator: A Historical-Theological Reading of Jesus of Nazareth*. Translated by Paul Burns. Maryknoll, NY: Orbis Books, 1993.

———. *Jesus the Liberator: A Historical-Theological View*. Maryknoll, NY: Orbis Books, 1994.

———. *The Principle of Mercy: Taking the Crucified People from the Cross*. Maryknoll, NY: Orbis Books, 1994.

South African Catholic Bishops' Conference. *Statement on Safeguarding and Historical Cases of Clerical Abuse*. Pretoria: SACBC Publications, 2022.

Southern Cameroons National Council. *Historical Grievances and Legal Claims of the People of Southern Cameroons*. Bamenda: SCNC Publications, 2010.

Steinberg, Avraham. "Contraception and Moral Theology: Distinguishing Abortive from Non-Abortive Methods." *Journal of Medical Ethics* 44, no. 6 (2018): 389–95.

Suarez, Juan. *Synodality and Liberation: The Church's Future*. Rome: Gregorian University Press, 2019.

Sullivan, Winnifred Fallers. *The Impossibility of Religious Freedom*. Princeton: Princeton University Press, 2005.

Tangwa, Godfrey B. *Karl Popper: A Thematic Critical Introduction*. Yaoundé: Lana Graphics, 1990.

Tanner, Kathryn. *Christ the Key*. Cambridge: Cambridge University Press, 2010.

Taylor, Charles. *A Secular Age*. Cambridge, MA: Harvard University Press, 2007.

Taylor, Keeanga-Yamahtta. *Race for Profit: How Banks and the Real Estate Industry Undermined Black Homeownership*. Chapel Hill: University of North Carolina Press, 2019.

Tempels, Placide. *Bantu Philosophy*. Translated by Colin King. Paris: Présence Africaine, 1959. First published 1945.

Tutu, Desmond. *Hope and Suffering: Sermons and Speeches*. Grand Rapids: William B. Eerdmans, 1984.

———. *No Future Without Forgiveness*. New York: Image Books, 1999.

United Nations Environment Programme. *Making Peace with Nature*. Nairobi: United Nations Publications, 2021.

United Nations General Assembly. *Declaration on the Granting of Independence to Colonial Countries and Peoples* (UNGA Resolution 1514). New York: United Nations, 1960.

United Nations High Commissioner for Refugees. *Desperate Journeys: Refugees and Migrants Arriving in Europe*. Geneva: UNHCR Publications, 2020.

———. *Global Trends: Forced Displacement in 2023*. Geneva: UNHCR Publications, 2023.

United States Conference of Catholic Bishops. *Pastoral Responses to Racism*. Washington, DC: USCCB, 2021.

Vatican Congregation for the Clergy. *Directory on the Ministry and Life of Priests*. Vatican City: Libreria Editrice Vaticana, 1993.

Vatican News. "New Church Statistics Reveal Growing Catholic Population, Fewer Priests." March 20, 2025.

Vosman, Frans. "When the Shepherd Devours the Sheep: The Theological Meaning of Clerical Abuse." *International Journal of Public Theology* 14, no. 3 (2020): 289–308.

Wall Street Journal. "The Catholic Church Has a Manpower Problem." September 23, 2025.

Weber, Max. *Economy and Society: An Outline of Interpretive Sociology*. Edited by Guenther Roth and Claus Wittich. Berkeley: University of California Press, 1968. First published 1922.

———. *The Theory of Social and Economic Organization*. Translated by A. M. Henderson and Talcott Parsons. New York: Oxford University Press, 1947.

Whitehead, Andrew L., and Samuel L. Perry. *Taking America Back for God: Christian Nationalism in the United States*. Oxford: Oxford University Press, 2020.

Wiredu, Kwasi. *Cultural Universals and Particulars: An African Perspective*. Bloomington: Indiana University Press, 1996.

Wolfe, Alan. *The Transformation of American Religion: How We Actually Live Our Faith*. New York: Free Press, 2003.

Woodberry, Robert D. "The Missionary Roots of Liberal Democracy." *American Political Science Review* 106, no. 2 (2012): 244–74. https://doi.org/10.1017/S0003055412000093.

World Health Organization. *Family Planning/Contraception*. Geneva: WHO Press, 2021.

———. *Moving One Step Closer to Better Health and Rights for Transgender People*. Geneva: WHO Press, 2019.

———. *Short Birth Intervals and Child Mortality*. Geneva: WHO Press, 2018.

———. *World Health Statistics 2022: Monitoring Health for the SDGs*. Geneva: WHO Press, 2022.

Wright, N. T. *How God Became King: The Forgotten Story of the Gospels*. New York: HarperOne, 2012.

———. *Scripture and the Authority of God*. San Francisco: HarperOne, 2010.

Zerai, Assata. *Eritrea's Struggle for Independence: A People's War*. Westport, CT: Lawrence Hill Books, 1999.

Zollner, Hans. "Safeguarding in the Global Church: A Theological and Cultural Analysis." *Theological Studies* 80, no. 4 (2019): 850–73.

Zoomers, Annelies. "Globalisation and the Foreignisation of Space: Seven Processes Driving the Current Global Land Grab." *The Journal of Peasant Studies* 37, no. 2 (2010): 429–47.

Zuboff, Shoshana. *The Age of Surveillance Capitalism*. New York: PublicAffairs, 2019.

INDEX

Abuse, clerical
    cover-up of, 248–55
    institutional complicity in, 239–48
    systemic nature of, 248–76
Accountability, ecclesial
    absence of, 239–60
    and clericalism, 241–43
    and reform, 312–24
Africa
    colonial legacy in, 64–78
    ecclesial complicity in, 199–240
    liberation theology in, 66–92
    witchcraft accusations in, 346–72
African cosmology
    eco-theological dimensions of, 473–89
Ambazonia struggle
    justice claims in, 325–34
    moral legitimacy of, 325–45
    political violence in, 331–40
Anselm of Canterbury
    fides quaerens intellectum, 9
Anthropological poverty
    definition of, 70–72
    Mveng on, 71–72
Arendt, Hannah
    bibliography, 519
Asongu, Januarius Jingwa (JJ)
    author
    Critical-Liberative Theology (CLT), xv–xvi
    Critical Synthetic Realism (CSR), 3–9

Augustine, St.
    Confessions, 5
    conscience in, 5–6

Bible (Scripture)
    as liberative text, 141–98
Bishop
    episcopal authority and conscience, 15–18
    institutional accountability of, 199–210
Bibi, Michael
    Bishop of Buea, 199–210
Boff, Leonardo
    ecclesial power critique, 3–5, 30–31
    Church: Charism and Power, 30–31
Bonhoeffer, Dietrich
    bibliography, 519
Body
    moral agency and, 401–10
Bushu, Immanuel Balanjo
    Bishop of Buea, xiv
    Bishop of Yagoua, xiv
    seminary rector and philosopher, 13–14
    mentor to author, 13–14

Cameroon
    Ambazonia conflict in, 325–45
    church–state relations in, 199–210
    seminary formation in, 9–14

INDEX

Capitalism
  economic oppression and, 379–88
Catholic Church
  credibility crisis in, 239–76
  institutional sin in, 239–60
Celibacy, clerical
  as structural injustice, 444–54
Church, institutional
  self-preservation, 312–24
  sin within, 239–60
Clericalism
  definition of, 241–43
Closed epistemic systems
  definition of, 6–9
  institutional religion and, 239–60
Colonialism
  ecclesial entanglement with, 70–78
Cone, James H.
  bibliography, 519
Conscience
  as theological locus, 15–18
Contraception
  women's health and, 433–43
Cosmic liberation
  ecological dimensions of, 473–97
Credibility crisis (of the Church)
  clerical abuse and, 239–76
  institutional self-protection and, 312–24
Critical-Liberative Theology (CLT)
  definition of, xv–xvi
  methodology of, 28–63
Critical Synthetic Realism (CSR)
  epistemological foundations of, 3–9

Development of doctrine
  Newman on, 14–16
Digital oppression
  AI and, 497–506
Dinayen, Henry
  inculturation and research mentorship, xiii–xiv

Diocese
  Buea, ix, 6
  Kumbo, xiv
  Yagoua, 6
Doctrinal rigidity
  definition of, xv–xvi
Dussel, Enrique
  bibliography, 519

Eco-theology
  definition of, 473–76
  African cosmology and, 473–89
  planetary crisis and, 473–97
Ecclesial reform
  necessity of, 18–21
Ecology
  theological crisis of, 473–97
Economic oppression
  structural sin and, 379–88
Ela, Jean-Marc
  African liberation theology, 66–72
Epistemic fracture
  definition of, xv–xvi
  doctrine–life separation, 16–18
Epistemological humility
  Popper and, 6–9
Exile
  migration as, 389–400
Exodus
  liberation paradigm, 141–45

Faith–praxis disjunction
  definition of, xv–xvi
Francis (Pope)
  bibliography, 519
Freire, Paulo
  bibliography, 519
Forced displacement
  theology of, 389–400

Gaudium et Spes
  "signs of the times," 14–15
Gender
  ecclesial exclusion and, 411–32
Ghana
  African Christianity and, 66–72

INDEX 533

GHS Kumbo
  secondary and high school
    education, xiv
Grace
  nature and, 5
Gutiérrez, Gustavo
  orthopraxy emphasis, 16–17,
    64–67

Hauerwas, Stanley
  bibliography, 519
Human dignity
  biblical foundations of, 141–45

Immigration
  pastoral failure and, 31–33
Institutional self-preservation
  moral cost of, 239–60

Jesus Christ
  liberating ministry of, 141–55
Jingwa, Nicholas Asongu
  parental influence, xiii
John Henry Newman
  doctrinal development, 14–16
  conscience as "aboriginal Vicar,"
    15–17
John XXIII (Pope)
  14–15, 519
Justice
  biblical foundations of, 141–98

Karl Popper
  critical rationalism, 6–9
Karl Rahner
  transcendental theology, 11–12
Kenya
  African ecclesial context, 66–72
Küng, Hans
  truth and reform, 12–13

Latin America
  liberation theology origins,
    64–67
Lekelefac, George Nchumbonga
  lay church critic, ecclesial
    leadership in Cameroon,
    255–72

Liberation theology
  global history of, 64–78
Lonergan, Bernard
  bibliography, 519
LGBTQ+ inclusion
  Christological argument,
    455–72
Luke
  Luke 4:18, xv, 142
Lysinge, Francis Teke
  Bishop of Mamfe, xiv

Metz, Johann Baptist
  bibliography, 519–
Migration
  as modern crucifixion, 389–400
Moltmann, Jürgen
  bibliography, 519
Moral authority
  loss of, 239–60
Mveng, Engelbert
  anthropological poverty, 70–72

Nationalism, Christian
  American context, 276–311
Neo-colonialism
  economic critique of, 379–88
Nigeria
  witchcraft discourse in, 346–72
Ngangsic, Christine
  intellectual and spiritual
    collaboration, x–xi
Ngangsic-Asongu, Jude Jingwa
  dedication to, v
Nkengbeza, Monique
  parental influence, xiii

Orthopraxy
  criterion of truth, 16–17

Peeters, Henri
  seminary formation and
    intellectual rigor, xiii
Pentecostalism
  Catholic migration to, 31–33
Planetary crisis
  theological interpretation,
    473–97

Poverty
    structural causes of, 379–88
Praxis, liberative
    criterion of theological truth, 16–17
Prophetic dissent
    definition of, 36–38

Reform, ecclesial
    Vatican II and, 14–15
Ricœur, Paul
    bibliography, 519
Resurrection
    liberative meaning of, 150–55
Romero, Oscar
    martyrdom and prophetic witness, 6

Salvation
    celestial vs. terrestrial, 18–21
Seminary formation
    Cameroon context, 9–14
Sobrino, Jon
    bibliography, 519
Structural sin
    economic forms, 379–88
St. Thomas Aquinas Major Seminary (STAMS)
    seminary formation, xiv

Tanla-Kishani, Bongasu
    thesis supervision and scholarly mentorship, xiv

Tanto, Robert
    priest and youth chaplain, xiv
Tardze, William
    thesis supervision, xiv
Technology
    digital oppression and, 497–506
Terrestrial salvation
    definition of, 18–21
Tangwa, Godfrey B.
    Popper interpretation by, 13–14
Tillich, Paul
    bibliography, 519
Tradition
    dynamic character of, 14–18
Truth
    historical mediation of, 14–18

United States
    Christian nationalism in, 276–311

Vatican II
    ecclesial self-critique, 14–16
Violence
    structural and political, 239–340

Women
    ecclesial exclusion of, 411–32
Witchcraft accusations
    fear and poverty and, 346–72

Young Christian Students (YCS)
    formative influence of, xiv

www.ingramcontent.com/pod-product-compliance
Lightning Source LLC
Chambersburg PA
CBHW052044290426
44111CB00011B/1611